비즈니스법

KOREAN BUSINESS LAW

Byung-Tae Kim

三 英 社

Preface

Business is not about charitable service, but it is about making money. Though nobody can guarantee any profit from a business, all activities in the business are related to making money, profit and benefit if possible. A business law, also known as a commercial law, is all about it, and so has a profit making purpose. A business law is one of the most challenging and dynamic areas of law to study and to practice.

This book begins with one question first. What should be included in a business law? No clear answer yet because there is no rule which must be included in a business law, and it is located in a rapidly changing business world. On national and international levels, it is continually evolving with new areas of law developing in relation to consumer protection, competition, company, banking, and computers and the Internet. Just generally, a business law governs the dealings between persons in commercial matters, and covers the regulations of commercial entities by the laws of company, partnership, agency, bankruptcy, banking & finance, employment and economic competition. It is also related to the laws of contract and often considered to be a branch of the civil law.

Accordingly, since the scope of a business law can be subjective matter, but definitely all matters should be commercial, this book deals with a business law within the generally accepted boundary of a commercial law used by many professionals and also within the jurisdiction of Korea. For those areas of a business law, Korea has a main source of statute law which is the Korean Commercial Act. The Korean Commercial Act covers all commercial matters including merchants, commercial activities, companies, insurance, maritime and air transportation. In a broad sense, however, it includes other commercial related statutes including insurance business, banking and finance, employment and labor, international business transaction and investment, commercial disputes, etc. This book covers those main commercial areas, and their rules and cases.

This book introduces students, experts and lawyers to legal problems encountered by the business or commercial law including commercial related issues. It covers the basic ideas and theories of the commercial law through legal approach and attempts to combine commercial law and theory with their practical applications. Emphasis is on commercial transactions, policies and regulations for businesses. Most of the readings are cases and statute rules organized by subject matter. By reading these cases or rules, readers will develop a better sense of a business law and practice a commercial law with it. The goal of this book is most of all to give students and professionals a sufficient understanding of commercial issues and legal problems so that they may analyze and understand many general principles of the commercial law and thus are able to solve legal problems related to commercial and corporate matters. Since this book is designed to give you full background and understanding on the Korean business laws and cases in English both for foreigners and Korean nationals, you may start your study using this and then do your further researches for your goals.

While every effort has been made to ensure that this book is accurate, there might be some errors or misstatements. If it really happens, hopefully not, it is definitely all my fault and responsibility, and will be fixed in the next edition.

Lastly, very special thanks to President Ko Sungik of Samyoungsa, a publishing company for the publication of this book despite the poor profitability of the English professional book in Korea, and Dr. Jang Beumhoo for his assistance in reviewing various chapters of this book.

Byung-Tae Kim
Seoul and Busan, Korea
February 2023

머 리 말

비즈니스와 상사에 관한 모든 법을 망라하여 비즈니스법 또는 상사법이라고 한다. 이 책은 상법에 국한된 선입견을 피하기 위하여 비즈니스법의 이름으로 상법(회사법), 금융법, 노동법, 국제거래 및 투자법, 상사분쟁 등을 중심으로 다양한 비즈니스 관련 법들을 다루고 있다. 그동안 대학 강의와 변호사 실무에서 축적한 자료와 연구 및 발표논문을 다시 정리하다 보니 의외로 새로운 판례와 법령의 변경 등을 반영하느라 원고작성에 많은 시간이 걸렸다. 특히 우리나라에 비즈니스법에 관하여 영어로 작성된 부분적인 논문과 도서가 일부 있지만, 비즈니스 및 상사 관련 법률을 총망라한 영문의 법학 전문 학술서가 아직 없다는 점을 안타깝게 생각하며 부족하더라도 그 공백을 메우는 역할에 자부심을 갖고 이 책을 집필하게 되었다.

비록 영어로 작성된 법학 전문 학술서이지만 외국에서도 한국어와 한국 비즈니스에 많은 관심이 있고 국내에도 한글이 필요한 많은 외국 유학생과 외국인 비즈니스 종사자가 있기에 굳이 한글로나마 머리말도 작성하고 중요 법률용어의 한글 병기도 하게 되었다. 또한 국내 변호사와 기업실무자 또는 학생들도 영어로 작성된 전문 법학서를 접할 수 있기에 한글로 이 책에서 의도한 중요한 내용을 전달하고자 한다.

이 책은 한국의 법을 중심으로 관련 주제의 법률과 사례를 소개하는 데 주력하였고 관련된 외국의 법, 사례 및 문헌을 최대한 반영하였다. 먼저 관련 주제별로 법률에서 정하고 있는 규정을 설명하고 관련 사례 및 판례를 적절히 반영하여 설명하였으며 해당 주제의 중요한 판례는 선별하여 사례검토를 할 수 있도록 배치하였다. 따라서 이 책을 통한 실제 사건의 문제해결이나 학습이 될 수 있도록 의도하였지만 필요하다면 별도로 한국어의 관련 리서치와 학습도 추천한다.

끝으로 영어로 작성된 법학 전문 학술서에도 불구하고 이 책의 출판을 맡아준 삼영사의 고성익 대표님과 편집부 직원분들 그리고 바쁜 일정 속에서도 이 책의 최종 검토를 도와준 김앤장의 장범후 박사에게도 큰 감사를 드린다.

2023. 2.
천성학관 연구실에서
김 병 태

Brief Contents

Table of Contents

Chapter 1. INTRODUCTION - Korean Legal System and Legal Research

Chapter 2. BUSINESS LAW BACKGROUND
- Korea and Korean Business Culture

Chapter 3. KOREAN COMMERCIAL ACT

Chapter 4. TYPE OF COMPANY

Chapter 5. INCORPORATION AND LIQUIDATION

Chapter 6. SHARES OF COMPANY

Chapter 7. SHAREHOLDER AND SHAREHOLDERS' MEETING UNDER CORPORATE GOVERNANCE

Chapter 8. BOARD OF DIRECTORS AND AUDITOR

Chapter 9. ISSUANCE OF NEW SHARES

Chapter 10. ACCOUNTING AND DIVIDENDS

Chapter 11. CORPORATE BONDS

Chapter 12. BANKING AND FINANCE LAW

Chapter 13. OTHER FINANCIAL MATTERS

Chapter 14. INSURANCE LAW

Chapter 15. EMPLOYMENT AND LABOR LAW

Chapter 16. INTERNATIONAL INVESTMENT LAW

CHAPTER 1
INTRODUCTION - Korean Legal System and Legal Research

Korea has its own legal system while it recognizes both civil law system and common law system. It is important to understand on what the Korean legal system is based and how we can study and research Korean laws. It is also essential to know what kinds of business laws should be considered in taking care of the commercial and business matters and cases. It is always necessary to check out the relevant statutes, their subordinate statutes and rules as well as related court decisions when taking care of certain cases because many different laws may affect a single business issue or transaction.

I. Korean Legal System

1. What is the Korean Legal System?

Like many other countries, the Korean legal system is shaped by its unique history and incorporates individual variations.[1] While the Korean legal system basically follows the civil law system and tradition that was influenced largely by the European civil law system, the US common law have also influenced Korea's more recent legislations. A little bit strictly speaking, the US common law doctrines and principles today govern only areas not covered by statutory or administrative law. If a statute regulates a certain issue, then the statute will apply rather than the common law doctrine that applied prior to the enactment of the statute.[2] Thus, the influence of the US common law over Korea should be

1) R. David, JEC. Brierley, Major Legal Systems in the World Today: An Introduction to the Comparative Study of Law, Simon & Schuster Inc., 1978, pp.286 and 368; Sweet & Maxwell, "English Common Law is the Most Widespread Legal System in the World," November 2008.

2) Frank B. Cross and Roger LeRoy Miller, The Legal Environment of Business: Text and Cases (8th edition), South-Western Cengage Learning, 2012, p.12.

said as the effect of the US laws and business environments, not just common law doctrines. Under the Korean legal system, the court decisions also, particularly those of the Korean Supreme Court, hold a lot of weight. Korea does not recognize a federal legal system since it is a unitary state. It means that all same laws apply in the same way in all districts of Korea.

The main sources of law are, in order of their superiority, (i) the Constitution (헌법), (ii) the Acts or Codes (법률) passed by the National Assembly, and treaties (조약) duly concluded and promulgated under the Constitution, and the generally recognized rules of international law (국제법규), (iii) Presidential decrees (대통령령), and (iv) Ordinances (시행령) issued by the prime minister and/or the head of each executive ministry. Since the Acts and subordinate statutes form a certain hierarchy, subordinate statutes that are enacted under powers delegated by Acts or are enacted for the purpose of enforcing Acts are not permitted to contain details in conflict with such Acts.

The Korean legal system effectively dates from the introduction of the original Constitution of Korea and the organization of Korea as an independent state.

1) Constitution

Korea has a written, codified constitution, known as the Constitution of Korea. The Constitution is composed of a single document, and is a unitary constitution. The Constitution stipulates fundamental matters pertaining to the rights and obligations of the people, fundamental structures of the Government, economic order, management of elections, etc.

The Constitution is the standard for the legislation and amendment of Acts and subordinate statutes of Korea. For example, if Acts, Presidential Decrees or other subordinate statutes are in violation of the Constitution, the Constitutional Court makes a decision on unconstitutionality of the relevant Acts or Presidential Decrees by referring to the provisions and preamble of the Constitution and interpreting the basic constitutional notions.[3)]

During the existence of Korea, the Constitution has been revised or rewritten several times, the most recent of which was in 1987 at the beginning of the

3) Article 111 of the Constitution of Korea and Articles 41 and 47 of the Constitutional Court Act.

sixth Republic of Korea.

2) Acts or Codes

Acts or Codes are the forms of legal norms stipulated by the legislative procedure of the National Assembly of Korea and prescribe the principle of legality, principle of legislated taxation, requirements for acquisition of Korean nationality, expropriation and indemnity of property rights, establishment of Ministries and categories of local Governments, etc. All of the rights and freedoms of the people may be restricted by Acts in cases where it is deemed necessary to do so for the purpose of safeguarding national security and maintaining public order or public welfare, and even if such rights and freedoms are restricted, essential elements of such rights and freedoms are protected from being infringed on.[4] For the business and commercial purpose in Korea, the main source of law in the level of Act is the Korean Commercial Act.

In addition, other emergency executive orders and emergency financial and economic executive orders could be issued by the President in the event of any national emergency.[5] They have the effect of Acts only when the President obtains such approval from the National Assembly.

3) International Treaties and International Laws

International treaties mean agreements concluded in writing among nations, while international laws mean the enforcement power of which is generally recognized by the international community even though Korea is not a signatory nation thereto and include international customary laws. The Article 6(1) of the Constitution of Korea stipulates the observance of international law and prescribes that treaties concluded and promulgated under the Constitution and international laws generally recognized have the same effect as those of domestic laws.

> Article 6 of the Constitution of Korea
> (1) Treaties duly concluded and promulgated under the Constitution and the generally

4) Article 37(2) of the Constitution of Korea.
5) Article 76 of the Constitution of Korea.

recognized rules of international law shall have the same effect as the domestic laws of the Republic of Korea.
(2) The status of aliens shall be guaranteed as prescribed by international law and treaties.

The paragraph of 'the same effect as those of domestic laws' in Article 6(1) of the Constitution refers to the fact that any treaties or international laws falling under any domestic Acts or subordinate statues have the same effect as those of the relevant domestic Acts or subordinate statutes, respectively. In cases where the Government concludes any treaty in conflict with domestic Acts, the Government is required to seek consent from the National Assembly. Some treaties require legislative measures for enactment as domestic Acts in order to be implemented.

4) Orders - Presidential Decrees, Ordinances, and Administrative Rules

Orders refer to all of subordinate statutes, excluding any treaties, international laws, and municipal ordinances and rules, prescribed by administrative power. Administrative legislation includes Presidential Decrees, Ordinances of Prime Minister and Ministries, and administrative rules.

Presidential Decrees issued by the President, the head of the Executive, consists of delegated orders and execution orders.[6] The jurisdiction of such orders extends over all of administrative affairs under the jurisdiction of the Executive. The Ordinances of the Prime Minister are enacted with respect to matters under the jurisdiction of the Ministry of Planning and Budget, the Ministry of Government Legislation, the Ministry of Patriots and Veterans Affairs, etc. that are administrative agencies under the direct supervision of the Prime Minister among the ministries of the Executive.[7] Ordinances of the Prime Minister are generally viewed to stand on par with Ordinances of Ministries in their hierarchy.

6) Article 75 of the Constitution of Korea.
7) Article 95 of the Constitution of Korea.

5) Ordinances and Rules of Local Governments

The Article 117 of the Constitution guarantees self-governance of local Governments. Local Governments exercise autonomous legislative powers to lay down local ordinances and rules. Municipal Ordinances are laid down after going through deliberation thereon by local councils and Municipal Rules are laid down by the heads of local Governments.

> Article 117 of the Constitution of Korea
> (1) Local Governments shall deal with administrative matters pertaining to the welfare of local residents, manage properties, and may enact provisions relating to local autonomy, within the limit of Acts and subordinate statutes.
> (2) The types of local Governments shall be determined by Act.

[Hierarchy of Korean Acts and Subordinate Statutes][8)]

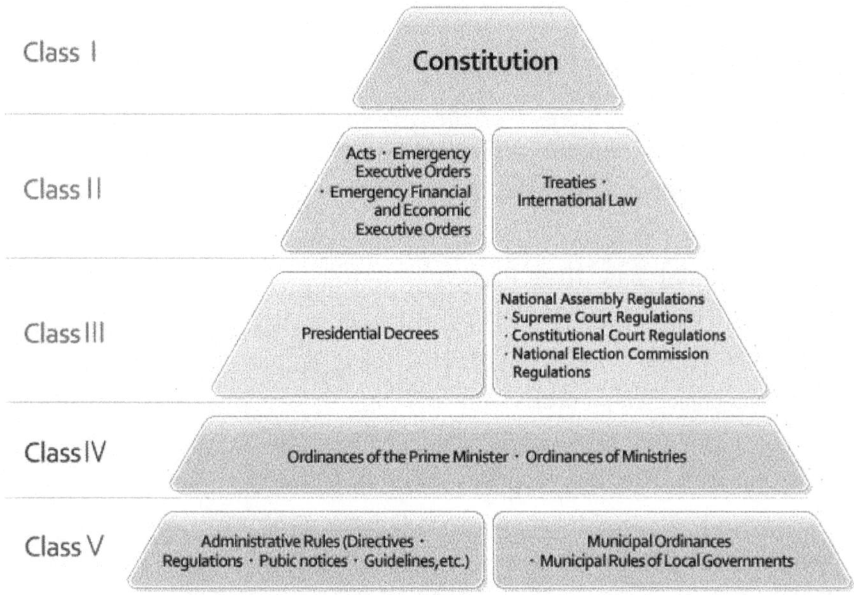

8) Korea Legislation Research Institute, "Legislative System," Retrieved on January 11, 2023 from <https://elaw.klri.re.kr/>.

2. General Principles on Contradiction of Laws

The law of contradiction or the law of non-contradiction (LNC) means that contradictory propositions cannot both be true in the same sense at the same time. Where norms that serve as legal bases of certain laws contradict, which one must be given priority becomes an issue of debate.

In such cases, generally the following principles will apply like in other jurisdictions.

1) The Upper Law-first Principle

If there is a contradiction between upper and lower levels in law, the law on the upper level will prevail. For example, the following hierarchy may apply: Constitution > Acts > Enforcement Decrees > Ordinances or Rules > Articles of Incorporation > Contract or Agreement.

However, the parties' autonomous contract will prevail if it is not against the upper levels of law.

2) The New Law-first Principle

Where two or more laws are applicable, the newest one must apply even if it is more disadvantageous to parties.

3) The Special Law-first Principle

Where a law is applicable to a specific object or purpose, it must be applied to the relevant object or purpose.

4) Exception: The More Advantageous Condition-first Principle

(i) Where a lower legal basis has a more advantageous content than an upper legal basis, the lower one must apply depending on the case.

(ii) Where an upper legal basis has a content more disadvantageous to parties than a lower legal basis, it must be nullified depending on the case.

(iii) Where the new law-first principle is in conflict with the more advantageous condition-first principle, the new law-first principle must prevail.

3. Legislative Procedures

The legislative procedures refer to a series of procedures ranging from the drafting of Bills to their promulgations. The Constitution of Korea grants the National Assembly the power of legislation and permits the Executive branch and other agencies to exercise lawmaking powers on subordinate statutes other than Acts.[9)]

The brief procedure for the legislation is as follows.[10)]

[Legislative Process in Korea][11)]

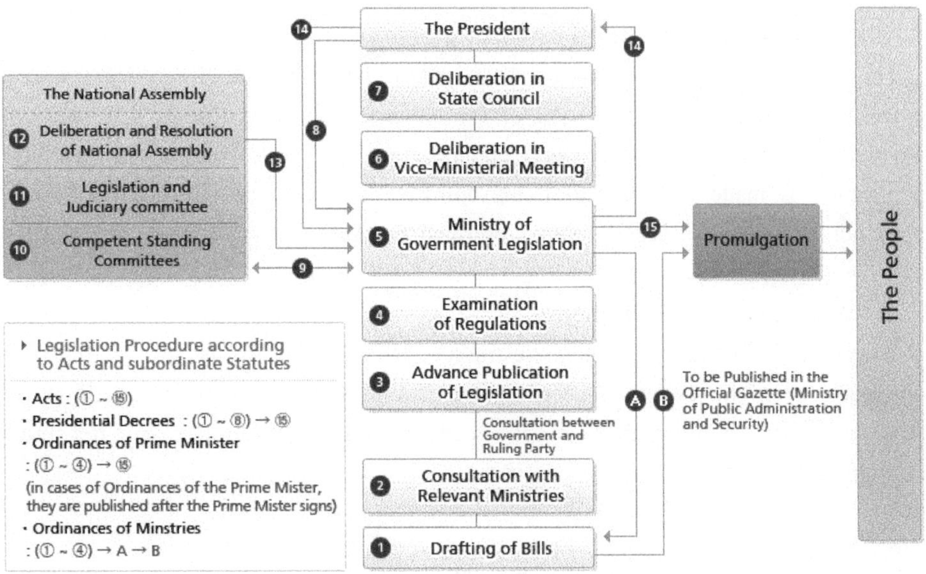

9) Articles 40 and 95 of the Constitution of Korea.

10) Korea Legislation Research Institute, "Legislative System," Retrieved on January 3, 2023 from <https://elaw.klri.re.kr/>.

11) *Id.*

(i) Drafting of Bills

A central administrative agency drafts Bills on affairs under its jurisdiction. In cases of administrative affairs under the jurisdiction of more than two Ministries, such Ministries jointly draft a bill.

Since Bills may be introduced not only by the Executive but also by the members of the National Assembly,[12] Bills drafted by the members of the National Assembly will go directly to the step '(x) Deliberation of Competent Standing Committees' below.

(ii) Consultation with Relevant Ministries

After the drafting of any Bills is completed, consultations on the details of such Bills with relevant Ministries are required. If necessary, consultations between the Government and Ruling Party or cooperation from opposition parties are to be sought.

(iii) Advance Publication of Legislation

The legislation of Bills, in advance, must be published to reflect various opinions of the people. The period of the advance publication is not less than 20 days. If anyone who holds his opinion on any Bills for which advance publication is made may put forth his opinion. However, the advance publication need not be made in special cases prescribed by Acts and subordinate Statutes.

(iv) Examination of Regulations

When any Bills include matters restricting the rights of the people or imposing obligation upon the people by the Government or local Governments in order to achieve specific administrative objectives, the Regulatory Reform Committee must examine such Bills.

(v) Examination by Ministry of Government Legislation

The Ministry of Government Legislation examines not only the formal aspects of the relevant legislative details, such as legal terms and system of legal wording, but also practical aspects, such as whether they are realistically appropriate, whether they are in conformity with the goals of state affairs, whether they are in conflict with higher Acts and subordinate statutes, and so

12) Article 52 of the Constitution of Korea.

forth.

(vi) Deliberation in Vice-Ministerial Meeting

Vice-ministerial meetings deliberate on key matters of Bills in advance to be placed on the agenda of the State Council. However, in cases of emergency, any Bills may be placed on the agenda of the State Council without going through deliberation of vice-ministerial meetings.

(vii) Deliberation in State Council

The State Council, as a top policy deliberative organ, hears proposal explanation of Bills from competent ministries and resolves after going through debates.

(viii) Signature of President

Bills resolved in the State Council and Presidential Decrees require the signature of the President after the Prime Minister and the relevant members of the State Council countersign.

(ix) Submission of Bills to National Assembly

Bills, after obtaining the signature of the President, are promptly submitted to the National Assembly by the Ministry of Government Legislation.

(x) Deliberation of Competent Standing Committees

When any Bill is proposed or submitted to the National Assembly, the Speaker reports it to the plenary session, refers it to the competent standing committee, and, after completing the examination of the competent standing committee, places it to on the agenda of the plenary session.

If necessary, any competent standing committee may examine specific Bills by comprising sub-committees. In cases of important Bills, a committee of all members may examine them.

(xi) Examination of Legislation and Judiciary Committee

When any Bill is proposed or submitted to the National Assembly, the Speaker reports it to the plenary session, refers it to the competent standing committee, and, after completing the examination of the competent standing committee, places it to on the agenda of the plenary session.

If necessary, any competent standing committee may examine specific Bills by comprising sub-committees. In cases of important Bills, a committee of all members may examine them.

(xii) Deliberation and Resolution of National Assembly

After completing examinations of Bills, such Bills are referred to the Legislation and Judiciary committee for going through the examination of terms and system of legal wording. Then, such Bills are to be deliberated upon and resolved at the plenary session.

(xiii) Transfer of Bills to Government

The Ministry of Government Legislation prepares a draft promulgation of a Bill resolved by the National Assembly and submits such draft to the State Council. If any objection is raised to such Bill, the President may request the National Assembly to deliberate again on the Bill by attaching an objection statement within 15 days from the day when such Bill is transferred to the Government.

(xiv) Deliberation of State Council and Signature of President

Bills resolved in the State Council require the signature of the President after the Prime Minister and the relevant members of the State Council countersign.

(xv) Promulgation

Such Bills are promulgated by being published in the Official Gazette.

4. Judiciary

1) Judicial System

(1) The judiciary (사법부) is separate from the administrative and legislative branches. It is a branch of the Government that has judicial powers. The Article 101 of the Constitution of Korea provides that the judicial powers must be vested in the courts comprising of judges, thereby granting the powers of the judiciary to the courts and allow them to carry out the rule of law. In addition, the Article 27 of the Constitution provides that all citizens have the right to be

tried in conformity with the Act by judges qualified under the Constitution and the Act. All citizens also have the right to a speedy trial, making it clear that it is a fundamental right of the people to have a fair trial by a court consisting of qualified judges.

Accordingly, all cases must be decided by judges. As an exception, however, the jury trials by members of the jury who are not a judge deal with felony cases only under the Act on Citizen Participation in Criminal Trials (국민의 형사재판 참여에 관한 법률), which has been in force since January 1, 2008.[13) In order to help the courts to fully perform their duty as a judiciary, the Constitution of Korea provides that judges must rule independently according to their conscience and in conformity with the Constitution and laws, declaring the independence of the judiciary.[14)]

The independence of the judiciary is one of the pillars of the division of powers, which is the fundamental principle in democracy and the most organizational mark of a country ruled by rule of law.

The Constitution of Korea
Article 27

(1) All citizens shall have the right to be tried in conformity with the Act by judges qualified under the Constitution and the Act.
(2) Citizens who are not on active military service or employees of the military forces shall not be tried by a court martial within the territory of the Republic of Korea, except in case of crimes as prescribed by Act involving important classified military information, sentinels, sentry posts, the supply of harmful food and beverages, prisoners of war and military articles and facilities and in the case of the proclamation of extraordinary martial law.
(3) All citizens shall have the right to a speedy trial. The accused shall have the right to a public trial without delay in the absence of justifiable reasons to the contrary.
(4) The accused shall be presumed innocent until a judgment of guilt has been pronounced.
(5) A victim of a crime shall be entitled to make a statement during the proceedings of the trial of the case involved as under the conditions prescribed by Act.

13) Junho Kim, "The Challenges and Outlook of Trial by Jury in Korea," Journal of Korean Law, Vol. 8, June 2009, p.470. *See* also Article 5 of the Act on Citizen Participation in Criminal Trials.

14) Article 103 of the Constitution of Korea.

Article 101
(1) Judicial power shall be vested in courts composed of judges.
(2) The courts shall be composed of the Supreme Court, which is the highest court of the State, and other courts at specified levels.
(3) Qualifications for judges shall be determined by Act.

Article 103
Judges shall rule independently according to their conscience and in conformity with the Constitution and laws.

The Courts are provided with the power to judge all legal disputes unless otherwise provided by the Constitution. The exceptions are found where the Constitution vests the power to judge some constitutional issues in the Constitutional Court and vests the power to examine the qualifications and to take disciplinary measures against lawmakers in the National Assembly.[15] The courts also exercise the power to administer and supervise extra-judicial matters such as immovable and movable property registration, corporation registration, family registration, deposit, and the duties of marshal.

(2) Korea's trial system follows the tri-trial system (삼심제). The Court Organization Act, which was passed into law on September 26, 1949, officially created a three-tiered, independent judicial system in Korea. The Constitution of Korea guarantees that judges would not be removed from office for any reason other than impeachment, criminal acts, or incapacity.

Additionally, the Constitution of Korea officially provides for a judicial independence,[16] which means that "judges rule independently according to their conscience and in conformity with the Constitution and the law." In addition, the 1987 revised Constitution established the Constitutional Court, marking the first time that Korea had an active body for constitutional review.

15) Articles 111(1) and 64(2) of the Constitution of Korea.
16) Article 103 of the Constitution of Korea.

[Tri-trial System in Korea][17)]

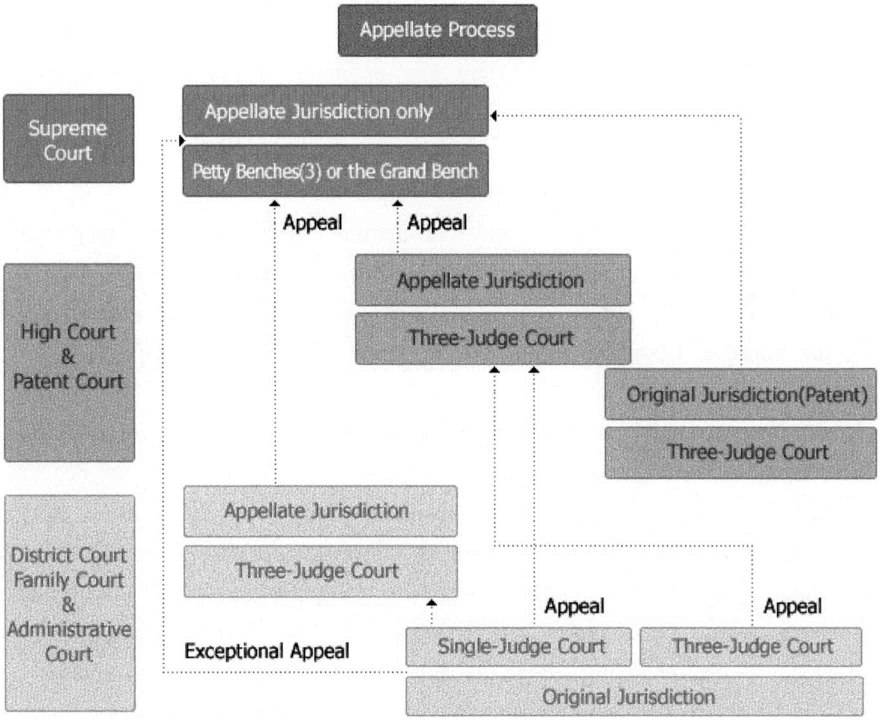

2) Korean Courts

(1) Korean courts (법원) are organized and empowered in the Chapters V and VI of the Constitution of Korea. Accordingly, there are seven types of courts in Korea, which are (i) the Supreme Court (대법원), (ii) High Court (고등법원), (iii) District Court (지방법원), (iv) Patent Court (특허법원), (v) Family Court (가정법원), (vi) Administrative Court (행정법원), and (vii) Bankruptcy Court (파산법원).[18)] The Korean judicial system is based on the three instance trial system, which is composed of district courts, the high courts and the Supreme Court. Other courts exercise specialized functions with the Patent Court positioned

17) Supreme Court of Korea, "The Judiciary," Retrieved on January 12, 2023 from <https://eng.scourt.go.kr/>.

18) Article 3(1) of the Court Organization Act.

on the same level as the high courts and the family court and the administrative court positioned on the same level as the district courts.

A district court and the family court may establish branch courts, municipal courts and Registration Offices or any one or more of the three institutions if additional support is necessary to carry out their tasks. A branch court of both the district court and the family court may be established within the same court complex.[19] There is also other special court such as the martial court. The difference between martial court and non-martial court is that military officers who are not qualified as judges hear cases in martial court, whereas in non-martial court only judges may adjudicate cases. However, including military trials, the Supreme Court has final appellate jurisdiction over all cases.[20]

(2) All hearings and rendering of judgments are open to the public. However, if there is any possibility that opening of hearings to the public could be subject to impairing national security, public peace and order, or be contrary to good morals, the court may decide to close the hearings to the public.[21] In either case, rendering of judgments must be open to the public under all circumstances. Videotaping, taking photographs or live broadcasting in a courtroom without prior permission of the presiding judge is not permissible. The court conducts its affairs in Korean while interpretation can be arranged whenever deemed necessary.

On the other hand, there is no general system of juries in the judicial system of Korea, although the limited system of juries has been adopted for criminal felony cases since February 2, 2008, and all questions of law and fact are decided by judges.

3) Supreme Court Decision and Its Citation

In the case of the Supreme Court, each court decision or order contains date, number, title of the case, main issues, summary of decision, reference provisions, reference cases and their dates of entries in the Collection of Supreme Court Decisions or Supreme Court Decisions Report, parties to the lawsuit, date and

19) Article 3(2) of the Court Organization Act.
20) Article 14 of the Court Organization Act.
21) Article 57(1) of the Court Organization Act.

number of the case from the Court of First or Second Instance, disposition, and reasoning as provided by the Collection of Supreme Court Decisions or Supreme Court Decisions Report.[22] Main issues, summary of decision, reference provisions, reference cases, and underlines in sections of reasoning are not part of the original text from the Supreme Court.

There is a special rule for the citation of a court decision. For example, in the Case Number of '2019Da276338' of [대법원 2021. 6. 30. 선고, 2019다276338 판결] which is a corporate case,[23] the number '2019' indicates the year in which the appeal was made (or in case of 'Gadan' or 'Gahap' the lawsuit was filed). 'Da' refers to the procedural classification and '276338' is a serial number of each case. In principle, 'Da' refers to an appellate case to the Supreme Court in the civil procedure. 'Na' refers to an appellate case to the Court of Second Instance in the civil procedure; 'Gadan', a case to the Single Judge Division of the Court of First Instance in the civil procedure; 'Gahap', a case to the 3 Judge Panel Division of the Court of First Instance in the civil procedure; and 'Do', 'No', 'Godan', and 'Gohap', respectively in the criminal procedure.

On the other hand, in the part of the citation that reads 'Gong2000Sang, 461' in the Reference Cases, 'Gong' refers to the Supreme Court Reports, '2000' indicates the year of its publication, 'Sang' means Volume Ⅰ ('Ha' means Volume Ⅱ), and '461' is the page number. As an another example, in 'Hungong3, 255,' 'Hungong' refers to the Constitutional Court Reports, '3' means Volume No. 3, and '255' is the page number.

In general, identities of persons, companies of their employment, their addresses and registration numbers of their vehicles are disguised under the statuses and numbers such as plaintiff, plaintiff 1, defendant, defendant 1, person, person 1, non-party, non-party A and so on, where the privacy of persons related to cases needs protection.

The online website (www.scourt.go.kr) for the Supreme Court contains selected Supreme Court Decisions or Orders delivered from the period January 1, 2000 through the most recent times. The selections include criminal law cases on

22) Supreme Court of Korea, "The Judiciary," *id.*

23) 'Supreme Court Decision 2019Da276338, decided on June 30, 2021' is the case with respect to the claim for restitution of fees, etc.

human rights and due process, private law areas comprising of international transactions cases, business law cases on foreign capital investment and business activities in Korea, tort law cases, and other cases, which share interests on global legal issues and embody clear and distinctive legal reasoning deserving to be introduced to a global legal community despite certain aspects peculiar only to the Korean legal system.

[Original Supreme Court Decision (in Korean)]

[대법원 2021. 6. 30. 선고 2019다276338 판결] (수수료등반환청구, 공2021하,1381)[24]

【판시사항】
[1] 사정변경을 이유로 계약을 해제하거나 해지할 수 있는 경우 / 사정변경에 대한 예견가능성이 있었는지 판단하는 기준
[2] 갑 등이 해외이주 알선업체인 을 주식회사와 미국 비숙련 취업이민을 위한 알선업무계약을 체결한 후 이민허가를 받고 이에 따라 을 회사에 국외알선 수수료를 모두 지급하였는데, 주한 미국대사관이 갑 등에 대한 이민비자 인터뷰에서 추가 행정검토 및 이민국 이송 결정을 하여 비자발급 절차가 진행되지 않고 중단된 사안에서, 갑 등은 사정변경을 이유로 위 계약을 해지할 수 있다고 한 사례

(이하 생략)

4) Constitutional Court Decision and Its Citation

In decision by the Constitutional Court of Korea, a case number is made up of the year, case code and serial number. For example, a case number, *i.e.,* '2017Hun-Ba369,' decided on November 29, 2018 of [헌법재판소 2018. 11. 29. 선고, 2017헌바369 판결],[25] is made up of the year (2017), case code (Hun-Ba) and serial number (369).

The first four-digit Arabic numbers indicate the year when the case is filed. The serial number is given in the order of case filing of each year.

24) Supreme Court Decision 2019Da276338, decided June 30, 2021.

25) '2017Hun-Ba369' by the Constitutional Court of Korea is the case with respect to the technical protection measures in the Copyright Act.

The typical case codes are as follows:[26)]

(i) Hun-Ka for constitutional review of statutes,

(ii) Hun-Na for the impeachment,

(iii) Hun-Da for dissolution of a political party,

(iv) Hun-Ra for Competence Disputes,

(v) Hun-Ma for constitutional complaint (Article 68 Paragraph 1 of the Constitutional Court Act),

(vi) Hun-Ba for constitutional complaint (Article 68 Paragraph 2 of the Constitutional Court Act),

(vii) Hun-Sa for court-appointed counsel and provisional disposition, and

(viii) Hun-A for special cases such as retrial and etc.

II. Online Resources for Korean Business Laws

1. The National Law Information Center (국가법령정보센터) (http://www.law.go.kr)

The Ministry of Government Legislation maintains this website which provides official information on the laws and regulations up to date. For the unified search service for national statutory information, the National Law Information Center provides a search service on which various statutory information such as legislations, treaties, administrative rules of the central administrative agencies, regulations and ordinances of the local Governments, precedents, etc. are available. Also, this service allows to connect statutes and lower statutes, statutes and administrative rules and the like, and to confirm them.

2. The Korea Legislation Research Institute (한국법제연구원) (http://elaw.klri.re.kr)

The Korea Legislation Research Institute maintains this website which provides English translations of the laws and regulations for guidance only.

---

26) Constitutional Court of Korea, "Search Guide," Retrieved on January 12, 2023 from <https://english.ccourt.go.kr/>.

3. Easy to Find Practical Legal Information Service (찾기 쉬운 생활법령 정보)

(http://easylaw.go.kr)

Practical Legal Information Service reclassifies laws and regulations in accordance with daily life and occupations and makes them easier to understand. It also provides information on them. Since 2013, it has been providing personalized practical legal information service according to gender, age, job, with or without children, single or married, etc.

4. The National Legislation System (정부입법 지원센터)

(http://www.lawmaking.go.kr)

In the National Legislation System, legislative affairs, such as reviewing bills, interpreting statutes, and supporting local Governments when drafting legislation, are conducted all together. In addition, the Public Participation Legislation Center (opinion.lawmaking.go.kr) provides the current status of the Government's legislation and pre-announcement of legislation of the State and local Governments. The people can also voice their opinions about pre- announcement of legislation, etc. and report the laws that cause inconvenience in this center.

5. Supreme Court of Korea (대법원)

(http://www.scourt.go.kr)

As the court of last resort in Korea, the Supreme Court is highest judicial tribunal in the nation. The Supreme Court provides the Judiciary, overview of the Korean Courts and courts adjudication procedure. It also provides information on the Supreme Court of Korea and court decisions.

6. The Korea Trade Investment Promotion Agency (KOTRA, 대한무역투자진흥공사)

(http://www.kotra.or.kr)

The KOTRA is the authority handling all details related to foreign investment and permitting reports received. It can give you Korean business information including relevant laws.

7. Others

Other academic web pages or research tools including Westlaw, Google, Law-related Institutions or Organizations, and other your favorite research tools.

III. Case Study on Claim for Restitution of Fees, Etc.[27)]

1. Main Issues and Holdings

1) Where a contract may be canceled or terminated on the grounds of any change in the circumstances / Standard for determining whether any change in the circumstances was foreseeable.

2) In a case where Party A and others were allowed to immigrate to the U.S. after entering into a contract for an overseas employment service based on employment of unskilled workers falling under the third preference of U.S. green cards available through employment with Stock Company B, which is an emigration agency, and, accordingly, paid for the entire fee for an overseas employment service to Stock Company B, but as the U.S. Embassy & Consulate in the Republic of Korea decided to make additional administrative review and transfer it to the U.S. Citizenship and Immigration Services in the process of an immigration visa interview with Party A and others, the visa issuance procedure is interrupted, the case holding that Party A and others can terminate the above contract on the grounds that any change has taken place in the circumstances.

2. Summary of Decision

1) The Article 2(1) of the Civil Act, with respect to the principle of trust and good faith, stipulates that "the exercise of rights and the performance of duties shall be in accordance with the principle of trust and good faith." The principle,

27) Supreme Court Decision 2019Da276338, decided on June 30, 2021.

as an abstract norm that the parties to a legal relation should not exercise rights or perform duties by means of the contents and methods contrary to equity or faith by being considerate of the interests of the other party, serves as the general principle running through the whole legal order. According to the precedents, the principle of change of circumstances is admitted as a derivative principle of the principle of trust and good faith to solve imbalance caused by any circumstance which was unforeseeable at the time of the conclusion of a contract. In other words, where a circumstance, which is the basis of the constitution of the contract, was remarkably changed, and the parties to the contract could not predict such circumstance at the time of the constitution of the contract, and maintaining the contract due thereto results in serious imbalance in the interests of the parties or prevents the purpose of the contract from being achieved, the contract cannot be cancelled or terminated on the grounds of any change in the circumstances as an exception of the principle of contract observance.

The term 'circumstance,' herein, refers to any circumstance which is the basis of the constitution of a contract between the parties, and does not contain any circumstance which the parties do not consider as the basis of the contract or one of the parties is supposed to take disadvantages or risks according to any change in the circumstances. whether any change in the circumstances was foreseeable should not be abstractly or generally determined and should be individually determined after comprehensively taking account of various circumstances, such as the type and details of the contract, the status of the parties, transaction experience and recognizability, and whether the risks caused by any change in the circumstances are great and concrete, in a specific case. In such a case, from the perspective of a reasonable person, where it is expected that the they would not have concluded the instant contract or would have concluded in different contents if the parties had foreseen any change in the circumstances, any change in the circumstances can be seen as unforeseeable, unless there are special circumstances.

If any change in the economic circumstances is foreseeable from the perspective of a reasonable person even if any damage is caused to the parties due to such change, a contract cannot be canceled or terminated on the grounds of any change in the circumstances. In particular, as a long-term contract has a wide gap between the conclusion and performance of the contract and, any change in the circumstances which could not be foreseen by the parties is highly likely to occur, and, in such a case, in order to terminate the contract, it is not enough on the sole basis of the fact that disadvantages were caused to the parties due to any change in the economic circumstances and the foregoing requirements should be fulfilled.

2) In a case where Party A and others were allowed to immigrate to the U.S. after entering into a contract for an overseas employment service based on employment of unskilled workers falling under the third preference of U.S. green cards available through employment with Stock Company B, which is an emigration agency, and, accordingly, paid for the entire fee for an overseas employment service to Stock Company B, but as the U.S. Embassy & Consulate in Korea decided to make additional administrative review and transfer it to the U.S. Citizenship and Immigration Services in the process of an immigration visa interview with Party A and others, the visa issuance procedure is interrupted, the case holding that the above contract corresponds to where any circumstance concerning the procedure or period of visa issuance, which was the basis of the constitution of the contract, was remarkably changed; the parties could not foresee such circumstance at the time of the constitution thereof; and even if the contract is maintained, the purpose of the contract cannot be achieved or serious imbalance in the interests of the parties is caused, and thus the Party A and others can terminate the above contract on the grounds of any change in the circumstances.

3. Comment

The court's decision can be evaluated as being appropriate and reasonable. A contract may be canceled or terminated on the grounds of any change in the circumstances.

However, the revocation of contract due to change in circumstance must be interpreted strictly, and thus the contract between parties needs, in general, to include what could be circumstances clearly in itself not to have further disputes on this issue.[28)]

---

28) Ji-Hong Joo, "Analysis of the Supreme Court Cases in 2021: The Law of Obligations (in Korean)," Human Rights and Justice, Vol. 505, May 2022, p.10.

Related Legal Issues and Questions:

1. What is the Korea's legal system briefly?
2. Where can you find and research Korean business laws and statutes?
3. Where can you find a court's decision if you are looking for a certain case law?

CHAPTER 2

BUSINESS LAW BACKGROUND - Korea and Korean Business Culture

Business law does not require law itself only. In order for businessmen to make their business judgments and operations, they should also know other business-related matters for better results. In this regards, it is also important to understand Korean business culture and environments to take well care of the business law cases in the position of foreigners or foreign investors. Like all countries, Korea has also a strong side and a weak side, and so it will be helpful for businesses to understand them accurately.

I. Brief Introduction to Korea

1) The Korean Peninsula lies in the middle of Northeast Asia with neighbors of China to its west and Japan to its east. Korea's official name is the Republic of Korea (ROK, 대한민국), but referred many times to South Korea or just Korea. The total area of Korea is 100,364 km^2, excluding the northern end, which is joined to the Asian continent and surrounded by water on three sides. According to Statistics Korea, Korea's 2019 population was estimated at 51.71 million, and the number of foreigners entering Korea reached 293,000 in 2010, 373,000 in 2015, and 438,000 in 2019, respectively.[29] Seoul is the capital city of country, with a population of over 10 million inhabitants.

Korea was divided at the end of World War II, when it was divided into the Soviet and US zones. Korea was created following an election in 1948 in the US zone and the Democratic People's Republic of Korea (DPRK) was established in the Soviet zone. The Korean War, which never technically ended, had a major impact on the country's development and continues to influence Korea politics today.[30]

29) Korean Culture and Information Service, Facts About Korea, Ministry of Culture, Sports and Tourism, 2020, pp.42-43.

30) National Law Review, "South Korea," Retrieved on January 5, 2023 from <https://www.natlawreview.com/jurisdiction/all-international/south-korea>.

Today, Korea has the 11th highest nominal GDP and 12th largest PPP (purchasing power parity) in the world. The country is a leader in technology and industrial sectors, as the 5th largest exporter and 8th largest importer worldwide. The country is considered a highly developed country and high-income economy, with a ranking of 18th in the world in the Human Development Index. Korea is a member of the United Nations, East Asia Summit, OECD, and APEC, among other international foreign relations groups.

2) The Constitution of Korea adopts liberal democracy as the basic principle of governance. Korea has three divided branches (judicial, executive, legislature) under the Constitution. Local Governments are semi-autonomous, and the judicial branch operates at state and federal levels. The Government's basic structure is based on the Constitution of Korea.

The Constitution of Korea
Article 40
The legislative power shall be vested in the National Assembly.

Article 66
(1) The President shall be the Head of State and represent the State vis-a-vis foreign states.
(2) The President shall have the responsibility and duty to safeguard the independence, territorial integrity and continuity of the State and the Constitution.
(3) The President shall have the duty to pursue sincerely the peaceful unification of the homeland.
(4) Executive power shall be vested in the Executive Branch headed by the President.

Article 101
(1) Judicial power shall be vested in courts composed of judges.
(2) The courts shall be composed of the Supreme Court, which is the highest court of the State, and other courts at specified levels.
(3) Qualifications for judges shall be determined by Act.

3) The country's legal system is basically based on a civil law system, but also influenced by a common law system. Under the Constitution of Korea, the President is elected by universal, equal, direct and secret ballot by the people, not be reelected, and the his term of office is five years.[31)] The Prime Minister is appointed by the President. Korea is divided into nine provinces, and with the inclusion of the Sejong Special Self-Governing City in July 2012, the number of high-level local Governments increased to 17 (*i.e.,* Seoul Special City, six metropolises, eight provinces, and Jeju Special Self-Governing Province). The number of low-level local Governments stands at 226 (75 cities (si), 82 counties (gun), and 69 districts (gu)).[32)]

The judicial system consists of the Supreme court, appellate courts, and the Constitutional Court. All cases are decided by judges, while the jury trials deal with felony cases only under the Act on Citizen Participation in Criminal Trials.[33)] 14 Supreme Court Justices are appointed by the President and the Supreme Court is known as the court of last resort. The Constitutional Court is comprised of 9 justices, also appointed by the President. This court hears constitutional issues under the Constitution of Korea. The appellate courts are comprised of six high courts, 13 district courts, and several specialized courts.

4) Korea has become a popular tourist destination in recent years, with over 17 million visitors. There are three designated UNESCO World Heritage Sites in the country. Additionally, Seoul, Jeju, Busan, Ulsan and Incheon, are leading tourist attractions in the country. Korea hosted the 1988 Olympic at Seoul, the 2018 Winter Olympic at Pyeongchang and the 2002 FIFA World Cup at Seoul jointly with Japan.[34)]

---

31) Articles 67 and 70 of the Constitution of Korea.

32) Korean Culture and Information Service, *id.*, p.247.

33) Article 5 of the Act on Citizen Participation in Criminal Trials; Junho Kim, "The Challenges and Outlook of Trial by Jury in Korea," Journal of Korean Law, Vol. 8, June 2009, p.470.

34) There is more official information on Korea from the online resource (https://www.mofa.go.kr/eng/index.do) supported by the Ministry of Foreign Affairs of Korea.

II. Korean Business Culture and Background

Even though a business law seems to have nothing to do with a country's business culture, it is derived from the business culture and economic conditions, and often business attitude. It sure is that success in business requires familiarity with law and culture. Below is the summary of the distinguished business culture and environment of Korea for the purposes of further and better review of Korean business laws.

1. Economic Fundamentals

Korea has the world's 10th largest economy, with a value of approximately USD 1.8 trillion. Also, Korea's economic fundamentals are solid, with its trading volume ranking 8th as of 2021 (9th in the world as of 2020), and with the 9th largest foreign exchange reserves as of end-June 2022 in the world (the 8th largest foreign exchange reserves in the world as of July 2021).[35]

The country's economy is stable and capable of supporting continuous business operation and growth. Despite the effects of the COVID-19 pandemic, the OECD forecast 3.8% economic growth outlook for Korea in 2021, with positive assessment of Korean New Deal and expansionary fiscal policy (June 2021). According to the International Monetary Fund (IMF), Korea's GDP growth rate is 2.0 percent as of December 2022 and forecast at 2.6 percent in 2023.[36]

The summary of the Korean economy fundamentals is as follows:[37]

(i) The 10th rank on the GDP: USD 1.8 trillion (as of 2021),

(ii) The 8th rank on the trade volume: USD 1,259.5 billion (as of 2021),

(iii) The 18th rank on the trade balance: USD 29.3 billion (as of 2021),

(iv) The sovereign credit rating: AA, stable (as of 2022), and

(v) The 9th rank on the foreign exchange reserves: USD 438.6 billion (as of July 2022).

---

35) *See* KOTRA, "Invest Korea," Retrieved on January 12, 2023 from <https://www.investkorea.org/ik-en/pgm/i-295/statistics/front/list.do>.

36) IMF, "IMF Data Mapper," Retrieved on January 12, 2023 from <https://www.imf.org/external/datamapper>.

37) The summary is aggregated with the sources of the International Monetary Fund (IMF), the Korea International Trade Association (KITA), the Bank of Korea (BOK), the Korea Exchange, the Brand Finance and the Korean Statistical Information Service (KOSIS).

2. Digital Infrastructure

According to the World Economic Forum (WEF), the dissemination of information and communication technologies (ICT) in Korea has ranked 1st in the world for 3 consecutive years.

Digital infrastructure in Korea is world-class. Korea succeeded in commercializing the world's first 5G network (Apr, 2019), proving that the country is a global leader in the ICT field. The Korean Government is planning to significantly expand investment and strengthen digital infrastructure in Korea through its Digital New Deal policy.[38)]

The summary of Korea's digital infrastructure is as follows:[39)]

(i) The 1st rank on the ICT penetration rate (2018 ~ 2020),

(ii) The 1st rank (99.7 percent) on the percentage of households with internet access at home (as of 2020),

(iii) The 1st rank (84.8 percent) on the broadband internet penetration rate (as of 2020),

(iv) The 1st rank (432.7 Mbps) on the 5G download speed (as of 2022).

Korea also stands atop in the UN e-Government survey's index. The e-Government development index (EGDI) is a composite benchmark of e-Government development consisting of the weighted average of three independent component indices: the online services index (OSI), the telecommunications infrastructure index (TII) and the human capital index (HCI). In the 2022 Survey findings by EGDI rankings at the global level, Korea is one of the 15 countries in the highest (VH) rating class within the very high EGDI group which are the leading countries, and in details, is the 1st rank in Asian countries and the 3rd rank in the world.[40)] Being highly recognized for its outstanding quality, Korea's e-Government system has been exported to many countries around the world. The excellence of Korea's e-Government demonstrates the Government's commitment to digitalization as well as the strength of the

---

38) *See* KOTRA, "Invest Korea," *op. cit.*

39) The summary is aggregated with the World Economic Forum (WEF) 2020, the OECD and the Open Signal (2022).

40) Department of Economic and Social Affairs of the UN, E-Government Survey 2022: The Future of Digital Government, 2022, p.8.

country's digital infrastructure.

3. Innovation and Highly Skilled Workforce

Korea is an innovative country, ranked 1st during 8 consecutive years in the '2021 Bloomberg Innovation Index.' The country is among the top 5 in the categories of R&D intensity, manufacturing value-added, high-tech density, researcher concentration, and patent activity. Its infrastructure for innovation is a primary reason that a number of global companies have been investing in Korea.

The summary of the innovation index for Korea is as follows:[41]
(i) 1st rank in the world in the field of Patent Activity,
(ii) 2nd rank in the world in the field of R&D Intensity,
(iii) 2nd rank in the world in the field of Value-added Manufacturing,
(iv) 3rd rank in the world in the field of Research Concentration, and
(v) 4th rank in the world in the field of Hight-tech Density.

Supporting Korea's rapid economic growth in the last half-century is characteristics prominent in the country, such as sincerity, responsibility, and flexibility. Korea's youth college education completion rate is the highest among the OECD member countries. The higher education completion rate for young adults between 25 and 34 years old is 69.8 percent, compared to the 45.5 percent of the OECD average, and for adults between 25 and 64 years old is 50.7 percent, compared to the 40.3 percent of the OECD average.[42]

This makes Korea the 1st rank in the highest number of college graduates. People are the most important resource in Korea, and they are what keep innovation alive in the country.

---

41) Bloomberg, "2021 Bloomberg Innovation Index," 2022; Michelle Jamrisko, Wei Lu, and Alexandre Tanzi, "South Korea Leads World in Innovation as U.S. Exits Top Ten," Bloomberg, February 3, 2021.

42) The OECD, "Education at a Glance 2021," September 16, 2021.

4. Global Power and Market

1) Strong Domestic Purchasing Power and Market

Though Korea ranks just 108th in the world by land area, it boasts the world's 14th largest domestic market. The consumer spending or personal consumption expenditure (PCE) in Korea is relatively high, ranking particularly among the top in terms of the number of Starbucks licensed stores, the average monthly payment of mobile game users, and average monthly expenses. In addition, the biggest steel consumption per capita in the world demonstrates the capacity of Korea's manufacturing industry for further growth.

The summary of the domestic market with strong purchasing power in Korea is as follows:[43)]

(i) 1st rank in the steel consumption per capita (as of 2021),
(ii) 1st rank in the seafood consumption per capita (as of 2019),
(iii) 1st rank in the food delivery app usage rate (as of 2020),
(iv) 1st rank in the semiconductor revenue (as of 2022),
(v) 1st rank in the global mobile game users' average monthly payment (as of 2021),
(vi) 4th rank in the sales revenue in skincare segment (as of 2021),
(vii) 2nd rank in the number of Starbucks stores (as of 2022), and
(viii) 3rd rank in the mobile application usage time (as of 2021).

2) Gateway to the Global Market

The demand for high-tech devices exists among all generations in Korea, based on the country's competitiveness in a variety of industries as well as its top-class IT infrastructure. Powerful consumer groups prefer the newest products and are sensitive to global trends. It is said that "You can succeed in the world only once you have succeeded in Korea," thus showing that Korea has solidified its place as a test bed for the world.[44)]

---

43) *See* KOTRA, "Invest Korea," *op. cit.*; The World Steel Association (2022), the Norwegian Seafood Council (2020), Gatner, Dunnhumby (2020), App Annie, Statista, at Kneoma.com (2022, 3Q).

44) KOTRA, "Invest Korea," *id.*

5. E-Commerce Market

The e-commerce industry is showing rapid growth in Korea. According to the 2021 global e-commerce share of retail sales, Korea ranked 5th in the world. China stands in the first position, United States in the second position, United Kingdom in the third position, Japan in the fourth position, and Korea in fifth position. The key items that led the expansion of Korea's online market are electronic home appliances, fresh foods, and processed foods. They continue to growth boosted by the development of logistics system such as improved convenience of the online payment system, rocket delivery and early-morning delivery.[45]

The summary of the e-commercial market in Korea is as follows:

[Country-by-Country Forecast of Retail E-Commerce As of 2021 (Unit: %)][46]

Ranking	**1**	**2**	**3**	**4**	**5**
Country	China	US	UK	Japan	Korea
Amount	52.1	19.0	4.8	3.0	2.5

[Annual E-Commerce Sales][47]

	2018	**2019**	**2020**	**2021**
Sales (USD 1bln)[1)]	75.3 (USD 1bln)	87.4 (USD 1bln)	109.5 (USD 1bln)	128.0 (USD 1bln)
Share (%)[2)]	18.8%	21.4%	26.7%	28.7%

1) Exchange rate (Aug 31, 2021) 1USD = KRW1,160
2) E-commerce share of total retail sales (%)

---

45) *Id.*

46) UNCTAD, "COVID-19 Boost to E-commerce Sustained into 2021, New UNCTAD Figures Show," April 25, 2022; China Ministry of Commerce, the UK Office for National Statistics, the US Census Bureau, and Korea SMEs and Startups Agency, eMarketer.

47) *See* KOTRA, "Invest Korea," *op. cit.*; Statistics Korea, Online shopping Trends.

6. Business Hub of Northeast Asia

1) The Center of East Asia

Korea possesses optimal logistics infrastructure connecting it with major countries and cities around the world. Located between China and Japan, it is the center of aviation and maritime logistics connecting the Asia-Pacific region as well as Eurasia and the Americas. Furthermore, it has the potential to establish a land-based route penetrating the Eurasian continent.[48)]

The summary of the logistics hub of Korea is as follows:[49)]
(i) 2nd rank in the Linear Shipping Connectivity Index (LSCI),[50)]
(ii) 2nd rank in the international flight air cargo workload (2021) and 5th rank in the total air cargo workload (2021) from the Incheon International Airport of Korea, and
(iii) 2nd rank in the trans-shipment workload (2021) and 7th rank in the container cargo workload performance (2021) from the Busan Port of Korea.

2) Export Powerhouse

Korea is the 7th largest exporter in the world. Since the worldwide outbreak of COVID-19, exports of consumer goods, medicine, and medical supplies have surged. The Korea International Trade Association (KITA) reported pharmaceutical exports in 2020 recorded USD 5.1 billion, a 139.1% jump year-over-year, and ranking moved up two places from the 9th to the 7th in the world.[51)]

Korea ranked 3rd in the Competitive Industrial Performance Index (CIP), which was released by the United Nations Industrial Development Organization (UNIDO) in July 2020, among 152 countries, followed by Germany and China.[52)] Even though the pandemic made it difficult for the country to safeguard growth

---

48) *id.*

49) The Ministry of Oceans and Fisheries, the Airports Council international (ACI), the Busan Port Authority (2021), the UNCTAD.

50) The Linear Shipping Connectivity Index (LSCI) is the UNCTAD's indicator which shows a country's maritime shipping network from the year 2006 until now. The LSCI evaluates data based upon six components which include the number of shipping liners servicing in a country, the number of vessels deployed from/to other ports on a monthly basis and the total container including carrying capacity, etc.

51) The KITA, "Medicines Exports by Month," 2021.

52) Valentin Todorov, "Competitive Industrial Performance Index 2020: Country Profiles," July 3, 2020.

through the expansion of domestic demand, Korea's exports rose rapidly backed by the competitiveness of manufacturing industry. As such, Korea is the 7th largest exporter in the world. Exports from Korea are led by the manufacturing industry, and major items of export include semiconductors, automobiles, oil products, automobile parts, and displays.[53]

3) Global Trade Hub

A Free Trade Agreement (FTA) is an agreement according to international law to form a free-trade area between the states (bilateral FTA) or among cooperating states (multilateral FTA). The FTAs determine the tariffs and duties that countries impose on imports and exports with the goal of reducing or eliminating trade barriers, thus encouraging international trade.

For challenging international trend with the FTA, Korea has signed 18 FTAs, covering 58 countries as of September 2022, which include major economies like the EU, the US., and China, while continuing to pursue FTAs with emerging countries.[54] With its geographical advantage, Korea is a gateway to the global markets that links most of the largest economies.

[Korea’s FTAs Network][55]

Status	Country
In Effect (18 FTAs)	Chile, Singapore, EFTA[56], ASEAN[57], India, EU[58], the U.S., Türkiye, Australia, Canada, China, New Zealand, Vietnam, Columbia, 5 countries in Central America[59], UK, RECP[60]
Signed / Concluded	Indonesia CEPA, Israel, Cambodia
Concluded	Philippines
Under Negotiation	Korea-China-Japan, MERCOSUR[61], Russia, Malaysia, Ecuador, Uzbekistan, Korea-ASEAN FTA expansion, Korea-India CEPA upgrading, Korea-Chile FTA upgrading, Korea-China FTA under follow-up negotiation on service & investment, GCC,[62] Korea-Central America FTA under accession negotiation with Guatemala

53) KOTRA, “Invest Korea,” *op. cit.*
54) FTA Korea, “Korea’s FTAs,” Retrieved on January 15, 2023 from <www.fta.go.kr>.
55) *Id.*

Resumed / On the Agenda / Under Reviews	Mexico, PA[63]), UK

7. Biz-friendly Environment

1) World's 19th on 'Economic Freedom Index'

Korea's economy is the 19th freest (Mostly Free Countries Group) among 177 countries in the survey of the 2022 Index of Economic Freedom released by World Heritage.[64]) The country's economic freedom climbed up 5 ranks compared to 2021. Also, it was evaluated that the level of freedom regarding the exercise of property rights and judicial efficiency increased, with significant improvements in financial soundness.

The summary of the economic freedom index is as follows:

[Economic Freedom Index][65])

Country	**Singapore**	**Korea**	**UK**	**US**	**Japan**
Ranking	1	19	24	25	35

56) EFTA (European Free Trade Association) (4 countries): Switzerland, Norway, Iceland, and Liechtenstein.

57) ASEAN (10 countries): Brunei, Cambodia, Indonesia, Laos, Malaysia, Myanmar, the Philippines, Singapore, Vietnam, and Thailand.

58) EU (27 countries): Austria, Belgium, Bulgaria, Croatia, Republic of Cyprus, Czech Republic, Denmark, Estonia, Finland, France, Germany, Greece, Hungary, Ireland, Italy, Latvia, Lithuania, Luxembourg, Malta, Netherlands, Poland, Portugal, Romania, Slovakia, Slovenia, Spain, and Sweden.

59) The Central America (5 countries): Panama, Costa Rica, Honduras, El Salvador, and Nicaragua.

60) RCEP (Regional Comprehensive Economic Partnership) (14 countries except Korea): Korea, 10 ASEAN member states, China, Japan, Australia, and New Zealand.

61) MERCOSUR (Southern Common Market) (4 countries): Argentina, Brazil, Paraguay, and Uruguay.

62) GCC (Gulf Cooperation Council) (6 countries): Saudi Arabia, Kuwait, the United Arab Emirates, Qatar, Bahrain, and Oman.

63) PA (Pacific Alliance) (4 countries): Chile, Colombia, Mexico, and Peru.

64) Heritage Foundation, "Highlights of the 2022 Index of Economic Freedom," 2022.

65) *Id.*

2) Country with Biz-friendly Condition

According to the World Bank's Doing Business 2020 report, Korea ranked 5th out of 190 countries in ease of doing business ranking, and the 3rd among OECD countries.[66] In particular, Korea ranked high in the category of Getting Electricity and Enforcing Contracts. The result highlights that electricity is supplied through a fast and simple process at an affordable price.

The International Energy Agency (IEA) reported that Korea's average cost of utilities per person (tax included: 8.28 pence/KWh) is 2nd the lowest of 28 OECD members as of 2020.[67] Energy prices in Korea remains merely half the OECD average and 25% of that in Denmark (tax included: 33.06 pence/ KWh) which tops in the global energy price index.

The summary of the comparison of electrical service is as follows:

[Comparison of Electrical Service][68]

Ranking	**1**	**2**	**3**	**4**	**5**
Country	UAE	Korea	Hong Kong	Malaysia	Germany

3) Stable Water Supply

Korea has developed infrastructure capable of providing a stable supply of water. Furthermore, Korea's water utility bills are on average KRW 719 per m2, compared to KRW 1,700 of major countries around the world as of 2021.[69]

Korea's water supply bill is 44.7% of that of the overall average of major countries around the world. For example, the water supply bill of UK is 4.1 times, US is 3.0 times, Japan is 1.6 times, and China is 0.6 times than that of Korea, amounting to 42.3% of the average bill of major overseas countries.

---

66) International Bank for Reconstruction and Development of the World Bank, "Doing Business 2020: Comparing Business Regulation in 190 Economies," 2020.

67) IEA, "Domestic Electricity Prices in the IEA," 2020.

68) World Bank, "Ease of Doing Business Score," Retrieved on January 18, 2023 from <https://www.doingbusiness.org/data/doing-business-score>.

69) Global Water Intelligence, "The Global Water Tariff Survey 2021," 2021.

The summary of the water supply bills as of 2021 is as follows:

[Water Supply Bills As of 2021 (Unit : Won/m2)][70)]

Country	Korea	Italy	Japan	USA	France	UK	Germany	Denmark
Bill	719	993	1,174	2,178	2,460	2,957	3,431	4,108

* Exchange rate (June 30, 2021): USD1 = KRW1,128.5

4) Active Application for Intellectual Property Rights

As of 2021, the number of applications for intellectual property rights in Korea is the 4th largest in the world, following China, the U.S., and Japan, and Korea reclaimed the 4th ranking in the world in Patent Cooperation Treaty (PCT) patent applications in 11 years with surpassing 20,000 cases per year for the first time.[71)]

In addition, resident patent applications filed per GDP, far outdistanced other leading countries, topping the global list, showing Korea's excellence in application for intellectual property rights.

[WIPO IP Facts and Figures][72)]

Ranking	PCT International Patent Applications from Major Countries (2021(tentative), Unit: case)		Hague International Design Application from Major Countries (2021(tentative), Unit: case)		Resident patent applications filed per GDP (2020, Unit: case)	
1	China	69,562	Germany	4,411	Korea	8,249
2	USA	59,440	USA	2,643	China	5,845
3	Japan	50,262	Italy	2,051	Japan	4,696

70) *Id.*

71) World Intellectual Property Organization, "June 2022-2021 Intellectual Property Statistics," WIPO IP Facts and Figures 2021, 2022.

72) *Id.*

4	Korea	20,676	Switzerland	1,824	Germany	1,609
5	Germany	17,320	France	1,585	Switzerland	1,605
6			Korea	1,418		

The speed of its patent process is one of Korea's strengths in this area. The examination and processing period for patent and utility model registry in Korea is shorter than in the US (16.3 months) and similar to Japan (10.4 months).

[Intellectual Property Statistics (Unit: months)][73)]

Status	**Patent and Utility Model Registry**	**Trademark Model Registry**	**Design Model Registry**
USA	16.3	13.3	2.7
Japan	10.4	4.9	5.0
Korea	10.3	5.5	4.9

On the other hand, innovations and inventions are strongly protected in Korea through intellectual property rights such as patents, copyrights, utility models, designs and trade secrets. From the legal perspective, patents, utility models, designs and copyrights are governed by the Patent Act, the Utility Model Act, the Design Protection Act and the Copyright Act, respectively, while trade secrets are governed by the Unfair Competition Prevention and Trade Secret Protection Act in accordance with legal principles for the protection of intellectual property rights that are commonly applied in other jurisdictions.

73) World Intellectual Property Organization, "Yearly Intellectual Property Statistics," WIPO IP Facts and Figures 2021, 2022.

III. Supplement to Korean Business Culture and Law

Understanding Korean Business Culture and Etiquette[74)]

Everything you need to know about Korean business culture: South Korea has become one of the most dynamic and innovative economies in the world. From Samsung to Hyundai and K-pop to Kia, this small country has made its way into our lives.

However, behind all the technology, Korea is still pretty traditional, especially when it comes to business. Fortunately, none of these practices are too complicated (aside from the language). So, if you plan on doing any business in Seoul, here a few things you should pay attention to:

1) Business Cards

A business card is a serious business in Korea. They allow Koreans to quickly exchange information and determine important facts like the company, title, and rank.

In Korean, you traditionally receive the card with two hands. In fact, in most situations in Korea, it is standard to receive items with two hands. Then you take the card and review it for a few seconds. If you're sitting at a table, place it face up in front of you.

People will do the same with your card. If possible, get one of yours translated to Korean. While most people you interact with will probably speak English, it's still a sign of cultural respect.

2) Respecting Privacy

While all businesses around the world have things, they want to be kept private, Koreans take this to a whole new level. The most successful Korean businesses like Samsung, Hyundai, and LG are built around clans (known as Chaebols). But even smaller firms imitate this structure.

If you ever work with or in a Korean company, you should keep all matters confidential. This includes securing your digital devices. Make sure they are protected with passwords and PIN codes. Also, that nobody can hack your internet connection, especially while connected to public WiFi, by installing a VPN. Being able to maintain such high standards goes a long way and is regarded as a sign of professionalism.

3) Dress Appropriately

In the last few years, things have gotten progressively more casual in the western world. While it's growing increasingly rare to see suits in the office in the West, business attire is still conservative in Korea.

Men should opt for dark-colored suits (there are tons of great and affordable tailors in Seoul) alongside white shirts and ties. Women should also dress conservatively in muted and subdued tones. All tattoos should be covered, and men should keep jewelry to a minimum of watches and wedding rings at the most. Of course, things are changing fast. If you're meeting with a startup, you may be able to get away with something less formal but always err on the side of caution.

4) Be Firm, but Not Pushy

Koreans tend to be solid negotiators, so prepare to be firm. However, remain dignified, and don't be too hard. Koreans will try to negotiate on price. Expect this but don't give up too easily. Koreans respect persistence in others and value this characteristic in business partnerships.

5) Enjoy a Night Out

You might think that all Korean business culture is serious, but they do know how to unwind. Hui-sik (eating out) is a common practice. As a guest, your hosts will want to take you out and show you a good time. While some etiquette remains, this also a good time to let your hair down a little and bond.

Koreans love eating and drinking massive amounts of soju (rice alcohol). You may also be invited out to enjoy a night of noraebang (Karaoke). Don't turn down such fun.

A few tips, though:

Don't try to split the bill. If you want to treat your host, offer to get the next round or outing.

Pour drinks for others.

Don't leave your chopsticks stuck in a rice bowl (that's a death offering).

Koreans drink a lot. If you want to slow down, never leave your glass empty. That's a sign you want a refill!

Eat a lot of food to soak up the alcohol.

Ask for pointers on etiquette from your hosts. They won't expect you to know everything.

6) Mastering Business Culture in South Korea

Business culture in South Korea is complex. Even natives take years to really get the hang of it. As a foreigner, it will be doubly hard for you. But by paying attention to a few of these details, you will show your respect and not only help your own business advance, but hopefully make lifelong friends. Then, it will be your turn to be a good host when they come to visit you.

Related Legal Issues and Questions:

1. Why do you want, as a foreign businessman, to set up your business in Korea? Are there any incentives for your proposed business?
2. What could be more competitive or profitable business items in your foreign position?

74) Jessica Susan Bogtrotter, "Understanding South Korean Business Culture and Etiquette," Korea Times, April 27, 2021.

CHAPTER 3
KOREAN COMMERCIAL ACT

The main source of business laws in Korea is the Korean Commercial Law and subordinate statutes. It is important to understand what the Korean Commercial Act is as a main statute of business laws in Korea and how it could be applied to business and commercial matters. The Korean Commercial Act consists of largely six Parts and will cover most of business law cases in Korea. Separate laws for negotiable instruments such as the 'Bills of Exchange and Promissory Notes Act' and the 'Check Act' are deemed to be one of commercial laws in Korea.

I. Introduction to Korean Commercial Act

1. Korean Commercial Act as a Business Law

A business law, also known as a commercial law governs the dealings between persons in commercial matters, and also governs the broad areas of business, commerce, and consumer transactions.[75] In the absence of any established legal definition of it, however, various definitions of it have been put forward.[76] Nevertheless, it covers generally the regulation of commercial entities by the laws of company, partnership, agency, bankruptcy, banking & finance and economic competition. It also covers the regulation of commercial transactions by the laws of contract and related fields. Since a business law applies to the rights, relations, and conduct of persons and business engaged in commerce, merchandising, trade, and sales, it is often considered to be a branch of civil law and deals, in certain cases, with issues of both private law and public law.

---

75) Legal Information Institute, "Commercial Law: An Overview," Retrieved January 18, 2023 from <https://www.law.cornell.edu/wex/commercial_law>.

76) LS Sealy and BJA Hooley, Commercial Law: Text, Cases, and Materials (4th edition), Oxford Uni. Press, 2009, p.3.

The Korean business law affects everyday lives and commercial transactions through every contractual dealing undertaken as well as Korean Civil Act does. On national and international levels, it is continually evolving with new areas of law developing in relation to consumer protection, competition, company, banking, and computers and the Internet.

For those areas of a business law, Korea has a main source of statute law, which is the Korean Commercial Act (KCA, 상법). In a narrow sense, the KCA means a specific statute, entitled the 'Commercial Act' and in a broad sense, it includes all other commercial laws.[77] For example, in a broad sense of the KCA, there are many other statutes dealing with commercial issues and matters in other parts of the business law. The most important statutes relating to the KCA are the Bills of Exchange and Promissory Notes Act (어음법), the Check Act (수표법), the Financial Investment Services and Capital Markets Act (자본시장과 금융투자업에 관한 법률), the Banking Act (은행법), the Electronic Financial Transactions Act (전자금융거래법), and the Monopoly Regulation and Fair Trade Act (독점규제 및 공정거래에 관한 법률), etc.

2. Enactment and Contents

The Korean Commercial Act (KCA), also called as the Korean Commercial Code (KCC) is a statute law that regulates the existence and the relationships of the merchants or enterprises that have the purpose of profit-making. It was enacted on January 20, 1962 as Act No. 1000, and entered into force on January 1, 1963 (the latest amendment to KCA on December 29, 2020). It is composed of six parts, such as general provisions, commercial activities, companies, insurance, maritime commerce, and air transport (newly inserted into the KCA in May 23, 2011).

As mentioned above, the KCA consists of six parts as follows:
(i) Part 1: General Provisions (총칙),
(ii) Part 2: Commercial Activities (상행위),
(iii) Part 3: Company (회사),
(iv) Part 4: Insurance (보험),
(v) Part 5: Marine Commerce (해상), and

77) Ki Jong Lee, General Principles of Korean Commercial Law, Sam Young Sa, October 2020, p.11.

(vi) Part 6: Carriage by Air (항공운송)

Additionally, separate laws for negotiable instruments are deemed to be one of commercial laws in Korea and law school students study them with the KCA in the commercial law courses. They are promissory notes, bills of exchange and checks which have been regulated by the relevant laws such as the Bills of Exchange and Promissory Notes Act (어음법) and the Check Act (수표법).

II. Brief Contents of Korean Commercial Act

1. Part 1: General Provisions

The Part 1 of the KCA includes general provisions applied commonly to other Parts and all commercial matters in the KCA. If the KCA does not provide for a particular commercial matter, however, the commercial customary law shall apply and if no such law exists, the Civil Act shall apply according to the Article 1 (Applicable Rules to Commercial Matters) of the KCA.

The Articles 1 through 45 in the Part 1 of the KCA provide generally for,
(i) Common Provisions,
(ii) Merchants,
(iii) Commercial Employees,
(iv) Trade Names,
(v) Trade Books (Financial Statements),
(vi) Commercial Registration, and
(vii) Transfer of Business.

In particular, it is important to define who would be a merchant (상인) when the KCA applies. Under the KCA, there three kinds of merchants: merchant-by nature of business, merchant-by legal construction and petty merchant.

A merchant-by nature of business (당연상인) means that any person who engages in commercial activities under his own name will a merchant.[78] This kind of merchant must engage in basic commercial activities listed in the Article

78) Article 4 of the Korean Commercial Act.

46 of the KCA and do them 'as a business.' In other words, he must repeatedly and continuously engage in the same type of activities on profit making purpose.[79)]

A merchant-by legal construction (의제상인) means that any person who engages in any business in the same manner as a merchant through a store or similar facility will be deemed a merchant, even if he does not carry out commercial activities listed in the Article 46 of the KCA.[80)] This will also apply to a company even if it does not carry out commercial activities. This concept of a merchant-by legal construction enables the KCA to apply to business types that are not covered by the Article 46.[81)]

A petty merchant (소상인) is defined as a merchant whose equity capital does not amount to KRW 10 million and who is not a company.[82)] The KCA provisions relating to managers, trade names, trade books, and commercial registration will not apply to a petty merchant.[83)]

2. Part 2: Commercial Activities

The Part 2 of the KCA includes commercial activities (상행위) and their related matters from Article 46 to Article 168-12. The following 22 commercial activities conducted for profit as a business are called as basic commercial activities, excluding that activities conducted by persons who manufacture goods or render services solely for the purpose of earning wages.[84)]

22 basic commercial activities are as follows:

(i) Sale of movables, immovables, securities, or any other assets,
(ii) Lease of movables, immovables, securities, or any other assets,
(iii) Activities relating to manufacturing, processing, or repair,
(iv) Activities relating to the supply of electricity, electric wave, gas, or water,
(v) Undertaking of subcontracting execution of works or labor services,
(vi) Activities relating to publishing, printing, or photographing,

79) Ki Jong Lee, *op. cit.*, p.70.
80) Article 5 of the Korean Commercial Act.
81) Ki Jong Lee, *op. cit.*, p.71.
82) Article 2 of the Enforcement Decree of the Korean Commercial Act.
83) Article 9 of the Korean Commercial Act.
84) Article 46 (Basic Commercial Activities) of the Korean Commercial Act.

(vii) Activities relating to advertisements, communications, or information,
(viii) Receiving and giving credit, exchanges, or other financial transactions,
(ix) Transactions by facilities used by the public,
(x) Undertaking of agency for commercial transactions,
(xi) Activities relating to brokerage,
(xii) Activities relating to commission agency or any other intermediation,
(xiii) Undertaking of carriages,
(xiv) Undertaking of bailments,
(xv) Undertaking of trusts,
(xvi) Mutual savings accounts and other similar acts,
(xvii) Insurance,
(xviii) Activities involving the collection of minerals or soil and stones,
(ixx) Activities involving financial lease of machinery, facilities, or any other assets,
(xx) Activities involving business by consent to the use of a trade name, trademark, etc.,
(xxi) Activities involving purchase, recovery, etc. of business receivables, and
(xxii) Undertaking of payment settlement affairs using a credit card, electronic currency, etc.

Other commercial activities effected by a merchant for the purpose of his business are deemed to be subsidiary commercial activities. In the KCA, there are more detailed provisions for certain commercial activities and their relevant responsibilities. For example, commercial sale (상사매매), mutual account (상호계산), undisclosed association (익명조합), limited partnership (합자조합), commercial agent (대리상), brokerage (중개상), commission agency (위탁매매업), forwarding agent business (운송주선업), carriage business (운송업), public entertainment business (공중접객업), warehousing (창고업), financial lease (금융리스업), franchise (가맹업), and bonds purchasing business (채권매입업).

In case of a commercial sale, if the buyer in a sale between merchants refuses or is unable to receive the subject matter of such sale, the seller, according to the KCA,[85] may deposit it or sell it by auction after giving peremptory notice within a reasonable period set by the seller. In such cases, the seller must send notice thereof to the buyer without delay. For other matters regarding to a

85) Article 67(1) of the Korean Commercial Act.

commercial sale, Articles 67 to 71 of the KCA will apply to them.

In a mutual account or an account current, it becomes effective when, in cases where there are regular transactions between merchants or a merchant and a non-merchant, they agree to offset the total claims and obligations arising out of transactions within a fixed period and to pay the balance thereof according to the Article 72. For other matters regarding to a mutual account, The Articles 72 to 77 of the KCA will apply to them.

In an undisclosed association, it is duly formed upon agreement between parties that one of them will make an investment in the business of the other and the other will share profits accruing from such business according the Article 78. For other matters regarding to an undisclosed association, the Articles 78 to 86 of the KCA will apply to them.

In a limited partnership, it is duly formed when general partners who, as managers of the partnership, bear unlimited liability for the partnership's obligations and limited partners who bear limited liability within the amount of their investment agree to make a mutual investment in, and jointly manage, a joint business according to the Article 86-2. For other matters regarding to a limited partnership, the Articles 86-2 to 86-9 of the KCA will apply to them.

In a commercial agent, a person who engages in the business of acting on behalf of a particular merchant, not as a commercial employee of any person but as agent or broker in transactions falling within the same type of business as such merchant, is called a commercial agent according to the Article 87.[86)] For other matters regarding to a commercial agent, the Articles 87 to 92-3 of the KCA will apply to them.

In a brokerage, a person who engages in the business of acting as an intermediary in commercial activities between other persons is called a broker according to the Article 93. For other matters regarding to a brokerage, the Articles 93 to 100 of the KCA will apply to them.

In a commission agency, a person who makes it his/her business to effect sale and purchase of goods or securities under his/her own name on the account of another party is called a commission agent according to the Article 101. For other matters regarding to a commission agency, the Articles 101 to 113 of the

86) Supreme Court Decision 2011Da28342, decided on February 14, 2013; Chung, Byung-Duck, "Review of The Supreme Court of Korea Case concerning relating to Provision and Commercial Transaction under the Korean Commercial Act in 2014 (in Korean)," The Commercial Cases Review, Vol. 28 No. 3, September 2015, p.318.

KCA will apply to them.

In a forwarding agent business, a person who engages in the business of intermediation for the carriage of goods in his/her own name is called a forwarding agent according to the Article 114. For other matters regarding to a forwarding agency, the Articles 114 to 124 of the KCA will apply to them.

In a carriage business, a person who engages in the business of carrying goods or passengers by land or on lakes and rivers, and in ports and bays is called a carrier according to the Article 125. Carriage of goods and carriage of passengers are provided under the KCA. For other matters regarding to a carriage business, the Articles 125 to 150 of the KCA will apply to them.

In a public entertainment business or a hospitality business, any person who engages in the business of making transactions by theaters, hotels, restaurants, or other facilities used by the public is called a hospitality service provider according to the Article 151. For other matters regarding to a public entertainment business or a hospitality business, the Articles 151 to 154 of the KCA will apply to them.

In a warehousing, a person who engages in the business of storing goods in a warehouse for another person is called a warehouse business entity according to the Article 155. For other matters regarding to a warehousing business, the Articles 155 to 168 of the KCA will apply to them.

In a financial lease business, a person who engages in the business of acquiring and borrowing machinery, facilities and other property selected by a financial lessee from any third party('supplier'), and then making financial lessees use such machinery, facilities and other property is called a financial lease business entity according to the Article 168-2. For other matters regarding to a financial lease business, the Articles 168-2 to 168-5 of the KCA will apply to them.

In a franchise business, a person who carries on business according to the quality standards and business polices designated by a person (franchisor) who engages in the business of providing his/her own trade name, trademark, etc. after obtaining a permit for the use of the trade name, etc. from the franchisor is called a franchisee according to the Article 168-6. For other matters regarding to a franchise business, the Articles 168-6 to 168-10 of the KCA will apply to them.

In a bonds purchasing business or factoring business, a person who engages in the business of purchasing and recovering business bonds acquired or to be acquired by another person through the sale of goods or securities, provision of services, etc. is called a bonds purchasing business entity according to the Article 168-11. For other matters regarding to a bonds purchasing business or factoring business, the Articles 168-11 and 168-12 of the KCA will apply to them.

3. Part 3: Company

The term 'company' used in the KCA means a corporation incorporated for the purpose of engaging in commercial activities and any other profit-making activities.[87] This Part 3 is generally called the 'Company Act' (회사법) or 'Corporation Act' in Korea even though it is not independent from the KCA. Whenever we say the Company Act in Korea, it always means the Part 3 of the KCA.

Companies under the KCA are categorized into five types, namely, partnership companies, limited partnership companies, limited liability companies, stock companies, and limited companies.[88] This means that companies are grouped into five categories and any company should be one of them in Korea if it is a commercial corporation. The five types of companies are as follows:

(i) partnership company (*hapmyong hwesa* in Korean, 합명회사),
(ii) limited partnership company (*hapja hwesa* in Korean, 합자회사),
(iii) limited liability company (*yuhanchaekim hwesa* in Korean, 유한책임회사),
(iv) stock company (*joosik hwesa* in Korean, 주식회사), and
(v) limited company (*yuhan hwesa* in Korean, 유한회사).

(1) A partnership company can be incorporated jointly by at least two members, and no member of a partnership company may, without the consent of the other members, transfer his shares to other persons, effect any transaction which falls within the class of business carried by the company, or become a member with unlimited liability at, or a director of, another company whose business purpose is the same kind of business as the company. If no managing member is designated, each member shall represent the company, and if the

87) Article 169 of the Korean Commercial Act.
88) Article 170 of the Korean Commercial Act.

assets of the company are insufficient to fully satisfy all its obligations, each member shall be jointly and severally liable to discharge the obligations. With the consent of all of the members the company may be transformed into a limited partnership company.

The Articles 178 to 267 of the KCA cover incorporation, internal relationship of company, external relationship of company, withdrawal of members, dissolution of company, and liquidation.

(2) A limited partnership company must be composed of members with limited liability and members with unlimited liability. Members with limited liability may not provide personal services or credits as a form of contributions, and every member with unlimited liability shall have the responsibility and duty to manage the affairs of the company unless otherwise provided in the articles of incorporation. A member with limited liability may effect a transaction which falls within the class of business carried on by the company without the consent of the other members and become a member with unlimited liability, or a director, of another company of which the business purpose is the same kind of business as the company. Also, he may transfer shares to other persons with the consent of all of the members with unlimited liability and be transformed into a partnership company with the consent of all of the members the company.

The Articles 268 to 287 of the KCA cover incorporation, internal and external relationship of company, dissolution of company, and liquidation.

(3) The recently amended KCA has introduced a new type of company. It is a limited liability company (*yuhan-chaekim-hwesa*), similar to a limited liability company (LLC) in the United States. This entity is intended to provide flexibility in the composition of the organization and recovery of investments while providing limited liability protection against creditors of the company up to their invested amounts.

The limited liability company can be established upon a capital investment by one or more persons and registration of its incorporation. Capital contributions can be made in any form, such as cash or other tangible assets except those that are difficult to determine the reasonable market value (e.g., services or credit). There is no minimum capital requirement to establish a limited liability company. While a manager is required (may be a person or a legal entity), there is no mandate to have directors or an auditor. A member is allowed to transfer her interests in the limited liability company to a third party with the consent of other members or if permitted in its Articles of Association.

The Articles 287-2 to 287-45 of the KCA cover incorporation, internal relationship of company, external relationship of company, admission and withdrawal of members, dissolution of company, and liquidation.

(4) A stock company can be incorporated jointly by at least one person, and the total number of shares authorized to be issued, the par value per share, and the total number of shares to be issued at the time of incorporation shall be determined. The number of shares to be issued at the time of incorporation shall be no less than one fourth of the total number of shares authorized to be issued by the company, and the capital shall be no less than fifty million won. The par value per share shall be at least one hundred won, and shares may be transferred. A stock company shall have a general shareholders' meeting, directors and the board of directors, auditors and an audit committee. The general shareholders' meeting shall be the highest organ, and the minority shareholders (shareholders who hold no less than three hundredths (3%) of the total issued and outstanding shares) may propose certain matters as issues to be resolved at the general shareholders' meeting. Directors and the board of directors shall manage the affairs of the company.

The Articles 288 to 542-13 of the KCA cover incorporation, shares, all-inclusive transfer of shares, organs of company (general meeting of shareholders, directors and board of directors, auditors and audit committee), issuance of new shares, amendments to Articles of Incorporation, reduction of capital, accounting of company, bonds, dissolution of company, merger, division of company, liquidation, and special cases for listed companies.

(5) A limited company can be incorporated jointly by at least one member. The liability of a member must be limited to the amount of his contribution to the company. A member may transfer his shares pursuant to the resolution of a general members' meeting, and the company must have one or more directors who will represent the company.

The Articles 543 to 267 of the KCA cover incorporation, rights and obligations of members, management of company, amendments to Articles of Incorporation, and dissolution and liquidation.

6) The KCA provisions for foreign company from Articles 614 to 621 are just for convenience regulations for appointment of representatives, establishment of business offices and registrations thereof. For example, a foreign company intending to engage in business in Korea must appoint a representative in Korea and must establish a business office in Korea, or have its one or more representatives have his address in Korea. For the purposes of a registration under the preceding paragraph, a foreign company must register the governing law under which it was incorporated and the name and address of its representative in Korea.[89)]

A foreign company is not a separate type of companies which are grouped into five categories under the KCA. Company incorporated in a foreign country is, if it has established its principal office in Korea or its main objective is to engage in business in Korea, subject to the same provisions as a company incorporated in Korea.[90)]

7) The Part 3 of the KCA has lots of provisions with many legal issues and matters. It is also cited in many company-related cases. In turn, many other legal issues and cases will be discussed in separate Chapters for the Company Act.

4. Part 4: Insurances

This Part provides for an insurance contract and an insurance responsibility. An insurance contract shall take effect when one of the parties pays the contractual premiums, and the other party promises to pay a certain amount of insurance coverage or other benefits upon occurrence of an uncertain event against the property, life, or body of the former.[91)]

The types of insurance under the KCA are as follows:

(i) Non-life insurance (*e.g.*, fire insurance, transportation insurance, marine

---

89) Article 614 (Appointment of Representatives, Establishment of Business Offices and Registrations thereof) of the Korean Commercial Act.

90) Article 617 (Similar Foreign Company) of the Korean Commercial Act.

91) Article 638 (Effect of Insurance Contracts) of the Korean Commercial Act; Supreme Court Decision 2013Da217108, decided on July 24, 2014.

insurance, liability insurance, automobile insurance, and guarantee Insurance), and (ii) Personal insurance (*e.g.*, life insurance, accident insurance, and sickness Insurance).

The Part 4 from the Articles 638 to 739-3 of the KCA is also called the 'Insurance Act' (보험법) in Korea even though it is not independent from the KCA. For insurance, there is also another important statute which is the 'Insurance Business Act' (보험업법) in Korea. Since the Part 4 for insurance is also cited in many insurance-related cases, many other legal issues and cases will be discussed in separate Chapters for Insurance.

5. Part 5: Marine Commerce

This Part was wholly amended by Act No.8582 in August 2007 and came into force on January 1, 2008. In particular, with respect to electronic bill of ladings, the 'Regulation for the implementation of Electronic Bill of Lading-related Provisions of the Korean Commercial Act' (상법의 전자선하증권 규정의 시행에 관한 규정) was established as a Presidential Decree and came into force on March 23, 2013.

The provisions of this Part will apply mutatis mutandis to a ship used for navigation, even if it is not intended for commercial activities or for other profit-making purposes. However, the same will not apply in cases where it is not appropriate for the provisions of this Part to apply mutatis mutandis to a state-owned ship or public ship, as prescribed by Presidential Decree in view of the purpose, character, etc. of the navigation.[92] The provisions of this Part will not apply to a small boat or a boat mainly propelled with oars or a pole.

The Articles 740 to 790 of this Part deal with a marine commercial enterprise which covers ship, shipmaster, co-ownership of ships and limits on liability of shipowners. The Articles 791 to 864 of this Part deal with a transportation and charter which covers affreightment[93] in general ships, marine passenger transportation, voyage charter,[94] time charter,[95] bareboat charter,[96] and Bills of

92) Article 741 (Scope of Application) of the Korean Commercial Act.

93) A contract of affreightment in a general ship shall come into effect when a carrier agrees to transport individual goods by ship at sea and a consignor agrees to pay the freight therefor (*see* Article 791 of the Korean Commercial Act).

94) A voyage charter comes into effect when a shipowner agrees to provide a charterer

Lading (B/L). The Articles 865 to 895 of this Part deal with a maritime perils which covers general average, collision of ships, and salvage.

6. Part 6: Carriage by Air

This Part 6 for a carriage by air or air transportation has been effective from November 24, 2011 since a new Chapter of Carriage by Air or Air Transport has been established in the Articles 896 to 935.

The provisions of this Part will apply mutatis mutandis to any aircraft for flight purposes, regardless of commercial activities or any other profit-making flight activities. However, the same will not apply in cases where it is inappropriate for the provisions of this Part to apply mutatis mutandis to a state-owned or public aircraft prescribed by Presidential Decree, taking the purpose, character, etc. of the flight into account.[97)]

This Part deals with carriage of passengers, carriage of goods, air waybill, and liability for damage.

III. Amendments to Korean Commercial Act

1. Necessity of the Amendment to the KCA

The KCA has arrived at its present form as the result of being amended many times, and the latest amendment was created in December 2020. The KCA has been amended to reflect the business reality which witnesses drastic changes of corporate environment and commercial circumstance while the fundamental

---

with the whole or any part of a ship serviced by the crew on board and equipped with navigation facilities for transportation of goods, and a charterer agrees to pay the fare in response thereto (*see* Article 827 of the Korean Commercial Act).

95) A time charter comes into effect when a shipowner agrees to provide a charterer with a ship serviced by the crew on board and equipped with navigation facilities for a given period to be used for navigation, and the charterer agrees to pay the fare determined by the period in response thereto (*see* Article 842 of the Korean Commercial Act).

96) A bareboat charter comes into effect when a shipowner agrees to provide a charterer with a ship for the purpose of operating such ship under the control and management of a charterer, and the charterer agrees to pay the charterage in response thereto (*see* Article 847 of the Korean Commercial Act).

97) Article 897 of the Korean Commercial Act.

framework remains intact.

Why is the KCA so often revised? Like other countries' commercial laws, the KCA is very sensitive to national or international business changes. The main reasons to frequent changes are that the KCA has to:

(i) Meet the quickly changing business environment like such new business activities as lease, factoring, franchise and electronic payment gateway,

(ii) Promote fair play of businesses and improvement of corporate governance,

(iii) Incorporate the practical provisions with respect to publicly listed corporations right after the repeal of the Securities Transactions Act, based on Korea's own business law history,

(iv) Regulate the developing industries like shipping and air transportation, and

(v) Historically, satisfy the requirements of the IMF Standby Credit Program after 1997 financial crisis.

2. Distinguished Partial Amendments to the KCA

The latest amendment to the KCA was made on December 29, 2020 since the establishment of the KCA in 1962. There have been many amendments of the KCA, but distinguished partial amendments since 2009 are as follows for the reference:

1) Amendment on December 29, 2020[98)]

The Amendment introduces a multi-level derivative suit and separate election system for audit committee members in order to prevent the majority shareholder of the parent company from misappropriating assets or business opportunities of subsidiary established by him/her, and from influencing the appointment of audit committee members of such subsidiary.

The regulations that caused confusion on the shareholders' dividend base date will be revised to ensure that dividends can be made equally to both old and new shares regardless of the share issue date. In the case of electronic voting, the resolution requirements of the general shareholders' meeting for the appointment of audit will be relaxed so that more than a quarter of the total number of issued shares is not applied.

98) Partial Revision on December 29, 2020, Act No. 17764 (Effective from December 29, 2020).

(1) In order to resolve confusion in dividend practice and induce decentralization of shareholders' meetings, the provisions that presuppose the end of the business year as a dividend base date are deleted (the existing Article 350 (3) deleted, etc.).

(2) Introduction of a multi-level derivative suit.

Shareholders with 1% or more of the total number of shares issued by the parent company are allowed to file a lawsuit against the subsidiary to hold the responsibility of the subsidiary director. Even if the parent company's shares fall to less than 50% of the total number of shares issued by the subsidiary, it does not affect the effectiveness of the complaint, with an exception when the parent company is not to hold any shares issued by the subsidiary (Article 406-2).

A person who holds at least 0.5% of the total number of shares issued by a listed company continuously from six months ago may exercise the rights of shareholders under Article 406-2 (Article 542-6(7)).

(3) Where a company is allowed to exercise voting rights electronically, it is possible to resolve the appointment of an auditor or audit committee member as a majority of the voting rights of the shareholders present (Article 409(3) and Article 542-12(8)).

(4) Shareholders of listed companies can selectively claim the requirements for exercising minority shareholders' rights under the special provisions of listed companies or the requirements for exercising minority shareholders' rights under general regulations (Article 542-6(10)).

(5) When appointing directors at a general shareholders' meeting, one of the members of the audit committee shall be appointed as a director who becomes a member of the audit committee separately from other directors (Article 542-12(2)).

(6) In the case of members of the audit committee who are not outside directors, the voting rights are restricted for stocks exceeding 3% by adding shares owned by related parties, etc. against a largest shareholder, and exceeding 3% against other shareholders. In the case of members of the audit committee who are outside directors, the voting rights are restricted for stocks exceeding 3% against all shareholders (Article 542-12(4)(7)).

2) Amendment on September 10, 2020[99]

Under the current law, 'provisional registration of a trade name' is available only for stock company and limited company so that 'limited liability company'

99) Partial Revision on June 9, 2020, Act No. 17362 (Effective from September 10, 2020).

cannot register a trade name. A limited liability company is similar to a limited company in the establishment procedure, broadly recognizing private autonomy in terms of operation and organization and having to fulfill investment before registration of establishment.

By revising the provisional registration of the trade name, even a limited liability company can apply it so that it prevents others from registering the trade name first during the establishment process.

3) Amendment on December 1, 2015[100)]

In order to expand the corporate acquisition and merger market and to revitalize the economy, various types of corporate acquisition and merger methods are introduced to facilitate corporate restructuring and investment activities, while improving the stock purchase claim by opposing shareholders.

(1) Introduction of triangular stock exchange, reverse triangular merger, and triangular division merger system (Article 360-3 and Article 530-6, etc.). It is expected that the economic demand for corporate mergers and acquisitions can be smoothly supported by establishing various corporate mergers and acquisitions using subsidiaries.

(2) Development of the stock purchase claim by opposing shareholders (Article 360-5(1) and Article 374-2, etc.).

(3) Relaxation of requirements for small-scale stock exchange, etc. (Article 360-10(1) and Article 527-3(1), etc.).

(4) Introduction of a simple business transfer and rental system (Article 374-3). It is expected that efficient restructuring of the company will be facilitated by introducing a simple business transfer and rental system.

(5) Development of regulations related to division and merger of the company (Article 530-5, etc.).

4) Amendment on May 20, 2014[101)]

There have been no cases of issuance of bearer stock so that there are concerns about tax blind spots such as avoidance of transfer tax and lack of transparency in tax.

It is intended to reflect the air carrier's liability limit raised by the ‘Convention for the Unification of certain Rule Relating to International

---

100) Partial Revision on December 1, 2015, Act No. 13523 (Effective from March 2, 2016).

101) Partial Revision on May 20, 2014, Act No. 12591 (Effective from May 20, 2014).

Transportation by Air' from January 1, 2010 on the grounds that international inflation has risen by 13.1% over five years to the existing Act.

(1) Abolish the current bearer stock and reorganize other related regulations (Article 329-2 and Article 352, and delete the existing Articles 357 and 358).

(2) In the event of a passenger's death or injury, the carrier's liability limit is raised from 100,000 to 113,100 per passenger, from 4,150 to 4,694 per passenger for delayed passenger, from 1,000 to 1,131 per passenger for loss, damage or delay of luggage, and from 17 to 19 per kilogram for loss, damage or delay of freight (Articles 905, 907(2), 910(1) and 915(1)).

(3) In the case of domestic air transport, the carrier's liability limit is raised from 500 to 1,000 units per passenger (Article 907(2)).

5) Amendment on March 11, 2014[102)]

There are great revisions on the Insurance part.

(1) The clear statement of the insurer's obligation to explain the insurance terms and conditions, and the period extension of the policyholder's right to cancel an insurance contract against the violation of the obligation to issue and explain the insurance terms and conditions (Article 638-3).

(2) The new regulations on the authority of insurance agents, etc. (Article 646-2).

(3) The extension of an extinctive prescription period (Article 662).

(4) The establishment of regulations prohibiting insurance subrogation by insurers against family members (Article 682).

(5) The concretization of an effect of violating the obligation for the insured in liability insurance to notify the insurer of the fact of claiming compensation (Article 722).

(6) The new guarantee insurance regulations (Articles 726-5 to 726-7)

(7) The improvement of pension insurance-related regulations and concreteness of life insurance accidents (Articles 727 and 730, and deletion of existing Articles 735 and 735-2)

(8) The concretization of the insurer's reasons for indemnification in life insurance (Article 732-2).

(9) The clarification of requirements for group insurance (Article 735-3(3)).

(10) The establishment of disease insurance regulations (Articles 739-2 and 739-3).

---

102) Partial Revision on March 11, 2014, Act No. 12397 (Effective from March 12, 2015).

6) Amendment on May 23, 2011[103)]

This amendment is for the establishment of air transport part in the KCA. In view of the growth of Korean air transportation industry, a new chapter of air transport has been established in the KCA (Articles 896 to 935).

The new chapter is expected to secure the stabilized contractual relationship and ensure the right and interest of customers and consignors.

(1) The reduction and exemption of liability of carriers and aircraft operators (Article 898).

(2) The application to non-contractual claims, etc. (Article 899).

(3) The extinction of the carrier's liability and claims (Articles 902 and 919).

(4) The carrier's liability and liability limit for passenger's damage (Articles 904, 905 and 907).

(5) The obligation to pay advance payments (Article 906).

(6) The carrier's liability and liability limit for the loss, damage, and delay of baggage (Articles 908 to 910).

(7) The carrier's liability and liability limit for damage to transportation goods (Articles 913 to 915).

(8) The transportation certificate (Articles 921 to 929).

(9) The liability for damages to a third party on the ground (Articles 930 to 935).

7) Amendment on April 14, 2011[104)]

(1) In line with the global trend and the needs from business community, new types of businesses like partnership, limited liability company (LLC) have been introduced (Articles 86-2 to 86-9 and 287-2 to 287-45).

(2) In order to facilitate the incorporation, no-par stocks may be issued and the minimum capital requirement has been abolished (Articles 291, 329 and 546).

(3) A company is allowed to acquire its own shares with its retained earnings as of the previous fiscal year-end on an equal and unbiased basis to all shareholders (Articles 341, 341-2, 341-3 and 342).

(4) A variety of stocks, with or without voting rights, may be issued to promote necessary fund raising (Articles 344, 345, 346, 344-2 and 344-3).

(5) Electronic filing of stocks and debentures will be permitted in view of the

103) Partial Revision on May 23, 2011, Act No. 10696 (Effective from November 24, 2011).

104) Partial Revision on April 14, 2011, Act No. 10600 (Effective from April 15, 2012).

dematerialization trend (Articles 356-2, 420-4, 474(2), 478(2), and 488).

(6) A controlling shareholder with more than 95 percent of ownership may purchase the remaining stocks held by minority shareholders at fair price in spite of their intention (Articles 360-24 to 360-26).

(7) The alleged misappropriation of corporate opportunity by a director shall be prohibited (Article 397-2).

(8) The scope of self-dealing by directors, which is subject to the approval of the board of directors, shall be expanded to cover dealings with specifically related persons or companies (Article 398).

(9) The Compensation for the damages incurred by a director shall be limited to six times of his yearly remuneration (three times in case of an outside director) but for willful intent or gross negligence (Article 400(2))

(10) Listed companies may designate executive officers (Articles 408-2 to 408-9).

(11) Accounting provisions shall be conformed to the generally accepted accounting principles (Articles 446-2, 447, 447-4, and the deletion of the existing Articles 452, 453-2, and 454 to 457-2).

(12) The current legal reserves, dividend policy and debentures shall be improved (Articles 460, 461-2, 462(2), 462-4, 469, 481 to 485, 480-2, and 480-3).

(13) The standing compliance officer shall be hired by listed companies in terms of asset size (Article 542-13).

(14) Some regulations on the limited company, including the total number of shareholders, transfer of ownership, transformation to stock company, etc., shall be abolished (Articles 556, 571, 607, and the deletion of the existing Article 545).

8) Amendment on June 10, 2010[105)]

This amendment is for the application of the new 'Act on Security Interests in Movable Properties, Receivables, etc.' (동산·채권 등의 담보에 관한 법률) to the KCA.

Revision of Article 468 (Employees' Rights to Preferential Payment): A person who has a claim for the return of money as a guarantee for fidelity of an employee or any other claim arising out of the employment relationship between the company and its employees shall be entitled to preferential payment from the company's total assets: Provided, That such entitlement shall not be

105) Partial Revision on June 10, 2010, Act No. 10366 (Effective from June 11, 2012).

claimed in preference to a pledge or mortgage.

9) Amendment on May 14, 2010[106)]

(1) Such new commercial activities as lease, franchise and factoring have got detailed provisions. Also payment and settlement services have become a new commercial activity prescribed in the KCA (Articles 168-2 to 168-12).

(2) It is noteworthy that the offer between the parties in remote places shall be effective at the time of its receipt by deleting Article 52. Accordingly there is no difference, regardless of the period of acceptance, between the KCA and the Civil Act in the principle of receipt of expressed intention.

(3) When a merchant has loaned money to another person in respect of his/her business, the merchant may claim statutory interest. If a merchant has made substituted donation for another person within the scope of his/her business, the merchant may request for statutory interest thereon from the date of the substituted donation (Article 55).

(4) When a contractual obligation is performed at the branch, it should be at the branch of the obligee, same as the Civil Act based on the principle that the debtor should come to the creditor to perform obligation (Article 56).

(5) A broker may intervene to take the result of transactions of not only goods but also securities (Article 107).

(7) If a consignment sheet has been issued, the carriage contract is presumed to be executed and the goods are also presumed to be properly delivered. Even in case of the failed presumption, the carrier shall be responsible to a third party with good faith as described in the sheet (Article 131).

(8) The strict liability invoked against the businesses serving a number of incoming customers has been reduced to ordinary negligence liability like other businesses (Articles 151 to 154).

10) Amendment on May 28, 2009[107)]

This amendment was purported to facilitate the incorporation of a small-sized company by omitting the initial paid-in capital requirement and notarization of the articles of incorporation, and by streamlining the procedures to convene the Shareholders' Meeting.

(1) In case of incorporation of small-sized company with the paid-in capital

---

106) Partial Revision on May 14, 2010, Act No. 10281 (Effective from November 15, 2010).

107) Partial Revision on May 28, 2009, Act No. 9746 (Effective from May 29, 2010).

less than one billion won, only by promoters, the notarization of the articles of incorporation shall be omitted (Article 292).

(2) The bank's certificate of stock-subscription amount may be replaced by the bank's certificate of outstanding deposit balance (Article 318).

(3) The procedure to convene the Shareholders' Meeting of the small-sized company may be streamlined and shortened. The resolution of Shareholders' Meeting may be conducted on paper (Article 363).

(4) Electronic voting at Shareholders' Meeting may be adopted (Article 368-4).

(5) Election of Auditor of the small-sized company may be exempted (Article 409(4), (5) and (6)).

11) Amendment on January 30, 2009[108)]

In preparation of the entry into force of the Financial Investment Services and Capital Markets Act (자본시장과 금융투자업에 관한 법률), the following special provisions on the corporate governance of listed companies provided in the Securities and Exchange Act shall be transferred to the KCA:

- Stock options (Article 542-3),
- Notice of Shareholders' meeting (Article 542-4),
- Minority shareholders' rights (Article 542-6),
- Special rule on cumulative voting (Article 542-7),
- Outside directors (Article 542-8),
- Restriction on the transactions with interested party (Articles 542-9 and 624-2),
- Standing Auditor and Audit Committee (Articles 542-10 and 542-11), and
- Composition of Audit Committee (Article 542-12).

[Important Partial Amendments to the KCA since 2009]

Revision Date	Revision Type	Act Number	Effective Date
2020-06-09	Partial Amendment	No. 17362	2020-09-10
2018-09-18	Partial Amendment	No. 15755	2018-12-19
2017-10-31	Partial Amendment	No. 14969	2018-11-01
2015-12-01	Partial Amendment	No. 13523	2016-03-02

108) Partial Revision on January 30, 2009, Act No. 9362 (Effective from February 4, 2009).

2014-05-20	Partial Amendment	No. 12591	2014-05-20
2014-03-11	Partial Amendment	No. 12397	2015-03-12
2011-05-23	Partial Amendment	No. 10696	2011-11-24
2011-04-14	Partial Amendment	No. 10600	2012-04-15
2010-05-14	Partial Amendment	No. 10281	2010-11-15
2009-05-28	Partial Amendment	No. 9746	2010-05-29
2009-01-30	Partial Amendment	No. 9362	2009-02-04
... (omitted)			

IV. Selected Issue from the KCA: Commercial Contract

1. Contract in General

A contract (계약) is a promise or set of promises, for breach of which the law gives a remedy, or the performance of which the law in some way recognizes as a duty.[109] It is a legally enforceable agreement between two or more parties that creates, defines, and governs mutual rights and obligations between them. A contract law, the field of the law of obligations concerned with contracts, is based on the principle that agreements must be honored.[110] If commercial matters are applied to a contract, then it becomes a commercial contract and a commercial contract law.

The types of contract generally include (i) express contract, implied contract, and quasi contract which is not a valid contract, (ii) unilateral contract and bilateral contract, (iii) void contract, voidable contract, and unenforceable contract (*e.g.*, the Statute of Frauds).

A contract can be generally created by 3 elements: (i) mutual assent, (ii) 'consideration' or substitute which is required in the common law system, but not in the civil law system and Korea, and (iii) no defense to formation.

In Korea, there is a contract based on the Korean Civil Act (민법) and also a

109) Frank B. Cross and Roger LeRoy Miller, *op. cit.*, p.185.

110) Reuer, Jeffrey J., Ariño, Africa, "Strategic alliance contracts: dimensions and determinants of contractual complexity," Strategic Management Journal. Vol. 28 No. 3, March 2007, pp. 313-330.

contract based on the KCA, which is our concern for the business law purpose.

'Consideration' in Common Law System

I. Introduction

A consideration is a concept of common law and is a necessity for simple contracts. To create an enforceable contract, two elements are required in the common law jurisdiction: (i) bargained for exchange, and (ii) legal value or detriment.[111)]

II. The Bargain Element

1. Promises to make gifts: It is not generally unenforceable, because it lacks the bargain element of consideration.

1) Existence of condition: Even if the person promising to make a gift requires the promisee to meet certain conditions in order to receive the gift, there will be still no consideration. For example, A promises his widowed sister-in-law B a place to live "if you will come down and see me." In response, B travels to see A, thereby incurring expenses. In this case, his promise is unenforceable due to the lack of consideration. However, if the promisor imposes a condition, and the occurrence of this condition is of benefit to him, then the bargain element probably will be present. For example, A promises his nephew B $5,000 if B will refrain from smoking, drinking and gambling until age 21. Contrary to this, the fact that one who promises to make a gift expects to derive altruistic pleasure, or love and affection, from making the gift is not sufficient to constitute a 'bargain.'

2) Executed gifts: Once the promisor makes the gift, he cannot rescind it for lack of consideration.

2. Sham and nominal consideration: It is not real consideration at all.[112)]

1) Nominal amount (*e.g.*, $1): No real bargain present at all. However, if the consideration is big enough to suggest that there was a bargain, the fact that it is 'inadequate' is irrelevant.

2) Payment not in fact made: If a non-trivial payment is recited, but the payment was not in fact made, most courts will take this as evidence that no bargain was present.

3. Promisee awareness: Generally, the promisee must be aware of the promise like in a reward case.

4. Past consideration no good: If the promise is made in return for detriment previously suffered by the promisee, there is no bargain, and thus no consideration. For example, In consideration of your having done X, I promise you $100. In this case, the promise is not enforceable.[113]

2. Offer and Acceptance

1) Intent to Contract

A contract law requires the offer (청약) and acceptance (승낙), which are generally recognized as essential requirements for the formation of a contract, and analysis of their operation is a traditional approach in contract law.[114]

A contract law follows the objective theory of contracts which considers a standard of a reasonable person. Where the evidence is ambiguous about whether the parties intended to be bound, a court will follow: (i) In a 'business' context, the court will presume that the parties intended their agreement to be legally enforceable, and but (ii) In a social or domestic situation, the presumption will be that legal relations were not intended. Where there are contract parties' intents to put in writing later, then the parties' intentions will control.

2) Offer and Acceptance Generally

An offer means the manifestation of willingness to enter into a bargain and an acceptance means the manifestation of assent to the terms thereof made by the offeree in a manner invited or required by the offer.[115] In a bilateral contract,

111) Frank B. Cross and Roger LeRoy Miller, *op. cit.*, p.199.

112) Neal R. Bevans, Business Law: A Hands-On Approach, Thomson Delmar Learning, 2006, p.79.

113) Richard A. Mann and Barry S. Roberts, Smith & Roberson's Business Law (13th edition), Thomson West, 2006, p.211; Neal R. Bevans, *id.*, p.77.

114) Ewan Maclntyre, Business Law (3rd edition), Pearson Longman, 2007, p.78.

115) G.H. Treitel, The Law of Contract (10th Edition), Sweet & Maxwell, 1999, p.8.

both contract sides make promises and in unilateral contract, a contract involves an exchange of the offeror's promise for the offeree's act and the offeree does not make a promise.

(1) Offer

An offer must be sufficiently clear, detailed and definitive so that the counterpart (offeree) may simply accept it to constitute a binding agreement.[116) An offer made in jest or anger is not a valid offer and thus no contract is created. Preliminary negotiations between parties is not also an offer. An auction is not usually an offer and it can be considered as a solicitation of offer.[117)]

In commercial advertisement for sale of goods, it is usually not an offer, but an invitation to treat.[118)] However, if the advertisement contains specific words of commitment, especially a promise to sell a particular number of units, then it can be an offer.[119)] For example, A issued a public notice announcing that it would sell the land at the current market price to the party from whom the land had been requisitioned. B submitted all of the purchase application documents required by A. A gave a formal notice of sale to B informing that the land would be sold to B at the current market price, and that B must enter into the sale contract paying the contract deposit not later than next month. It was held that this was not an offer.[120)]

An offer of a contract may not be withdrawn.[121)] However, there are some exceptions. For example, an offer of a reward may be revoked if no deadline is specified. If a deadline is specified, the offer may not be revoked and it can only expire upon reaching the deadline.[122)] An offer to terminate an employment contract is also revocable until the acceptance reaches the employee (offeror).[123)]

116) Supreme Court Decision 2001Da53059, decided on April 11, 2003 (An offer, which is a legal element of a contract, is an expression of detailed and definitive intention to create a contractual relationship upon an acceptance corresponding to it. The offer must include sufficient details so that the content of the contract can be determined).

117) Ewan MacIntyre, *op. cit.*, p.87.

118) *Id.*, p.79.

119) Supreme Court Decision 2005Da5812, decided on June 1, 2007.

120) Seoul Appellate Court Decision 94Na12526, decided on February 15, 1995.

121) Article 527 of Korean Civil Act.

122) Article 679 of Korean Civil Act.

123) Supreme Court Decision 94Da14629, decided on August 9, 1994 and *see* also 2000Da60890, decided on August 23, 2002 (Where an employee makes an offer to

In some cases, however, to revoke an offer and to refuse to complete the negotiation may constitute a civil wrong, and thus provide a ground for an action in tort.[124)]

An offer of a contract specifying a period for acceptance must lose its effect if the offeror does not receive a notice of acceptance within the period specified.[125)] Where a notice of acceptance had arrived after the expiration of the period, if it was dispatched at such a time that under normal circumstances it would have arrived within such period, the offeror must dispatch, without delay, to the other party a notice of the delayed arrival. If the offeror has neglected to give such notice, the notice of acceptance is deemed not to have been delayed. An offer of a contract which does not specify a period for acceptance loses its effect if the offeror does not receive a notice of acceptance within a reasonable period.[126)] The offeror may regard a delayed acceptance as a new offer in the cases of the preceding two Articles.[127)]

If the offeree has accepted an offer but subject to a condition or with any other modification, he is deemed to have rejected the original offer and thereby simultaneously made a new offer.[128)]

(2) Acceptance

Who may accept the offer? An offer can be accepted only by a person in

---

terminate the employment contract, the offer may be withdrawn as long as the employer's acceptance to terminate has not reached the employee).

124) Supreme Court Decision 2001Da53059, decided on April 11, 2003 (If, in the course of negotiation, a party provided the ground for the other party to hold a reasonable expectation or reliance that a contract will certainly be entered into, and if the other party acted on the basis of that reliance, the party's refusal to enter into a contract will be wrongful, considering the principle of good faith. The party's refusal, which causes loss to the other party, is beyond the limits of freedom of contract and it constitutes a tort). *See* also Supreme Court Decision 92Nu16942, decided on July 27, 1993 (A resignation handed in by a public servant can, in principle, be withdrawn as long as the Government's decision to terminate the employment has not been made. However, the withdrawal will not be permitted even before the Government's decision has been made, if there are special circumstances which make it against good faith to withdraw the resignation).

125) Article 528(1) of Korean Civil Act.

126) Article 529 of Korean Civil Act.

127) Article 530 of Korean Civil Act.

128) Article 534 of Korean Civil Act. An acceptance must be entirely match with an offer. This is called as the ‘Mirror Image Rule’ in the common law system.

whom the offeror intended to create a power of acceptance. An offeree must know of an offer. Thus, if a reward is offered for a particular act, a person who does the act without knowing about the reward cannot claim it.[129)]

Where method not specified, an acceptance may be given in any reasonable method. An acceptance of unilateral contract may be done by full performance of the requested act. When an offer invites either promise or performance, an acceptance may be done by either a promise or performance. If the seller is 'accommodating' the buyer by shipping what the seller knows and says are non-conforming goods, this does not act as an acceptance. For a notice of acceptance of unilateral contract, most courts now hold that the offeree must give notice of his acceptance after he has done the requested act in the unilateral contract.

In case of an acceptance by a silence, an offer, generally, cannot be accepted by silence. However, there are some exceptions and a silence may be acceptance in followings: (i) Reason to understand (if the offeror has given the offeree, reason to understand that silence will constitute acceptance), (ii) Benefit of services, (iii) Prior conduct, and (iv) Acceptance by dominion (where the offeree receives goods, and keeps them). For example, A proposed an exchange of his parcel of land with B's parcel of land. A subsequently withdrew the proposal. But B believed that the exchange was made and B started cultivating A's parcel of land until the time when A evicted B. A's parcel was near A's home and A knew about B's occupation all along.[130)] In this case, the court finds an acceptance on the basis of the parties' conduct.

There are various ways of terminating the power of acceptance.

(i) Rejection by the offeree, but rejection will not terminate the power of acceptance if either: (a) the offeror indicates that the offer still stands despite the rejections; or (b) the offeree states that although he is not now accepting, he wishes to consider the offer further later.

(ii) Counter-offer by the offeree,[131)] but counter-offer does not terminate the power of acceptance if either offeror or offeree indicates otherwise.

(iii) Lapse of time, but the power of acceptance terminates at the end of a

---

129) G.H. Treitel, *op. cit.*, p.9.

130) Supreme Court Decision 92Da29696, decided on October 13, 1992.

131) Ewan MacIntyre, *op. cit.*, p.86.

reasonable time period when there is no time limit for acceptance and face-to-face or over the phone, power of acceptance continues only during the conversation.

(iv) Revocation by the offeror, but it does not become effective until it is received by an offeree. If the letter or telegram revoking an offer is lost through misdelivery, the revocation of an offer never becomes effective.

(v) Death or incapacity of the offeror or offeree and this is so even if the offeree does not learn of the offeror's death or incapacity until after he has dispatched the acceptance.

An offeror may waive the receipt of acceptance and an offer is bound by the contract without an explicit acceptance. For example, a merchant who received an offer in his usual line of business must reply without undue delay. Failure to do so is deemed to be an acceptance under the Article 53 of the KCA.

3. Timeliness between Remote Parties

While a declaration of intention made to another party takes effect as from the time it has reached him,[132] a contract between parties in remote places is concluded when the acceptance is dispatched to the offeror.[133] If an offer stipulates that an acceptance must be made by a certain date or time, a contract is made only if an acceptance arrives in time.

4. Effect of Contract

In principle, one of the parties to a bilateral contract may refuse performance of his own obligation until the other party tenders performance of his obligation.[134] However, if the performance of an obligation of one of the parties to a bilateral contract becomes impossible by any cause for which neither of the parties is responsible, the obligor may not be entitled to counter-performance.

If one of the parties or both parties have a right of rescission for the future,

---

132) Article 111 of Korean Civil Act.

133) Article 531 of Korean Civil Act. This is called as the 'Mailbox Rule,' which means an acceptance is effective upon proper dispatch (*see* Frank B. Cross and Roger LeRoy Miller, *op. cit.*, p.198).

134) Article 536(1) of Korean Civil Act.

or a right of rescission, either right of rescission will be effected by a declaration of intention made to the other party.[135] The declaration of such intention may not be withdrawn. If one of the parties does not perform his obligation, the other party may fix a reasonable period and give peremptory notice demanding its performance, and may rescind the contract, if no performance is effected within such period.[136] If, according to the nature of the contract or by a declaration of intention of the parties, the objective for which the contract has been entered is unattainable unless it is performed at a designated time and date or within a designated period, and one of parties has not effected performance on his part, the other party may, without giving such notice, rescind the contract.[137] If one of the parties has rescinded the contract, each party is liable to restore his other party to his original position.[138] Interest must be paid upon any money to be repaid in such case as from the day on which such money has been received.

If one of the parties rescinds a contract for the future, the contract will lose its effect for the future and rescission for the future or rescission of a contract may not affect any claim for damages.[139] If a person entitled to a right of rescission has by his intentional act or negligence, materially damaged the subject matter of the contract, or has become unable to return it, or has caused it to be converted into a different kind of object by processing or altering it, the right of rescission must be extinguished.[140]

5. Commercial Contract

In Korea, the KCA provides for a different set of typical commercial contracts (상사계약):

(i) Commercial sale from the Article 67 of the KCA,
(ii) Account current or mutual account from the Article 72 of the KCA,
(iii) Undisclosed association from the Article 78 of the KCA,
(iv) Limited partnership from the Article 86-2 of the KCA,

135) Article 543 of Korean Civil Act.
136) Article 544 of Korean Civil Act.
137) Article 545 of Korean Civil Act.
138) Article 548(1) of Korean Civil Act.
139) Articles 550 and 551 of Korean Civil Act.
140) Article 553 of Korean Civil Act.

(v) Commercial agents from the Article 87 of the KCA,
(vi) Brokerage from the Article 93 of the KCA,
(vii) Commission agency from the Article 101 of the KCA,
(viii) Forwarding agent business from the Article 114 of the KCA,
(ix) Carriage business from the Article 125 of the KCA,
(x) Hospitality business from the Article 151 of the KCA,
(xi) Warehousing from the Article 155 of the KCA,
(xii) Financial lease business from the Article 168-2 of the KCA,
(xiii) Franchise business from the Article 168-6 of the KCA, and
(xiv) Bonds purchasing business from the Article 168-11 of the KCA.

There are special provisions for such commercial contracts in the KCA. Otherwise, the Korean Civil Act will apply even to commercial contracts.

V. Case Study on Business Transfer and Contract

1. Case Study on Business Transfer[141)]

1) Main Issues

(1) The meaning of a business transfer and criteria for its determination.

(2) In case where a business transferee who ceases to use a transferor's business name gives an individual notice of acceptance of obligation to a creditor of an transferor, whether he bears the responsibility of paying off the obligation to the creditor (affirmative).

2) Summary of Decision

(1) A business under the Article 42(1) of the KCA refers to a functional asset as an organic entity organized for a certain business purpose, which means that an organic combination of tangible and intangible assets and factual relation with

141) Supreme Court Decision 2007Da89722, decided on April 11, 2008 and *see* also Supreme Court Decision 2005Da602, decided on July 22, 2005.

economic values functions as a source of revenue and the source of revenue becomes an object of transaction as if it were a kind of goods. Thus, the issue of whether a business transfer occurred should be determined depending on whether an transferee continues to operate the business which the transferor used to operate after he got transferred with a functional asset as a source of revenue.

(2) The legal principle of the Article 44 of the KCA acknowledges the existence of liability of paying off obligations where a business transferee makes an advertisement of acceptance of obligations, although he ceases to use a transferor's trade name. It is applied not limited to the situation where a business transferee makes an advertisement of acceptance of a transferor's obligation, but also applied to the situation where a transferor's creditor was given an individual notice and thus, the liability of paying off obligations occurs as to such creditor.

3) Reasoning

(1) As to whether a business transfer occurred

A business under the Article 42(1) of the KCA refers to a functional asset as an organic entity organized for a certain business purpose, which means that an organic combination of tangible and intangible assets and factual relation with economic values functions as a source of revenue and the source of revenue becomes an object of transaction as if it were a kind of goods. Thus, the issue of whether a business transfer occurred should be determined depending on whether an transferee continues to operate the business which the transferor used to operate after he got transferred with a functional asset as a source of revenue.[142]

In light of the above legal principle and the records applied to the facts established by the adopted evidences, we agree with the court below in its justified fact-findings and judgment that the defendant got transferred with the business of this part by being transferred with a business organization composed of antenna manufacturing-sales facilities and human resources organization of Mirae Tech Incorporation about Oct. 15 of 2004 without any modifications. We cannot hold a different view merely based on the disposition of tax authorities as

---

142) *See* Supreme Court Decision 2005Da602, decided on July 22, 2005.

to the business transfer of this case and the allegations in the grounds for appeal.

This part of judgment below contains no errors in the misunderstanding of legal principles or the misconception of facts as otherwise alleged in the grounds of appeal.

(2) As to the liability of a business transferee

The legal principle of the Article 44 of the KCA acknowledges the existence of liability of paying off obligations where a business transferee makes an advertisement of acceptance of obligations, although he ceases to use a transferor's trade name. It is applied not limited to the situation where a business transferee makes an advertisement of acceptance of a transferor's obligation, but also applied to the situation where a transferor's creditor was given an individual notice and thus, the liability of paying off obligations occurs as to such creditor.

In light of the above legal principle and the records applied to the facts established by the adopted evidences, we agree with the court below in its justified fact-findings and judgment that shortly after the defendant was transferred with the business from the above Mirae Tech, the document was faxed to the plaintiff to the purport that the trade name of Mirae Tech was changed from the 'Mirae Tech (Inc.)' to the defendant's '(Inc.) Antenna Tech' and contact number and address were also changed; thereafter, another document with '(Inc.) Antenna Tech (the former Mirae Tech)' as a sender was faxed, attached with the defendant's certificate of registration of business; moreover, while the defendant was doing business transactions with the plaintiff, the defendant paid off not only the commodities sales price incurred by the defendant, but also KRW 68,840,000 out of the prior commodities sales price obligation of KRW 132,699,189 owed to the plaintiff; and based on the above facts, the defendant is obligated to pay off sales price obligations owed by the above Mirae Tech, a business transferor, to the plaintiff.

The grounds of appeal alleged that no objective similarity exists between the defendant's trade name and that of the above Mirae Tech, or the commodities sales price obligations were not succeeded to by the transferee at the time of the business transfer contract between the defendant and that of the above Mirae Tech. However, such facts alone do not constitute a ground for negating the defendant's liability to pay off obligations as stipulated by the Article 44 of the

KCA. On the other hand, such allegation is not sufficient to acknowledge that the plaintiff knew that the commodities sales price obligations were not succeeded to by the transferee in the above business transfer contract. Further, other allegations in the grounds of appeal are all without merit since they dispute fact-findings that belong to the exclusive authorities of the court below, which mainly sits for finding facts.

This part of judgment below contains no errors in the misunderstanding of legal principles or the misconception of facts as otherwise alleged in the grounds of appeal.

4) Conclusion

Therefore, the appeal is dismissed, and the costs of appeal shall be borne by the losing party. It is so decided as per Disposition by the assent of all participating Justices.

The court decision can be evaluated as being appropriate and reasonable.[143)]

2. Case Study on Contractual Amount[144)]

1) Main Issues and Holdings

(1) Significance of an exclusive management agreement and standard for determining its legal nature.

(2) In a case where Party A, an entertainer, concluded an exclusive agreement with Party B in which she delegated management tasks relating to her entertainment career to Party B and thereafter rescinded the exclusive agreement on the ground of a breach of fiduciary relationship, the case holding that the legal nature of the foregoing exclusive agreement constitutes an innominate contract that is akin to mandate, and that Party A may rescind the exclusive agreement upon termination of the mutual fiduciary relationship between the

143) Soo Hyun Ahn, "A Review of the Korean Supreme Court Case on the General Provision and Commercial Activities under the Commercial Act announced in 2008 (in Korean)," Commercial Cases Review, Vol. 21 No. 4, December 31, 2008, p.15.

144) Supreme Court Decision 2017Da258237, decided on September 10, 2019. *See* also Supreme Court Decision 2010Da20532, decided on October 28, 2010.

contracting parties.

(3) Exceptional circumstances where the court is obliged to resume argument upon filing of an application by the parties concerned.

2) Summary of Decision

(1) An 'exclusive management agreement' refers to a contract whose main terms and conditions obligate an agency or manager to provide management services relating to an artist's business in the field of entertainment in return for an artist's obligation not to perform entertainment activities either directly or through a third person and to do so only through the designated agency or manager. Its legal nature ought to be determined by specifically examining various circumstances including: the purpose of the relevant contract; the contents and nature of the obligation borne by the parties concerned; the difference in status, popularity, and negotiating power of the parties concerned; and the manner of payment of remuneration and distribution of profits.

(2) In a case where Party A, an entertainer, concluded an exclusive agreement with Party B in which she delegated management tasks relating to her artistic career to Party B, and thereafter rescinded the exclusive agreement on the ground of a breach of fiduciary relationship, the case held as follows: (a) the said exclusive agreement mainly concerns Party B's obligation to provide management services relating to Party A's entertainment activities in good faith; (b) for this reason, the instant exclusive agreement basically has the nature of a mandate agreement, which is established when one party entrusts the administration of business affairs to a counterparty, who accepts the offer; (c) however, the instant exclusive agreement may not be deemed to have the nature of a typical mandate agreement under the Civil Act; rather, it constitutes an innominate contract that is similar to a mandate, as the instant agreement assumes distinctive characteristics that separate it from a typical mandate agreement prescribed under the Civil Act when taking into account the following circumstances: (i) Party B, who was in charge of providing management services, stated that he would receive all profits expected to arise from Party A's entertainment activities as remuneration for his service, from which he would deduct expenses and pay 50% of the remainder to Party A on a designated date each month; (ii) Party B paid an exclusive fee to

Party A; (d) for the above reasons, the instant exclusive agreement, unlike a mandate agreement under the Civil Act, strongly binds the interests of the parties concerned and thus may not be arbitrarily rescinded by Party A, an artist; (e) however, considering that the instant exclusive agreement basically has resemblance to a mandate agreement, it should not be deemed that rescission of the contract is granted only when there are serious reasons that render it impossible to expect continuation of the contract; (f) as such, maintaining a high degree of fiduciary relationship between contracting parties is vital for the fulfillment of the purpose of a contract, as is required by the nature of the instant exclusive agreement; (g) Party A's duty to perform entertainment activities as an artist on an exclusive basis pursuant to an exclusive agreement is irreplaceable by another person; (h) forcing an artist to perform entertainment activities on an exclusive basis against his or her free will, even where the fiduciary relationship between parties concerned has been undermined, on the grounds that it does not constitute a circumstance where there are serious reasons that render it impossible to expect continuation of contract, is likely to result in an undue infringement of an artist's personality right; (i) for the above reasons, Party A, an artist, may rescind an exclusive agreement upon a breach of the mutual fiduciary relationship between the contracting parties.

(3) In a case where a party concerned files an application for resumption of argument after closing of argument in order to submit allegations or proof, whether to grant the application falls under the court's discretion in principle. Cases where the court has a duty to resume argument and proceed with hearings are limited to circumstances where ruling against the party concerned without granting the said party with an opportunity to submit allegations or proof violates procedural justice pursued by the Civil Procedure Act. Examples of such circumstances include situations where a party concerned who filed an application for resumption of argument was not properly provided an opportunity to submit allegations or proof, the subject of which constitutes factum probandum, or, an ultimate fact that needs to be proved, that may influence the conclusion of judgment.

3) Conclusion

The Defendant's appeal is meritless and thus is dismissed. The cost of the final appeal is borne by the losing party. It is so decided as per Disposition by the assent of all participating Justices on the bench.

Related Legal Issues and Questions:

1. What does the Korean Commercial Act cover?
2. Where do you find the legal answers on Corporate matters and cases?
3. Can you explain the Korean Commercial Act in general?
4. How can we make a contract successfully in Korea? (offer & acceptance)
5. How can we accept the offer?
6. Do we need consideration in making contract under the common law? What if under the Korean laws?

CHAPTER 4
TYPE OF COMPANY

The Korean Commercial Act, as a main source of a business law, has lots of provisions for a corporation in the Part 3, which is called the Korean Company Act. Though a stock company type is the most popular in Korea, there are also other available types of companies. In this Chapter, it is important to understand what kinds of corporate types are available in the Korean Company Act and why a certain type of corporation is popular in Korea. Same questions can also be asked even in different jurisdictions in the world.

I. Korean Company Act

A company (회사) is regarded as being a legal person in its own right.[145] Any rules and regulations for companies are so called as the Korean Company Act (회사법), which can be found from the Part 3 (Companies) of the Korean Commercial Act (KCA, 상법). The KCA can be applied to all listed or unlisted companies, but the Capital Market and Financial Investment Business Act (자본시장과 금융투자업에 관한 법률) should be considered for and applied only to the listed companies. Under the KCA, the term 'company' means a corporation incorporated for the purpose of engaging in commercial activities and any other profit-making activities.[146]

In the KCA and its relevant laws, there are many noteworthy and important corporation issues including the following issues among others:

- Incorporation and liquidation of a company
- Introduction of new business entities and other legal issues

145) Ewan Maclntyre, *op. cit.*, p.492.
146) *See* Article 169 of the Korean Commercial Act.

- Adoption of electronic securities registration system
- Issuance of various classes of shares
- Introduction of executive officer system
- Prohibition of the usurpation of corporate opportunities
- Development of corporate governance
- Mitigation and exemption of directors' liabilities
- Developments of capital increase
- Capital reduction procedure
- Increased flexibility in types of merger consideration and introduction of cash-out merger
- Adoption of the squeeze-out right of a controlling shareholder
- Introduction of electronic voting system in shareholders' meeting
- Enhancement of audit committee requirements and statutory audit system

Most issues and many legal cases are derived from a stock company since it is the most popular type in Korea. Some of those issues, not all will be reviewed in this book.

II. Types of Companies under the KCA

Possible business vehicles as a corporate type are regulated by the KCA. Under the KCA, companies are grouped into five basic categories:[147] (i) Partnership Company (*Hapmyong Hwesa*, 합명회사), (ii) Limited Partnership Company (*Hapja Hwesa*, 합자회사), (iii) Limited Liability Company (LLC, *Yuhan Chaekim Hwesa*, 유한책임회사). (iv) Stock Company (*Joosik Hwesa*, 주식회사), and (v) Limited Company (*Yuhan Hwesa*, 유한회사). Other business types are available under the KCA or other special Acts. For example, a limited partnership (*Hapja Johap*, 합자조합) is available under the KCA and an Investment Trust is also available under the Capital Market and Financial Investment Business Act.

According to the Ministry of Justice of Korea, over 85% of companies in Korea are formed as a stock company, while the KCA, at this time, defines five

147) Article 170 of the Korean Commercial Act.

different types of Korean potential business entities. In the past, only four different types of companies were allowed under the KCA, but a limited liability company (*yuhan chaekim hwesa*) as an additional company type and a limited partnership (*hapja johap*) as an additional partnership type have been created by the 2011 Amendment to the KCA in order to allow a little more flexibility for the possible business forms. Even though the 2011 Amendment to the KCA introduced two new business forms of Korean business entities, the possible type of company under the KCA is still five different forms because a *hapja johap* is not a company but a partnership.

All types of companies come into existence upon registration for its incorporation at the location of its principal office under the KCA.[148)]

> Article 170 (Types of Companies) of the KCA
>
> Companies are categorized into five types, namely, partnership companies, limited partnership companies, limited liability companies, stock companies, and limited companies.
>
> Article 172 (Incorporation of Company) of the KCA
>
> A company shall come into existence upon registration for its incorporation at the location of its principal office.

While Korean companies today commonly utilize the type of a stock company (*joosik hwesa*) or a limited company (*yuhan hwesa*), taking advantage of limited liability associated with those forms, there are fundamental differences between those two types as discussed below. It is noted that the most common type of business vehicle used by companies is a stock company. The type of a limited liability company is also commonly used by foreign companies or family companies due to (i) lower regulatory standards and (ii) simple incorporation procedure and corporate governance structure.

A brief description of each type or form of a company that is available under the KCA will be set forth below.

---

148) Article 172 of the Korean Commercial Act.

1. Partnership Company (*Hapmyong Hwesa*)

A *hapmyeong hwesa* corresponds to a partnership company. In a partnership company, two or more partners form the company.[149] Partner members consist of only those with direct, joint and several, and unlimited liabilities. Every member has the authority to represent the company unless the articles of incorporation of the company provides for a member who has such authority.

Each partner member will be jointly liable to repay the debts of the company in case the company may not fully repay its debts by use of the company's corporate assets. Transfer of ownership interest is limited and requires unanimous consent of all members. The partnership company is responsible for corporate taxes and thus is not a pass-through entity.

2. Limited Partnership Company (*Hapja Hwesa*)

A *hapja hwesa* corresponds to a limited partnership company. This company has a dual structure in the composition of partner members. Partner members consist of one or more partner members with unlimited liabilities (unlimited members) and one or more partner members with limited liabilities (limited members).[150]

Unlimited partner members have the authority to execute the corporate affairs of the company and are also liable to the liabilities of the company, while limited partner members participate in the company only through capital investment and do not have the right to execute the company business or to represent the company. The liabilities by limited partner members are limited by the amount of their capital investment to the company. A limited partnership company is responsible to pay Korean corporate taxes and thus may not be treated as a pass-through entity.

3. Limited Liability Company (LLC, *Yuhan Chaekim Hwesa*)

A *yuhan chaekim hwesa*, a new corporate type introduced by the 2011 Amendment to the KCA, corresponds to a limited liability company (LLC). This

---

149) Article 178 of the Korean Commercial Act.
150) Article 268 of the Korean Commercial Act.

company is viewed to be similar to a limited liability company in the United States or to a godo kaisha in Japan. It is intended to provide the advantages of a limited company (*yuhan hwesa*) and a stock company (*joosik hwesa*). It means that the entity is intended to provide flexibility in the composition of the organization and the recovery of members' investments while providing limited liability protection against creditors of the company up to their invested amounts.

In a limited liability company, the liability is limited, shares are freely transferable between members, bonds may be issued, no capitalization requirements are imposed, no director or auditor requirements are imposed, and the entity has easy exit requirements.

Summarized below are the main characteristics of a limited liability company.

(i) A limited liability company can be established upon a capital investment by one or more persons and registration of its incorporation. Capital contributions can be made in any form, such as cash or other tangible assets except those that are difficult to determine the reasonable market value (*e.g.*, services or credit).[151] In case of a limited liability company, although it is not subject to the Article 600 of the KCA which is the basis of prohibition of issuance of corporate bonds for a limited company, whether a limited liability company can issue bonds is still up for debate as it continues to be subject to the Article 604(1) of the KCA which states that a stock company may not change the company form to a limited company unless the redemption of bonds has been completed.[152]

(ii) There is no minimum capital requirement to establish a limited liability company. The company must appoint, by its articles of incorporation, a manager from among its members or non-members.[153] While a manager who may be a person or a legal entity is required, there is no mandate to have directors or an auditor. The company may also change its legal business status to a stock company with the unanimous consent of all of the members.[154]

(iii) A member is allowed to transfer his/her interests in the limited liability company to a third party with the consent of other members or if permitted in the company's Articles of Incorporation. Unless otherwise stated in the Articles of

151) Article 287-4 of the Korean Commercial Act.

152) Choi Junesun, Company Law (16th edition) (in Korean), Samyoungsa, February 2021, p.892.

153) Article 287-12 of the Korean Commercial Act.

154) Article 287-43(2) of the Korean Commercial Act.

Incorporation, a member may obtain a refund of his/her investment in the company by exiting at the end of the company's fiscal year after the member has given at least six months' prior notice to the company.[155] Thus, if the company's fiscal year is the calendar year, the member must submit notice to the company by June and leave by December. However, if the amount refunded to the exiting member exceeds the capital surplus of the company, the company must provide notice to its creditors informing them that objections may be submitted to the member's exit and must also provide the objecting creditors adequate security if there is a possibility that the refund may damage such creditor.[156]

(iv) The tax treatment issues pertaining to a limited liability company are not yet clear, but many believe that it may be treated for tax purposes in the same manner as a stock company.

4. Stock Company (*Joosik Hwesa*)

A *joosik hwesa* corresponds to a stock company and is abbreviated to Co. Ltd., Corp. or Ltd. A stock company is the only corporate entity that is allowed, at the present, to publicly issue shares. Shareholders of a company have limited liabilities, being liable only to the extent of their capital investment in the corporation made through the acquisition of its stock. The capital of a company is a normal sum of the total face value (par value) of stock issued by the company. The stock of a company may be freely transferable. However, the transfer of stock may be subject to some limitations, for example such as the approval of the board of directors in accordance with its articles of incorporation.

By its nature, a company cannot increase the liabilities on its stockholders, neither by a provision in the Articles of Incorporation nor by a decision of the general meeting of shareholders. The vast majority of incorporators in Korea chose a corporate type of the stock company. It is also the most common corporate type for foreign companies establishing subsidiaries in Korea.

Since a stock company type is the most popular in Korea and most company cases come from it, more legal issues and relevant cases will be reviewed in detail by the following Chapters.

155) Articles 287-24 and 217 of the Korean Commercial Act.
156) Article 287-30 of the Korean Commercial Act.

5. Limited Company (*Yuhan Hwesa*)

A *yuhan hwesa* is a closely held company and corresponds to a limited company. This company is designed to take advantage of operating a small-sized business in a closed manner. The company, however, had not become as much popular business models as expected in the past. Accordingly, the KCA was amended on April 14, 2011 and effective from April 15, 2012, among other revisions, to enhance the availability of a limited company by providing more flexibility in operation, management and governance structures (*i.e.*, removal of minimum capital requirement and restriction on the total number of members, and transfer of units).

In recent years, a few foreign companies including some international hedge funds have chosen a limited company type. A few companies, recently, have chosen this company type because of possible U.S. and E.U. tax benefits (pass-through benefits).

Below is a summary of the KCA regulations reflecting the 2011 revisions relating to the limited company.

i) Unlimited number of members[157)]

Under the old KCA, a limited company consisted of members with limited liabilities who were responsible only to the extent of their capital investment. Also the number of members must have been not more than 50 unless the court approval provided otherwise. However, the amended KCA removed this provision and no longer restricts the number of members.

ii) No minimum capital requirement[158)]

Under the old KCA, a limited company was required to have a minimum amount of capital equal to or above KRW 10,000,000. However, under the amended KCA, there is no minimum capital requirement to establish a limited company. Instead, for foreign investors desiring to establish a limited company in Korea, the Foreign Investment Promotion Act still requires a minimum capital contribution of KRW 100 million. In addition, a par value may be set at KRW 100 per unit under the amended KCA.

---

157) Article 545 of the Korean Commercial Act.

158) Article 546 of the Korean Commercial Act.

iii) No restrictions on transfer of units[159)]

Under the old KCA, members in a limited company could transfer its units only after a special resolution had been adopted by the general members' meeting. Although a stricter process for unit transfers could be adopted in the company's Articles of Incorporation, any process that allowed less than a special resolution among members was not permitted. The amended KCA, however, permits members in a limited company to transfer units freely and at their will. In addition, any limitations or restrictions if desired can be reflected in the company's Articles of Incorporation.

iv) Electronic notice permitted for general meeting of members[160)]

Under the old KCA, a limited company had to deliver written notice to each member at least one week prior to the date set for the general members' meeting. Under the amended KCA, however, an electronic notice of the general members' meeting may be sent to the members, as long as each member consents to such notice and it is followed up with a written notice.

v) Easier conversion of a limited company into a stock company[161)]

Under the old KCA, converting a limited company into a stock company required a unanimous resolution at a general members' meeting by all members. Under the amended KCA, however, the conversion may be approved through a special resolution (*i.e.*, affirmative vote by (a) at least one half (1/2) of the total number of members and (b) at least 75 percent of all outstanding voting rights).

Until now, the operation of a limited company has been generally limited to (a) a small number of members managing a business with limited liability, (b) a special purpose company, as defined under the Asset-Backed Securitization Act, or (c) a company defined under the Financial Investment Services and Capital Markets Act. The amended KCA provides limited companies with simple and flexible operation and decision-making procedures. Cumbersome requirements (*e.g.*, minimum capital requirement, member limitations and unit transfers) and inconvenient procedure provisions (*e.g.*, notice and conversion) have been revised

159) Article 556 of the Korean Commercial Act.
160) Article 571 of the Korean Commercial Act.
161) Article 607 of the Korean Commercial Act.

and now it is expected for more businesses to take advantage of these changes by establishing a limited company. However, it is clear that a limited company is still not permitted to issue bonds under the KCA and to be publicly listed.

III. Limited Partnership (*Hapja Johap*) - Additional Business Entity

1. Introduction

As already mentioned above, the 2011 Amendment to the KCA includes the addition of two new types of business entities: *hapja johap* (literally translated as a limited partnership) and *yuhan chaekim hwesa* (literally translated as a limited liability company) to meet the increasing demands of investors and dynamics in Korea's economy. The additional business entities have been created to provide greater flexibility in the formation, operation and dissolution of a business enterprise, and to promote commerce while providing limited liability protection to investors.

With the additional legal entities, the business entities recognized under the KCA are now five company types and one partnership type. However, a *hapja johap* is not included in one of possible company types because it is not a company but a partnership. A *hapja johap* is similar to a *hapja hwesa* (limited liability company). The critical difference between *hapja hwesa* and *hapja johab* is that *hapja johap*, like *johap* (partnership) is not a separate legal entity.[162] It is also a business entity similar to a limited liability partnership (LLP) recognized in the United States.

2. Main Features

Like other company types, a *hapja johap* may be also regarded as another important business entity which can be used in other purposes. The main features of a *hapja johap* are as follows:

162) Chung Chan-Hyung, Commercial Law (I) (24th edition) (in Korean), Parkyoungsa, February 2021, p.278.

1) A *hapja johap* (limited partnership) can be established upon an agreement among (i) one or more managing partners who agree to bear unlimited liability in the partnership and (ii) one or more limited partners, whose liability is limited to their capital contribution in the partnership to make joint capital contributions to conduct business together.[163] A *hapja johap* is not a separate legal entity per se and instead, is recognized as an 'partnership or association' authorized by law to engage in business (similar to *johap*).

2) The major matters required to be included in a *hapja johap* agreement (limited partnership agreement) are as follows:[164]

(i) Objectives,

(ii) Name,

(iii) Names or trade names, addresses, resident registration numbers of general partners,

(iv) Names or trade names, addresses, resident registration numbers of limited partners,

(v) Locality of the principal office,

(vi) Matters on investment of the partners,

(vii) Matters on distribution of losses and profits to partners,

(viii) Matters on transfer of shares of limited partners,

(ix) In the case of having determined that at least two general partners jointly execute affairs of or act as an agent for the limited partnership, the regulation,

(x) In the case of having determined that only some of the general partners execute affairs of or act as an agent for the limited partnership, the regulation,

(xi) Matters on distribution of the residual property upon dissolution of the limited partnership,

(xii) Matters on the term of existence of the limited partnership or other matters on grounds for dissolution thereof,

(xiii) Effective date of the limited partnership agreement.

Once a *hapja johap* is established, certain information stipulated in the KCA (*e.g.*, above items (i) to (vi)) must be registered with the court having jurisdiction over the *hapja johap*.

---

163) Article 86-2 of the Korean Commercial Act.

164) Article 86-3 of the Korean Commercial Act.

3) A general partner has a fiduciary duty to the other partners to manage and represent the partnership with care and loyalty.[165] However, a general partner may not sell, assign or transfer of her interest in the partnership to a third party without the unanimous consent from all partners.

4) Unless otherwise permitted in the *hapja johap* agreement, a limited partner must refrain from managing or representing the partnership and making capital contributions in the form of credit or labor services. A limited partner is largely a passive investor with a right to review the management of the partnership and its financial matters. A limited partner may sell, assign or transfer her interest in the partnership to a third party in accordance with the limited partnership agreement.[166] Further, the outgoing partner's right and obligations in the partnership will bind the incoming partner.

5) The tax treatment issues for a *hapja johap* are not yet clear, but the double taxation should not arise as a *hapja johap* is legally treated as an association and thus, it should be treated as a pass-through entity.

A *hapja johap* offers additional options for investors to conduct their business in Korea as it provides flexibility in business organization and operation while limiting liability to the investors' capital contribution. While a stock company (*joosik hwesa*) and a limited company (*yuhan hwesa*) will likely remain the popular choice for larger companies, a *hapja johap* will likely appeal to small-sized companies or investors with limited objectives. The utilization of the new business vehicles, however, will depend much on their business purpose and tax treatment.

165) Article 86-5 of the Korean Commercial Act.
166) Article 86-7(2) of the Korean Commercial Act.

IV. Case Study on Piercing the Corporate Veil[167)]

1. Main Issue

In applying the theory of piercing the corporate veil, the requirements for recognizing ‘the corporate shell entity’ or ‘the abuse of the corporate entity.’

2. Summary of Decision

Where a corporation externally maintains the appearance of a juristic person by taking the form of a juristic person but, in substance, it is equivalent to the person's private enterprise hiding behind the corporate veil or used without any justifiable reason in order to circumvent the application of laws against the person hiding behind the corporate veil, the denial of any responsibility of the person hiding behind the corporate veil with respect to an action of the corporation, based on the ground that such person is a separate entity and the legal effect of such action should only be attributed to the company, cannot be permitted as it is an abuse of the corporate entity in violation of the principle of the trust and good faith and is significantly against justice and equity. Therefore, the person hiding behind the corporate veil, as well as the corporation, must be held responsible for the actions of the corporation. Here, for determining whether a corporation is equivalent to a person’s private enterprise hiding behind the corporate veil, in principle, starting from the moment that legal or factual acts concerned are performed, the corporation merely takes the form of a juristic person, and shall be a shell entity to the degree that it is substantially equivalent to a private enterprise, considering whether the corporate property and business were commingled with those of the person hiding behind such corporate veil to the extent that they cannot be classified, whether any decision making process as provided in the law or bylaws was not followed, whether shareholders' or Board of Directors' meetings were held, the degree of the impaired corporate assets, the scale of business, and the number of employees, etc.

In addition, even though the juristic person does not fall under the shell

---

167) Supreme Court Decision 2007Da90982, decided on September 11, 2008. *See* also Supreme Court Decision 2019Da293449, decided on April 15, 2021 and Supreme Court Decision 97Da21604, decided on January 19, 2001.

entities, when a person hiding behind the corporate veil abuses its status as a juristic person, such person as well as the corporation shall be held liable for the acts of the corporation. However, in this case, on the basis of the moment that the act of abuse occurs, such as avoiding responsibility arising from debts, the person hiding behind the corporate veil must have had control over the corporation as he pleases, and must have abused the corporate legal entity by using such status. Additionally, whether a person hiding behind the corporation veil abused the corporate legal entity shall be determined individually in the light of the totality of the circumstances, including the degree of the corporate shell entity and the recognition or reliance of the transaction counterparty.

3. Reasoning

1) According to the reasoning in the judgment below, the court below, considering the following circumstances as a whole, found the facts that when the non-party 1 corporation was faced with the crisis of impending bankrupt, the Defendant, instead of dissolving the non-party 1 corporation, incorporated and has practically operated the non-party 2 corporation, which took over customers, employees, and etc., of non-party 1 corporation as is: (1) the non-party 2 corporation was incorporated almost at the same time when the non-party 1 corporation under the practical control by the defendant was dissolved; (2) the place of business, the location of the head office, and the type of business of the non-party 2 corporation are identical to those of the non-party 1 corporation, and the non-party 3, who was in charge of accounting in the non-party 1 corporation, continued to work for the non-party 2 corporation (the non-party 3 was registered as a shareholder holding 10% of shares of both corporations); (3) the non-party 2 corporation undertook KRW 44,874,749 as a whole, which is the price of the fabric incurred by the non-party 1 corporation, and even after such transaction, the non-party 2 corporation has continued to maintain trade relations equivalent to annual average of 300 million won, with the plaintiff, who was a customer of the non-party 1 corporation; (4) even before December 11, 2001, when the defendant received all of the non-party 4's shares and took office as the sole director, he received the money from the return of the fabric from the non-party 2 corporation into his own private banking account, and money transfers frequently transpired between the non-party 2 corporation's account and the

defendant's private account; and (5) from January 20, 1999, right after establishing the non-party 2 corporation, the defendant was registered at the National Health Insurance Corporation as an employee of the non-party 2 corporation. After that, the court below, considering the following circumstances as a whole, determined that the non-party 2 corporation has maintained the external appearance of a corporation, but it merely took on the form of a corporation and, in substance, it is equivalent to the defendant's private enterprise hiding behind the corporate veil: (a) the circumstances relating to the incorporating process of the non-party 2 corporation; (b) according to the shareholder register, the defendant held 40% of the non-party 2 corporation's shares, but most of the remaining shareholders were the defendant's relatives or employees, and as a result, the defendant actually owned almost all of the shares of the non-party 2 corporation; (c) most of executive officers who were appointed for the first time in the non-party 2 corporation were the defendant's wife or relatives, and on December 11, 2001, all the executive officers retired from their positions and the defendant was appointed as the sole director, thereby operating the non-party 2 corporation only by his decision making; (d) the non-party 2 corporate account was commingled with the defendant's private account, as shown by the fact that the non-party 2 corporation's money from the return of fabric was deposited into the defendant's private account; (e) around the dissolution of the non-party 2 corporation, the defendant had incorporated and operated the non-party 6 corporation again in the name of the non-party 5; (f) and while in the course of closing the non-party 1 corporation and the non-party 2 corporation, the defendant paid only 20 to 30% of the customer's product price and was exempt from any remaining payments, as he continued to incorporate and operate other businesses. Thus, the court below ruled that the defendant's lack of responsibility for the fabric price payment indebted to the Plaintiff, in arguing that the defendant is a separate entity from the non-party 2 corporation, cannot be admissible since it is the abuse of corporate entity in violation of the principle of trust and good faith and is significantly against justice and equity.

2) Where a company externally maintains the appearance of a juristic person by merely taking the form of a juristic person and, in substance, it is equivalent to the person's private enterprise hiding behind the corporate veil or used without any justifiable reason in order to circumvent the application of laws against the

person hiding behind the corporate veil, the denial of any responsibility of the person hiding behind the corporate veil with respect to an action of the corporation, based on the ground that such person is a separate entity and the legal effect of such action should only be attributed to the company, cannot be permitted as it is an abuse of the corporate entity in violation of the principle of the trust and good faith and is significantly against justice and equity. Therefore, the person hiding behind the corporate veil, as well as the corporation, must be held responsible for the actions of the corporation.[168)]

Here, for determining whether a corporation is equivalent to a person's private enterprise hiding behind the corporate veil, in principle, starting from the moment that legal or factual acts concerned are performed, the corporation merely takes the form of a juristic person, and shall be a shell entity to the degree that, it is substantially equivalent to a private enterprise, considering whether the corporate property and business were commingled with those of the person hiding behind such corporate veil to the extent that they cannot be classified, whether any decision making process as provided in the law or bylaws was not followed, whether shareholders' or Board of Directors' meetings were held, the degree of the impaired corporate assets, the scale of business, and the number of employees, etc.

In addition, even though the juristic person does not fall under the shell entities, when a person hiding behind the corporate veil abuses its status as a juristic person, such person as well as the corporation shall be held accountable for the acts of the corporation. However, in this case, on the basis of the moment that the act of abuse occurs, such as avoiding responsibilities arising from debts, the person hiding behind the corporate veil must have had control over the corporation as he pleases, and must have abused the corporate legal entity by using such status. Additionally, whether a person hiding behind the corporation veil abused the corporate legal entity shall be determined individually in the light the totality of the circumstances, including but not limited to the extent of the corporate shell entity, and the recognition or reliance of the transaction counterparty.

3) However, in light of the legal principle aforementioned as to the corporate shell entity, even though the defendant as a controlling shareholder of the

---

168) *See* Supreme Court Decision 97Da21604, decided on January 19, 2001.

non-party 2 corporation was appointed as a sole director from December 11, 2001, and exercised absolute power over the corporate management, thereby controlling the corporation as mentioned in the above in parts (b) and (c) of Section 1, if the degree of commingling between the non-party 2's corporate account and the defendant's private account was only partial as mentioned in the above in parts (4) and (d) of Section 1, then it cannot be viewed that properties of the non-party 2 corporation and the defendant were significantly commingled to the extent that its juristic person becomes a shell entity, so that its legal entity can be invalidated. Moreover, the circumstances stated by the court below in relation to the non-party 1 corporation cannot be an appropriate or sufficient ground to raise the argument that the non-party 2 corporation became the shell entity. To that end, even taking all things stated by the court below into consideration, it cannot be viewed that, at the time when the debt as to the product price occurred, the defendant merely did his private business by taking the form of a juristic person (*i.e.*, the non-party 2 corporation), and as a result the non-party 2 corporation is completely the defendant's private enterprise behind the corporate veil.

4) Additionally, among matters falling under (a) of the above No. 1 stated by the court below, (1) to (3), and (5) are the facts that the defendant dissolved the non-party 1 corporation and practically transferred its customers and employees, thereby establishing the non-party 2 corporation. Those facts are just circumstances to raise questions of identity between the non-party 1 corporation and the non-party 2 corporation, and matters falling under parts (b) to (c), and (e) are the facts that the defendant has practically controlled the non-party 1 corporation or the non-party 2 corporation, and the non-party 6 corporation.

However, such circumstances alone are not sufficient to deny the non-party 2 of its corporate legal entity based on the abuse of a juristic person according to the legal principle examined above. Necessarily, it shall be recognized that the defendant abused the status of a juristic person and has used the form of juristic person of the non-party 2 corporation as a way to circumvent the application of laws against himself, whereby escaping liabilities attributed to himself without justifiable reasons. The acts of dissolving the corporation which is performing poorly in business, liquidating its credit and debt, and thereafter investing new funds and incorporating and operating a new corporation, cannot be unlawful unless those acts causes damage to its creditors in light of the material and limited responsibility of a corporation. Thus, it is difficult to find that the defendant's acts itself, as in part (f) of the above Section 1, when he paid only 20% to 30% of the product price of the customer and was exempt from any remaining payments, and incorporated and operated the non-party 2 corporation or the non-party 6 corporation in the course of dissolving the non-party 1 corporation or the non-party 2 corporation, fit the circumstances suspecting abuse enough to deny its juristic person. Even considering the degree of control over the non-party 2 corporation exercised by the defendant as examined above, in light of the degree of the commingling between the property of the non-party 2 corporation and that of the defendant, it is not sufficient to see that the defendant abused the juristic person system as a way of avoiding his legal responsibilities.

Therefore, the judgment of the court below that the plaintiff can claim that the defendant hid behind the non-party 2 corporate veil and is liable for the payment of the fabric price debt arising from transactions made by the non-party 2 corporation, contains an error of law by misapplying the legal principles regarding the corporate shell entity and the abuse of a juristic person. It is obvious that such an error of law affected the conclusion of the judgment.

4. Conclusion

Therefore, the court determines by unanimous opinion of all participating Justices that the judgment of the court below shall be reversed without further reviewing the remaining grounds for appeal, and the case shall be remanded to the court below for a new trial and determination as set forth in the Disposition above.

5. Comments on the Supreme Court Decision

It is possible, in some situations, for shareholders to be sued for the acts of a corporation. This is called as the doctrine of 'piercing the corporate veil,' or 'disregarding corporate entity.'[169]

169) This doctrine came from the US common law. In the US, the courts will ignore the corporate structure and pierce the corporate veil, exposing the shareholders to personal liability. It is now recognized in the corporate statute in many states and in the Article 2.04 of the RMBCA (Frank B. Cross and Roger LeRoy Miller, *op. cit.*, p.427).

The Korean Supreme Court has noted that the corporate veil may be pierced and a shareholder may be sued, and the 'test' imposed by the Supreme Court has lead to Korea courts to look to, inter alia, whether:

(i) funds were commingled between a shareholder and the company,

(ii) corporate formalities were observed,

(iii) all the assets were transferred to another company controlled by a dominate shareholder,

(iv) company failed to maintain an arm's length relationship with a related entity or individuals,

(v) siphoning of corporate funds by a dominant shareholder occurred,

(vi) two or more companies acted as a single economic unit,

(vii) company falsified corporate records, and/or

(viii) company is otherwise being utilized as a facade to shield a shareholder from liability.

Related Legal Issues and Questions:

1. What kinds of corporate types are legally available in Korea?
2. Compare each type of corporation in detail.
3. What is the most common corporate form in Korea, and Why?
4. When is the corporate entity disregarded?

CHAPTER 5
INCORPORATION AND LIQUIDATION

An incorporation is a first step to set up a company in starting a business, and a liquidation is to close a business and finally to annul business's legal status. The most popular type of a company in Korea is a stock company and probably also in most countries. Thus, in the incorporation and liquidation of a company under the Korean Commercial Act, this Chapter will review them focusing on a stock company rather than other forms of companies. In this Chapter, it is important to understand how to incorporate a stock company and what legal documents to be prepared under the Korean Commercial Act, and finally how to liquidate a stock company.

I. Incorporation of the Company

1. Incorporation in General

All kinds of companies must satisfy the establishment requirements and procedures regulated by the Korean Commercial Act (KCA). Each company type has its own requirements and procedures for its establishment under the KCA. However, the procedure for establishing a stock company (*joosik hwesa*) under the KCA will be explained here since a stock company accounts for the majority of business entities in Korea.

Briefly, to establish a stock company starts with the preparation of the Articles of Incorporation (정관) or the Articles of Association,[170] and ends with the registration of incorporation under the KCA.[171] The Articles of Incorporation regulates the company's autonomous agenda and must be registered with the

170) Articles 289 and 292 of the Korean Commercial Act.
171) Article 317 of the Korean Commercial Act.

registry office along with other required documents. The Articles of Incorporation can be generally drafted based on a standard form for Articles of Incorporation.[172] When establishing businesses, especially a joint investment or a joint venture, shareholders' agreement is also another important document for operation of the company among shareholders, and usually such agreement may be reflected in drafting the Articles of Incorporation.

2. Incorporation Procedure

The following activities, among others, must be completed to incorporate a stock company through the incorporation by promotion or by subscription. The simple procedure for the incorporation is as follows:

(i) Step 1: Drafting the Articles of Incorporation

The promoter(s) must prepare the draft of Articles of Incorporation and a promoter signing the Articles of Incorporation will be named an incorporator.

(ii) Step 2: Composing a capital of the company

In this step, subscription of shares by the promoter(s) and other subscriber(s) and payment of subscription money are required.

(iii) Step 3: Composing the company's governance

Director(s) and corporate auditor(s) must be elected in the initial shareholders' meeting. In this step, investigations to the incorporation are required by the directors and statutory auditors into whether the incorporation has complied with applicable laws and the Articles of Incorporation, and investigation by the court-appointed inspector into whether any elements of abnormal incorporation, such as promoters' special benefits, contributions in kind and transferred property in advance, have been duly assessed and dealt with in accordance with applicable laws.

(iv) Step 4: Registering the company with a competent commercial registry

The Steps 1 through 3 are for the incorporation of a company and thus, the Step 4 is required just for the acquisition of a legal status and for business operation by registering a company with the registry office.

---

172) *See* the Model Articles of Incorporation in the Appendix of this book.

[Procedure for Incorporation of a Stock Company][173)]

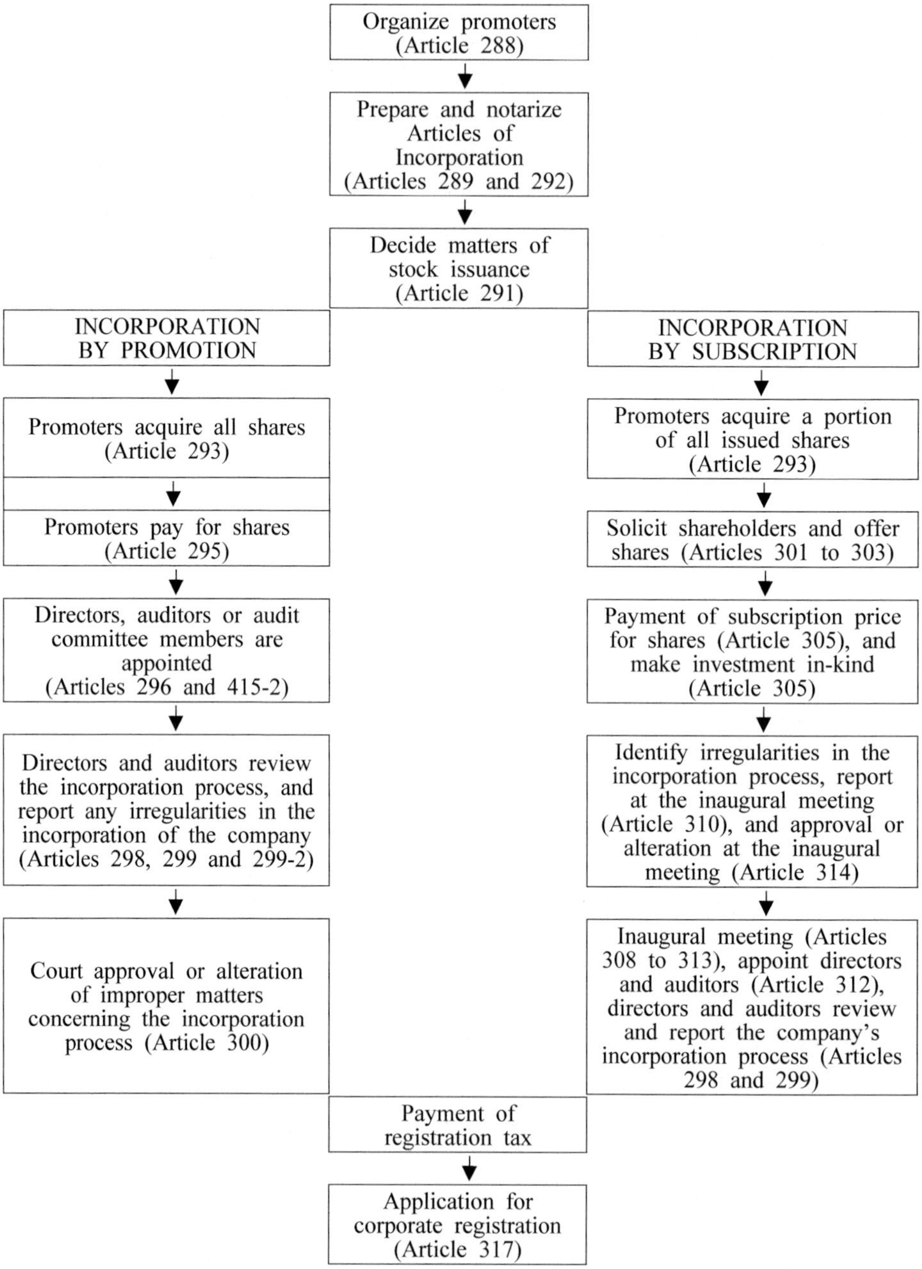

173) Revised from KOTRA, "Guide to Establishing a Business in Korea," 2016, p.9.

II. Registration of the Company

1. Registration in General

A company must be registered at a competent commercial registry in order to be a legal entity. This must be filed within 2 weeks following the date of completion of the investigation about elements of abnormal incorporation and any subsequent procedure of change.

A business registration certificate from the local tax office must then be obtained.[174)]

To incorporate a stock company, the following taxes and fees apply:

(i) Registration and license tax: 0.004 to 0.012 percent of the paid-in capital, depending on the place of incorporation.

(ii) Local education tax: 20 percent of the registration and license tax.

(iii) Notarization fees for the Articles of Incorporation: KRW 80,000 or more depending on the amount of paid-in capital.

(iv) Fees for registration of incorporation: not fixed expenses depending on the filing methods and the filing agents.

2. Documents Required for the Registration

After the incorporation of a company, many legal documents are required for the registration of incorporation with a commercial registry. The most important documents, among others, are as follow and most sample documents or forms are available from the commercial registry office:

(i) Application form for incorporation registration.

(ii) Articles of Incorporation. Notarization for the Articles of Incorporation by a public notary is required, but notarization is exempted where a company with total capital of less than KRW one billion is incorporated by promotion.

(iii) Documents certifying subscription to shares.

(iv) Stock subscription agreement which is applicable only to incorporation by

---

174) For more information on the registration with the tax office, *see* online resources from <http://www.iros.go.kr>.

subscription.

(v) Written consent to matters concerning issuance of shares.

(vi) Written consent to reduction of the notice period for convocation of the inaugural general meeting in case for a company with a total capital of less than KRW one billion incorporated by subscription.

(vii) The minutes of the inaugural general meeting when it is the incorporation by subscription or the meeting minutes of promoters when it is the incorporation by promotion. The minutes must be notarized by a public notary, but notarization is exempted for company with a total capital of less than KRW one billion incorporated by promotion.

(viii) The meeting minutes of the board of directors. The minutes must be notarized by a public notary, but notarization is exempted for company with a total capital of less than KRW one billion incorporated by promotion.

(ix) A securities subscription deposit certificate issued by a deposit bank. This can be replaced with a certificate of balance for company with a capital of less than KRW one billion incorporated by promotion.

(x) An inspection report by a director, auditor or the audit committee.

(xi) A certificate of delivery of the pertinent property which is applicable only to an investment-in-kind.

(xii) The public notary's report on particulars of abnormal incorporation.

(xiii) A written statement by an appraiser.

(xiv) A certified copy of the inspector's report.

(xv) A certificate of foreign investment notification only if it is a foreign invested company.

(xvi) A certificate of inauguration acceptance. (a) Korean nationals must put his seal on the certificate, and attach a certificate of the seal and a certified copy of resident registration. (b) Foreigners must attach a notarized original certificate of signature, certificate of address and a copy of his passport.

(xvii) A certificate of registration of seal impression.

(xviii) Translations of the required documents only when the required documents including the directors' inauguration acceptance are written in a foreign language.

(xix) A certificate of payment of registration tax as issued by the district office having jurisdiction over the area in which the business' headquarters is located.

(xx) The Supreme court revenue stamp.

(xxi) Power of attorney only when an agent files the application.

(xxii) Seal of each director and promoter including foreigners.

(xxiii) Corporate seal.

(xxiv) Application form for issuance of corporate seal card after the registration of incorporation.

The documents in (xi), (xii), (xiii) and (xiv) above apply only when there are particulars of abnormal incorporation, such as an investment-in-kind.

III. Other Considerations for Incorporation

1. Articles of Incorporation

The Articles of Incorporation (정관) is a set of formal documents or charters filed with a Government body (usually the state or the registry) that signifies the creation of a corporation. They are generally filed with the company registry and referred to as the certificate of incorporation or the corporate charter. For example, in the U.S., the Articles of Incorporation is filed with the Office of the Secretary of State where the business chooses to incorporate, and in Korea it is filed with a commercial registry. The Articles of Incorporation generally contains pertinent information such as the firm's name, street address, corporate governance, and the amount and type of stock to be issued. It is used to legally form the corporation.

Under the KCA, an incorporator[175] (발기인) must prepare the Articles of Incorporation and enter the following eight essential matters in the Articles of Incorporation, and each of them must write his name and affix his seal, or affix his signature:[176]

(i) objectives,

(ii) trade name,

(iii) the total number of shares authorized to be issued,

(iv) par value per share where par value shares are issued,

---

175) A person who just drafted the Articles of Incorporation, but did not sign it will become a 'promoter' in legal sense, instead of an 'incorporator.'

176) Article 289(1) of the Korean Commercial Act.

(v) the total number of shares to be issued at the time of incorporation,

(vi) the location of a principal office,

(vii) method of giving a public notice by the company,[177] and

(viii) the name, resident registration number and address of each incorporator.

Promoter *v*. Incorporator

In the company law, a promoter means the founder or organizer of a corporation or business and so the person who takes the initiative to create or organize a business. A promoter would perform the conduct required for incorporating the business. Then, the acts by the promoter would be ratified by the formation of the board of directors and their subsequent conduct.

However, the person signing the Articles of Incorporation would be named the incorporator.[178] Strictly speaking, the promoter is not always the incorporator of the corporate entity and vice versa. Since a person is usually acting as a promoter while signing the Articles of Incorporation as an incorporator, they are often used in the same sense together without distinction.

However, the following matters will take effect only upon entry in the Articles of Incorporation:[179]

(i) any special benefits to be received by incorporators and names of such incorporators,

(ii) the name of a person who is to make an investment in kind, the type, quantity and value of the subject matter of such investment in kind and the class and number of shares to be given in consideration thereof,

177) Under the KCA, public notices of a company must be made in the Official Gazette or in a daily newspaper carrying current events: Provided, that a company may give a public notice by electronic means as determined by its Articles of Incorporation. A company must continue to give a public notice by the period prescribed by Presidential Decree if such public notice is made by electronic means, and by the period determined under Article 450 if public notice of financial statements is made by electronic means. The company must also make the details thereof available for public inspection even after the expiration of the period of the public notice. Where a company gives a public notice by electronic means, it must prove the period and details of such notice (Article 289(3), (4) and (5) of the Korean Commercial Act).

178) Chung Chan-Hyung, *op. cit.*, p.659; Choi Junesun, *op. cit.*, p.148.

179) Article 290 of the Korean Commercial Act.

(iii) the class, number and value of the assets agreed to be transferred to the company after its incorporation and the name of the transferor, or

(iv) the expenses for incorporation to be borne by the company and the amount of remunerations for the incorporators.

The Articles of Incorporation takes effect upon being notarized by a public notary. However, where a company with total capital of less than KRW one billion is incorporated by incorporators, the Articles of Incorporation takes effect after each incorporator writes his name and affixes his seal, or affix his signature.[180] Notarization is not required for the amendments to the Articles of Incorporation after incorporation of a company,

2. Company Name

A company must have its own company name (회사명). The lettering 'partnership company,' 'limited partnership company,' 'limited liability company,' 'stock company' or 'limited company must be contained in the trade name of a company according to its nature.[181] Accordingly, in case of a stock company, it must have its name which contains the lettering 'stock company.' Sometimes it can be abbreviated as 'Co. Ltd.,' 'Corp.' or 'Ltd.'

It is important to make sure whether the same trade name is already used or registered. When establishing a company, it is advised to check if the trade name that the company intends to use is already registered by another business. Registered trade names can be searched on the registry website[182] of the Supreme Court of Korea.

3. Share Capital

A share capital (자본금) is the portion of a company's equity derived by the issue of shares in the company to a shareholder. It is commonly referred to as capital stock in the U.S. or many times just as a company's capital in Korea. In

180) Article 292 of the Korean Commercial Act.

181) Article 19 of the Korean Commercial Act.

182) All trade names of companies registered with the competent registry may be found from <http://www.iros.go.kr>.

European corporate and foundation law or the UK company law, a legal capital is used to refer to the sum of assets contributed to a company by shareholders when they are issued shares.[183] Generally, the law often requires that the capital is maintained, and that dividends may not be paid when a company is not showing a profit above the level of a capital.

In Korea, there is no currently prescribed minimum or maximum amount of share capital. With the 2011 Amendment to the KCA, the provision stipulating that the total capital of a company must have been no less than KRW fifty million was abolished. However, the minimum capital requirement for a foreign invested company under the Foreign Investment Promotion Act must still be KRW one hundred million.[184]

In addition, unless otherwise provided for in the KCA, the capital of a company must be equal to the total sum of par values of all issued and outstanding shares.[185] Where a company issues no par value shares, the capital of the company must be the amount equal to or higher than half of the share issuance price, and must be the total amount which the board of directors agrees to include in the capital.[186] In such cases, the amount not to be included in capital out of the issuance price must be included in the capital reserve. The capital of a company may not be changed by transferring par value shares into no par value shares or by transferring no par value shares into par value shares.

4. Non-cash Consideration

If expressly set out in the Articles of Incorporation, a company can issue shares for non-cash consideration. The KCA provides that an investment in kind takes effect upon entry in the Articles of Incorporation.[187]

In this case, the matters such as the name of a person who is to make an investment in kind, the type, quantity and value of the subject matter of such investment in kind and the class and number of shares to be given in

183) Thakur, Madhuri, Vaidya, Dheeraj (ed.), "Legal Capital," CFA Institute, August 29, 2020.

184) Article 2(1) of the Foreign Investment Promotion Act and Article 2(2) of the Enforcement Decree of the Foreign Investment Promotion Act.

185) Article 451(1) of the Korean Commercial Act.

186) Article 451(2) of the Korean Commercial Act.

187) Article 290 of the Korean Commercial Act.

consideration thereof will need to be expressly prescribed in the Articles of Incorporation and inspected by the court-appointed inspector.

5. Incorporation by Promotion and by Subscription

There are two ways to incorporate a stock company under the KCA: (i) Incorporation by promotion (발기설립) and (ii) incorporation by subscription (모집설립).

In the incorporation by promotion, each incorporator must subscribe to shares in writing.[188] Where incorporators subscribe to the total number of shares to be issued at the time of incorporation, they must without delay make full payment of the subscription price. In such cases, they must designate a bank or other financial institutions at which the subscription price is to be paid as well as the place for payment. When the payment of a subscription price and the investment in kind are completed, incorporators must without delay appoint directors and auditors by a majority vote. Further, incorporators must prepare and write their names and affix their seals, or affix their signatures, on the minutes of meetings, in which the proceedings of deliberation and the outcomes thereof must be entered.

However, in the incorporation by subscription, incorporators do not subscribe to the total number of shares issued at the time of incorporation and they must invite subscribers.[189] A person who intends to subscribe to shares must complete a share subscription form[190] in duplicate, in which the class and number of shares to which he is to subscribe and his address are stated, and must write his name and affix his seal or must affix his signature, thereon. A person who has subscribed to shares is obliged to pay the subscription price in accordance with

188) Article 293 of the Korean Commercial Act.

189) Article 301 of the Korean Commercial Act.

190) Incorporators must prepare a share subscription form in which the following matters are entered: (i) the date of notarization of the articles of incorporation, and the name of the notary public, (ii) the matters listed in the Articles 289(1) and 290, (iii) the period of existence or reasons for dissolution of the company, if determined, (iv) the class and number of shares subscribed to by incorporators, (v) the matters listed in the Article 291, (vi) provisions that transfer of shares requires the approval of the board of directors, if so determined, (vii) retirement of shares out of profits to be distributed to shareholders, if so determined, (viii) a statement to the effect that the subscription of shares may be canceled if the inaugural general meeting is not closed by a fixed date, (ix) the bank and any other financial institution in charge of the payment of the subscription price and the place for payment, and (x) the name, address and business office of a transfer agent, if any (*see* Article 302(2) of the Korean Commercial Act).

the number of shares allotted to him by the incorporators. Where the payment and the making of investment in kind have been completed, incorporators must, without delay, convene an inaugural general meeting, and the resolutions of an inaugural general meeting must be adopted by affirmative votes of at least two-thirds of the total votes of attending subscribers and also by affirmative votes representing a majority of the total number of shares which have been subscribed to. At an inaugural general meeting, directors and auditors must be appointed.

Either way, the registration for incorporation of a stock company must be made within two weeks from the date of completion of the procedures in cases where the incorporators subscribed to the total number of shares issued at the time of incorporation, and within two weeks from the date of closing of the inaugural general meeting or from the date of completion of the procedures in cases where the incorporators have offered shares for subscription.

6. Special Provisions for a Small Company under the KCA

A small company (소규모회사) is the company type with a total capital of less than KRW one billion incorporated by incorporators under the Article 295(1) of the KCA.

1) A small company incorporated by promotion is granted exemption from the requirement to notarize the Articles of Incorporation.[191] To incorporate a company, it was mandatory for all companies regardless of capital amount and method of incorporation to notarize their Articles of Incorporation, which caused unnecessary time and expense. However, with the amendment to the KCA, a company incorporated by promotion with a capital of less than KRW one billion was exempted from the requirement to notarize the Articles of Incorporation if the signature of the promoters or the written name and seal of the promoters are affixed to the Articles of Incorporation. Exempting a small company from notarization of the Articles of Incorporation has expedited the business opening procedure and facilitated investment.

2) A bank or any other financial institutions to which the subscription price paid is deposited must issue a certificate as to the deposited amount, upon the

191) Article 292 of the Korean Commercial Act.

request of incorporators or directors. However, for a small company with a total capital of less than KRW one billion incorporated by incorporators, such certificate can be substituted by a balance certificate issued by a bank or other financial institutions.[192]

3) Simplification of the convocation procedure for the general shareholders' meeting is allowed for a small company.[193] For a small company operated like a family business, the requirement to follow the complicated convocation procedure for the general shareholders' meeting may burden company operations.[194] In this regard, the convocation procedure for the general shareholders’ meeting has been simplified for a small company. In the case of a company with a total capital of less than KRW one billion, the convocation notice period has been reduced to less than 10 days. Further, the convocation procedure may be omitted if all shareholders agree, and a resolution may be passed in writing at the general shareholders' meeting. The simplification of the convocation procedure for the general shareholders' meeting has helped a small company save the time and expense.

4) The number of directors in a stock company must be three or more. However, in the case of a small company with a total capital of less than KRW one billion, the number of directors may be one or two.[195] If a small company has only two directors, each will represent the company. If a representative director has been designated under the Articles of Incorporation, the representative director will represent the company. Compared to a company with only one director, a company with two directors must also delegate the functions of the board of directors to the general shareholders’ meeting or each director (or the representative director).

In the case of a small company with two directors, the following matters must be decided at a general shareholders’ meeting instead of the board of directors’ meeting: the approval of transfer of restricted shares, cancellation of stock options, prohibition of directors from holding more than one position, approval of

192) Article 318 of the Korean Commercial Act.
193) Article 363 of the Korean Commercial Act.
194) Choi Junesun, *op. cit.*, p.94.
195) Article 383(1) of the Korean Commercial Act.

self-dealing by directors, the issuance of new shares, convertible bonds (CBs) or bonds with warrants (BWs), transfer of reserves to capital, and interim dividends. In a small company with two directors, the right to convene a general shareholders‘ meeting and the right to execute business such as the nomination or dismissal of managers and the opening, transfer or closure of a branch must belong to each director (or the representative director) instead of the board of directors.

5) In addition, when incorporating a company, it was mandatory to appoint auditors, which required time and expense. With the amendment the KCA, the nomination of auditors became optional for a small company with a capital of less than KRW one billion. This means that a small company may choose not to appoint auditors.[196] Even though the appointment of auditors is optional, the appointed auditors must be registered once appointed. If a small company chooses not to appoint an auditor, the general shareholders' meeting must audit directors' performance and monitor the financial status of a company. Also, if a small company files an action against a director and vice versa, the company, director or an interested party must request the court to nominate a person to represent the company. Allowing a small company to decide whether to appoint auditors has helped reduce the time and expense for opening a small company.

6) Where a company has issued bearer bonds (무기명식 채권), it must give a public notice of its intent to convene a meeting of bondholders and the agenda for the meeting three weeks prior to the date of a general meeting of shareholders, while two weeks prior to the date of a general meeting of shareholders are required in case of a small company with a total capital of less than KRW one billion.[197]

---

196) Articles 409(4) of the Korean Commercial Act.
197) Article 491-2(2) of the Korean Commercial Act.

IV. Dissolution and Liquidation of the Company

1. Introduction

When an investor establishes a stock company in Korea by placing an equity investment into the company, it would be natural that the investor would want to make the company prosperous and operate the company for a long period of time to realize significant returns on the investment made. However, if things do not work out for some reasons, there comes a situation where the company needs to be closed down permanently.

To close a company, the company must be liquidated and its registration with the competent court registry office must be de-registered. Under the KCA, it requires that the company must undergo dissolution (해산) and liquidation (청산) in order to wind up the company. The dissolution is the legal process whereby the company's legal capacity is limited to liquidation activities. To the extent necessary for achieving the objectives of liquidation, a company is deemed to continue to exist even after its dissolution.[198] That is, the dissolution does not mean the company ceases to exist, but it transforms into a liquidating the company. The liquidation is a process of closing unsettled business, collection, repayment, and distribution of the corporate assets to the shareholders. In some cases, the company is closed down through a procedure of not only dissolution and liquidation, but also cancellation of authorization or permission, cancellation of business registration, and cancellation of the foreign invested company registration.

In the case of a foreign invested company, the KCA, the Foreign Investment Promotion Act and the Foreign Exchange Transaction Regulations set forth the procedures to be taken for such liquidation and de-registration of the company. Generally, it will take two to six months to complete the whole liquidation process of the company. It is impossible to shorten the period to less than two months since the period of notice to creditors must not exceed two months in accordance with the Article 535 of the KCA.

2. Grounds for Dissolution of the Company

A stock company will be dissolved on any of the following grounds:[199]

198) Article 245 of the Korean Commercial Act.
199) Article 517 and 227 of the Korean Commercial Act.

1) Expiration of the time of existence of the company or occurrence of any events specified in the articles of incorporation. Where a company has been dissolved due to expiration of the duration or of the occurrence of any other event specified in the articles of incorporation as a ground for dissolution or by a resolution adopted at a general meeting of shareholders, the company may continue to exist by such Special Resolutions as the affirmative votes of at least two thirds of the voting rights of the shareholders present at a general meeting of shareholders and of at least one third of the total number of issued and outstanding shares.[200)]

2) Merger

3) Bankruptcy

4) Order or judgment of a court. If, in any of the following cases, there exist unavoidable reasons, any shareholder who holds shares representing no less than 10 percent of the total number of issued and outstanding shares may request a court to dissolve the company:[201)]

(i) When the company's business operation continues to be considerably in deadlock and as a result irreparable damage to the company is or is likely to be caused, or

(ii) When the management or disposal of the company's assets is considerably improper and thereby threatens existence of the company.

Any order or judgment by a court must be subject to the exclusive jurisdiction of the district court having jurisdiction over the place of the principal office of the company.[202)] If plaintiffs in such order or judgment by a court have lost in such procedure and it is found that they, in bad faith or by gross negligence, filed such order or judgment by a court, they must be jointly and severally liable for damage against the company.[203)]

5) A division or merger after division of the company under Article 530-2, or

200) Article 519 and 434 of the Korean Commercial Act.
201) Article 520 of the Korean Commercial Act.
202) Article 186 of the Korean Commercial Act.
203) Article 191 of the Korean Commercial Act.

6) A resolution passed at a general meeting of shareholders. A resolution for dissolution must be adopted by the affirmative votes of at least two thirds of the voting rights of the shareholders present at a general meeting of shareholders and of at least one third of the total number of issued and outstanding shares.[204] In such cases, the company may also continue to exist by such special resolutions.

On the other hand, where the Administrator of the Office of Court Administration has given public notice in the Official Gazette, requiring any company whose last registration was made five years ago to make a report to the effect that it has not closed its business to the court with jurisdiction over the place of its principal office, if a company for which five years has already lapsed since its last registration as of the date of public notice fails to report within two months from the date of public notice in accordance with Presidential Decree, the company will be deemed to have been dissolved at the expiration of the period set for such a report.[205] However, it does not apply where the company has filed for registration within the period.

In the case of public notice, a court must also give the relevant company separate notice informing that such public notice has been given. A company deemed to have been dissolved by such reasons may continue as a company by a special resolution for up to three years thereafter. If a company does not continue as a company in such cases, it will be deemed to have been liquidated upon expiration of the period of the above three years.

Upon dissolution of a company, except in cases of bankruptcy, directors must, without delay, give a notice thereof to shareholders.[206] In cases of dissolution of a company for reasons other than a merger or the initiation of bankruptcy proceedings, such fact must be registered within two weeks at the location of the principal office and within three weeks at the location of each branch office, both period starting from the day on which the ground for dissolution arises.[207]

204) Article 518 and 434 of the Korean Commercial Act.
205) Article 520-2 of the Korean Commercial Act.
206) Article 521 of the Korean Commercial Act.
207) Article 521-2 and 228 of the Korean Commercial Act.

3. Dissolution and Liquidation under the KCA

The dissolution and liquidation of a company in Korea is a straightforward process. Assuming the dissolution by a resolution passed at a general shareholders' meeting, the following steps must be taken in chronological order to effectively dissolve and liquidate a company under the KCA.

[Procedure of Dissolution and Liquidation of Company][208)]

Dissolution	->	Liquidation	->	Cancellation of authorization or permission	->	Cancellation of business registration	->

Cancellation of the foreign invested company registration if any	->	Closing unsettled business, collection, repayment, distribution of the corporate assets to the shareholders, or overseas remittance

1) The first step is making the resolution of a shareholders' meeting. The shareholders at a general shareholders' meeting must pass a special resolution to dissolve the company. Under the KCA, a special resolution of shareholders must be adopted by the affirmative votes of no less than two thirds of the voting rights of the shareholders present at the meeting and of at least one third of the total issued and outstanding shares, unless the Articles of Incorporation contains more stringent requirement.

2) Upon Dissolution, the directors will become liquidators (청산인) of a company unless the Articles of Incorporation of a company provides otherwise. Usually, a representative director becomes a liquidator. Also, another person can be appointed as a liquidator at a general shareholders' meeting. If none of these are available, then the court will appoint a liquidator.

3) A liquidator, except as appointed by the court, may be removed from office at any time by a resolution of a general shareholders' meeting. In addition, if a liquidator has acted in contravention of his material duties, any shareholder who

208) Revised from Iinvestkorea, "Invest Guide," at <https://www.investkorea.org/>.

holds shares representing no less than two thirds of the total issued and outstanding shares may apply to the court for removal of such liquidator from office.

4) The dissolution must be registered with the court at the locality of its principal office within two weeks after the date on which the shareholders have resolved to dissolve a company, thereby officially commencing for the closure of the company. Appointment and details of liquidators must also be registered with the court within two weeks after the dissolution date in case where the directors become liquidators, or within two weeks of the date of the appointment of the liquidator in case where another person is appointed as a liquidator.

5) After the commencement of liquidation procedures, the company is deemed to continue its existence to the extent of its objectives of the liquidation.

6) The liquidator must file a report on the grounds for and date of dissolution, and the name, resident registration number and address of the liquidator with the court within two weeks of the date of appointment.

7) The liquidator must also investigate, promptly upon being appointed, the actual condition of the company's property and prepare inventory and balance sheet and submit these to the shareholders for their approval, and upon obtaining such approval, submit them to the court.

8) Among others, the duties of a liquidator are limited to the following basic matters:

(i) closing currently existing business matters,
(ii) collecting all accounts receivable and paying off all outstanding liabilities,
(iii) disposing of all assets owned or held by the company,
(iv) preparing a liquidator's report on the accounts settlement of the company,
(v) repatriation of liquidation proceeds left over after the foregoing is completed, and
(vi) performing any acts related to the foregoing, whether in or out of a court.

In connection with 'paying off all outstanding liabilities' in (ii) above, a notice of liquidation must be published at least twice within two months after the appointment of liquidator to the creditors on a daily newspaper. The notice must request the creditors to report their claim to the company within a certain period and state that the failure to report a claim within such period would exclude such creditor from participating in the liquidation. The period during which creditors have to submit their claims against the company must be specified in the notice and must be no less than two months from the date of the second notice. The liquidator must also send individual notices to all the known creditors of the company, requesting them to report their claims to the company. The failure by such known creditors to report their claim to the company does not exclude such creditors from participating in the liquidation.

All reported claims against the company must be settled with the creditors and the remaining surplus assets if any must be distributed to the shareholders in proportion to shareholding ratios. However, when it has become clear in the course of liquidation that the assets of the company are insufficient to fully satisfy its liabilities, the liquidator is required to immediately file an application for bankruptcy and give a public notice thereof. One thing to note is that if a company has more debts than assets, it cannot wind up by dissolution. Instead of it, the liquidator of a company must file a bankruptcy with the court. Then the court will take care of the dissolution and liquidation of a company.

9) When the matters in Items (i), (ii) and (iii) above are completed, the liquidator must, without delay, prepare a report on the settlement of accounts of the company and submit the report to shareholders and obtain their resolution approving the completion of the liquidation at the general shareholders' meeting.

10) Upon receiving the shareholders' resolution on the completion of liquidation, the liquidator must register the completion of liquidation with the court at the locality of the principal office of the company within two weeks.

11) In addition to the dissolution and liquidation procedures under the KCA, where registration of business, report of business, and authorization or permission of business are granted by the type of a company, the company closure must be reported. When a company closes registered business, the liquidator must submit

a declaration of business closure, without delay, to the head of the tax office.

4. Other Considerations for Liquidation of the Company

1) Tax Matters

Under the Korean Corporate Tax Act (CTA) and the Value-added Tax Act, the liquidator of a company must undertake the following procedure to obtain tax clearance for the liquidation of a company:

(i) Report the closure of the business,

(ii) File a value-added tax (VAT) return for the last period ending on the dissolution date,

(iii) File an annual corporate tax return for the last fiscal period ending on the dissolution date,

(iv) File a liquidation income return, and

(v) For a foreigner or a foreign invested company, obtain a certificate on taxes paid (or due) for the Korean source income of nonresidents (tax clearance certificate).

Under the CTA, a company is subject to corporate income tax on its liquidation income, if any, at the normal corporate income tax rate. Briefly, a liquidation income is the amount of net assets minus the amount of net equity. Further, the closure of a company may cause the tax office to conduct a field tax audit in order to ascertain that the tax returns duly reflect the actual business of the company. However, whether such audit is conducted or not will depend on the schedule and discretion of the pertinent tax office.

2) Termination of Employment

The employment of the employees of a company under liquidation must be terminated and the employees must be paid severance pay.[209] Accordingly, the year-end declaration and calculation of the annual payroll taxes for the employees and computation of withholding income taxes on severance pay must be carried

209) Article 34 of the Labor Standards Act.

out.

A company must also terminate the employment agreement and close the national health accounts and national pension accounts of the employees.

3) Liabilities of Debtor Company

Even during the dissolution and liquidation of a company, a director, parent company or shareholder/equity holder of a debtor company can be liable for the liabilities of the debtor company in the following circumstances:

(i) Guarantee. If a director, debtor's parent company or any party provides a guarantee, it is liable for the debt covered by the guarantee.

(ii) Piercing the corporate veil. If the court decides that a company does not have corporate existence separate from and independent of its shareholders/equity holders, those shareholders or equity holders can be held liable for the company's debt.

(iii) Directors' duties. If the directors breach their duties owed to a company, they are liable to compensate the company for any damages and losses incurred.

When a company is dissolved and liquidated, the liquidator of a company must immediately file for a bankruptcy proceeding if it becomes clear that the assets of a company are insufficient to satisfy its creditors' claims. No such obligation to file for a bankruptcy proceeding is imposed on a director of the company or its parent company.

4) Foreign Invested Company

When a foreign invested company closes its business in Korea, its registration must be canceled, and the collection of surplus equity for investment and overseas remittance are guaranteed by the Article 3(1) of the Foreign Investment Promotion Act and the Article 6(1) of the Foreign Exchange Transactions Act. The repatriation of capital remaining after liquidation, if any, is subject to the approval of a foreign exchange bank and such bank normally requests the foreign investor/shareholder to submit the certificate issued by the Korean tax authorities proving that it has satisfied its tax obligations in Korea.

In the case of dissolution and liquidation of a foreign invested company, an application for the cancellation of the foreign investor of the foreign investment must be filed by the foreign investor with its foreign exchange bank. In addition, if a foreign invested company had required specific permits, licenses and authorizations from the Korean Government, it will have to report its business closure and to return or cancel the permits, licenses and authorizations to the Korean Government.

V. Case Study on Incorporation and Dissolution

1. Incorporator's Liability[210)]

An incorporator is the individual who organizes the incorporation and arranges for the Articles of Incorporation to be filed with the registry office. An incorporator signs the Articles of Incorporation, verifying the information submitted is true and correct. He has special liabilities for subscription of shares and security for payment, and damages under the KCA.

Under the Article 321 of KCA, where, after a company comes into existence, any shares issued at the time of incorporation of the company are found to have not been subscribed to or the subscription for certain shares has been canceled, incorporators are deemed to have jointly subscribed to such shares. Where, after a company comes into existence, shares for which payment of the subscription price has not been completed, incorporators must make such payment jointly and severally. This can be one of examples for the disregard of personality feature in the KCA.[211)]

Under the Article 322 of the KCA, if an incorporator has neglected his duties in connection with the incorporation of the company, he will be jointly and severally liable for damages suffered by the company. If an incorporator has neglected his duties in bad faith or by gross negligence, he will be jointly and severally liable for damage to a third party.

If directors or auditors have neglected their duties and are thereby liable for damages suffered by the company or third parties and if incorporators are also

210) Supreme Court Decision 99Da35737, decided on January 28, 2000. *See* also Supreme Court Decision 89Nu916, decided on September 12, 1989.

211) Ki Jong Lee, *op. cit.*, p.37.

liable therefor, the directors, auditors and incorporators are liable for such damages jointly and severally under the Article 323 of the KCA.

2. Company Bankruptcy [212)]

1) Main Issues and Holdings

(1) Whether, pursuant to the territorial principle of the former Company Reorganization Act, the original effect of a foreign country reorganization proceeding reaches property located within Korea (negative).

(2) Legal nature and effect of 'the approval order of foreign country bankruptcy procedure.'

(3) Legal nature of 'assistance order' under the Debtor Rehabilitation Act.

(4) The standards, under the Debtor Rehabilitation Act, of determining the approval of the discharge trial, etc. of a foreign court conducted in foreign country bankruptcy procedure.

(5) The case where it is against the 'good customs or other social order of Korea' to acknowledge the effect of the discharge trial, etc. of a foreign court.

(6) The case holding that to acknowledge the effect of discharge in domestic property according to the rehabilitation plan approval order of the US Bankruptcy Court unfairly invades the right of the domestic creditor and its concrete result is against the good customs or other social order of Korea and thus, the above rehabilitation plan approval order of the US Bankruptcy Court can not be approved since it does not satisfy the requirements of the Article 217(3) of the Civil Procedure Act.

2) Summary of Decision

(1) The Article 4(2) of the former Company Reorganization Act (repealed by

212) Supreme Court Decision 2009Ma1600, decided on March 25, 2010.

Act No. 7428 of March 31, 2005, Article 2 of Addendum to the Debtor Rehabilitation Act) adopts 'the territorial principle' as to the effect of a reorganization proceeding commenced in a foreign country. The issue of whether the administrator of a debtor in such case can obtain a right to manage and sell the debtor's property in Korea under a foreign country's law is a separate one. The original effect of a foreign country reorganization proceeding, which enables special measures under the bankruptcy procedure in order to limit individual creditors' exercise of rights and preserve and recover property of a debtor or bankruptcy estate, and which is given for maintenance,rebuilding of business through coordination of the creditor and shareholder's interests like changing creditor shareholder's rights through a reorganization plan, does not reach property located in Korea. Thus, a creditor's exercise of rights as to the debtor's domestic property based on reorganization proceedings commenced in a foreign country is not limited by original effect of a foreign country reorganization proceeding and a change of rights or effect of discharge by the reorganization plan approval order in a foreign country reorganization proceeding does not have any consequence.

(2) The 'approval of foreign country bankruptcy procedure' under the Debtor Rehabilitation Act, unlike 'foreign country judgment approval under the Article 217 of the Civil Procedure Act,' does not approve a foreign court's 'trial.' It approves the pertinent 'foreign country bankruptcy procedure.' And its legal effect is to confirm that a foreign country bankruptcy procedure qualifies for an assistance order. The effect of its approval pursuant to foreign country bankruptcy procedure is not the same as bankruptcy procedure expanded directly within Korea or commenced domestically.

(3) An assistance order under the Debtor Rehabilitation Act provides mere procedurally support so that a foreign country bankruptcy procedure representative may preserve and secure financial resources for dividend and repayment necessary for the foreign country bankruptcy procedure and carry out the plan such as interruption of lawsuit progressing domestically as to the debtor's business and property, mandatory execution, auction for realizing a security right, prohibition or suspension of preservation procedure, debtor's repayment prohibition or prohibition of disposal of debtor's property, etc. It does not conduct a trial directly to change

or extinguish claims or responsibilities that a foreign court has done in the foreign country bankruptcy procedure such as a discharge order or approval order of a rehabilitation plan. It is not a procedure to change or extinguish a creditor's rights substantially by conducting a trial to grant the same effect domestically as to the foreign court's discharge trial.

(4) The discharge trial, etc. of a foreign court relates to an existence of a claim right or an execution power under substantial laws and its effect is simple and unambiguous as the reduction of claims or responsibilities between debtor and individual creditor, and the dispute surrounding approval of its discharge trial should be resolved individually through mutual attack and defense between debtor and creditor in the lawsuit for performance or compulsory execution procedure or bankruptcy procedure dealing with the claim which becomes a target for discharge. etc. In this respect, approval of the discharge trial, etc. of a foreign court does not differ from the approval of general foreign country judgments under the Article 217 of the Civil Procedure Act, although it is done as part of the foreign country bankruptcy procedure. Thus, the issue of approving the discharge trial, etc. of the foreign court conducted in the foreign country bankruptcy procedure under the Debtor Rehabilitation Act repealing the territorial principle should be individually determined by examining whether its discharge trial satisfies approval requirements of the Article 217 of the Civil Procedure Act. and the issue of whether to give an approval is not a matter to be determined pursuant to the approval procedure or assistance procedure under the Debtor Rehabilitation Act.

(5) The requirement should be satisfied that to acknowledge the discharge trial, etc. of a foreign court is not against good customs or other social order of Korea (Article 217(3) of the Civil Procedure Act), Here, the case against good customs or other social order of Korea means that the establishment procedure of the discharge trial, etc. of a foreign court is against good customs or other social order of Korea such that a domestic creditor's lawful participation right in the foreign country bankruptcy procedure is invalidated; the contents of the discharge trial, etc. of a foreign court is against good customs or other social order of Korea; and also its concrete result is against the good customs or other social order of Korea such that to acknowledge the effect of discharge according to the

discharge trial, etc. of a foreign court invades unfairly domestic creditor's rights or interests.

(6) The case holding that to acknowledge the effect of discharge in domestic property according to the rehabilitation plan approval order of the US Bankruptcy Court unfairly invades the right of the domestic creditor, who trusted the territorial principle of the former Company Reorganization Act (repealed by Act No. 7428 of March 31, 2005, Article 2 of Addendum to the Debtor Rehabilitation Act) and did not participate in the rehabilitation procedure of the US Bankruptcy Court and completed provisional attachment as to domestic property owned by the debtor and tried to collect claims through compulsory execution or bankruptcy procedure, and its concrete result is against the good customs or other social order of Korea and thus, the above rehabilitation plan approval order of the US Bankruptcy Court can not be approved since it does not satisfy requirements of the Article 217(3) of the Civil Procedure Act.

3) Conclusion

Therefore, the reappeal is dismissed and it is decided as per Disposition by the assent of all participating Justices.

Related Legal Issues and Questions:

1. What is the Articles of Incorporation and an incorporator?
2. When does a company get a legal entity?
3. How is the liquidation of a company processed? Are there any requirements for liquidation?
4. Does Korea accept an incorporator's liability?

CHAPTER 6
SHARES OF COMPANY

Only stock company may issue shares, which are classified into different classes of shares. The Korean Commercial Act allows shareholders to freely transfer their shares, but it also provides a company with a way to restrict the transfer of shares. One of possible methods enough to restrict a share transfer is to require any shareholder, who is intending to transfer the relevant shares, to obtain prior written approval from the board of directors as specifically provided for in the Articles of Incorporation. In this Chapter, it is important to understand what kinds of shares are classified and how to transfer shares of a stock company under the Korean Commercial Act.

I. Introduction to Shares

A share (주식) is a unit of equity ownership in the capital stock of a stock company. Investors are given share certificates as evidence of their ownership of shares. In modern times, certificates are not always given and ownership may be recorded electronically by a system such as the CREST[213] in the UK, the DTCC in the US[214] or in the KSD (Korea Securities Depository, 한국예탁결제원) in Korea, a central securities depository.

A stock company must issue par value shares. However, where provided for in the Articles of Incorporation, a company may issue all of its shares with no par value. In cases of issuing no par value shares, par value shares may not be

213) The Certificateless Registry for Electronic Share Transfer (CREST) is a UK-based central securities depository that holds UK equities and UK gilts, as well as Irish equities and other international securities (Investopedia. "CREST," August 24, 2021).

214) The Depository Trust & Clearing Corporation (DTCC) is the US post-trade financial services company providing clearing and settlement services to the financial markets (DTCC, "DTCC 2021 Annual Report," Retrieved on January 15, 2023 from <https://www.dtcc.com/about/annual-report>).

issued.[215] The value of par value must be equal and the par value per share must be at least KRW 100. A company may convert its outstanding par value shares into no par value shares, or no par value shares into par value shares, as determined by the Articles of Incorporation.

Based on shares, the liability of a shareholder is limited to the subscription price that he has paid for his shares. Persons who have subscribed to shares jointly must be jointly and severally liable for the payment of the subscription price.[216] Where a share belongs jointly to two or more persons, they must designate one from among themselves who is to exercise the rights of a shareholder. Where no one is designated to exercise the rights of a shareholder, notice or peremptory notice required to be given to the co-owners may be given to any one of them.

II. Classes of Shares under the KCA

1. Introduction

In the past, under the limited types of shares in then existing KCA, companies were hamstrung in being able to raise funds in response to rapid changes in the market environment. In response, the 2011 Amendment to the KCA allowed a company to issue various types of shares according to the demands of the capital market.

Under the current KCA, a company may now issue different classes of shares (종류주식) which are different in respect of their particulars as to the profit dividends, distribution of the surplus assets, exercise of voting rights at a general shareholders' meeting of a company, repayment, conversion, etc.[217] For example, a company might create two classes of shares such as class A share and class B share, where the class A shares have fewer rights than class B shareholders.

Below is a brief review of the classes of shares under the KCA.

215) The Article 329(1) of the Korean Commercial Act.
216) Article 333 of the Korean Commercial Act.
217) Article 344(1) of the Korean Commercial Act.

2. Different Classes of Shares

1) Possible Classes of Shares

Possible classes of shares under the KCA are generally placed into the following four categories:

(i) A class different from a common class concerning the dividend of profits or the distribution of remaining assets,

(ii) A class different from a common class concerning the exercise of the voting right in the general shareholders' meeting,

(iii) A redeemable class of shares, and

(iv) A convertible class of shares.

Notably, redeemable shares and convertible shares are also categorized as a class of shares under the Article 344 of the KCA, though it was a prevailing view in the past that the two types of shares were not recognized as a separate class of shares.

When a company wants to issue different classes of shares, the Articles of Incorporation of a company must provide for the particulars and number of each class of shares. If a company issues different classes of shares, special provisions may be made for each class of shares with respect to the subscription to new shares, the consolidation, split, or retirement of shares or the allotment of shares as a result of a merger or split of the company, even where no such matters have been provided for in the Articles of Incorporation.[218] With respect to the resolution of a general shareholders' meeting of certain classes of shares must be adopted by the affirmative votes of at least two thirds of the voting rights of the shareholders present at a general shareholders' meeting and of at least one third of the total number of issued and outstanding shares of such class.

If a company has issued different classes of shares, and an amendment to the Articles of Incorporation will injure the shareholders of a certain different class of shares, a resolution adopted by a general meeting of such specific class of shareholders must be required for effecting such amendment in addition to that of a general shareholders' meeting.[219] The resolution for such cases must be

218) Article 344(2) and (3) of the Korean Commercial Act.

219) Article 435 of the Korean Commercial Act.

adopted by the affirmative votes of at least two thirds of the voting rights of the shareholders present at a general meeting of shareholders and of at least one third of the total number of issued and outstanding shares of such class.

2) Different Classes of Shares for Profit Dividends or Distribution of Surplus Assets

A company may issue different classes of shares concerning profit dividends or distribution of surplus assets.

(1) Different Classes of Shares for Profit Dividends

Where a company issues different classes of shares in connection with profit dividends, it must determine in the Articles of Incorporation particulars concerning the dividends of profits, such as the types of assets to be distributed for shareholders of different classes of shares, methods of determining the value of such assets, conditions for the distribution of profits, etc.[220] In the past, under then existing KCA, the minimum dividend payout ratio on a preferred class of shares (preferred as to dividends) was determined in the Articles of Incorporation. This determination was deleted by the amended KCA, and instead, now the current KCA stipulates (i) the type of dividend assets, (ii) how to determine the value of dividend assets and (iii) conditions for the dividend of profits. In doing so, it is possible to issue a share preferred as to dividends for which a fixed amount is paid out as a preferred dividend. In this case, for example, the profit of KRW 500 per share can be paid out as a preferred dividend. In other way, a company may issue a share preferred as to dividends with the variable dividend ratio in which the dividend ratio of a share preferred as to dividends is linked to market interest rates.

(2) Different Classes of Shares for Distribution of Surplus Assets

Also, where a company issues different classes of shares in connection with the distribution of surplus assets, it must determine in the Articles of Incorporation particulars concerning the distribution of surplus assets, such as the

---

220) Article 344-2(1) of the Korean Commercial Act.

types of surplus assets, methods of determining the value of such surplus assets, and other matters regarding the distribution of surplus assets.[221)]

3) Different Classes of Shares for Exclusion or Limit of Voting Rights

Under the KCA, it is possible to issue not only a share preferred as to dividends without voting right but also a share preferred as to remaining-asset distribution without voting right and a share with the same conditions as those of a common share but without voting right. When a company issues different classes of shares having no, or limited voting rights, it must determine in the Articles of Incorporation matters concerning no exercise of voting rights and particulars, such as the conditions for exercise or revival of voting rights, if any.[222)] The total number of such classes of shares must not exceed a quarter of the total number of issued and outstanding shares. In such cases, if the different classes of shares having no, or limited voting rights are issued and exceed a quarter of the total number of issued and outstanding shares, the company must, without delay, take measures necessary to keep the said number of different classes of shares not exceeding the limitation.

Since the Article 370 of the old KCA requiring that voting rights be restored if preferred dividends cannot be paid out was deleted by the amendment to the KCA, it is now possible to include various provisions relating to the restoration of the voting right in the Articles of Incorporation without limitation.

In addition, under the KCA, it is now possible to issue both a completely nonvoting share as well as a share with a limited voting right for which the voting right is recognized only for certain matters. For example, it is possible to issue a share for which the voting right is recognized only for important corporate matters requiring special resolution of the general shareholders' meeting including business transfer, merger or amendment of the Articles of Incorporation. However, as the KCA does not yet introduce a class of shares with a veto over certain matters, for example, the so-called 'veto share' requiring a resolution of the general shareholders' meeting of a certain class of shares for business transfer, merger or amendment of the Articles of Incorporation, it is still

---

221) Article 344-2(2) of the Korean Commercial Act.

222) Article 344-3 of the Korean Commercial Act.

impermissible to have the veto of minority shareholders, which is commonly provided in an agreement among shareholders.

4) Different Classes of Shares for Redemption or Conversion of Shares

The KCA expressly provides that a share of a convertible or redeemable class may be converted or redeemed at the request of a shareholder or unilaterally by the company when certain causes for redemption or conversion occur for a redeemable share or a convertible share, and imposes a duty of notice on the company in the case of unilateral decision of conversion or redemption by the company.

(1) Different Classes of Redeemable Shares

First of all, under the KCA, it is possible to redeem in securities or other assets as well as in cash for a redeemable share. A company may issue different classes of shares that may be retired out of profits in accordance with the Articles of Incorporation. In such cases, the price, period, and methods of the redemption of shares, and the number of redeemable shares must be stated in the Articles of Incorporation.[223] In such cases, no later than two weeks prior to the date of acquisition of the redeemable shares, a company must separately notify the particulars of the said redemption to the shareholders of the redeemable shares and to the interest-holders stated in the register of shareholders, in accordance with the Articles of Incorporation. The said notification may be substituted by public notification.

A company may also, as prescribed in its Articles of Incorporation, issue different classes of shares with which the shareholders may demand redemption of shares against the company.[224] In such cases, the company must determine in the Articles of Incorporation the rights of shareholders to demand redemption against the company, and the price, period, and methods of the redemption of shares.

---

223) Article 345(1) of the Korean Commercial Act; Jung-Hai Moon, "A Study on the Cases of the Supreme Court on the Commercial Act in 2020," Ewha Law Journal, Vol. 25 No. 2, December 2020, p.241.

224) Article 345(3) of the Korean Commercial Act.

In both a share of a convertible class at the request of a shareholder and unilaterally by the company, as a consideration for acquisition of shares, a company may provide securities or assets other than cash, excluding other different classes of shares. In such cases, however, the book value of the assets must not exceed the distributable profits. Such convertible shares may be issued with a limit to different classes of shares, excluding those concerning redemption and conversion.[225] Therefore, issuing a common share as a redeemable share is not allowed. Such issuance is prohibited in order to prevent the management of a company from protecting its position in a way similar to a 'poison pill' (which has yet to be introduced in the KCA), by unilaterally redeeming a common share.

(2) Different Classes of Convertible Shares

If a company issues different classes of shares, the Articles of Incorporation may provide that a shareholder may request that shares subscribed to by the shareholder are converted into shares of another class. In such cases, the conditions for conversion, the period within which the conversion may be requested, and the number and particulars as to the shares to be issued as a result of the conversion must be prescribed in the Articles of Incorporation.[226]

In cases where a company issues different classes of shares, the company may also determine in the Articles of Incorporation that it may convert the shares subscribed to by the shareholder into shares of another class upon occurrence of certain event. In such cases, the reason of conversion, conditions for conversion, the period within which the conversion may be requested, and the number and particulars as to the shares to be issued as a result of the conversion shall be prescribed in the Articles of Incorporation.[227] In such cases, the board of directors must separately notify the following matters to the shareholders of the relevant shares and to the interest-holders stated in the register of shareholders: (i) the shares to be converted, (ii) a statement to the effect that the share certificates should be submitted to the company within a prescribed period of no less than two weeks, and (iii) a statement to the effect that the share certificates will become invalidated if they are not submitted to the company within the said period.

---

225) Supreme Court Decision 2017다251564, decided on April 9, 2020.

226) Article 346(1) of the Korean Commercial Act.

227) Article 346(2) of the Korean Commercial Act.

The said notification may be substituted by public notification. The number of shares to be newly issued must be reserved out of the number of shares of different classes, with respect to their issuance, during the period for requesting the conversion or the period of conversion.

In cases of convertible shares, the following matters must be stated in share subscription forms or certificates of preemptive rights to new shares:[228)]

(i) A statement to the effect that the relevant shares may be converted into shares of another class,

(ii) Conditions of conversion,

(iii) Particulars of the shares to be issued as a result of the conversion, and

(iv) The period for requesting the conversion, or the period for conversion.

If shares are to be issued as a result of the conversion, the issuance price of such new shares must be that of the shares which existed before the conversion.[229)] A person requesting conversion of shares must submit to the company two copies of the written request form together with the share certificates.[230)] The written request form must state the classes and number of shares to be converted and the date of the demand and the shareholder demanding the conversion must write his/her name and affix his/her seal, or affix his/her signature, thereon.

Conversion of shares will take effect at the time it is requested in cases where a shareholder requests the conversion, and at the prescribed time elapses in cases where the company has completed the conversion.[231)] The holders of shares converted during the period of closure of register of shareholders may not exercise their voting rights at the general shareholders' meeting held during such period. With regard to dividends of profits accruing from the shares issued as a result of conversion, the conversion must be deemed to have been made when the shareholder requests the conversion or at the end of the business year in which the prescribed period elapses. In such cases, the Articles of Incorporation may provide that with respect to dividends of profits as to the new shares, the conversion is deemed to have been made when the shareholder demands the

228) Article 347 of the Korean Commercial Act.

229) Article 348 of the Korean Commercial Act.

230) Article 349 of the Korean Commercial Act.

231) Article 350(1) of the Korean Commercial Act.

conversion or at the end of the business year immediately before the business year in which the prescribed period.

The registration of changes arising from the conversion of shares must be made at the place of the principal office, within two weeks from the last day of the month in which the conversion is demanded or the prescribed period elapses.[232)]

5) Implications of Different Classes of Shares

The 2011 Amendment to the KCA concerning the classes of shares is meaningful in that the amendments have (i) reduced the rigidness that was built into then existing KCA which strictly limited the types of shares that could be issued by a company and (ii) created the basis for the diversification of shares a company may issue. Under the current KCA, the details on classes of shares must be provided in the Articles of Incorporation. However, the KCA is silent on the degree of detail with which the Articles of Incorporation should regulate the conditions of a class of shares and to what extent a company can independently establish relevant provisions.[233)] Such standards must be established under the general principles of company law including the principles of the fair treatment of all shares and from the perspective of the director's due diligence, and the interests of various stakeholders of a company including shareholders need to be fully taken into consideration in the process of establishing such standards.

In turn, a company needs to fully understand and acquaint different classes of shares in rearranging its Articles of Incorporation and following relevant procedures in order to reduce possible legal issues that may arise in relation to classes of shares.

III. Transfer of Shares under the KCA

1. Share Transfer in General

In principle, the KCA allows shareholders to freely transfer their shares like in

232) Article 351 of the Korean Commercial Act.

233) Choi Junesun, *op. cit.*, p.148; Chung Chan-Hyung, *op. cit.*, p.722.

all other countries. Accordingly, it is not allowed to completely prohibit a share transfer. In the transfer of shares (주식양도), share certificates (주권) must be delivered and the possessor of a share certificate is presumed to be the legal holder thereof.[234] Any transfer of shares made before the issuance of share certificates is not effective against the company, and this will not apply where six months have passed from the date of the establishment of the company or the date of the payment of the subscription price for new shares.[235]

However, the KCA also provides a company with a way to restrict the transfer, via including a provision in the relevant Articles of Incorporation that requires any shareholder, who is intending to transfer the relevant shares, to obtain prior written approval from the board of directors according to the Article 335(1) of the KCA.

This is often done especially by unlisted or non-public companies of which shareholders have entered into shareholders agreements restricting share transfer to third parties, among other things. Such restriction in the transfer of share is reflected in the Articles of Incorporation of a relevant company by requiring the approval of board of directors for a specific share transfer. In this connection, the board of directors would approve a share transfer by a shareholder, if the shareholder has complied with share transfer procedures stipulated under the relevant shareholders agreement.

2. Restrictions of Share Transfer

Are restrictions on the transfer of fully paid shares permitted? If so, what restrictions are commonly adopted under the KCA? Despite the free transferability of shares in principle, there could be a way of restricting or limiting a share transfer under the KCA.

1) Transfer of Potential Shares

A potential share (권리주) means a share not yet issued, but having the right

234) Article 336 of the Korean Commercial Act.

235) Article 335(3) of the Korean Commercial Act; Park, Sei-hwa, "A Shareholder's Right in Share Transfer Prior to Issuing Share Certificates and Preferred Position Relation between First and Second Transferees - A Review of a Korean Supreme Court Case (in Korean)," Analysis of Recent Cases, Vol. 721, February 2017, p.821.

based upon subscription of shares. Since potential shares are apt to be the target of circulation, the transfer of such potential shares or such rights based on subscription of shares is not effective against the company.[236]

2) Transfer of Shares Made before the Issuance of Share Certificates

Any transfer of shares made before the issuance of share certificates is not effective against the company.[237] However, this does not apply where six months have passed from the date of the establishment of the company or the date of the payment of the subscription price for new shares.[238]

3) Acquisition of Treasury Shares or Share Redemption

(1) Provisions of the KCA

Are compulsory share repurchases allowed? Can they be made mandatory in certain circumstances? A stock company is prohibited from forcing a shareholder to accept a refund of his capital contributions even if such refund is specifically provided for in its Articles of Incorporation. Unless explicitly provided for in the KCA or other relevant laws and regulations, a compulsory share repurchase by a company, in its discretion, from its shareholders is invalid.

However, a stock company may acquire treasury shares or redeem its shares under its own name and on its own account, in accordance with the following methods:[239] (i) in cases of shares having market values on the stock exchange, the method of acquisition at the exchange, or (ii) the methods of acquisition under equal conditions in proportion to the number of shares owned by each shareholder as determined by Presidential Decree, except for the different classes of shares concerning the redemption of shares. The total acquisition price must not exceed the amount obtained by subtracting the amounts prescribed in the Article 462(1) from the net assets value on the balance sheet for the immediately

236) Article 319 of the Korean Commercial Act.

237) Supreme Court Decision 2015Da71795, decided on March 24, 2016.

238) Article 335(3) of the Korean Commercial Act.

239) Article 341(1) of the Korean Commercial Act.

preceding period for the settlement of accounts.

A company seeking to acquire its own shares must determine the following matters in advance by a resolution of a general shareholders' meeting:[240] (i) the class and number of the shares that can be acquired, (ii) limit on the total acquisition price, and (iii) the period of not exceeding one year for acquisition of its own shares. In cases where the Articles of Incorporation provide that distribution of profits can be made with a resolution of the board of directors, such resolution of the board of directors may substitute for that of the general shareholders' meeting.

No company will acquire its own shares in cases where it is likely that the net assets value on the balance sheet for the period for the settlement of accounts in the relevant business year is less than the sum of the amounts prescribed in the Article 462(1).[241] In cases where a company acquires its own shares although the net assets value on the balance sheet for the period for the settlement of accounts in the relevant business year is less than the sum of the amounts prescribed in the Article 462(1), directors are jointly and severally liable to compensate the company for the relevant insufficient amount. However, this does not apply where the directors determined that there was no likelihood of the relevant insufficient amount and proved that he/she had not neglected his/her duty of care in making such decision.[242]

As an exception, however, it is allowed to acquire treasury shares for particular purposes. For example, in cases falling under any of the following cases, a company may acquire treasury shares:[243] (i) in the case of merger of the company or acquisition of the entire business of another company, (ii) in cases where it is necessary to achieve the objective in the course of exercising the rights of the company, (iii) in cases where it is necessary to deal with fractional shares, or (iv) in cases where a shareholder exercises his/her appraisal rights.

In cases where a company disposes of treasury shares that it holds, the following matters must be determined by the board of directors unless the Articles of Incorporation provide otherwise:[244] (i) the class and number of the

240) Article 341(2) of the Korean Commercial Act.
241) Article 341(3) of the Korean Commercial Act.
242) Article 341(4) of the Korean Commercial Act.
243) Article 341-2 of the Korean Commercial Act.
244) Article 342 of the Korean Commercial Act.

shares to be disposed of, (ii) the price of the shares to be disposed of and date of payment, and (iii) persons to whom the shares are to be transferred and the method of the disposition.

(2) Significance of Share Redemption under the KCA

(i) Background

Under the previous KCA, the redemption of shares was not allowed except for several limited situations. One of the main reasons for restricting share redemption was a concern that companies would abuse such mechanism by distributing retained profits to only certain shareholders and in effect, violate the principle of equality among shareholders.[245] However, to deny all fiscally responsible and financially healthy companies the opportunity to redeem their own shares was deemed unfair, particularly considering that the value added to shareholders was equal to that of the distribution of dividends. Furthermore, the previous KCA was criticized for discriminating against unlisted companies, as listed companies are permitted to redeem their shares under the Financial Investments Services and Capital Markets Act.

As a way to ease the foregoing concerns, the KCA now permits a share redemption as a general rule and instead has abolished a share retirement which has the same economic effect as share redemption. Below is a summary of the major provisions relating to share redemption under the KCA.

(ii) Major Provisions for Share Redemption

(a) Share Redemption is Allowed as a General Rule

If the financial statement for the year suggests that the company has the capacity to dispose of retained profits, it may do so by (i) redeeming the shares on the open-market, or (ii) making an offer to all shareholders to redeem their shares under equal conditions for all under the KCA.[246] The rule intends to protect shareholder equality during the redemption of shares process. If a company

245) Choi Junesun, *op. cit.*, p.308; Chung Chan-Hyung, *op. cit.*, p.776.

246) Article 341(1) of the Korean Commercial Act.

chooses to redeem its shares by making an equal offer to all shareholders, the process will be further detailed in a Presidential Decree of the KCA.

(b) Share Redemption Process

A share redemption process may be implemented by the resolution at a shareholders' meeting, if the following matters are discussed: (i) the type and number of shares that are being redeemed, (ii) the total redemption value limit, and (iii) a time period, not exceeding one year, in which the share(s) can be redeemed.

If the company's Articles of Incorporation allow the redemption process to be adopted by resolution of the board of directors, then the board may prescribe the above process without requiring a shareholder meeting.[247]

(c) Financial Responsibility of Directors

A company may not redeem its shares if it is projected that the company would have insufficient retained profits during the relevant fiscal year. In case that a company has already redeemed its shares but the redemption value exceeds that of retained profits at the end of the fiscal year, the directors will be personally liable and reimburse the deficit caused by the redemption of shares.

If the directors, however, can prove that the projection of retained profits was based on good faith and due care, the directors is not liable for reimbursement.[248] As such, the board of directors and each director must thoroughly evaluate the company's business records and data before making a decision on the redemption of shares.

(d) Exceptions to the Share Redemption Process

Under the KCA, a company may redeem its shares without consideration of the company's retained profits in the following cases: (i) the merger of companies or of the acquisition of the entire business of another company, (ii) it is necessary to do so for achieving its objectives in the course of exercising the

247) Article 341-2 of the Korean Commercial Act.
248) Article 341(4) of the Korean Commercial Act.

rights of the company, (iii) it is necessary to deal with the fractional shares, or (iv) the exercise of an appraisal right by a shareholder.[249)]

Because share redemption is deemed necessary under the foregoing circumstances, the process does not require the evaluation of the company's retained profits in such cases.

(e) Disposition of Redeemed Shares

Under the previous KCA, disposition of the redeemed shares was required within 'a reasonable time period.' As such, it was unclear how long a company was allowed to possess such shares before disposition.

Under the amended KCA, provided that the Articles of Incorporation do not state otherwise, the redeemed shares may be disposed of at a reasonable time determined by resolution of the board of directors.

(f) Abolishment of Share Retirement

Under the previous KCA, a share retirement is a process whereby a company retires its shares by using retained profits reserved for distribution to shareholders. The retirement price, method and director duties are also prescribed by the previous KCA. However, because the amended KCA permits share redemption, the share retirement system is no longer of any use to companies. The economic effect of distribution of retained profits without capital fluctuation is the same.

As a result, to eliminate any confusion or overlapping, share retirement was abolished and in the event a company redeems its shares by resolution of the board of directors, the company is no longer subject to the capital reduction regulations under the KCA.[250)]

(iii) Implications of the KCA regarding Share Redemption

By giving unlisted companies the right to redeem their own shares, the KCA is meaningful in that it provides shareholders with flexible options regarding return on investments and capital financing.[251)] In return, the KCA holds

249) Article 341-2 of the Korean Commercial Act.
250) Article 343(1) of the Korean Commercial Act.

company directors to strict standards involving the duty to protect the principle of equality of all shareholders and to maintain the financial well-being of the company.

It is expected that the foregoing issues will continue to evolve as the relevant provisions of the KCA is being implemented, and thus, it is important to reduce possible legal issues that may arise in relation to the redemption of shares and director duties.

4) Creation of Pledges on Treasury Shares

A company may not create a pledge on treasury shares in excess of a twentieth of the total number of shares issued and outstanding. However, such ceiling does not apply in cases falling under (i) in the case of merger of the company or acquisition of the entire business of another company, or (ii) in cases where it is necessary to achieve the objective in the course of exercising the rights of the company.[252)]

5) Acquisition of Parent Company's Shares by Subsidiary Company

Where a company (parent company) holds more than half of the total number of issued and outstanding shares in another company (subsidiary company), the subsidiary company may not acquire shares in the parent company, except in the following cases: (i) in cases of an all-inclusive exchange and all-inclusive transfer of shares, the merger of companies or the acquisition of the entire business of another company, or (ii) where it is necessary to do so to achieve the objective in the course of exercising the rights of the company.[253)] In such cases, the subsidiary company must dispose of the shares of the parent company within six months of the acquisition thereof.

If a parent company and its subsidiary company in aggregate hold, or a subsidiary company by itself holds, more than half of the total number of issued and outstanding shares in another company, such another company is deemed a subsidiary company of the parent company.

---

251) Chung Chan-Hyung, *op. cit.*, p.776; Choi Junesun, *op. cit.*, p.308.

252) Article 341-3 of the Korean Commercial Act.

253) Article 342-2(1) of the Korean Commercial Act.

6) Acquisition of Another Company's Shares

If a company acquires more than ten percent of the total number of issued and outstanding shares in another company, it must, without delay, notify the company of such acquisition.[254)]

7) Transfer of Shares subject to the Board's Approval

The transfer of shares may require a resolution of the board of directors as specifically provided for in the Articles of Incorporation. A shareholder who intends to transfer his shares may request the company's approval by indicating the party to whom the shares will be transferred and the type and number of shares to be transferred. If a shareholder receives from the company a notice denying the approval of the transfer of shares, such shareholder may request the company to designate the party to whom the shares will be transferred and the number of shares to be transferred.

However, it should be noted that the transfer of shares in listed companies may not be restricted. Devices restricting a share transfer pursuant to shareholders' agreements are frequently used. Such restrictions may cause the parties in breach of the shareholders' agreements to be held liable for damages, but are not effective against the company even if the company is a party to the shareholders' agreements and such agreements are specifically provided for in the Articles of Incorporation.[255)]

As such, the KCA allows other means for the shareholders to collect their invested capital in the case that the board of directors does not give its approval of a specific share transfer. That is, shares may be transferred to other persons in case that a company subjects the transfer of shares to the approval of the board of directors, as determined by the Articles of Incorporation. Any transfer of shares that is not approved by the board of directors is not effective against the company.[256)]

---

254) Article 342-3 of the Korean Commercial Act.

255) Seoul High Court Decision 2016Na2089876, decided on July 7, 2017.

256) Article 335(2) of the Korean Commercial Act.

The brief procedure for the transfer of shares subject to the board's approval is as follows:

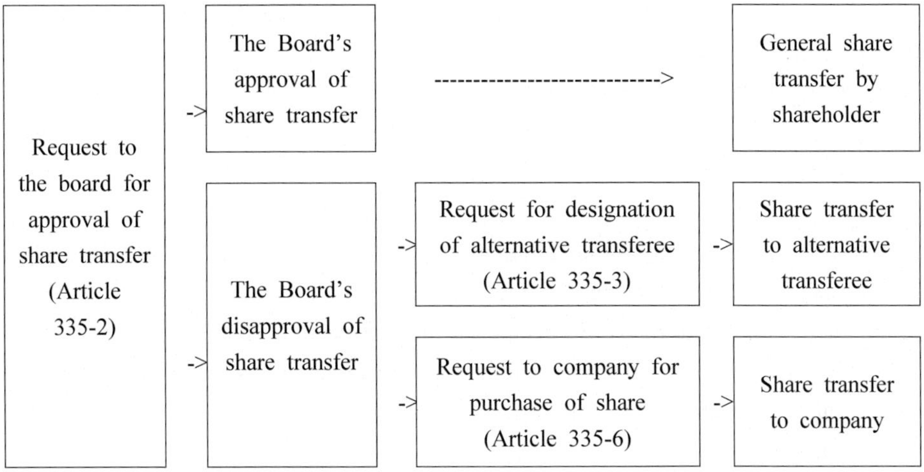

(1) Requests for Approval of Transfers

In cases where the transfer of shares requires the approval of the board of directors, a shareholder intending to transfer his/her shares may request in writing the company to approve the transfer, by specifying the intended transferee and the class and number of the shares to be transferred.[257] Subsequently, a company must give a written notice to a shareholder of whether or not it approves the transfer of shares, within one month of the shareholder's request. If a company fails to notify the shareholder of its refusal within the period of one month, the board of directors is deemed to have approved the transfer of shares.

A shareholder who receives a notice of the refusal to approve the share transfer may request the company to designate the alternative transferee or to purchase the shares, within twenty days of receipt of the notice.

(2) Requests for Designation of Alternative Transferee

If a shareholder requests the company to designate an alternative transferee, the

257) Article 335-2(1) of the Korean Commercial Act.

board of directors must designate the alternative transferee and give a written notice thereof to the shareholder and the designated person, within two weeks of the request.[258)]

If the board of directors fails to notify the shareholder of the designation of the alternative transferee within the period of two weeks of the request, the board of directors is deemed to have approved the transfer of shares.

(3) Requests for Sale by Designated Transferee

Any person designated as an alternative transferee may make a written request to the shareholder who made the request for such designation to sell the shares to him/her within ten days of receipt of the notification of such designation.[259)] Where a person designated as an alternative transferee fails to make a request for sale within the such period), the board of directors is deemed to have approved the transfer of shares.

In case of the sale by designated transferee, the sale price of the relevant shares must be determined through a negotiation between the shareholder and the person who requests sale. Where such negotiation is not made within thirty days from the date of receipt of the request for the sale by designated transferee, the company or the shareholder who has requested the purchase of shares may request the court to determine the purchase price. Where the court makes a ruling on the purchase price of shares, it must compute it by a fair price in view of the current status of assets of the company and other situations.[260)]

(4) Request for Purchase by Shareholders

As mentioned above, a shareholder who receives a notice of the refusal to approve the share transfer may request the company to purchase the shares, within twenty days of receipt of the notice.[261)] In such cases, the relevant company must purchase the shares within two months from the expiration of a period during which a request for purchase can be made. The purchase price of

---

258) Article 335-3(1) of the Korean Commercial Act.
259) Article 335-4(1) of the Korean Commercial Act.
260) Articles 335-5(2) and 374-2(4) & (5) of the Korean Commercial Act.
261) Article 335-2(4) of the Korean Commercial Act.

shares must be determined through consultation between the shareholder and the company. Where the consultation between the shareholder and the company fails to produce an agreement within thirty days from the expiration of the period during which a request for purchase can be made, the company or the shareholder who has requested the purchase of shares may request the court to determine the purchase price. Where the court makes a ruling on the purchase price of shares, it must compute it by a fair price in view of the current status of assets of the company and other situations.[262)]

(5) Request for Approval by Transferee of Shares

In cases where the transfer of shares is subject to the approval of the board of directors, any person who has acquired the shares may make a written request to the company to approve such acquisition, by specifying the class and number of the acquired shares.[263)] However, if the board of directors rejects the request, then the transferee must go through the same process as the transferor, i.e. requesting designation of an alternative transferee or requesting the company to acquire the shares. In such cases, the Articles 335-2 (Requests for Approval of Transfers), 335-3 (Requests for Designation of Alternative Transferee), 335-4 (Requests for Sale by Designated Transferee, 335-5 (Determination of Sale Price) and 335-6 (Request for Purchase by Shareholders) as already explained above, mutatis mutandis, will apply.

3. Other Considerations for Transfer of Shares

In the transfer of shares, some other important matters must be considered in corporate practice.

1) First of all, in the transfer of shares, share certificates must be delivered and the possessor of a share certificate is presumed to be the legal holder thereof.[264)] There are some requirements to assert the effect of transfer of shares. The effect of transfer of shares can not be asserted against the company, unless

---

262) Article 335-6 of the Korean Commercial Act.

263) Article 335-7(1) of the Korean Commercial Act.

264) Article 336 of the Korean Commercial Act.

the name and address of the transferee have been entered in the register of shareholders.[265] A company may designate a transfer agent in accordance with the Articles of Incorporation. In such cases, if the transfer agent has entered the name and address of the transferee in part of a set of the register of shareholders, the entry of changes in holders will be deemed duly effected.

2) In pledging of shares, the share certificates must be delivered to the pledgee in order to pledge shares,[266] No pledgee can assert his/her pledge against a third party unless he/she continues to hold the share certificates. Where there has been retirement, consolidation, split or conversion of shares, the pledge rights over the original shares may continue to exist as against the cash or shares which the original shareholder is to receive based thereon.[267]

3) In cases where the subject of pledge rights is a share and the company has, at the request of the pledgee, entered the name and address of the pledgee in the register of shareholders and entered his/her name in the share certificate, the pledgee may receive from the company the profit dividends, distribution of residual assets or money, and may apply the sum toward repayment of the obligations owed to him/her in preference to other creditors.[268] In such cases, a pledgee may request the company to deliver the share certificate of the such shares.

IV. Share Certificate

1. Issuance of Share Certificate

A share certificate (주권) or a certificate of stock is a legal document that certifies the legal interest or right of ownership of a specific number of shares or stock in a company. Today, however, most shares are uncertificated – that is, no actual, physical share certificate are issued. Instead, a company keeps an official

265) Article 337(1) of the Korean Commercial Act.
266) Article 338(1) of the Korean Commercial Act.
267) Article 339 of the Korean Commercial Act.
268) Article 340(1) of the Korean Commercial Act.

record of its shareholders and may send each of them a letter or other notice that contains the pertinent information that formerly was included on the face of share certificate.[269)]

Also in Korea, a shareholder may notify a company of his intent not to have share certificates of his shares, and in such case, a company may not issue the relevant share certificates. As a general principle, however, a company must issue share certificates without delay after its incorporation or after the date of payment for new shares.[270)] No share certificate may be issued before the incorporation of the company or the subscription date for new shares. Share certificates issued in contravention of these timing for issuing share certificates will be null and void, but this will not affect any claim for damages against the parties who have issued them.

Each share certificate must state the following matters and the serial number, and the representative director must write his name and affix his seal, or affix his signature, thereon:[271)]

(i) Trade name of the company,

(ii) Date of incorporation of the company,

(iii) Total number of shares authorized to be issued by the company,

(iv) Par value per share where par value shares are issued,

(v) Date of issuance of such certificates, if the shares are issued after the incorporation of the company,

(vi) Particulars and classes of shares, if different classes of shares are issued, and

(vii) Provisions that the transfer of shares is subject to the approval of the board of directors, if so determined.

2. Electronic Registration of Shares Instead of Issuing Share Certificates

A company may register shares with the electronic registration ledger of an electronic registration authority which refers to the authority handling the affairs

269) Frank B. Cross and Roger LeRoy Miller, *op. cit.*, p.439

270) Article 355(1) of the Korean Commercial Act.

271) Article 356 of the Korean Commercial Act.

of electronic registration of securities, etc., instead of issuing share certificates, as prescribed by the Articles of Incorporation.[272] Transfer or pledge of shares registered with the electronic registration ledger will become effective when the transfer or pledge is registered with the electronic registration ledger.

A person who has registered shares with the electronic registration ledger is deemed to legitimately have the right to the registered shares, and the person who has relied on such electronic registration ledger in good faith and without gross negligence and thereby acquired the right pursuant to registration will validly acquire such right.

3. Non-Possession of Share Certificate

Unless otherwise provided for in the Articles of Incorporation, a shareholder may notify the company of his intent not to have share certificates of his shares. Upon receipt of such notification, the company must without delay enter in the register of shareholders and part of a set thereof its intent not to issue the share certificates and notify the shareholder accordingly.[273] In such cases, the company may not issue the relevant share certificates.

In cases of non-possession of share certificates, any share certificates issued previously must be submitted to the company and the company must invalidate them or deposit them with a transfer agent. Notwithstanding in cases of non-possession of share certificates, a shareholder may request at any time that the company issue or return the share certificates.

4. Judgment of Nullification and Re-issuance of Share Certificates

A share certificate may be invalidated through the process of a public summons.[274]

No person who has lost his share certificate must request its re-issuance to the company, unless he/she has obtained a judgment of nullification with respect thereto.

272) Article 356-2(1) of the Korean Commercial Act.
273) Article 358-2(2) of the Korean Commercial Act.
274) Article 360(1) of the Korean Commercial Act.

V. Case Study on Issuance of Share Certificate and Price of Stocks

1. Case Study on Issuance of Share Certificate[275)]

1) Main Issues and Holdings

(1) Whether the division of inherited property by agreement shall be made by the participation of all co-inheritors (affirmative) and the validity of the division of inherited property by agreement which was made in consecutive order (valid).

(2) Whether a lawsuit to seek the affirmation of existence of a right of share relating to a portion of co-inherited property is an indispensable co-litigation (negative).

(3) A method of acquiring the possession of share certificate.

(4) Whether a specific preemptive right is transferred along with the transfer of shareholder right (negative) and a person entitled to have a specific preemptive right (a shareholder who was entered on the register of shareholders at the record date).

2) Summary of Decision

(1) The division of inherited property by inheritors' agreement is a sort of contract between co-inheritors and shall be made by the participation of all co-inheritors, and the division by agreement between some inheritors shall be considered as invalid. However, such division does not need to be made at the same place, and can be made in consecutive order, and it is fine if other inheritors recognize original division plan which has already been made by one inheritor by turns.

275) Supreme Court Decision 2008Da96963, 96970, decided on February 25, 2010. *See* also Supreme Court Decision 2000Du9731, decided on November 27, 2001 and Supreme Court Decision 2003Da65438, 65445, decided on October 28, 2004.

(2) A lawsuit to seek affirmation of existence of a right of share relating to a portion of co-inherited property is not an indispensable co-litigation but a normal co-litigation.

(3) The transfer of shares after share certificate was issued takes effect where share certificate is delivered (Article 336(1) of the KCA), and as a method of possessing share certificate, there are summary delivery and transfer of a right to request a return, besides actual hand-over delivery.

(4) Preemptive right which arises when a company issues shares through capitalizing the reserve by a resolution of the board of directors pursuant to the Article 461 of the KCA, or issues new shares by a resolution of a general shareholder's meeting or the board of directors pursuant to the Article 416 of the KCA, does not fall under the shareholders' own rights but just a specific right arising out of a resolution of a general shareholders' meeting or the board of directors based on the above provisions of the KCA. Thus, the preemptive right is not transferred along with the transfer of shareholder right. In the course of issuing new shares, if a company limits a person who will be entitled to hold such right only to shareholder entered on the register of shareholders at a certain time by a resolution of a general shareholders' meeting or the board of directors, such preemptive right will belong to shareholders who can legally raise an objection against the company, i.e., shareholders who were entered on the register of shareholders, regardless of whether they are beneficial owners at such a certain time.

3) Conclusion

Therefore, the Court determines by unanimous opinion of all participating Justices that of the judgment of the court below, the portion that ruled against the defendants shall be reversed without examination as to the remaining grounds of appeal, the corresponding part of this case shall be remanded to the court below for a new trial and determination, and the plaintiff's appeal shall be dismissed, as set forth in the Disposition above.

2. Case Study on Corporate Tax and Transaction Price of Stocks[276)]

1) Main Issues and Holdings

(1) Meaning of the principle of substantial taxation under the Article 14(1) of the former Framework Act on National Taxes.

Whether the principle of substantial taxation is applicable to an international transaction in which a resident or domestic corporation establishes, and uses only the corporate form of, a merely formal 'base company' in a tax haven to avoid domestic taxes (affirmative).

(2) In cases where it is difficult to apply the transfer price tax system under the former Adjustment of International Taxes Act to an international transaction between persons in special relationship, and the substance of the transaction constitutes a transfer of domestic corporate profits to a foreign related person without consideration, whether said transaction falls under any of the items under the Article 3-2 of the former Enforcement Decree of the Adjustment of International Taxes Act (affirmative).

In cases where a domestic corporation jointly holding derivative-based rights with a foreign related party distributes profits to the said foreign related party by allowing it to exercise the entire right, whether such an act falls under the scope of the repudiation of wrongful calculation under the Article 52(1) of the former Corporate Tax Act and the Article 88(1)(g-2) of the former Enforcement Decree of the Corporate Tax Act (affirmative).

(3) In cases of a corporate transfer of issued stocks together with its managerial control, whether the transaction price may be deemed an ordinary market price (negative). In cases of stock transactions involving a complete transfer of managerial control, whether the transaction price may be deemed an arm's length price (negative in principle).

2) Summary of Decision

(1) The principle of substantial taxation as provided under the Article 14(1) of

276) Supreme Court Decision 2014Du335, decided on November 26, 2015.

the former Framework Act on National Taxes (amended by Act No. 9911, Jan. 1, 2010) means that, when there is a person to whom such taxable items as income, profit, property, or transaction substantially accrue, apart from the one nominally designated, tax authority shall deem liable for tax the one to whom such items substantially accrue, instead of the nominally designated person in formality or appearance.

Thus, in cases where: (a) the person to whom a property nominally accrues lacks the capacity to control/manage the property; (b) there is another person who substantially controls or manages the property by means of governance, etc. of the nominal owner; and (c) the disparity between name and substance arose out of the intent to avoid tax, the income on property shall be deemed attributable to the person substantially controlling/managing the property, rendering said person liable for taxation.

In addition, the principle of substantial taxation may be applicable not only to those international transactions in which a non-resident or foreign corporation establishes, and uses only the corporate form of, a nominal corporation in a country eligible for tax treaty benefits in order to avoid domestic taxes as the source country, but also to those international transactions in which a resident or domestic corporation establishes a so-called 'base company' only in form without the capacity to carry out business activities in a tax haven where income tax is exempted or imposed at a low rate, and uses only the corporate form of said base company as a means to avoid domestic taxes as the country of residence, thereby unfairly reserving the income which ought to have accrued to the substantial controller or manager.

(2) In cases where it is difficult to apply the transfer price tax system under the former Adjustment of International Taxes Act to an international transaction between persons in special relationship, and the substance of the transaction constitutes a transfer of domestic corporate profits to a foreign related person without consideration, said transaction shall be construed to fall under each of the items under the Article 3-2 of the former Enforcement Decree of the Adjustment of International Taxes Act, in full view of the following: (a) chronology of the enactment and amendment of the Adjustment of International Taxes Act, (b) developments leading up to the establishment of the Article 3(2) of the former Adjustment of International Taxes Act (amended by Act No. 9914, Jan. 1, 2010;

hereinafter 'former International Taxes Adjustment Act'), (c) interrelationship between the former Corporate Tax Act (amended by Act No. 10423, Dec. 30, 2010, hereinafter 'Corporate Tax Act') and the former International Taxes Adjustment Act, and (d) features and organization of each items under the Article 88(1) of the former Enforcement Decree of the Corporate Tax Act (amended by Presidential Decree No. 20720, Feb. 29, 2008; hereinafter 'Enforcement Decree of the Corporate Tax Act'), setting out the object and types of the repudiation of wrongful calculation, and those under the Article 3-2 of the former Enforcement Decree of the International Taxes Adjustment Act (amended by Presidential Decree No. 21299, Feb. 4, 2009, hereinafter 'former Enforcement Decree of the International Taxes Adjustment Act'), setting out the scope of exclusion from the applicability of the former International Taxes Adjustment Act.

Therefore, it falls under the scope of the repudiation of wrongful calculation under the Article 52(1) of the Corporate Tax Act and the Article 88(1)(g-2) of the Enforcement Decree of the Corporate Tax Act for a domestic corporation jointly holding derivative-based rights with a foreign related party to abstain from exercising its rights corresponding to its holding ratio, and to instead distribute profits to said foreign related party by allowing it to exercise the entire right, which is tantamount to an asset transfer without consideration under the Article 3-2(1) of the former Enforcement Decree of the International Taxes Adjustment Act.

(3) The transaction price of a corporate transfer of issued stocks together with its managerial control may not be deemed an ordinary market price reflecting the objective exchange value in a transfer of stocks only.

Likewise, it is difficult to regard a stock transaction involving a complete transfer of managerial control as a transaction highly comparable to a domestic corporate transfer of only a part of the stocks to a foreign related party. Thus, barring any special circumstances, the transaction price in such a context may not be deemed an arm's length price.

3) Conclusion

Therefore, the judgment of the court below is reversed, and the case is remanded to the court below for further proceedings consistent with this Opinion. It is so decided as per Disposition by the assent of all participating Justices.

Related Legal Issues and Questions:

1. What kinds of shares can be issued in Korea?
2. Can the share transfer be restricted or limited?
3. What if the board of directors approves a share transfer?
4. What if the board of directors disapproves a share transfer?

CHAPTER 7

SHAREHOLDER AND SHAREHOLDERS' MEETING UNDER CORPORATE GOVERNANCE

A corporate governance is the collection of mechanisms used by various parties to control and to operate a stock company. Generally, it covers shareholder's meeting, board of directors, representative director, auditor, etc. Meanwhile, a good corporate governance is related to what powers and rights should be vested to a shareholder and a shareholders' meeting. The shareholder is an individual or legal entity that is registered by a company as the legal owner of shares of a stock company. The shareholders' meeting is where shareholders can exercise their rights to make certain decisions relating to a company. In this Chapter, it is important to understand how the corporate governance is well structured, what shareholders and shareholders' meeting are, and what their rights and requirements to be exercised are under the Korean Commercial Act.

I. Introduction to Corporate Governance

A corporate governance (기업지배구조) is broadly defined as the collection of mechanisms, processes and relations used by various parties to control and to operate a corporation.[277] Governance structures and principles identify the distribution of rights and responsibilities among different participants such as the board of directors, managers, shareholders, creditors, auditors, regulators, and other stakeholders in the company and include the rules and procedures for making decisions in corporate affairs. A corporate governance is necessary because of the possibility of conflicts of interests between stakeholders, primarily between shareholders and upper management or among shareholders.

A corporate governance includes the processes through which companies'

277) Frank B. Cross and Roger LeRoy Miller, *op. cit.*, p.644.

objectives are set and pursued in the context of the social, regulatory and market environment. These include monitoring the actions, policies, practices, and decisions of companies, their agents, and affected stakeholders. Corporate governance practices can be seen as attempts to align the interests of stakeholders.

Until now, there has been no single model of good corporate governance. However, contemporary discussions of corporate governance tend to refer to principles raised in the Principles of Corporate Governance by the Organization for Economic Co-operation and Development (OECD).[278] The OECD reports present general principles around which businesses are expected to operate to assure proper governance. Meanwhile, in 1997, the east Asian financial crisis severely affected the economies of Asian countries including Korea through the exit of foreign capital after property assets collapsed. The lack of good corporate governance mechanisms in these countries highlighted the weaknesses of the institutions in their economies. In Korean perspective, to overcome the financial crisis and to develop the good corporate governance, Korea has amended the relevant provisions of the KCA several times since 1998, reflecting the G20/OECD Principles of Corporate Governance which is regarded as one of international standards for a good corporate governance.

II. G20/OECD Principles of Corporate Governance

1. Why and What?

Interest in the corporate governance practices of modern corporations, particularly in relation to accountability, increased following the high-profile collapses of a number of large corporations in 2001-2002, many of which involved accounting fraud, and then again after the financial crisis in 2008.

Corporate scandals of various forms have maintained public and political interest in the regulation of corporate governance. In the U.S., these have included scandals surrounding Enron and MCI Inc. (formerly WorldCom). Their demise led to the enactment of the Sarbanes-Oxley Act in 2002, a U.S. federal law intended to improve corporate governance in the United States. Comparable

278) The OECD, “G20/OECD Principles of Corporate Governance,” 2015, p.9.

failures in Australia (*e.g.,* HIH and One.Tel) are associated with the eventual passage of the CLERP 9 reforms there (2004), that similarly aimed to improve corporate governance. Similar corporate failures in other countries stimulated increased regulatory interest (*e.g.*, Parmalat in Italy).[279)]

Under this background, the 'G20/OECD Principles of Corporate Governance'[280)] (G20/OECD Principles) started to be prepared and reviewed among the OECD member countries. First published in 1999, the G20/OECD Principles have since become the international benchmark. In 2015, the updated Principles were endorsed by the OECD Council and the G20 Leaders Summit. The G20/OECD Principles are currently being reviewed, and the revised Principles will be issued in 2023 according to the schedules by the OECD. They have been also adopted as one of the Financial Stability Board's Key Standards for Sound Financial Systems and endorsed by the G20.

2. Role of the OECD for Corporate Governance

It is important role in functions of the OECD to publish and review the international standards for a good corporate governance. The G20/OECD Principles is one of them.

The G20/OECD Principles can help policy makers evaluate and improve the legal, regulatory, and institutional framework for corporate governance, with a view to supporting economic efficiency, sustainable growth and financial stability.[281)]

3. Six Principles for Corporate Governance

The G20/OECD Principles cover general six key areas of corporate governance: ensuring the basis for an effective corporate governance framework, the rights of shareholders, the equitable treatment of shareholders, the role of stakeholders in

---

279) Lee, Janet & Shailer, Greg. "The Effect of Board-Related Reforms on Investors' Confidence," Australian Accounting Review, Vol. 18 No. 2, June 2008, pp.123-134.

280) The 'OECD Principles of Corporate Governance' were issued in 1999 and updated in 2015. Since the OECD Council adopted the updated Principles on July 8, 2015 and the G20 Leaders Summit endorsed them on November 15-16, 2015, it is now referred to as the 'G20/OECD Principles of Corporate Governance' (*See* the OECD, *op. cit.*, p.3).

281) The OECD, "G20/OECD Principles of Corporate Governance," 2015, p.3 and p.9.

corporate governance, disclosure and transparency, and the responsibilities of the board.282)

The six different chapters presented in the G20/OECD Principles are as follows:283)

(i) Ensuring the basis for an effective corporate governance framework,
(ii) The rights and equitable treatment of shareholders and key ownership functions,
(iii) Institutional investors, stock markets, and other intermediaries,
(iv) The role of stakeholders,
(v) Disclosure and transparency, and
(vi) The responsibilities of the board.

Each chapter is headed by a single principle that appears in bold italics and is followed by a number of supporting sub-principles. The G20/OECD Principles are supplemented by annotations that contain commentary on the G20/OECD Principles and are intended to help readers understand their rationale. The annotations may also contain descriptions of dominant or emerging trends and offer alternative implementation methods and examples that may be useful in making the G20/OECD Principles operational.

The G20/OECD Principles provide specific guidance for policymakers, regulators and market participants in improving the legal, institutional and regulatory framework that underpins corporate governance, with a focus on publicly traded companies.

4. OECD Corporate Governance Factbook

The OECD Corporate Governance Factbook (Factbook) is a good material to understand the G20/OECD Principles itself and their implementations in each country. The Factbook provides easily accessible and up-to-date information about the institutional, legal and regulatory frameworks for corporate governance across

282) Sumatriani SUMATRIANI, Gagaring PAGULUNG, Darwis SAID, Grace T. PONTOH, Jamaluddin JAMALUDDIN, "The Effects of Shareholders' Rights, Disclosures, and Transparency on Firm Value," The Journal of Asian Finance, Economics and Business, Vol. 8 No. 3, 2021, p.387.

283) The OECD, "G20/OECD Principles of Corporate Governance," 2015, p.11.

50 jurisdictions worldwide.

The full text with pdf-file format of the book is downloadable from the official OECD website for the further study and review.[284)]

Currently, the 2021 edition of the 'OECD Corporate Governance Factbook' is available.

The Factbook complements the G20/OECD Principles and can be used by Governments, regulators and the private sector to compare their own frameworks with those of other countries and also to get information on practices in specific jurisdictions. The 2021 edition of the Factbook, currently available in the OECD, will be an important reference for the upcoming review of the G20/OECD Principles.

The Factbook is divided into four main areas that are crucial for understanding how corporate governance functions in different jurisdictions:

(i) The global market and corporate ownership landscape,
(ii) The corporate governance and institutional framework,
(iii) The rights of shareholders and key ownership functions, and
(iv) The corporate board of directors

The 2021 edition of the Factbook includes new material on global market landscape, including how capital markets have evolved during the COVID-19 pandemic, new coverage of the oversight of audit, proxy advisory services, gender balance on boards, as well as significant updates across many other issue

284) The OECD, "OECD Corporate Governance Factbook 2021," available at <https://www.oecd.org/corporate/OECD-Corporate-Governance-Factbook.pdf>.

areas, reflecting dynamic changes to regulatory and institutional frameworks around the world.

The Factbook covers 50 jurisdictions, including all 38 OECD countries plus Argentina, Brazil, China, Hong Kong (China), India, Indonesia, Malaysia, Peru, Russian Federation, Saudi Arabia, Singapore and South Africa. Not only Korea's status on corporate Government but also other country's perspectives can be found from this Factbook.

III. Corporate Governance in Korea

1. Sources of Law for Corporate Governance

The main source of laws and regulations with respect to a corporate governance in Korea are the 'Part 3: Company' of the Korean Commercial Act (KCA, 상법) and its Enforcement Decree which regulate unlisted and listed stock companies, and also the Financial Investment Services and Capital Markets Act (자본시장과 금융투자업에 관한 법률) and its Enforcement Decree which regulate listed stock companies and financial investors. The KCA is enforced by the Ministry of Justice and the Financial Services Commission is responsible for the Financial Investment Services and Capital Markets Act and the Financial Holding Companies Act. Other types of financial companies, including but not limited to banks, insurance companies and financial companies, have their own rules for a corporate governance by the Act on Corporate Governance of Financial Companies (금융회사의 지배구조에 관한 법률) and the Financial Services Commission is responsible for it.

In addition, the Monopoly Regulation and Fair Trade Act (독점규제 및 공정거래에 관한 법률) regulates large enterprise group companies whose total assets are above KRW five trillion as well as holding companies. The Fair Trade Commission is responsible for the Monopoly Regulation and Fair Trade Act. Further, financial holding companies are governed by the Financial Holding Companies Act and the Financial Services Commission is responsible for it.

For making a good corporate governance, the views of shareholder rights protection groups, including but not limited to the 'People's Solidarity for Participatory Democracy and the Citizens' Coalition for Economic Justice,' who have been active in initiating derivative suits in Korea, are often considered. However, until now, there have not been any reliable proxy advisory firms in Korea.

The corporate governance covers shareholders' meeting including shareholders, board of directors including directors, representative director, and auditor or audit committee.

2. Disclosure and Transparency for Corporate Governance

As the G20/OECD Principles require to ensure disclosure and transparency of a company among others, they are ensured in Korea through the access to company's information and any charters by shareholders, even by any investors or creditors.

1) Articles of Incorporation and By-laws

Are the corporate charter (*e.g.*, Articles of Incorporation) and by-laws of companies publicly available? If so, where? The Articles of Incorporation of a company must be kept at the head office under the KCA, but are not made publicly available. However, any shareholder or creditor of a company may, at any time during its business hours, inspect the Articles of Incorporation and others, and request a copy thereof.

Under the KCA, directors must retain the Articles of Incorporation and the minutes of the general meeting of shareholders at the principal office and each branch office, and must retain the register of shareholders and the bond register at the principal office. In such cases, if there is a transfer agent, the register of shareholders or the bond register or duplicates thereof may be retained at the business office of the transfer agent.[285)]Any shareholder or creditor of a company may request, at any time during its business hours, the company to inspect or copy documents thereof.[286)] In particular, the Articles of Incorporation of a listed company are attached to the annual report and always available on the website of the 'Data Analysis, Retrieval and Transfer System' (DART) maintained by the Financial Supervisory Service (FSS, 금융감독원).

285) Article 396(1) of the Korean Commercial Act.

286) Article 396(2) of the Korean Commercial Act.

2) Other Company Information

What other information must companies publicly disclose? How often must disclosure be made? Listed companies or companies that are required to submit an annual report must submit to the Financial Services Commission (FSC, 금융위원회) and the Korea Exchange (한국거래소) the report setting forth the information listed below on the company:[287)] overview of the company, corporate governance, board of directors, affiliates of the company, shareholders, directors and officers and employees, majority shareholders, transactions with officers and employees, financial information and ancillary information related thereto, audit opinion of the statutory auditor, etc.

Those companies must also submit a regular report each quarter in a fiscal year. The submitted reports are made available on the DART website. In addition, those companies must submit a timely report setting forth material information by the date following the day on which an event having a material adverse effect on the management or assets of the company occurs. Such events may include but not be limited to the following: application for commencement of a rehabilitation proceeding, merger, spin-off, comprehensive exchange of shares, transfer of a material business or assets, sale or transfer of treasury stocks and issuance of convertible bonds or bonds with warrants.

3. Employees in Corporate Governance

Does a corporate governance cover employees? What role do employees play in a corporate governance? Other than the exercise of voting rights by the Employee Stock Ownership Association comprising employees, as shareholders, after acquiring shares, the KCA does not provide for any matters by which employees may affect a corporate governance.

However, employees, through activist groups, may indirectly affect M&A transactions by conducting strikes and thus, in certain M&A transaction practices, collective agreements require prior negotiations with the employees' representatives.

---

287) Articles 33, 159 and 163 of the Financial Investment Services and Capital Markets Act.

IV. Shareholder

1. Shareholder in General

A shareholder (주주) or stockholder of a company is an individual or legal entity that is registered by the company as the legal owner of shares of a stock company.[288] A shareholder is different from a stakeholder. A shareholder is an owner of a company as determined by the number of shares it own. A stakeholder does not own part of the company but does have some interest in the performance of a company just like the shareholders. A stakeholder's interest may or may not involve money. For example, a company employs many people and has several stakeholders, including its employees because they rely on the company for their job.

A shareholder is also different from a subscriber. Before a company becomes public, it starts out first as a private limited company that is run, formed, and organized by a group of people called 'subscribers.' The subscribers are considered the first members of the company whose names are listed in the memorandum of the Articles of Incorporation. Once the company goes public, their names continue to be written in the public register and they remain as such even after their departure from the company.

Depending on the jurisdiction and subject to the applicable laws, the rules on a corporate governance and any shareholders' agreement, shareholders may generally have the right to sell their shares, to vote on the directors nominated by the board of directors, to nominate directors (although this is very difficult in practice because of minority protections) and propose shareholder resolutions, to vote on mergers and changes to the company's Articles of Incorporation or charter, to dividends if they are declared, to access certain information (for publicly traded companies, this information is normally publicly available), to sue the company for violation of fiduciary duty, to purchase new shares issued by the company, to vote on and file shareholder resolutions, to vote on management proposals, or to what assets remain after a liquidation.

In particular, a shareholder's voting right is valuable and can be implemented at the resolution of the shareholders' meeting.

---

288) Ewan Maclntyre, *op. cit.*, p.558.

2. Main Rules for Shareholder in Korea

In Korea, a shareholder must be registered by the company as the legal owner of shares of the share capital of a stock company. Where shares are issued, the following matters must be entered in the register of shareholders (주주명부):[289)]

(i) The name and address of each shareholder,

(ii) The classes and number of shares held by each shareholder,

(iii) The serial number of share certificates when such share certificates have been issued for shares held by each shareholder, and

(iv) The date of acquisition of each share.

If convertible shares (전환주식) are issued by the company, the register of shareholders must also additionally state the following matters:

(i) A statement to the effect that the relevant shares may be converted into shares of another class,

(ii) Conditions of conversion,

(iii) Particulars of the shares to be issued as a result of the conversion, and

(iv) The period for requesting the conversion, or the period for conversion.

The register of shareholders may be replaced by the electronic register of shareholders (전자주주명부) according to the Article 352-2 of the KCA. As determined by the Articles of Incorporation, a company may prepare a register of shareholders in electronic form, Such electronic registers of shareholders must contain e-mail addresses, in addition to matters to be entered above in the register of shareholders.[290)]

Any notice or peremptory notice to a shareholder or a pledgee may be effective if sent to the address entered in the register or electronic register of shareholders, or other address notified to the company by such person.[291)]

In order to designate the person who can exercise the voting right, receive dividends or exercise other rights as a shareholder or a pledgee, the company may suspend changes of the entries in the register of shareholders for a specified

289) Article 352(1) of the Korean Commercial Act.

290) Article 352-2(2) of the Korean Commercial Act.

291) Article 353(1) of the Korean Commercial Act.

period ('period of closure of register of shareholders,' 주주명부 폐쇄기간) or it may deem any shareholder or pledgee whose name appears in the register of shareholders on a specified date (record date, 기준일) to be the shareholder or pledgee who is entitled to exercise such rights.[292] The period of closure of register of shareholders may not exceed three months. The record date above must be determined as a day within three months before the date the person may exercise the rights as a shareholder or pledgee. If a company has determined the period of closure of register of shareholders or the record date, it must give a public notice two weeks prior to such period or date. However, this does not apply where such period or date has been designated by the Articles of Incorporation.

3. Shareholders' Duties and Responsibilities

Does shareholder owe duties to the company or to other shareholders? There are no such kinds of duties for shareholders, even no for controlling shareholders. The KCA does not specifically provide for a duty of care or duty of loyalty that any shareholders or the controlling shareholders would owe the company or non-controlling shareholders. However, controlling shareholders are under the obligation to indemnify for damage suffered by the company if such controlling shareholders, by using their influence, order directors to execute certain activities, directly execute certain activities in the name of a director or execute certain activities by using a title which is perceived as granting the authority to execute such activities. Indeed, such activities by controlling shareholders would constitute a breach caused by negligence or willful misconduct. In principle, damages in such cases are claimed by the company; provided that a shareholder holding a certain amount of shares may file a derivative lawsuit with a court.

Can shareholders ever be held responsible for the acts or omissions of the company? In principle, a shareholder may not be held responsible for the acts or omissions of the company, other than the obligation to contribute to the company in case of acquisition of shares, so long as a separate guarantee agreement has not be executed. However, a shareholder holding more than 50 percent of the

292) Article 354(1) of the Korean Commercial Act.

total issued and outstanding shares of a company other than a listed company may be subject to the secondary tax liability.

4. Shareholder Rights Plan or Poison Pill

1) Are anti-takeover devices permitted under the KCA? A shareholder rights plan, colloquially known as a 'poison pill,' is a type of defensive tactic used by a company's board of directors against a takeover. Poison pills referring to special rights of the target's shareholders to acquire additional shares at a low price or issuance of golden shares, which are shares with special voting rights that allow the holder to outvote other shareholders, are not currently available under the KCA.

Hostile corporate takeover refers to a merger or acquisition in which the bidder threatens the control of a business without the consent of the management of the said business. After the foreign exchange crisis in late 1990s, Korean companies became easy target of hostile takeovers as Korean Government eliminated restrictions in foreign shareholding and mandatory tender offer system. For example, back in 2004, the Sovereign Asset Management, a New Zealand based private equity fund, purchased bottomed out shares of the SK Corporation in large volumes, became the largest shareholder and officially requested the Korean Chairman (Mr. Choi Tae-won) to resign from office on the pretext of transparent management and governance improvement. In the end, the Chairman had no option but to purchase treasury shares in the SK Corporation to defend his control of the company. Afterwards, the share price rose, and the Sovereign Asset Management sold all shares, making a significant amount of profit.

2) Recognizing that the current lack of any defenses against hostile takeover attempts results in imbalance between bidders and targets as well as waste of company resources, the Ministry of Justice of Korea announced, last in 2010, a draft amendment to the KCA that was intended to introduce a shareholder rights plan, the most common type of takeover defense known as a poison pill.[293)]

---

293) Bill of the amendment to the KCA by the Ministry of Justice of Korea, introducing the shareholder rights plan, was submitted to the National Assembly in early 2010, but failed to be enacted. Again in September 2022, a proposal to protect shareholder rights in the case of a corporate split off has been drafted by the Government to present as a bill to the National Assembly. *See* also Korea JoongAng Daily, "Split off proposal could help protect shareholder rights," September 5, 2022.

The shareholder rights plan is a defensive means used to thwart hostile takeover attempts by allowing shareholders other than a hostile bidder to purchase shares at a low, prescribed price if the bidder purchases shares of a company with a view to taking over the corporate control. This dilutes the percentage of the target owned by the bidder, and makes it more expensive to acquire control of the target. In other words, this form of poison pill is called a shareholder rights plan because it provides shareholders other than the bidder with rights to buy more stock in the event of a control acquisition.

3) However, although a poison pill such as a shareholder rights plan may provide means to protect corporate control from hostile takeover attacks, they are not without their drawbacks: abuse of these pills may cause moral hazard on the owners, management and existing shareholders of the business and also could cause decrease in foreign direct investments.

Aimed at reining in potential abuse of a poison pill, the 2010 draft amendment to revision of the KCA stipulated that a shareholder rights plan must be adopted through amendment of the relevant company's Articles of Incorporation, and that the rights to acquire shares may not be granted to any persons other than shareholders. Further, any grant of rights to shareholders under the plan must be implemented via a special board resolution with affirmative votes of at least two-thirds of the directors in office. And, in relation to grant or redeeming of the rights to acquire shares, the draft amendment to the KCA required that discrimination of shareholders be based on a purpose of exercising influence on important management matters which would lead to enhancement of the values of the company and shareholders in general.

4) It is obvious that the Korean Government will introduce this draft amendment again with the hope that the shareholder rights plan would help the management of Korean companies fully use their authority to pursue corporate development without having to utilize valuable corporate resources in defending unwarranted hostile takeovers. In this connection, if enacted, the introduction of a shareholder rights plan in the context of hostile takeovers is expected to cause significant changes in the M&A market of Korea.[294]

---

294) The Federation of Korean Industries has also recently represented necessities of the shareholder rights plan. *See* the Federation of Korean Industries, "Analysis on the

5. Squeeze-Out Right of Controlling Shareholder

1) Provisions of the KCA

(1) A controlling shareholder's right to request a minority shareholder to sell its shares, often referred to as 'squeeze-out right,' is provided in the Article 360-24 of the KCA. In cases where it is necessary to achieve managerial objectives of a company, a shareholder who owns, on his own account, 95 percent or more of the total number of issued and outstanding shares of the company (hereinafter referred to as 'controlling shareholder') may request other shareholders of the company (hereafter referred to as 'minority shareholder') to sell the shares held by them.[295] In calculating the number of shares held, the shares held by parent and subsidiary companies must be aggregated. In such cases, the shares held by a company having shares in excess of half of the total number of issued and outstanding shares held by a shareholder who is not a company must be aggregated to the shares held by the said shareholder. When a request for sale by a controlling shareholder is made, the prior approval of a general meeting of shareholders must be obtained.

When the convocation of such general meeting of shareholders is notified, the following matters must be stated in the notification, and the controlling shareholder requesting the sale of shares must explain thereon at the general meeting of shareholders:

(i) The status of share-ownership of the controlling shareholder,

(ii) The objective of requesting the sale of shares,

(iii) Publicly certified appraiser's evaluation of the ground and adequacy of calculation of the sales price, and

(iv) Payment guarantee for the sales price.

A controlling shareholder must publicly notify the following matters by no later than one month prior to the date of request for the sale of shares, and must separately notify the same to the shareholders listed in the register of shareholders

---

Protection Measures for a Corporate Management," Press Release (in Korean), October 10, 2022.

295) Article 360-24(1) of the Korean Commercial Act.

and the pledgees, respectively:

(i) The purport that minority shareholders must submit the share certificates to the controlling shareholder simultaneously with the minority shareholders' receipt of the sales price, and

(ii) The purport that, if minority shareholders fail to submit the share certificates, the share certificates will become invalidated on the date the minority shareholders receive the sales price or when the controlling shareholder publicly deposits the sales price.

(2) Minority shareholders who receive a request for sale by a controlling shareholder must sell their shares to the controlling shareholder within two months from the date of receipt of the request for sale.[296)]

In such cases, the sales price must be determined through a negotiation between the minority shareholders who received the request for the sale of shares and the controlling shareholder who requested the sale. In cases where negotiation regarding the sales price between the minority shareholders and the controlling shareholder is not conducted within 30 days of the date of receipt of the request for sale, the minority shareholders who received the request for the sale of shares or the controlling shareholder who requested the sale may request the court to make a determination of the sales price. In cases where the court determines the sales price of shares, the court must compute a fair and reasonable value of the shares based on the status of the company's assets and other circumstances.

2) Significance of Squeeze-out Right

(1) The amended KCA, which took effect on April 15, 2012, introduced a 'squeeze-out' right. The squeeze-out right permits a controlling shareholder holding 95% or more of shares in a stock company to require minority shareholders to sell their shares to the controlling shareholder at a fair price, provided that the following conditions are satisfied:

(i) The squeeze-out is necessary to accomplish the company's business purpose,

(ii) The squeeze-out is approved in advance at a shareholders' meeting, and

(iii) The minority shareholders' shares are appraised by a certified appraiser

---

296) Article 360-24(6) of the Korean Commercial Act.

and the outcome of such appraisal together with the purpose and other details of the squeeze-out is (a) disclosed in the notice sent to the shareholders to convene the shareholders' meeting and (b) explained by the controlling shareholder at the shareholders' meeting.

(2) There are ambiguities in the squeeze-out provisions of the KCA. In particular, with respect to the first condition set out above, it is not clear what circumstances would be viewed as accomplishing a company's business purpose. In general view, a controlling shareholder's intention to remove the minority shareholders would not, in and of itself, be considered as a sufficient ground to satisfy the first condition.[297] If, however, it could be proven that a company incurs too much cost due to a minority shareholders or a minority shareholders abuses his shareholder rights, thereby making it difficult to manage or operate the company, then a squeeze-out could be considered necessary to achieve the company's business purpose.

(3) On the other hand, disputes could arise in connection with the meaning and application of the squeeze-out provisions. Among other things, claims could be made by minority shareholders as to whether (i) a squeeze-out is justifiable to achieve the company's business purpose, (ii) the squeeze-out procedure prescribed by the KCA has been duly followed, and (iii) a fair price has been paid. In particular, the appraisal of unlisted company shares would complicate the situation further, as the parties may find it difficult to agree on the method of appraisal or dispute the outcome of an appraisal.

In case of listed companies, controlling shareholders may elect to take the squeeze-out route after purchasing shares on the open market or acquiring shares through a tender offer and delisting the shares from the stock exchange.

(4) In addition to the squeeze-out, the KCA provides for 'cash-out merger.[298] In a cash-out merger, the surviving company in a merger may opt to pay cash in consideration for the shares of the company being absorbed, in effect removing the shareholders of the company being absorbed. A controlling shareholder who wishes to acquire full control could use the cash-out merger as an alternative to

297) Chung Chan-Hyung, *op. cit.*, p.856; Choi Junesun, *op. cit.*, p.818.
298) Article 523(d) of the Korean Commercial Act.

the squeeze-out.

One notable aspect is that alongside the squeeze-out right, the KCA grants minority shareholders a 'sell-out right,' allowing minority shareholders to require the controlling shareholder at any time to buy out their shares.[299] The sell-out right provides minority shareholders with an opportunity to exit their investment by selling their shares to the controlling shareholder at a relatively high price compared to prices to be paid by third parties. From the perspective of controlling shareholders, the sell-out right may prove burdensome or cumbersome, since minority shareholders are permitted to exercise the sell-out right separately and, accordingly, controlling shareholders may have to go through multiple buy-out processes.

V. Shareholders' Meeting

1. Shareholders' Meeting in General

1) What is a Shareholders' Meeting?

The shareholders' meeting (주주총회) or general meeting of shareholders is where shareholders can exercise their rights to make certain decisions relating to a company, to receive reports from the board of directors on their performance and accountability and to question the board of directors about their actions. The shareholders' meeting may be required by law, the Articles of Incorporation, or by-laws of a stock company. A company must have at least an annual general meeting during a fiscal year. The shareholders' meetings are held to conduct business on behalf of a company.

In Korea, the general meeting of shareholders may adopt resolutions on matters provided for by the KCA or the Articles of Incorporation of a company.[300] There are two types of shareholders' meeting under the KCA: (i) an ordinary general meeting of shareholders and (ii) an extraordinary general meeting of shareholders.[301] An ordinary general meeting of shareholders must be convened

299) Article 360-25 of the Korean Commercial Act.
300) Article 361 of the Korean Commercial Act.
301) Article 365 of the Korean Commercial Act.

at least once a year at a fixed date. Where a company has determined that the settlement of accounts takes place more than twice a year, a general meeting of shareholders must be convened with respect to each of such period for the settlement of accounts. An extraordinary general meeting of shareholders may be convened from time to time whenever necessary.

To participate at a general meeting of shareholders, a shareholder must be registered as a holder of the company's shares on the register of shareholders to exercise his voting rights. A shareholder whose name is not registered on the register of shareholders may nevertheless be considered a shareholder by the company. However, if such shareholder is revealed not to be an actual shareholder, no indemnification is given to the company and the resolutions adopted at the general meetings of shareholders may be canceled. A small company whose total equity is less than KRW one billion may omit the procedures for convening a shareholders' meeting (*e.g.*, the sending of notices to shareholders) if all shareholders consent.

2) Matters Reserved to Shareholders' Meeting

(1) Matters for Shareholders' Meeting

Next, what decisions must be reserved to the shareholders' meeting? What matters are required to be subject to a shareholder vote? The shareholders have the power to pass resolutions concerning certain matters specified in the KCA or the Articles of Incorporation. The KCA lists matters that require a resolution at a shareholders meeting.

Major matters that require a resolution at a shareholders meeting are as follows:

- transfer of all or a material part of its business,
- execution of agreements with another party relating to leasing all of the company's business, delegating management, or sharing all the profit, or execution, amendment or cancellation of similar agreements,
- acquisition of all or a material part of the business of a third party having a material effect on the business of the company,
- amendment of the Articles of Incorporation,

- capital reduction,
- merger, spin-off, comprehensive exchanges and transfers of shares,
- dissolution of the company and continuation of the company after dissolution,
- change of corporate type of the company,
- appointment and removal of directors, statutory auditors and liquidators,
- determination of the remuneration of directors, statutory auditors and liquidators,
- approval of financial statements,
- discharge of liabilities of directors, statutory auditors and liquidators, and
- granting of stock options.

(2) Case Example

For example, it can be a related issue whether an agreement to pay compensation for a director dismissal is valid or not, if there is no shareholders' resolution on it, For this issue, the Supreme Court ruled that an agreement between a director and a company providing for dismissal compensation in case of the director being dismissed is void in the absence of a shareholder resolution.[302)]

In the case, a former representative director of Bridge Securities Co. filed a lawsuit with the Seoul Central District Court against the former employer for payment of dismissal compensation amounting to some USD 700,000.00. The claim of the former representative director was based on the employment agreement between the former representative director and the company, which specified, among other things, that in the event of the employee being involuntarily dismissed, the company was required to pay him certain dismissal compensation. The Seoul Central District Court ruled that the employee was not entitled to the compensation for the dismissal and the Seoul High Court affirmed the decision. The former representative director appealed the ruling of the lower courts, but the Supreme Court also concurred with the decision of the lower courts as it denied the appeal filed by the former representative director.

In the Supreme Court's ruling, it referred to the Article 388 of the KCA that provides that if the amount of remuneration to be received by directors has not been fixed by the Articles of Incorporation, it must be determined by the

---

302) Supreme Court Decision 2004Da49570, decided on November 23, 2006.

resolution of a general meeting of shareholders. The Supreme Court stated that the Article 388 of the KCA is also applicable to the dismissal compensation matters, and, therefore, unless a specific amount is provided for in the relevant Articles of Incorporation or there exists a shareholder resolution approving the relevant dismissal compensation, the employer is not obligated to pay the dismissal compensation amount specified in the employment agreement.[303)]

The Supreme Court further stated that since a company is free to dismiss a director with or without a just cause pursuant to a special resolution of shareholders under the KCA, recognition of director dismissal compensation in an employment agreement could interfere with, especially if the compensation amount is large, the free right to dismissal of directors by shareholders, leading to the restriction of stipulated functions of shareholders' meeting under the KCA.

3) Developments of Convocation and Voting

In response to the recent developments of IT technologies and business circumstances, the KCA has been revised to allow the procedures for convening the general meeting of shareholders and voting by shareholders to be more simplified and developed, depending on the level of equity capital of a stock company. More simplified and developed procedures and requirements for a shareholders' meeting and a shareholder's voting as provided for in the KCA will be briefly set forth below.

2. Convocation of Shareholders' Meeting

1) Who Can Convene Shareholders' Meeting?

A decision to convene a general meeting of shareholders must be made by the board of directors, unless otherwise prescribed by the KCA.[304)] Mostly, under the KCA, (i) the board of directors make a decision to convene a shareholders' meeting, but exceptional convocation of a shareholders' meeting may be made by (ii) requests of minority shareholders holding no less than three percent of the total number of issued and outstanding shares, (iii) auditor or audit committee, or

303) *Id.*

304) Article 362 of the Korean Commercial Act.

(iv) order of a court.

As a first exception, shareholders' meeting may be convened by the requests for convocation by minority shareholders. Minority shareholders who hold no less than three percent of the total number of issued and outstanding shares may request convocation of an extraordinary general meeting of shareholders, by submitting to the board of directors a document or an electronic document stating the subject matter of and the reasons for the convocation of the meeting.[305] If procedures for the convocation of a general meeting of shareholders are not taken promptly after the demand by minority shareholders holding no less than three percent of the shares, the shareholder who has made such demand may convene shareholders' meeting with the permission of the court. In such cases, the chairperson of the general meeting of shareholders may be appointed by the court upon request of any interested person or ex officio. An inspector may be appointed at a general meeting of shareholders held by the requests of minority shareholders to investigate the affairs of the company and the current condition of its assets.

As a second exception, shareholders' meeting may be convened by the requests for convocation by an auditor or an audit committee. An auditor may request the board of directors to convene an extraordinary general meeting of shareholders by presenting a written statement specifying the agenda of the meeting and the grounds for the convocation.[306] For other matters, shareholders' meeting by the requests for convocation by minority shareholders mentioned above will apply mutatis mutandis where an auditor convenes a general meeting of shareholders. In the shareholders' meeting convened by the request of an auditor, such auditor may be replaced by an audit committee where a company has an audit committee instead of an auditor. A company may establish an audit committee constituted by a committee within Board of Directors according to the Article 393-2, in lieu of auditors, as prescribed by the Articles of Incorporation of a company. Once an audit committee has been established, there must not be an auditor. The audit committee must consist of at least three directors, but the ratio of outside directors must exceed two thirds of the total number of members.[307]

305) Article 366(1) of the Korean Commercial Act.

306) Article 412-3(1) of the Korean Commercial Act.

In such cases, an auditor will be construed as a member of the audit committee.

As a third exception, shareholders' meeting may be convened by the order of a court. If any ground exists to suspect any irregularity or material violation of any statute or the Articles of Incorporation in connection with the business affairs of the company, any shareholder owning three or more percent of the total number of issued and outstanding shares may request court to appoint an inspector to inspect the business affairs of the company and the status of its assets. In such case, an inspector must report to court on the outcomes of the inspection. If court deems it necessary after inspecting the inspector's report, it may order the representative director to convene a general meeting of shareholders.[308)] Directors and auditors must examine, without delay, whether the inspector's report is accurate and must report to a general meeting of shareholders on the findings thereof.

2) Relationship between Shareholders and the Board on the Convocation of Shareholders' Meeting

Are shareholders able to require shareholders' meeting to be convened, resolutions to be put to shareholders against the wishes of the board of directors or the board of directors to circulate statements by dissident shareholders? As already mentioned above, any shareholder who holds no less than three percent of the total issued and outstanding shares may demand the convocation of a general meeting of shareholders by filing with the board of directors a document stating the reasons for the convocation of the meeting. In case of a listed company, a shareholder who has held no less than 0.15 percent of the total issued and outstanding shares for at least six months may also demand the convocation of a general meeting of shareholders.

If a shareholders' meeting by the board of directors in such cases is not convened despite the shareholder's demand, the shareholder may file a claim with the court to convene such shareholders' meeting.

---

307) Article 415-2(1)(2) of the Korean Commercial Act.

308) Article 467(3) of the Korean Commercial Act.

3) Notice of Convocation of Shareholders' Meeting

(1) Provisions of the KCA

When a company convenes a general meeting of shareholders, it must give a written notice or notice in an electronic form to each shareholder by obtaining the consent of each shareholder, at least two weeks prior to the date set for such general meeting. If such notice has not arrived at the address of a shareholder entered on the register of shareholders for three consecutive years, the company may choose not to give such notice to that shareholder.[309] Those written notices must state the agenda for the general meeting of shareholders.

However, when a company with total capital of less than KRW one billion, convenes a general meeting of shareholders, it may give each shareholder a notice in writing, or in an electronic form, in which case after obtaining consent from each shareholder, at least ten days prior to the date of the general meeting of shareholders. In addition, a company with total capital of less than KRW one billion may hold a general meeting of shareholders without undergoing a convocation procedure if there is consent of all shareholders, and a resolution of a general meeting of shareholders may be replaced by a written resolution. If all shareholders consent to the subject matter of a resolution in writing, a written resolution is deemed adopted. Such written resolution will have the same effect as a resolution by a general meeting of shareholders and provisions mentioned above concerning a general meeting of shareholders will apply mutatis mutandis to a written resolution.

Of course, the notice requirements of convocation of shareholders' meeting will not apply to the shareholders of non-voting shares, unless the agenda of the general meeting includes matters triggering appraisal rights of dissenting shareholders.

(2) Significance of Notice Requirements

The convocation of a general meeting of shareholders requires notifying each shareholder no later than two weeks prior to the date of meeting. In addition to notification by mail, the KCA stipulates that shareholders may be notified using

---

309) Article 363(1) of the Korean Commercial Act.

electronic documents if each of such shareholders agree thereto, allowing for notification for a shareholders' meeting by an e-mail.

Furthermore, small or medium size companies of which total equity capital is less than KRW one billion may omit meeting notification requirements in convening a shareholders meeting if all shareholders consent thereto. Specifically, the KCA provides for an exception where a small company with shareholders' equity of less than KRW one billion may omit the procedures for convening a shareholders' meeting, effectively recognizing the fact that the strict procedures for convening and holding the meeting may impose a significant burden to the businesses with fewer resources available.

3. Shareholders' Rights to Make Proposals on the Agenda for Shareholders' Meeting

Shareholders who hold no less than three percent of the total number of issued and outstanding shares excluding non-voting shares may make a proposal to directors in writing or by an electronic document that certain matters be raised as agenda items for a general meeting of shareholders at least six weeks prior to the date set for the general meeting of shareholders.[310] In this case, such shareholders may request that directors enter or record a summary of the proposals submitted by the shareholders in writing or by an electronic document in a convocation notice under the Article 363, in addition to the agenda for the shareholders' meeting, at least six weeks prior to the date set for a general meeting of shareholders.

Where a shareholders' proposal has been made, directors must report it to the board of directors, which will accept the proposal as an agenda item of a general meeting of shareholders, except where such proposal is in violation of statutes or the Articles of Incorporation. In such cases, the shareholder who made the proposal must, on his/her request, be given an opportunity to explain the proposal at a general meeting of shareholders.

To sum up again, any shareholder who holds no less than three percent of the total issued and outstanding shares, exclusive of non-voting shares, may propose an agenda item six weeks prior to the date of a general meeting of shareholders and such shareholder may explain the subject matters at the shareholders'

310) Article 363-2(1) of the Korean Commercial Act.

meeting. However, in the case of a listed company, a shareholder who has held no less than 0.5 percent (for a listed company with at least KRW one billion of total capital) or 1 percent of the total issued and outstanding shares for at least six months may also propose an agenda for the shareholders' meeting.

4. Place for Convocation

Unless otherwise provided for in the Articles of Incorporation of a company, a general meeting of shareholders must be convened at the place of the principal office or at some place adjacent thereto.[311)]

5. Chairperson's Maintenance Order at Shareholders' Meeting

The chairperson of a general meeting of shareholders must be elected at the general meeting unless otherwise provided for by the Articles of Incorporation. The chairperson of a general meeting of shareholders must exercise control over maintaining order and proceedings at the general meeting of shareholders.

The chairperson of a general meeting of shareholders may order anyone who notably disturbs the order by intentionally speaking or acting for a filibuster, to stop speaking or to leave the meeting room.[312)]

6. Appointment of Inspectors

At a general meeting of shareholders, an inspector may be appointed to examine documents submitted by the directors and auditors' reports.

A company or shareholder who owns one percent or more of the total number of issued and outstanding shares of the company may request a court, before convocation of a general meeting of shareholders, to appoint an inspector in order to examine the legitimacy of procedures for convening the general meeting or the methods of resolutions thereof.[313)]

---

311) Article 364 of the Korean Commercial Act.

312) Article 366-2(3) of the Korean Commercial Act.

313) Article 367(2) of the Korean Commercial Act.

7. Resolution to Adjourn or Continue Shareholders' Meeting

A general meeting of shareholders may adopt a resolution for adjournment or continuation of the meeting. In such cases, the notice requirements of convocation of the Article 363 of KCA will not apply.[314)]

8. Minutes of Shareholders' Meeting

Minutes must be prepared for the proceedings of a general meeting of shareholders.[315)] Such minutes must record a summary of proceedings of the meeting and the outcomes thereof and the chairperson as well as the directors present at the meeting must write their names and affix their seals, or shall affix their signatures, thereon.

VI. Shareholder's Voting at Shareholders' Meeting

1. Quorum and Number of Votes

1) General Resolutions

Are there any special requirements for shareholders to vote at the general meetings of shareholders? And also can shareholders act by written consent without a meeting? Under the KCA, there are some requirements for methods of adopting resolutions and exercise of voting rights. Unless otherwise provided for by the KCA or the Articles of Incorporation, resolutions must be adopted at a general meeting of shareholders by affirmative votes of a majority of the voting rights of shareholders present thereat and representing at least a quarter of the total number of issued and outstanding shares.[316)]

Every shareholder has one vote for each share and in computations with respect to resolutions by a general meeting of shareholders, the number of non-voting shares must be excluded from the total number of issued and

---

314) Article 372 of the Korean Commercial Act.

315) Article 373(1) of the Korean Commercial Act.

316) Article 368(1) of the Korean Commercial Act.

outstanding shares.[317)]

In addition, with respect to a resolution by a general meeting of shareholders, the number of shares for which voting rights cannot be exercised due to the certain requirements must not be counted as the number of voting rights of the shareholders present at the shareholders' meeting.[318)]

The number of shares for which voting rights cannot be exercised and thus not be counted as the number of voting rights is as follows:

(i) Where no person who has special interests in a resolution by a general meeting of shareholders cannot exercise his voting rights under the Article 368(3) of the KCA,

(ii) Where no shareholder who holds more than three percent of the total number of issued and outstanding shares, exclusive of non-voting shares, cannot exercise his voting rights in respect of such excess shares beyond the three percent limit, in the appointment of auditors, or where the Articles of Incorporation of a company provides for a lower ratio than the three percent limit under the Articles 409(2) and (3) of the KCA,

(iii) Where the total amount of voting stocks of a listed company held by the largest shareholder, his specially related persons, and other persons determined by Presidential Decree of the KCA exceeds three percent of the total number of shares issued and outstanding, excluding nonvoting stocks, such shareholder may not exercise his voting rights on the stocks in excess when appointing or dismissing auditors or members of the audit committee who are not outside directors: Provided, that a lower ratio of holding shares may be determined in the Articles of Incorporation of a company under the Article 542-12(3), and

(iv) Any shareholder who has stocks in excess of three percent of the total number of issued stocks other than nonvoting rights of a listed company determined by the Presidential Decree of the KCA, may not exercise his voting rights on the stocks in excess when appointing members of the audit committee as outside directors: Provided, that a lower ratio of holding shares may be determined in the Articles of Incorporation of a company under the Article 542-12(4) of the KCA.

---

317) Article 371(1) of the Korean Commercial Act.

318) Article 371(2) of the Korean Commercial Act.

2) Special Resolutions

Any special or extraordinary corporate businesses such as transfer, takeover or lease of business which may have risks to affect against a company are required to adopt the special resolutions at a general meeting of shareholders.

A special resolution is required for a company to engage in any of the following activities:[319]

(i) A transfer of the whole or a substantial part of the business of the company,

(ii) The conclusion, alteration or rescission of a contract for lease of the whole business, entrusting the operations thereof, or for sharing with another person the entire profits and losses from the business or of a similar contract, or

(iii) The acquisition of the whole or any part of business of another company which significantly affects the business of the company.

In such cases, a special resolution must be adopted by the affirmative votes of at least two thirds of the voting rights of the shareholders present at a general meeting of shareholders and of at least one third of the total number of issued and outstanding shares.[320] When a company gives a notice of convocation of a general meeting of shareholders in relation to extraordinary activities above, it must specify the details and the methods of exercising appraisal rights under the Articles 374-2(1) and (2) in the notice.

However, in cases of a simplified transfer, acquisition, lease, etc. of corporate business, there are exceptions to such special resolutions at the shareholders' meeting above. For example, where all shareholders of a company engaging in an extraordinary activities under the Article 374(1) give their consent, or the other party of the relevant activities owns at least 90 percent of the total number of the issued and outstanding shares of such company, approval of the board of directors of the company may be given in lieu of the approval of the general meeting of the shareholders.[321] In such cases, the company must make a public notification, or give a notice to its shareholders, that it intends to transfer,

---

319) Article 374(1) of the Korean Commercial Act.

320) Article 434 of the Korean Commercial Act.

321) Article 374-3(1) of the Korean Commercial Act.

acquire or lease business without obtaining approval from the general meeting of shareholders, within two weeks from the preparation of an agreement therefor. Of course, this does not apply where all shareholders give their consent.

A shareholder who has expressed dissent to the transfer, acquisition, lease, etc. of corporate business in writing to the company within two weeks from the date of the public notification or notice above may request the company to purchase his shares in writing, specifying the classes and number of such shares, within 20 days from the expiration of the aforesaid period.

3) Example of Resolutions at Shareholders' Meeting

For example, let's suppose to appoint or remove directors in a company. What powers do shareholders have to appoint or remove directors or require the board to pursue a particular course of action? Or what shareholder vote is required to elect or remove directors?

The appointment of a director of a stock corporation requires an ordinary resolution adopted at a general meeting of shareholders. An ordinary resolution requires the affirmative vote of at least the majority of the shares present at a general meeting of shareholders, which must also be at least one-quarter of the total issued and outstanding shares. However, dismissing a director requires a special resolution adopted at a general meeting of shareholders. A special resolution requires the affirmative vote of at least two-thirds of shares present at the shareholders' meeting, which must also be at least one-third of the total issued and outstanding shares of the company.

Where a general meeting of shareholders of a company is convened to appoint two or more directors, shareholders who hold no less than 3 per cent of the total shares, excluding non-voting shares, may request that the company appoint by means of a 'cumulative voting.' Where a company issues different classes of shares, a shareholder of a certain class of shares having no voting rights or a shareholder with shares that are restricted from appointing and dismissing directors may not appoint or dismiss directors.

On the other hand, the KCA lists certain matters as being within the jurisdiction of the board of directors. However, the KCA also allows certain of these board matters to be determined by the shareholders at a general meeting of shareholders if such board matters are specified in the Articles of Incorporation.

However, an individual shareholder may not force the board of directors to engage in specific acts unless otherwise specified in the Articles of Incorporation.

2. Exercise of Voting Rights

Every shareholder has one vote for each share and no company is entitled to vote in respect of treasury shares.[322] Where a company, its parent company and its subsidiary company together, or its subsidiary company alone holds more than one tenth of the total number of issued shares of another company, such another company has no voting rights for shares it holds of the company or the parent company.

1) Exercise of Voting Rights in Disunity

Shareholder's exercise of voting rights in disunity is allowed under the some requirements of the KCA. If a shareholder has at least two votes, he may exercise them in disunity. In such cases, he must notify the company, in writing or by an electronic document, of his intent to do so and the grounds therefor three days prior to the date set for a general meeting of shareholders.[323]

However, a company may reject the exercise of vote in disunity by a shareholder, unless he has accepted a trust of shares or he holds the shares on behalf of another person.

2) Exercise of Voting Rights by Proxy

A shareholder may delegate authority to a third party to act as a proxy in exercising his voting rights, in which case, the proxy must submit to the general meeting of shareholders a document evidencing the authority to act as a proxy.[324]

---

322) Article 369(1) of the Korean Commercial Act.
323) Article 368-2(1) of the Korean Commercial Act.
324) Article 368(2) of the Korean Commercial Act.

3) Exercise of Voting Rights in Writing

(1) General Rules for Written Voting

General shareholders' meetings of companies, including small companies, may not adopt resolutions in writing without convening a meeting. However, the Articles of Incorporation of a company may provide that decisions which are included into a general meeting of shareholders agenda may be voted in writing by completing the general ballot paper attached to the notice convening the general meeting.

In turn, the Article 368-3 of the KCA provides that shareholders may exercise their voting rights in writing, without attending a general meeting of shareholders, pursuant to the Articles of Incorporation.[325] Any notice of convocation of a general meeting of shareholders must be accompanied by documents and reference materials necessary for shareholders to exercise their voting rights in writing. Even in such case, a general meeting of shareholders must physically be convened. However, a shareholders' meeting will be deemed to have been duly convened, without the convocation of an actual meeting, if all shareholders consent thereto. In such case, only the minutes of the shareholders' meeting is required to be drafted.

(2) Written Voting at Small Company

The KCA as amended in 2009 stipulates that any small business of which total equity capital is less than KRW one billion may adopt a resolution by a written means in lieu of the resolution of a general meeting of shareholders.[326] Although the previous KCA, in principle, required a physical meeting of shareholders to make their decisions, the 2009 amended KCA allows any small business of which total equity capital of less than KRW one billion, as is the case with limited liability companies, to adopt a resolution by a written means.

'Resolution by written means' in this context refers to the mode where a physical meeting of shareholders is omitted and all shareholders are asked to present their decisions through writing. Such resolutions by written means (e.g.,

---

325) Article 368-3(1) of the Korean Commercial Act.

326) Article 363(4) of the Korean Commercial Act.

written consent to an agenda item in the shareholders meeting notice) have the same effect as a resolution adopted at a shareholders' meeting.

4) Exercise of Voting Rights by Electronic Means

(1) Provisions of the KCA

A company may determine that a shareholder may exercise an absentee vote by electronic means, through a resolution of the board of directors.[327] Where a company gives shareholders a notice of convocation of the shareholders' meeting, it must notify that each shareholder may exercise his voting rights by such electronic means.

This electronic voting allows shareholders to exercise voting rights online without attending the shareholders' meeting. The electronic voting can improve rights exercising for shareholders and enhance the corporate image by prioritizing shareholders. Shareholders can also strengthen shareholders' rights and ensure wider participation in the decision making process in companies by using electronic voting.[328] The electronic voting can be carried out by company itself or by professional service providers. One of professional service providers is the 'K-evote,'[329] an electronic voting system for exercising voting rights through the internet, which was launched on September 23, 2010 by the Korea Securities Depository (KSD).[330]

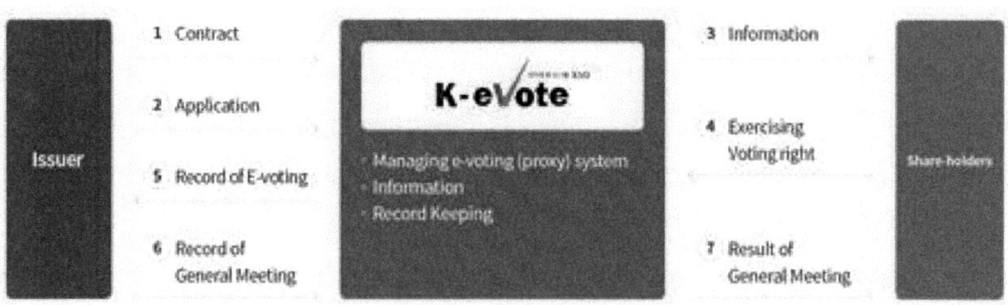

327) Article 368-4(1) of the Korean Commercial Act.

328) Byung-Tae Kim, "Cyber Shareholder's Meeting (in Korean)," in the Series of Stock Company (II), Bubmoonsa, March 2022, p.301.

329) The 'K-evote,' an electronic voting service is provided at <http://evote.ksd.or.kr>.

330) Korea Securities Depository, "E-voting & E-proxy," 2011.

Where a company has determined the exercise of voting rights by electronic means, each shareholder must exercise their voting rights according to the procedures for identifying the shareholders. In such cases, the company must provide each shareholder with documents and reference materials necessary to exercise their voting rights by electronic means.

Where a shareholder exercises his voting right in the same share in writing under the Article 368-3(1) or by electronic means under the Article 368-4(1), he must choose to do so either in writing or by electronic means.

A company must retain electronic records on the exercise of voting rights for public inspection at the head office for three months from the closing of a general meeting of shareholders and must preserve the same records for five years from the closing of a general meeting of shareholders. Procedures for exercising voting rights by electronic means, including procedures for identifying the shareholders, and other necessary matters are prescribed in detail by the Presidential Decree of the KCA.

(2) Significance of Electronic Voting for Shareholders' Meeting

(i) With the advancement of telecommunications technology, it has become possible to hold a general shareholders' meeting through electronic means. Before the 2009 amendment, the KCA recognized a shareholder's voting by physically attending the meeting or using a proxy in addition to the voting exercise by way of a written means (*e.g.*, mail voting). However, the KCA as amended in 2009 provides for another means: an electronic voting. In turn, an electronic voting system was introduced so that shareholders can exercise their voting rights through electronic means without being present at the general shareholders' meeting. Although a company may determine whether to use mail and/or electronic voting, a mail voting requires a provision in the Articles of Incorporation, whereas an electronic voting may be used by the resolution of the board of directors without any provision in the Articles of Incorporation.[331] An electronic voting still does not allow the general meeting of shareholders itself to be omitted with the exception of any company with equity capital of less than KRW one billion.

---

331) Byung-Tae Kim, "Compulsory Electronic Voting System and Its Problems," Business Law Review, Vol. 27 No. 3, p.80.

Under the Article 368-4 of the KCA, any company adopting an electronic voting is required to state in the notices of a general meeting of shareholders that votes may be cast using electronic means. The notices are also required to state the Internet address at which electronic votes may be cast, the period in which votes may be cast, and other technical details of the electronic voting.

Then any shareholder intending to cast an electronic vote is required to be authenticated as a shareholder through a publicly recognized electronic signature or other certified methods as set forth under the Electronic Signature Act, and cast a vote in such manner as provided for by the company at such Internet address as designated by the company. The period in which votes may be cast is prescribed by the company, but must end no later than the day immediately preceding the date of the shareholders meeting. As the disclosure of the results of electronic voting, which is being completed prior to the meeting, may undermine the fairness of the voting at the meeting, the company and any person involved in the operation of an electronic voting are required to keep confidential such results until ballots are counted at the meeting. If a company allows both a mail voting and an electronic voting, however, a shareholder is required to choose only one option in casting the relevant votes.

(ii) In particular, there was a shadow voting system in Korea, which had been a practice in Korea under which issuing companies could request the Korea Securities Depository (KSD) to vote, based on shares registered with the KSD, in the same proportion as voters that are present at the annual general meeting of shareholders to prevent from failing to satisfy quorum requirements. However, the Financial Investment Services and Capital Markets Act was amended on May 28, 2013 to abolish a shadow voting from January 1, 2015, provided that the supplementary provisions gave exceptions to those listed companies that satisfy certain requirements (electronic voting and encouragement of proxy voting) to exercise its voting rights using shadow voting for a number of agenda, such as appointment or dismissal of auditor(s) or member(s) of audit committee, extending the due date until December 31, 2017.[332)]

When the grace period ended and shadow voting was abolished completely, there has been a possibility that having a quorum may practically be difficult for many companies, especially when a certain percentage of the shares issued and

332) Byung-Tae Kim, "Cyber Shareholder's Meeting (in Korean)," *op. cit.*, p.325.

outstanding is required. Moreover, passing of a resolution for appointment and dismissal of auditor(s) or member(s) of audit committee may become problematic when the three percent limitation on voting rights is applicable. A company may be at a greater risk when operated based on audit committee, as the consequences of failing to establish such a committee may extend to being subject to administrative issues on corporate governance as well as delisting from stock exchange. Same risks exist when a listed company has its shares dispersed to multiple shareholders making it difficult to secure votes representing at least 1/4 of the shares issued and outstanding to approve on (i) financial statements (KOSDAQ), and (ii) appointment of outside director(s), hence failing to meet the legal requirements.

In relation to the possible side effects, especially for being subject to administrative issues or delisting due to failure to appoint member(s) of audit committee, it has been important for listed companies to adopt an electronic voting to satisfy quorum requirements.[333)]

It is now expected that an electronic voting under the KCA can help shareholders and companies save the expense of hosting and attending a general shareholders' meeting, increase the efficiency of the meeting, and promote the participation of minority shareholders.

5) Disproportionate Voting Rights

To what extent are disproportionate voting rights or limits on the exercise of voting rights allowed under the KCA? As a matter of principle, each share is entitled to one vote. Unequal treatment of shareholders in terms of interests given to shareholders is prohibited.

However, the following limitations exist in relation to the exercise of a shareholder's voting right:

- A company may issue different classes of shares, shares with no voting rights or restricted voting rights.
- Treasury stocks acquired by the company have no voting rights.
- If the company, parent company or subsidiary holds in excess of 10 percent

333) *Id.*, p.326.

of the total issued and outstanding shares of another company, the shares held by the other company or the parent company have no voting rights.

- A shareholder's exercise of his voting right is restricted if he has a special interest in the resolution to be adopted at the shareholders' meeting.
- When electing statutory auditors, any shareholder who holds more than 3 percent of the total issued and outstanding shares, exclusive of non-voting shares, may not exercise his vote in respect to such shares exceeding the 3 percent limit.

3. Appraisal Rights of Dissenting Shareholders

Do shareholders have appraisal rights? A shareholder objecting to the company's resolutions to be adopted at a meeting of shareholders in relation to a business transfer, business acquisition, merger, spin-off followed by merger or comprehensive exchange and transfer of shares may force the company to buy his shares.

A little bit more in detail, dissenting shareholders at a shareholders' meeting can be protected by the admission of an appraisal rights in certain cases. Where a shareholder, including a shareholder with no or limited voting right, dissenting from extraordinary resolutions under the Article 374, has notified the company of his dissent to such resolutions in writing before a general meeting of shareholders, he may request the company to purchase his shares in writing, specifying the classes and number of such shares, within 20 days from the date of the resolutions at the general meeting of shareholders.[334] Where the company receives such request by dissenting shareholder, the company must purchase the shares within two months from the expiration of a period during which a request for purchase can be made.

The purchase price of shares between the company and dissenting shareholder must be determined through consultation between them. Where the consultation between the company and dissenting shareholder fails to produce an agreement within 30 days from the expiration of the period during which a request for purchase can be made, the company or the shareholder who has requested the purchase of shares may request the court to determine the purchase price.[335]

---

334) Article 374-2(1) of the Korean Commercial Act.

335) Article 374-2(4) of the Korean Commercial Act.

Where the court makes a ruling on the purchase price of shares in such cases, it must compute it by a fair price in view of the current status of assets of the company and other situations.

VII. Lawsuit Against Resolution of Shareholders' Meeting

The resolutions of a general shareholders' meeting may be contested by a lawsuit for revocation of resolutions, a lawsuit seeking confirmation of non-validity or non-existence of resolutions, and a lawsuit seeking revocation or alteration of improper resolutions.

1. Lawsuit for Revocation of Resolution

Where the procedures for convocation of a general meeting of shareholders or methods for adopting a resolution are in violation of any statute, or the Articles of Incorporation of a company, or are substantially unfair or the details of a resolution are contrary to the Articles of Incorporation, a shareholder, director or auditor may file a lawsuit to revoke such resolution, within two months of the date of such resolution.[336] Any lawsuits against the resolutions of a shareholders' meeting is subject to the exclusive jurisdiction of the district court having jurisdiction over the place of the principal office of the company. If a lawsuit is filed for revocation of the resolutions of a shareholders' meeting, the company must give a public notice thereof without delay. If two or more lawsuits are filed for revocation of the resolutions, the court must hear the lawsuits jointly. A judgment confirming revocation of the resolutions of a shareholders' meeting will be effective against any third party. If a plaintiff in a lawsuit for revocation of the resolutions of a shareholders' meeting has lost in such lawsuit and it is found that he, in bad faith or by gross negligence, filed such lawsuit, he is jointly and severally liable for damage against the company.

In cases of a shareholder filing a lawsuit for revocation of a resolution, the court may, upon request of the company, order him to provide an appropriate amount of security, unless he is a director or auditor of the company.[337] In such

336) Article 376(1) of the Korean Commercial Act.
337) Article 377(1) of the Korean Commercial Act.

request of the company, the company must meet the minimal showing with respect to the fact that the application was filed in bad faith.[338] Where a lawsuit for revocation of a resolution has been filed, the court may dismiss the claims, if it deems the revocation is improper, taking into consideration the details of the resolution, the current status of the company, and other circumstances.

When the subject matter of a resolution has been registered and a judgment revoking such resolution has become final and conclusive, registration thereof must be made at the location of the principal office and each branch office.[339]

2. Lawsuit Seeking Confirmation of Non-validity or Non-existence of Resolution

The matters mentioned in the lawsuit for revocation of resolution above, such as court's exclusive jurisdiction, public notice of filing of lawsuits, combined hearings of lawsuits, legal effects of judgments, liability for losing plaintiffs, duty to provide security of shareholder filing lawsuit, and registration of revocation of resolutions, will apply mutatis mutandis to a lawsuit seeking confirmation of the non-validity of a resolution on the ground that the details of the resolution adopted at a general meeting of shareholders are contrary to a statute.

And they will also apply to a lawsuit seeking confirmation of the non-existence of a resolution on the ground that material defects exist in the procedures for the convocation of a general meeting of shareholders or in the method of adopting a resolution that no resolution of the general meeting of shareholders is deemed to have existed.[340]

3. Lawsuit Seeking Revocation or Alteration of Improper Resolution

In cases where a considerably improper resolution is adopted at a general meeting of shareholders where a certain shareholder is unable to exercise his voting rights and the adoption of such resolution could have been avoided if he had exercised his voting rights, such shareholder may file a lawsuit seeking revocation or alteration of the resolution within two months from the date of the

---

338) Article 176(4) of the Korean Commercial Act.
339) Article 378 of the Korean Commercial Act.
340) Article 380 of the Korean Commercial Act.

resolution.[341)]

The matters mentioned in the lawsuit for revocation of resolution above, such as court's exclusive jurisdiction, public notice of filing of lawsuits, combined hearings of lawsuits, legal effects of judgments, liability for losing plaintiffs, duty to provide security of shareholder filing lawsuit, and registration of revocation of resolutions, will also apply mutatis mutandis to this lawsuit seeking revocation or alteration of improper resolution.

VIII. Case Study on Shareholder's Rights and Resolution of Shareholders' Meeting

1. Case Study on Shareholder's Rights[342)]

1) Main Issues and Holdings

(1) Whether the pledger is required to be a merchant in order for a foreclosure agreement included in a pledge to be valid under the Article 59 of the KCA (negative).

(2) Whether the Article 59 of the KCA is applicable to pledges established for the purpose of securing claims arising from unilateral commercial activities (affirmative).

2) Summary of Decision

For a foreclosure agreement included in a pledge to be valid under the Article 59 of the KCA, it is sufficient that the secured claim under the pledge arose from a commercial activity, without the pledger having to be a merchant. In addition, the Article 3 of the KCA provides, "If an act of a party, among all related parties, is considered a commercial activity, this Act shall apply to all such parties involved." As such, the Article 59 of the KCA, allowing for a

341) Article 381(1) of the Korean Commercial Act.

342) Supreme Court Decision 2017Da207499, decided on July 18, 2017.

foreclosure agreement, is applicable also to pledges established for the purpose of securing claims arising from unilateral commercial activities.

3) Conclusion

Therefore, the Plaintiff's final appeal is meritless, and thus dismissed in its entirety. The costs of appeal are assessed to the losing party. It is so decided as per Disposition by the assent of all participating Justices on the bench.

2. Case Study on Resolution of Shareholders' Meeting[343)]

1) Main Issues and Holdings

(1) Legislative purport of the Article 383(3) of the KCA providing that the term of office of directors may be extended by the articles of incorporation up to the closing of the general shareholders' meeting convened with regards to the last period for the settlement of accounts within their term of office and whether that provision applies where the director's term of office expires between the last day of the period for the settlement of accounts and the beginning of the regular general shareholders' meeting (affirmative).

(2) The validity of a resolution of shareholders' general meeting convened without a convocation decision of the board of directors.

(3) Where director Gap who retired after the term of office expired convened the meeting of the board of directors where Gap, director Eul and director Byung who retired after the term of office expired attended, the resolution was adopted which dismissed Jeong from the position of representative director and appointed Gap as representative director. In the shareholders' general meeting that Gap promptly convened, Gap, Eul and Byung attended as shareholders and the resolution was adopted which dismissed Jeong from the position of director and Gap and Mou were appointed as directors. The case held that the above resolution of the board of directors was void since it violated the convocation

343) Supreme Court Decision 2010Da13541, decided on June 24, 2010. *See* also Supreme Court Decision 2004Da25123, decided on December 10, 2004.

procedure and quorum for resolution under the articles of incorporation, and the above resolution of the shareholders' general meeting was adopted in the shareholders' general meeting convened by an unauthorized person without the convocation decision of the board of directors, and that such defect is so significant that the resolutions do not exist legally.

2) Summary of Decision

(1) The Article 383(2) of the KCA provides that the term of office of directors may not exceed three years. Nonetheless, the Article 383(3) of the KCA provides that the term of office despite paragraph (2) may be extended by the articles of incorporation up to the closing of the general shareholders' meeting convened with regards to the last period for the settlement of accounts within the director's term of office. The above provision purports to give, to the director whose term of office expires, an opportunity to be responsible for the settlement of accounts within the term of office and to answer questions with justifications, where applicable, at the shareholders' general meeting dealing with the documents of the settlement of accounts.

On the other hand, the company is relieved from the inconvenience of holding a special shareholders' general meeting to appoint a director just before the regular general shareholders' meeting, every time a director's term of office expires. In light of the above legislative purport and provisions, under the above provision, "the regular general shareholders' meeting as to the last period for the settlement of accounts within the term of office" means that the regular general shareholders' meeting with regards to the last period for the settlement of accounts which occurs during the term of office. It means neither the regular general shareholders' meeting for the first period for the settlement of accounts coming after expiration of the term of office nor the first regular general shareholders' meeting convened after expiration of the term of office. Thus, the above provision allows an expansion of term of office to the final day of the regular general shareholders' meeting by the articles of incorporation, in case where the director's term of office expires between the last day of the period for the settlement of accounts and the beginning of the regular general shareholders' meeting.

(2) If a person who does not have an authority to convene a shareholders' general meeting convenes such a shareholders' general meeting without a resolution by the board of directors, the resolution adopted in such shareholders' general meeting does not exist legally despite the factual existence of the general meeting and resolution due to significant defect in its establishment process, barring special circumstances such that the general meeting is held by the one shareholder of a one person company, or that the entirety of shareholders attended the general meeting and agreed to its convocation and adopted the resolution without any objection.

(3) Where director Gap who retired after the term of office expired convened the meeting of the board of directors where Gap, director Eul and director Byung, who retired after the term of office expired, attended, the resolution was adopted which dismissed Jeong from the position of representative director and appointed Gap as representative director. In the shareholders' general meeting that Gap promptly convened, Gap, Eul, and Byung attended as shareholders and the resolution was adopted which dismissed Jeong from the position of director and Gap and Mou were appointed as directors.

The case held that the above resolution of the board of directors was void since it was convened by the unauthorized person, and one director attended except the non-director attendee against the convocation procedure and the quorum for resolution under the articles of incorporation, and the above resolution of the shareholders' general meeting was adopted in the shareholders' general meeting convened without the convocation decision of the board of directors, and that such defect is so significant that the resolutions do not exist legally.

3) Conclusion

Therefore, the appeal is dismissed. The costs of appeal are assessed against the defendant. It is decided as per Disposition by the assent of all participating Justices.

Relevant Legal Issues and Questions:

1. How are the G20/OECD Principles implemented in each country or in Korea? Why are the G20/OECD Principles important not only in OECD member countries but also even in non-OECD member countries?
2. What are the shareholders' rights?
3. Is the redemption of shares available now?
4. How is a shareholders' meeting held? What are the convocation requirements for a shareholders' meeting?
5. What are the resolution by an electronic voting and by written means for shareholders' meeting?
6. How can we contest the resolutions of shareholders' meeting?

CHAPTER 8
BOARD OF DIRECTORS AND AUDITOR

A good corporate governance is related to what powers and rights should be vested to the board of directors, a representative director and an auditor. A director is a member of the board of directors, and the board of directors referred to as the board is an executive committee that jointly supervises the activities of a company and the performance of duties by directors. A representative director represents the company, and an auditor supervises and audits whether the directors properly discharge their duties. In this Chapter, it is important to understand what their rights, duties and liabilities are under the Korean Commercial Act.

I. Directors

1. Introduction to Director

1) Who is Director?

Holding the capacity of a trustee empowered by a company, a director (이사) is a member of the board of directors (이사회), which, in turn, is an essential, permanent organization of a company having statutory authority to, inter alia, conduct the affairs of such company.[344] A director must be appointed at the general meeting of shareholders[345] and any director so appointed is basically referred to as 'registered director.' The term 'registered' comes from the legal requirement that companies are required to register their respective directors appointed by shareholders with the relevant court registry office. One of the most

344) Richard A. Mann and Barry S. Roberts, *op. cit.*, p.698.
345) Article 382(1) of the Korean Commercial Act.

important powers of a director is that the director participates, as a member of the board of directors, in the conduct of the affairs of the company. A director, however, is also authorized to perform certain other acts.

In corporate practice, any employee holding a supervisory position by the resolution of the board of directors or under the directions of the representative director may, at times, be referred to as director as well, or more specifically, 'non-registered director.' However, any director, whether registered or not, who is not appointed by shareholders is not essentially a director under the KCA. Therefore, this class of directors may not exercise the authority of a director under the KCA and have no responsibility of a director.

When a company has filed a lawsuit against a director and vice versa, auditors must serve as representatives of the company with respect to the lawsuit. The same will apply where the company receives a request under the Article 403 (representative suits by shareholders).[346] In cases where a member of the audit committee is a party to a lawsuit, the audit committee or a director must request the court to appoint a person to serve as a representative of the company.

2) Appointment and Removal of Director

The number of directors must be three or more.[347] As already discussed before, however, in cases of a company with total capital of less than KRW one billion, the number of directors may be one or two. The term of office of the directors must not exceed three years.[348] The term of office of the directors may be extended by the Articles of Incorporation until the closing of an ordinary general meeting of shareholders convened in respect of the last period for the settlement of accounts within the said term of office.

A director must be appointed at a general meeting of shareholders under the KCA.[349] If the Articles of Incorporation provide that a director must have a certain number of shares (*i.e.*, qualification shares), the directors must deposit such number of share certificates with the auditors, unless otherwise provided for by the Articles of Incorporation.[350]

---

346) Article 394(1) of the Korean Commercial Act.
347) Article 383(1) of the Korean Commercial Act.
348) Article 383(2) of the Korean Commercial Act.
349) Article 382(1) of the Korean Commercial Act.
350) Article 387 of the Korean Commercial Act.

On the other hand, a director may be removed from office at any time by a special resolution adopted at a general meeting of shareholders under the Article 434.[351] The special resolutions at a shareholders' meeting under the Article 434 require the affirmative votes of at least two thirds of the voting rights of the shareholders present at a general meeting of shareholders and of at least one third of the total number of issued and outstanding shares. Where the term of office of a director has been determined and his removal is made without good cause before the expiration of his term of office, he may file a claim for damages caused thereby against the company. If the removal of a director is rejected at a general meeting of shareholders, despite the director having engaged in inappropriate activities or any grave fact in violation of any statute or the Articles of Incorporation in relation to the performance of his duties, a shareholder who holds no less than three percent of the total number of issued and outstanding shares may request the court to remove the director, within one month from the date of adoption of the above resolution by the general meeting of shareholders.[352]

What if there are vacancies of directors? A director retiring from office due to the expiration of his term of office or due to resignation must continue to have the rights and obligations of a director until a newly elected director takes office, if the number of directors remaining in office would otherwise become fewer than the minimum number prescribed by other Acts or by the Articles of Incorporation.[353] A court may, if it deems necessary in such cases, appoint a person who is to temporarily perform the duties of a director, upon request of a director, auditor or any other interested person. In such cases, registration thereof must be made at the place of the principal office.

3) Representative Director

A company must appoint, by a resolution of the board of directors, a director who will represent the company.[354] However, the Articles of Incorporation may provide that such representative director would be appointed at a general meeting

351) Article 385(1) of the Korean Commercial Act.
352) Article 385(2) of the Korean Commercial Act.
353) Article 386(1) of the Korean Commercial Act.
354) Article 389(1) of the Korean Commercial Act.

of shareholders. There can be two or more representative directors. In the event that more than two directors are appointed as representative directors, the Articles of Incorporation must stipulate whether the directors are to act jointly or individually in representing the company.

Under the KCA, the representative director of a company is responsible for implementation of resolutions of the board of directors and shareholders. The representative director is also responsible for making decisions in regard to the ordinary matters not stipulated under the KCA and the Articles of Incorporation as being subject to authorization by the shareholders or the company board. If deemed necessary in implementation of the business affairs of a company in accordance with the resolutions of shareholders or the company board, the representative director has also power to legally represent the corporation. This is why control over the seal of the representative director and its use is of importance in Korea because, under Korean laws, a document executed in the name of the representative director and by use of the registered seal may be assumed as a document that is validly and effectively executed by the company, thereby having a binding effect over the company. If a company wants to deny the legal effect of such documents, it must prove that the seal was used without due authorization and the counter-party acted with bad faith with knowledge of such unauthorized use of the seal.

What if there are business activities by not real or but apparent representative director? This happens many often in corporate practices and contracts. In such cases, a company may be liable to a third party acting in good faith for any act done by a director who has used titles that can be understood as having authority to represent the company even where the said person has no such authority, such as president, vice president, executive director, or managing director.[355)]

The most frequently asked question by foreigners with respect to a representative director is that “do laws or regulations require separation of the functions of board chairman and CEO? and if flexibility on board leadership is allowed, what is generally recognized as best practice and what is the common practice?” The legal representative of a company is its representative director who has the authority to perform the internal activities of the company and the authority to represent the company. His role is similar to that of a CEO in the

355) Article 395 of the Korean Commercial Act.

US or the UK corporations. The representative director is appointed upon a resolution of the board of directors and plays the role of the chairman in most cases. Recently, it as been recommended to differentiate the titles of a chairperson and representative director for the balance between the board of directors and the representative director. Meanwhile, under the KCA, a company may adopt executive officer system to separate the managing body from the supervisory body.

Under such system, a company cannot have a representative director, as an executive officer plays that role instead. Companies with executive officers must have a chairperson appointed pursuant to the Articles of Incorporation or upon a resolution of the board of directors if not provided for in the Articles of Incorporation. Although the KCA does not explicitly prohibit it, it would conform to the tenor of the KCA for directors not to concurrently serve as executive officers.

2. Classification of Directors

The KCA classifies registered directors into three categories. The KCA provides that any director be registered as one of three categories:[356] an 'inside director,' an 'outside director,' or 'any other director not engaged in regular activities' which is also referred to as a 'non-regular director' for the purpose of convenience. That is, as further explained below, based on engagement in regular activities or affairs of the company, a director may be classified as an inside director, an outside director or a non-regular director.

1) Inside Director

An inside director refers to any ordinary director engaged in the day-to-day business of the company.

2) Outside Director

An outside director refers to any director not engaged in the day-to-day business of a company. Although an outside director was a term used in the

356) Article 317(2)(h) of the Korean Commercial Act.

context of the Securities Exchange Act which is now consolidated into the Financial Investment Services and Capital Markets Act, such term has been incorporated into the KCA via the 2009 Amendment to the KCA. In terms of authority and obligation, there are no differences between inside directors and outside directors.

Although the KCA does not impose particular restrictions on the qualifications of a director, it does provide certain criteria for disqualification of outside directors and prescribes that any person falling within such criteria may not be appointed as an outside director and that any outside director becoming subject to the same during his or her term of office lose the position. As the outside directors are expected to monitor the activities of representative director and other directors executing the affairs of the company, the above requirements are essentially means to ensure independence from controlling shareholders or the management.

Any of the following persons may not become an outside director:[357]

(i) any director or employee engaged in the regular business of the company or any director, statutory auditor or employee who was engaged in the regular business of the company within the last two years,

(ii) if the largest shareholder is a natural person, such shareholder or such shareholder's spouse, lineal ascendant or lineal descendant,

(iii) any director, statutory auditor or employee of the largest shareholder if such shareholder is a juristic person,

(iv) any spouse, lineal ascendant or lineal descendant of any director or statutory auditor,

(v) any director, statutory auditor or employee of the parent or subsidiary of the company,

(vi) any director, statutory auditor or employee of a juristic person maintaining transactional relationship or sharing material interests with the company,

(vii) any director, statutory auditor or employee of any other company of which any director is a director or employee of the company. For outside directors of a publicly-listed company, there are also additional criteria for disqualification under the Article 542-8 other than the ones listed above.

---

357) Article 382(3) of the Korean Commercial Act.

The KCA prescribes that a company appoint three or more directors unless its equity capital is less than KRW one billion, in which case one or two directors suffice. A publicly-listed company is required to appoint outside directors in a number no less than one fourth of the total number of directors under the Article 542-8(1) of the KCA. In the case of any publicly-listed company above a certain size, it is also required that the number of outside directors be no less than three and no less than one half of the total number of directors under the Article 542-8(1) of the KCA. If the resignation by or death of an outside director results in the number of outside directors falling below this floor limit, the first general meeting of shareholders held since then is required to appoint outside directors in such number as may be necessary to meet this floor limit.

3) Any Other Director Not Engaged in Regular Activities

The term 'any other director not engaged in regular activities' refers to any director who is not an outside director and not engaged in the day-to-day business of a company. In corporate practice, this kind of directors has been commonly been referred to as, inter alia, 'non-standing directors' or 'non-full time directors,' and such practice has finally been reflected in the relevant legislation.

The provisions for outside directors are not applicable to these directors, and in terms of authorities and duties that pertain to directors under the KCA, there are no differences between these directors and inside directors.

4) Non-executive and Independent Director

What is a non-executive or independent director? Is there a minimum number of non-executive or independent directors required by laws or regulations? If so, how do their responsibilities differ from executive directors? As discussed above, the members of the board of directors must be listed under the KCA as either inside directors who are standing, outside directors who are independent, or other directors not directly engaged in the regular business of the company who are similar to non-executive directors and whose responsibilities are almost the same as those of inside directors.

In particular, outside directors are directors who are not engaged in the regular business of the company. The appointment of outside directors and other directors not directly engaged in the regular business of the company is not generally mandatory. However, a company that has established an audit committee must have outside directors accounting for at least two-thirds of the members of the committee. Additionally, in case of a listed company, it must have outside directors accounting for at least one-fourth of the total number of directors.

In case of a listed company of which the total assets are at least KRW two trillion, at least three persons, representing the majority of the total number of directors of the company, must be appointed as outside directors. Such outside directors generally assume the duties of a executive and standard director. However, in connection with the duty to supervise, an outside director assumes the duty to supervise only to the extent that the director knew of or could have known of the illegal implementation of an activity by a director responsible for said activities. Liability of an outside director may be limited.

3. Cumulative Voting

1) Provisions of the KCA

Since directors must be appointed at a general meeting of shareholders, a majority shareholder will always win the appointment of directors who are favored for him and a minority shareholder will never appoint his candidate in his side. A cumulative voting (집중투표) is a voting system used by the companies that allow shareholders to vote proportionately to the number of shares they hold. This allows a shareholder with 100 shares to cast the equivalent of 100 votes toward any single issue. and can give a minority shareholder an opportunity to appoint his director candidate. As a result, this process is said to benefit minority shareholders because they can focus all of their attention on a single candidate for a director. If multiple minority shareholders focus in a single direction together, they often have the power to influence a change or appointment in their desired direction.[358)]

In this regard, the KCA has adopted a cumulative voting in the appointment of directors since December 1998. Where a general meeting of shareholders of a company is convened to appoint two or more directors, shareholders who hold no

358) Lim, Soomin, "The Cumulative Voting Rule in Taiwan," The Korean Association of Comparative Private Law, Vol. 27 No. 3, August 2020, p.545.

less than three percent of the total number of issued and outstanding shares excluding nonvoting shares may request the company to appoint directors based on a cumulative voting, except as otherwise provided for by the Articles of Incorporation.[359] Such request must be made in writing or by an electronic document at least seven days prior to the date set for a general meeting of shareholders. A written request for a cumulative voting must be retained at the principal office until the closing of a general meeting of shareholders and offered for inspection by the shareholders during its business hours.

Where such request has been made, each shareholder will have the same number of voting rights per share as directors to be elected, with respect to the resolutions for election of directors, and the voting rights may be exercised based on a cumulative voting for one or several candidates for directors. When directors are to be elected by a cumulative voting, the directors will be elected in order of candidates who obtain the most votes.[360] Where a request for the cumulative voting has been made, the chairperson of the shareholders' meeting must inform the members, ahead of adopting a resolution, of the existence of such request.

2) Example of Cumulative Voting

Let's suppose multiple candidates are being considered for multiple positions, such as board seats. In that case, each shareholder has the option of placing all of their votes toward one seat during elections or toward one choice when voting on other matters. However, the shareholder can also choose to split his votes across multiple options.

For example, if there are three board seats open, and a shareholder has 100 shares, the shareholder has 100 votes for each of the open seats. This is in contrast to a cumulative voting where the shareholder could take all 300 votes (100 shares X 3 directors) and direct them toward a single seat.[361]

As another example of a cumulative voting, if a shareholder participates in a vote for two open board seats for which candidates A and B are running for the first seat and candidates C and D are running for the second seat, the shareholder would possess 200 votes. The shareholder could choose to participate

---

359) Article 382-2(1) of the Korean Commercial Act.

360) Lim, Soomin, *op. cit.*, p.543.

361) Frank B. Cross and Roger LeRoy Miller, *op. cit.*, p.438.

only in the first seat vote, sending all 200 votes toward the candidate of his choice, candidate A. The shareholder could also vote solely on the second seat placing all 200 votes on candidate C. If the shareholder wishes to vote in both seats, the shareholder can split his votes equally giving 100 to candidate A and 100 to candidate C. Alternatively, the shareholder can direct the votes in an alternate proportion, such as 150 votes for candidate A and 50 votes to candidate C. The results will differ depending on how many votes must be casted to win.

3) Strategic Voting in Cumulative Voting

With strategic voting, the following formula can calculate how many shares are needed to elect a certain number of candidates, and to determine how many candidates a person holding a certain number of shares can elect. The formula to determine the number of shares necessary to elect a majority of directors is:[362]

$$X = \frac{SN}{D+1} + 1$$

where

X = number of shares needed to elect a given number of directors

S = total number of shares at the shareholders' meeting

N = number of directors needed

D = total number of directors to be elected

The formula to determine how many directors can be elected by a faction controlling a certain number of shares is:

$$N < \frac{X \times (D+1)}{S}$$

with N becoming the number of directors which can be elected and X the number of shares controlled. This inequality is correct under all circumstances. Under most reasonable circumstances, however, an approximation may be used to the value for N, by reducing the number of shares by 1:[363]

---

362) Richard A. Mann and Barry S. Roberts, *op. cit.*, p.695.

$$N = \frac{(X-1) \times (D+1)}{S}$$

This approximation addresses the case where the right side of the inequality is an integer. By reducing the number of shares by one, the number of directors is reduced in the equation compared to the inequality. Under reasonable circumstances, the number of directors is reduced by one, yielding the correct answer. This approximation fails, however, under certain circumstances, such as when the number of shares is 1.

4. Remuneration of Directors

How is the remuneration of directors determined? Is there any law, regulation, listing requirement or practice that affects the remuneration of directors? If the amount of remuneration to be received by the directors has not been determined by the Articles of Incorporation, such amount must be determined by a resolution of a general meeting of shareholders.[364)]

In principle under the KCA, the remuneration of the directors must each year be determined by separate resolutions of a general meeting of the shareholders or by specifying it in the Articles of Incorporation. In practice, however, the remuneration amounts payable to all the directors are determined at a general meeting of shareholders, and the determination of the remuneration amount payable to each of the directors is delegated to the board of directors. Companies, including listed companies, which are required to submit an annual report to the Financial Services Commission under the Capital Market and Financial Investment Business Act, must disclose the total amount of remuneration payable to registered officers including officers who have retired during the year in which the annual report is submitted, the remuneration payable to a director exceeding KRW 500 million and the calculation basis thereof.

How is the remuneration of the most senior management determined? There are no particular provisions under the KCA relating to the remuneration of the most senior management, and there are no particular differences in the remuneration of the most senior management and that of the directors.

---

363) *Id.*

364) Article 388 of the Korean Commercial Act.

In cases of listed companies, they are prohibited from lending money or offering credit to a director, including without limitation guaranteeing performance of certain obligations and acquiring a security for funding purposes.

II. Duties and Liabilities of Director

1. Duties by Director

1) Principal Duties of Director

Oftentimes, an investment to or a share acquisition of a company is accompanied by the relevant investor's participation in the board of directors of the company. As for the individuals becoming directors of a company, it becomes natural for them to wonder about the possibility of being exposed to any liability while serving as director of a company.

Taking a look briefly at duties and liabilities of directors under the KCA, the relationship between a company and directors is that of a fiduciary relationship where the company has entrusted the directors with the management of affairs and the directors have consented thereto. Then do the director's duties include a care or prudence element? Based on the relationship between a company and directors, the directors are required to manage the affairs entrusted to him with the care of a good manager.[365] The directors are also required to perform their duties in good faith for the interest of the company in accordance with laws, subordinate statutes, and the Articles of Incorporation.[366] Many times, this duty is also referred to as the duty of loyalty by the directors.

The directors also have a duty of confidentiality. No director must divulge any business secret of the company, which has come to his knowledge in the course of performing his duty, not only while in the office but also after the retirement.[367]

To what extent do the duties of the directors differ? The scope of duties of directors under the KCA does not differ based on the qualifications and

365) Article 382(2) of the Korean Commercial Act and the Article 681 of the Civil Act.
366) Article 382-3 of the Korean Commercial Act.
367) Article 382-4 of the Korean Commercial Act.

experience of the directors. However, pursuant to court precedents and certain legal scholars, outside directors are subject to a slightly less demanding duty of care in monitoring the employees of the company in light of the nature of their roles and functions.

2) Other Duties or Obligations of Director

The directors have other duties or obligations with some exceptions and requirements, such as (i) obligations to retain and disclose the Articles of Incorporation, etc., (ii) not to compete with the company, (iii) not to appropriate the company's opportunities and assets, and (iv) not to transact business with the company.

(1) Directors must retain the Articles of Incorporation and the minutes of the general meeting of shareholders at the principal office and each branch office, and must retain the register of shareholders and the bond register at the principal office. In such cases, if there is a transfer agent, the register of shareholders or the bond register or duplicates thereof may be retained at the business office of the transfer agent.[368] Any shareholder or creditor of a company may request, at any time during its business hours, the company to inspect or copy such documents.

(2) No director may, without the approval of the board of directors, engage in, on his own account or on the account of a third party, any transactions in the same type of business of the company or become a general partner or a director of any other company, the business purposes of which are the same as those of the company.[369] If any director has engaged in transactions on his own account in contravention of the prohibition of competition with the company, the company may, by a resolution of the board of directors, deem such transactions to be made on the account of the company and if he has made transactions on the account of a third party, the company may request the pertinent director to transfer any gains accrued therefrom. The company’s such rights will be extinct upon the lapse of one year after the date such transactions have been made.

---

368) Article 396(1) the Korean Commercial Act.
369) Article 397(1) the Korean Commercial Act.

(3) No director may use business opportunities of the company falling under any of the followings and likely to be of present or future benefit to the company, on his own account or on the account of a third party, without the approval of the board of directors:[370)]

(i) A business opportunity that has become known to the director in the course of performing his duty, or a business opportunity taking advantage of information of the company, and

(ii) A business opportunity closely related to the business that is being currently conducted or is to be conducted by the company.

In such cases, the approval of the board of directors must be granted with two thirds or more of the total number of directors. A director who has violated such prohibitions and thereby incurred damage to the company, and the director who approved the same must be jointly and severally liable for the damage. The benefits earned by the directors or a third party from the violation are presumed to be the damage suffered by the company.

(4) When any of the following persons intends to engage in a transaction with the company on his own account or on the account of a third party, he must in advance disclose material facts about the relevant transaction at the board of directors and must obtain approval therefrom:[371)]

(i) A director or a major shareholder under the Article 542-8(2)(f) of the KCA,

(ii) The spouse and lineal ascendents or descendents of a person falling under (i) above,

(iii) Lineal ascendents or descendents of the spouse of a person falling under (i) above,

(iv) A company in which half or more of the total number of issued and outstanding shares with voting rights are held by a person falling under any of (i) through (iii), solely or jointly with others, or its subsidiary company, and

(v) A company in which at least half the total number of issued and outstanding shares with voting rights are held by a person falling under any of (i) through (iii), together with a company falling under (iv).

In such cases, the approval of the board of directors must be granted with two thirds or more of the total number of the directors, and the relevant transactions

---

370) Article 397-2(1) the Korean Commercial Act.

371) Article 398(1) the Korean Commercial Act.

must be fair in terms of its particulars and procedures.

2. Liabilities of Director

If the directors violate the above-noted duty of care as a good manager and duty to faithfully perform for the interests of company, the directors may be held liable to the company or even to a third party under certain circumstances, and be required to pay damages.

1) Liabilities of Director to Company

If a director has intentionally or negligently acted in violation of any statute or of the Articles of Incorporation or has neglected his duties, he must be jointly and severally liable for damage against the company.[372] If any act has been done in accordance with a resolution of the board of directors, the directors who have consented to such resolution must take the same liability. Directors who have participated in the resolution of the board of directors and whose dissenting opinion has not been entered in the minutes will be presumed to have consented to such resolution.

More specifically, the Article 399 of the KCA stipulates that a director would be held liable to the company for damages if he acted in violation of any laws or of the Articles of Incorporation, or neglected to perform his duties as a director. If any acts by a director were done in accordance with the resolution of the board of directors, the director who assented to such resolution would be held jointly and severally liable. As a related matter, it is of importance that even if a director voiced his dissenting opinion in the meeting, but any record of the dissenting opinion was not entered in the minutes thereof, then the director may be presumed to have assented to the said resolution.

Then, are there any constraints on the company indemnifying the directors in respect of their liabilities incurred in their professional capacity? If not, are such indemnities possible or common? There are no provisions forcing the company to indemnify the directors in respect of their liabilities.

However, such liabilities of the directors may be released in certain cases.

372) Article 399(1) of the Korean Commercial Act.

Following the adoption of the restrictions on the liability of directors under the KCA, a number of companies have established relevant regulations in their Articles of Incorporation. For example, the consent by all the shareholders may absolve the directors from liabilities.[373)]

In addition, a company may, in accordance with its Articles of Incorporation, absolve a director from liability with respect to the amount exceeding six times (in cases of outside directors, three times) his remuneration including bonuses and the profit from exercise of stock option for the last one year prior to the date of the act or misconduct by the director.[374)] However the company may not absolve a director from liability where the director has incurred any loss or damage by intention or gross negligence and where he falls under the Article 397 (prohibition of competition), the Article 397-2 (prohibition of appropriation of company's opportunities and assets) and the Article 398 (transactions between directors, etc. and company).

2) Liabilities of Director to Third Party

If a director has neglected his duties by intention or gross negligence, he must be jointly and severally liable for damages suffered by a third party.[375)] If any act has been done in accordance with a resolution of the board of directors, the directors who have consented to such resolution must take the same liability. Directors who have participated in the resolution of the board of directors and whose dissenting opinion has not been entered in the minutes may also be presumed to have consented to such resolution.

As such, the Article 401 of the KCA also stipulates that a director would be held liable to a third party if he neglected to perform his duties willfully or by gross negligence causing damages to the third party. As with director's liabilities to a company, if any acts by a director were done in accordance with the resolution of the board of directors, the director who assented to such resolution would also be held jointly and severally liable, as well as the directors having voiced his dissenting opinion but not having any record of the said opinion in the relevant minutes.

---

373) Article 400(1) of the Korean Commercial Act.

374) Article 400(2) of the Korean Commercial Act.

375) Article 401(1) of the Korean Commercial Act.

3) Other Considerations for Director's Liabilities

(1) It is noted, however, that as with the US common laws, a director faced with a damage compensation lawsuit (*e.g.*, breach of duty of care as a good manager) could claim as a defense that the director exercised his or her business judgment, and if a court accepts such defense, then the director could be exculpated from liability unless the party bringing the lawsuit (*e.g.*, shareholder) proves otherwise.

In addition, looking at the potential liabilities of a director as noted above, one could make a case that a director should be held liable only to a company when the director has not properly discharged any of the required duties, but not to a third party, since the director acts pursuant to the mandate issued by the relevant company. Korean courts also recognize this foregoing point, and so award damages to a third party in limited cases where a director acted irrationally to a significant extent and/or discharged any of the required duties unreasonably so as to cause damages to a third party.

(2) Apart from civil liability towards the relevant company or a third party, it is noted that a director could also be criminally liable for breach of trust cases. Under the Article 355 of the Criminal Act of Korea (형법), the offense of breach of trust is applicable to a person, who, administering another's business, obtains pecuniary advantage or causes a third person to do so from another in violation of one's duty, thereby causing loss to such person, and the offense is punishable by imprisonment for not more than five years or by a fine not exceeding KRW fifteen million.[376)] Korean courts are especially known to recognize the breach of trust offense for cases where financial institutions have unreasonably made loan arrangements with other parties.[377)]

(3) It is also noted that, under the KCA, there is no ceiling on the directors' liabilities, and as such, the scope of the directors' liabilities is unlimited. Further,

---

376) Seung-Ki Shin, Beom-Jun Kim, "'Obtaining a Pecuniary Advantage' Requirement for Establishing the Crime of Breach of Trust (in Korean)," Korea Law Review, No. 95, 2019, p.76; Supreme Court Decision 2014Do1104, decided on July 20, 2017.

377) Sang Hoon Han, "Double Sales of Real Estate and the Breach of Trust in Korean Criminal Act sec. 355(2) Focusing on the Categorization of 'Another's Business' and the Efficient Breach of Contract Theory (in Korean)," Justice, Vol. 192, 2022, p.200.

there are no laws in Korea that require companies to obtain insurance for the directors' potential liabilities. Therefore, a company has complete freedom as to whether it should obtain the said insurance.

Recently, because of a much more active movement by civic organizations in Korea for protection of minority shareholders' rights, there have been some actual litigations with respect to the directors' liabilities, and the cases in which courts have acknowledged liabilities of directors are increasing. Also, with introduction of securities-class action system that is now applicable to all publicly listed companies in Korea, we will likely see more of lawsuits pertaining to directors' liabilities.

In view of the above noted recent developments, the number of companies obtaining directors and officers liability insurance (D&O liability insurance) for the purpose of protecting directors and encouraging directors to make decisions without fear of liability has been increasing. But still the number of companies which have obtained the D&O liability insurance is still far below under 40% for public companies, though most public companies with assets of at least KRW 2 trillion have obtained the said insurance, when compared to the advanced nations. Then is directors' and officers' liability insurance permitted under the KCA or common practice? Can the company pay the premiums? D&O liability insurance is not prohibited under the KCA, and in practice, a number of companies are enrolled in D&O liability insurance. Insurance premiums are often paid by the companies, but a considerable amount of the premiums is generally included in the remuneration of the directors.

4) Business Judgment Rule

The business judgment rule (경영판단의 원칙) comes from a case law-derived doctrine in company law that the courts generally defer to the business judgment of company's directors or executives. This rule exists in some form in most common law countries, especially in the United States.[378]

In Korea, even though the KCA does not expressly adopt a business judgment rule, Korean courts tend to apply a business judgment rule as a judiciary accepted doctrine in a director's defense against his liabilities linked particularly to the duty of care.

378) Gimbel v. Signal Cos., 316 A.2d 599, 608 (Del. Ch. 1974).

If a director is able to show that "a business decision was made in good faith for the best interest of the company, on the basis of a sufficient review of the necessary information reasonably available," then he will be deemed to have acted within 'a permissible range of discretion,' and the reviewing court will not find breach of fiduciary duty 'unless the substance of such judgment is egregiously irrational.'[379] However, the business judgment rule does not apply to director's illegal misconduct. For example, the use of corporate funds for bribery, window dressing, and other types of violations of law cannot be justified under this rule even if the misconduct might have brought more benefit than harm to the corporation.[380] In addition, the business judgment rule does not apply to conflict-of-interest situations. For example, directors are liable when a company allegedly incurred a loss in a transaction with parties related to it.[381]

3. Enforcement Action against Directors

Since the directors have duties and liabilities mentioned above, can an enforcement action against the directors be brought by, or on behalf, of those to whom duties are owed? Under the KCA, there are several enforcement actions available against the directors for the company.

1) Rights to Injunction

If a director commits an act in contravention of any statute or the Articles of Incorporation of a company, and such act is likely to cause irreparable damage to the company, the auditor or a shareholder who holds no less than one percent of

---

379) Kyung-Hoon Chun "Understanding Korean Corporate Law and Governance," Journal of Korean Law, Vol. 21, August 2022, p.265. *See* also Supreme Court Decision 2001Da52407, decided on June 14, 2002, Supreme Court Decision 2003Da69638, decided on October 28, 2005, and Supreme Court Decision 2006Da33333, decided on October 11, 2007.

380) Supreme Court Decision 2006Da33333, decided on October 11, 2007. *See* also Supreme Court Decision 2007Da60080, decided on December 13, 2007, Supreme Court Decision 2006Da19603, decided on November 30, 2007, and Supreme Court Decision 2003Da69638, decided on October 28, 2005.

381) Supreme Court Decision 2008Da14633, decided on April 14, 2011. *See* also Supreme Court Decision 2006Da33333, decided on October 11, 2007, Supreme Court Decision 2003Da69638, decided on October 28, 2005, Supreme Court Decision 2007Do8373, decided on April 11, 2008, and Supreme Court Decision 99Do1141, decided on June 25, 1999.

the total number of issued and outstanding shares may demand on behalf of the company that the relevant director stop such act.[382]

In case of a listed company, a shareholder who has continuously held no less than 0.05 percent of the total issued and outstanding shares of the company for six months, and in cases for a company with at least KRW one hundred billion of total capital, a shareholder holding no less than 0.025 percent of the total issued and outstanding shares of the company may, on behalf of the company, file a claim with a court demanding the suspension of the activities of such director.[383]

2) Representative Suits by Shareholders

In addition, a shareholder holding no less than one percent of the total issued and outstanding shares of the company may request the company to institute a lawsuit against directors investigating the directors' liabilities or to compel them to perform their obligations.[384] For a listed company, a shareholder who has continuously held no less than 0.01 per cent of the total issued and outstanding shares of the company for six months may request the company to institute a lawsuit against directors investigating the director's liability. Such requests must be made in writing, stating the grounds therefor.

If a company fails to file a lawsuit within 30 days from the date of receiving such requests, the relevant shareholder may immediately file such action on behalf of the company. If irreparable damage is likely to be caused to the company upon the lapse of the period of 30 days, the relevant shareholder may immediately file such action. In such cases, a shareholder who has filed a lawsuit must immediately give a notice of the lawsuit to the company and the company may intervene in a lawsuit.[385] If a shareholder who has filed a lawsuit wins the case, he may demand reimbursement from the company for the cost incurred in relation to the action and a reasonable amount of other expenses disbursed for the action. In such cases, the company which has paid the expenses incurred in

382) Article 402 of the Korean Commercial Act.

383) Young-Cheol Lee, "Elliott v. Samsung C&T: Evaluating Challenges to the Legality and Fairness of the Samsung C&T-Cheil Industries Merger," Business Law Review, Vol. 31 No. 4, December 2017, p.376.

384) Article 403 of the Korean Commercial Act.

385) Article 404 of the Korean Commercial Act.

relation to the legal action will have a right of recourse against the directors or auditors.[386] If a shareholder who has filed a lawsuit loses the case, he may not be liable for damage suffered by the company, except for damage attributable to malicious intent.

The effect of filing a lawsuit may not be affected even where the number of shares held by a shareholder who files an action falls below one percent of the total number of issued and outstanding shares after the lawsuit is filed, but excluding where the shareholder no longer holds the issued and outstanding shares. Where a company files a lawsuit to a shareholder's request or a shareholder files a lawsuit, relevant party may not dismiss the suit, renunciate or admit the claim, or come to a compromise, without permission from the court.

However, in cases where the plaintiff and defendant in a representative suits by shareholders have procured a judgment to be rendered by their collusion for the purpose of fraudulently injuring the rights of the company, which is the subject matter of the case, the company or shareholders may file a lawsuit seeking retrial against the final and conclusive judgment.[387]

III. Board of Directors

Under the KCA, members of the board of directors must convene at a meeting to discuss and vote on resolutions concerning material affairs of a company. The physical presence of directors is not required so long as the members can hear each other simultaneously (*e.g.*, video conference or audio conference), unless the company's Articles of Incorporation provides otherwise.

1. Who is the Board of Directors?

1) Board of Directors?

A board of directors (이사회) referred to many times simply as the board or the BOD is an executive committee that jointly supervises the activities of a company.[388] The board of directors plays a supervisory role, overseeing corporate

386) Article 405(1) of the Korean Commercial Act.
387) Article 406(1) of the Korean Commercial Act.

activities and assessing performance.

In general, the powers, duties, and responsibilities of a board of directors are determined by the KCA or the Articles of Incorporation of a company. These authorities may specify the number of members of the board, how they are to be chosen, and how often they are to meet.

Is the predominant board structure for companies best categorized as one-tier or two-tier? In Korea, companies have adopted a single-tier board system where the governing body comprises a single board. Under the KCA, the one-tier board combines both supervisory and monitoring functions and managerial functions, although some corporate governance models through various mechanisms could achieve a certain degree of separation of such functions.

Whom does the board represent and to whom does it owe legal duties? The board of directors is a body of individuals to whom duties are delegated by the shareholders to perform activities for and on behalf of the company. Thus, the board of directors only owes duties to the company and does not assume any obligations with respect to individual shareholders.

2) Composition of Board of Directors

Relating to the board composition, several questions may be raised. For example, are there criteria that individual directors or the board as a whole must fulfil? Are there any disclosure requirements relating to the board composition? Are there minimum and maximum numbers of seats on the board? How is the size of the board determined? Who is authorized to make appointments to fill vacancies on the board?

To answer them one by one, first of all, no specific restrictions exist on the qualifications of a director. However, a corporation may not serve as a director of the company, and statutory auditors may not serve as directors of the company as well as directors of a subsidiary company.

For outside directors, they must not correspond to any of the followings and where any outside director falls under any of the followings he must be removed from office:[389)]

388) Richard A. Mann and Barry S. Roberts, *op. cit.*, p.699.

389) Article 382(3) of the Korean Commercial Act.

(i) Directors, executive directors and employees who are engaged in the regular business of the relevant company, or directors, auditors, executive directors and employees who have engaged in the regular business of the relevant company within the latest two years,[390]

(ii) The principal, his spouse, lineal ascendants, and lineal descendants, in cases where the largest shareholder is a natural person,

(iii) Directors, auditors, executive directors and employees of the corporation, in cases where the largest shareholder is a corporation,

(iv) The spouses, lineal ascendants, and lineal descendants of directors, auditors and executive directors,

(v) The directors, auditors, executive directors and employees of a parent company or a subsidiary company of the relevant company,

(vi) Directors, auditors, executive directors and employees of a corporation which has a significant interest in the relevant company, such as business relations with the company, and

(vii) Directors, auditors, executive directors and employees of another company for which directors, executive directors and employees of the relevant company serve as directors and executive directors.

In addition to the matters set forth above, no outside director of a listed company must fall under any of the followings and if he falls under any of the followings, he must be removed from his office:[391]

(i) A minor, person under adult guardianship, or person under limited guardianship,

(ii) A person declared bankrupt and not yet reinstated,

(iii) A person for whom two years have not elapsed since his or her imprisonment without labor or greater punishment declared by a court was completely executed or exempted,

(iv) A person for whom two years have not elapsed since he was dismissed or removed from office after violating an Act separately prescribed by Presidential Decree,

(v) In cases where a shareholder of the listed company and persons who have

---

390) Chung Joon Woo, "A Review of Current Issues Concerning the Appointment and Dismissal of Directors under the Commercial Act (in Korean)," Inha Law Review, Vol. 20 No. 2, June 2017, p.195.

391) Article 542-8(2) of the Korean Commercial Act.

a special relationship with the shareholder as prescribed by Presidential Decree own the largest number of shares, based on the total number of issued and outstanding shares other than nonvoting shares, such largest shareholder and his specially related persons,

(vi) A shareholder who owns more than ten percent of the total number of issued and outstanding shares other than nonvoting shares on his or her own account regardless of in whose name the shares are held, or exerts de facto influence on important matters related to the management of the listed company, including the appointment and dismissal of directors, executive directors or auditors, and his or her spouse, lineal ascendants and lineal descendants, and

(vii) A person determined by Presidential Decree, who has difficulty faithfully performing any of his or her duty as an outside director, or who may have an influence on the management of the listed company.

Information on directors, including the names and dates of birth of directors, and information on the representative director, including his name, date of birth and address, are provided for in the commercial registry.

As the next answer to questions above, directors must be at least three in number.[392] In a small company of which total capital is less than KRW one billion, the number of the directors may be one or two. Directors are appointed at a shareholders' meeting. In case that the number of directors provided for in the Articles of Incorporation is not satisfied, a director whose term of office has expired or who has resigned owes duties as a director to the company until a new director is appointed. If the appointment of a temporary director is deemed necessary by a court as a result of a claim filed by a director, statutory auditor or other interested parties, a temporary director may be appointed.

2. Authority of Board of Directors

1) General Authority of Board of Directors

A resolution of the board of directors must be required for disposal or transfer of major assets, borrowing of large-scale assets, appointment or dismissal of managers, and management of affairs such as establishment, transfer or abolition

392) Article 383(1) of the Korean Commercial Act.

of branch offices.[393] The board of directors must supervise the performance of duties by directors. The directors may request that the representative director report on the affairs of other directors or employees to the board of directors. The directors must report on the progress of his duties to the board of directors more than once every three months.[394]

Then, what could be the board of directors' primary legal responsibilities? As mentioned above, the board resolution is required for the company to make decisions on corporate policy and business matters such as disposition and transfer of material assets of the company, borrowing of substantial amounts of money, appointment and dismissal of managers, and establishment, change and closure of branches. Matters that are specifically enumerated in the KCA as the powers of the board of directors are, among others, convocation of a general meeting of shareholders, approval of the director's competition with the company, usurpation of corporate opportunity and self-dealing transaction, approval of a transaction conducted by the largest shareholder of a listed company with the company, issuance of bonds and payment of interim dividends.

2) The Board Committees

The board of directors may also establish committees within the board, as prescribed by the Articles of Incorporation of a company. What board committees are mandatory? What board committees are allowed? Are there mandatory requirements for committee composition? Large listed companies with at least KRW two trillion of total capital are required to have a committee for recommending candidates for outside directors and an audit committee. Those large listed companies must have outside directors representing at least half of the total number of members of the company's committees, and an audit committee with outside directors accounting for at least two-thirds of its members. The audit committee of a listed company of which the total assets is at least KRW two trillion, must comprise at least one member who is an accountant or a financial professional, and the head of the audit committee must be an outside director.

---

393) Article 393(1) of the Korean Commercial Act.
394) Article 393(4) of the Korean Commercial Act.

The board of directors may delegate to the committees its power other than the following matters:[395]

(i) Proposal of matters subject to approval at a general meeting of shareholders,

(ii) Appointment or dismissal of the representative director,

(iii) Establishment of committees and appointment or dismissal of their members, and

(iv) Other matters as prescribed by the Articles of Incorporation.

In cases that the board of directors establishes committees within the board, the committee must be composed of two or more directors. Such committee must notify each director of the resolutions it has adopted. In such cases, any of the directors may, upon receipt of the notification, request the convocation of a meeting of the board of directors, and the board of directors may adopt, once again, the resolutions of the committee. The provisions of the Articles 386 (1), 390, 391, 391-3, and 392 of the KCA, which are required in the board of directors will apply mutatis mutandis with respect to committees.

To what extent can the board of directors delegate responsibilities to management, a board committee or other persons? The board of directors may delegate the authority to make decisions on certain matters relating to the execution of activities of the company to the extent that the specific scope of the authority is determined. However, certain activities may not be delegated by the board of directors such as disposal and transfer of material assets, borrowing of large scale assets, appointment or dismissal of managers, and management of affairs, such as establishment, transfer or abolition of branch offices. The authority to implement the day-to-day activities of the company is delegated to a representative director.

3. Board of Directors' Meeting

Is a minimum or set number of board meetings per year required by laws or regulations? The representative director of a listed company is required to report at least once in a quarter to the board of directors the implementation of business activities. As such, the board of directors is required to be convened at

---

395) Article 393-2(2) of the Korean Commercial Act.

least once per quarter.

The board of directors' meeting must be convened by each director.[396] However, this will not apply where a director with the power to convene such meetings has been designated by a resolution of the board of directors. Any director who has not been designated as the director with the power to convene a board of directors' meeting may request the director so designated to convene such meeting. Where the director so designated refuses to convene the meeting without good cause, other directors may convene the board of directors' meeting.

In convening a board of directors' meeting, the date of such meeting must be fixed and a notice of convocation must be sent to each director and auditor at least one week prior to such date. The said period may be shortened by the Articles of Incorporation. When there is consent of all the directors and auditors, the board of directors' meeting may be held at any time without undergoing the said procedures.

The board of directors' meetings may adopt a resolution for adjournment or continuation of the meeting and the convocation of the board of directors will not apply.

4. Resolutions by Board of Directors

1) Methods of Resolutions

A resolution of the board of directors must be adopted in the presence of a majority of directors in office by the affirmative votes of a majority of directors present at the meeting.[397] This voting requirement may be increased by the Articles of Incorporation.

The board of directors may, unless otherwise provided for in the Articles of Incorporation, allow all or some of the directors to take part in the adoption of a resolution without presence in person at the meeting by means of a remote communications system that enables all directors' simultaneous transmission and receipt of sounds.[398] In such cases, the relevant directors are deemed present at the meeting. Before the 2011 Amendment to the KCA, means of a remote

---

396) Article 390(1) of the Korean Commercial Act.
397) Article 391(1) of the Korean Commercial Act.
398) Article 391(2) of the Korean Commercial Act.

communications system required the multi way with audio and video. Those means of a remote communications system was criticized a lot since business had become increasingly global and fast paced and the KCA did not accommodate modern advances and directors were often required to make a important commercial decisions with very little advance notice.[399] By the amendment to the KCA, means of a remote communications system require just simultaneous transmission and receipt of sounds. As a result, telephone conference will now suffice and simultaneous visual image (*e.g.*, video conference) is no longer required.

Since the provisions of the Articles 368(3) and 371(2) apply mutatis mutandis in the resolution of board of directors, the director who has special interests in a resolution by the board may not exercise his voting rights,[400] and may also not be counted as the number of voting rights of the directors present at the meeting.[401]

2) Other Considerations

Auditors may attend the board of directors' meetings and state their opinions.[402] When any auditor deems that a director acts or is likely to act in contravention of statutes or the Articles of Incorporation of a company, the auditor must report it to the board of directors.

Is disclosure of board practices required by laws or regulations? The minutes of the board of directors' meeting must be prepared with regard to the proceedings of the board of directors' meeting.[403] The agenda items, summary of the proceedings and the outcomes thereof, and the objectors and grounds for their objection must be entered in the minutes, and the directors and auditors present at the board's meeting must write their names and affix seals, or affix their signatures, thereon. Any shareholders may, during business hours, request to either inspect the minutes of the board of directors' meeting, or to copy them. A company may reject shareholders' such request with an explanation of grounds therefor. In such cases, shareholders may inspect or copy the minutes of the board of directors' meeting after obtaining permission from the court. In addition,

399) Choi Junesun, *op. cit.*, p.488.
400) Article 368(3) of the Korean Commercial Act.
401) Article 371(2) of the Korean Commercial Act.
402) Article 391-2(1) of the Korean Commercial Act.
403) Article 391-3(1) of the Korean Commercial Act.

companies which are required to submit an annual report to the Financial Services Commission under the Financial Investment Services and Capital Markets Act must disclose matters relating to the board of directors (e.g., composition of the board of directors, material resolutions, committees within the board of directors, etc.).

IV. Executive Officer System

1. Introduction to Executive Officer

Under the KCA, the board of directors in a Korean company manages and executes the affairs of the company, while simultaneously supervising the status of execution. This may have created inherent limitations of self-monitoring as the board of directors oversees its own activities. As the board of directors has primarily focused on the managerial function, there has been much discussion of ways to strengthen the supervisory function of the board of directors in order to enhance transparency in a corporate governance.

Especially, after the Asian financial crisis of the late 1990s, listed companies with assets over KRW two trillion must have the board of directors which has at least 50% outside directors. What this means is that most large listed companies in Korea have been managed and run by the representative director and non-registered directors who are, in fact, executive officers (집행임원). However, the KCA and other laws were silent on executive officers.

Accordingly, various issues have been raised in connection with the existence of and the rights and obligations of executive officers, and their relationship with the board of directors. To resolve issues and problems in executive officers, the 2011 Amendment to the KCA have officially introduced the executive officer system.

2. Appointment of Executive Officer and Relationship with Board of Directors

1) The KCA allows companies to choose to appoint one or more executive officers with the approval of board of directors[404] and as in the case of

directors, the names and resident registration numbers of those executive officers have to be registered with the court. The term of office for executive officers cannot exceed two years unless otherwise provided for in the Articles of Incorporation.[405] The term of office for executive officers may be extended by the Articles of Incorporation until the closing of an ordinary general meeting of shareholders convened in respect of the last period for the settlement of accounts within the said term of office. Executive officers can be re-elected after expiration of this term.

The board of directors, however, can remove an executive officer at any time. As the provisions regarding delegation of authorities in the Civil Act apply mutatis mutandis to the relationship between the company and its executive officers, the relationship is the same as the company's relationship with its directors.

2) The board of directors of a company with executive directors will have the following authority:[406]

(i) Appointing or removing an executive director and the representative executive director,

(ii) Supervising the executive directors' performance of duties,

(iii) Appointing a person who is to represent the company with executive directors in a lawsuit between the company with executive directors and any of its executive directors,

(iv) Delegating the decision-making affairs concerning performance of duties to executive directors, excluding where such is prescribed as the matter of authority of the board of directors,

(v) Where there exist more than one executive director, decision-making on allocation of duties, chain of supervision/command, and other matters concerning interrelationship between executive directors, and

(vi) Decision-making on remuneration for executive directors, in cases not provided for in the Articles of Incorporation of a company or approval thereon has not been made in a general meeting of shareholders.

---

404) Article 408-2(1) of the Korean Commercial Act.
405) Article 408-3(1) of the Korean Commercial Act.
406) Article 408-2(3) of the Korean Commercial Act.

A company with executive directors must have a chairperson of the board of directors to preside over meetings of the board of directors. In such cases, the chairperson of the board of directors must be appointed by a resolution of the board of directors, unless otherwise provided for in the Articles of Incorporation.

Executive officers are responsible for the company's management, and make decisions regarding matters delegated by the articles of incorporation or resolution of the board of directors.[407)] Once a company appoints an executive officer, it cannot have a representative director, but can have a representative executive officer who plays the same roles as the representative director. If the company has a sole executive officer, then such executive officer will be automatically appointed as the representative executive officer, while the representative executive officer will be elected by resolution of the board of directors if the company has two or more executive officers.

3) Apart from the executive officers, the board of directors will be composed of directors in accordance with the KCA and have the authority to monitor the performance of executive officers. In other words, the board of directors will have the authority to appoint and remove executive officers including representative executive officer, to oversee and audit the status of the execution of duties of executive officers, to delegate decision making power, to allocate duties among executive officers and to determine remuneration to executive officers. The KCA does not expressly prohibit directors to concurrently serve as executive officers and some view that it would be possible in practice for directors to serve as executive officers. On the other hand, given that the KCA aims to separate the managing body from the supervising body, some view that it would be desirable for directors not to concurrently serve as executive officers. Therefore, it appears that an express legislative provision will be necessary regarding this matter.

3. Duties and Liabilities of Executive Officer

Executive officers owe the same duties as directors: fiduciary duty, duty of loyalty, duty not to compete, duty not to self-deal, duty not to appropriate business opportunities and duty of confidentiality. Executive officers, in lieu of

---

407) Article 408-4 of the Korean Commercial Act.

directors, must report to the board of directors at least once in a quarter.[408] In addition, executive officers have to attend and report to the board of directors whenever so requested. The representative executive officer is also required to report the performance of other executive officers or employees to the board of directors upon request by the board of directors.[409] An executive director may, if necessary, demand convocation of a meeting of the board of directors by filing with directors a written request which states the subject matter of the meeting and the reasons for which it is to be convened.[410]

In cases where there is a person eligible to convene the board, such person may demand convocation of a meeting of the board of directors. After making a demand by an executive director, if the directors fail to take procedures without delay to convene a meeting of the board of directors, the executive director who has requested the convocation may convene such meeting with the permission of the court. In such cases, the chairperson of the board of directors may be appointed by the court upon request of any interested person or ex officio.

Moreover, executive officers must accept audits and investigations on their duties by the auditor or the audit committee. If an executive officer finds any fact that is likely to inflict a substantial loss on the company, he must immediately report such to the auditor or the audit committee.

An executive officer, like a director, will be liable to the company for damages if he acted in violation of any laws or of the Articles of Incorporation, or neglected to perform his duties as an executive officer.[411] Furthermore, an executive officer will be held liable to a third party if he neglected to perform his duties willfully or by gross negligence causing damages to the third party. In such a case, other executive officers, directors, or auditors who are liable for damages must be jointly and severally liable. As in the case of directors, such liability of executive officers is not only imposed upon the registered executive officers, but it is also imposed on a person who gives an instruction to an executive officer to execute the affairs of the company by exerting his influence over the company and a person who is not an executive officer but is deemed to have the authority to execute the affairs of the company by using the job title,

---

408) Article 408-6(1) of the Korean Commercial Act.
409) Article 408-6(3) of the Korean Commercial Act.
410) Article 408-7(1) of the Korean Commercial Act.
411) Article 408-8(1) of the Korean Commercial Act.

such as honorary chairman, chairman, president, managing director or director.

4. Rationale and Implementation of Executive Officer System

The rationale behind the KCA is that, it empowers executive officers to decide and execute management on an exclusive basis, while giving the board of directors the authority to oversee and audit the execution of duties of such executive officers with a view to allowing executive officers to perform their duties in a prompt and efficient manner and the board of directors to fulfill its supervisory functions efficiently. Moreover, the authority to make decisions is delegated to executive officers in order to ensure prompt and efficient decision making. The KCA also provides for appointment of persons who are not directors but have managerial skills as executive officers to increase management efficiency.

The executive officer system in the KCA is not mandatory provisions. However, considering benefits from the system, listed companies with de facto non-registered executive officers should consider changing the status of such officers into the executive officers that are introduced pursuant to the KCA. Before adopting the executive officer system, companies need to pay attention to duties and liabilities of executive officers obligated by the KCA.

V. Auditor and Audit Committee

1. Role and Function of Statutory Auditor

The office of statutory auditor (감사) is unique in Korea. It differs from outside auditor, who is an accountant and audits financial statements of a company. The most important function of the statutory auditor is to supervise and audit whether the directors properly discharge their duties. To this end, the auditor may attend meetings of the board of directors, express opinions at such meetings and sign the meeting minutes. The auditor may also require the directors to report to him on the business operation of a company. In any litigation between a company and any of its directors of a company, the auditor represents the company. The powers of statutory auditor also include the power to investigate the financial condition of a company and audit whether the financial statements are prepared and maintained in an appropriate manner. This is independent from and in addition to audit by the outside auditor. The auditor may also prepare an audit report and submit the same to the shareholders, request convocation of and attend the shareholders meeting.

By the KCA, all stock companies must have at least one (non-standing) statutory auditor. In case of a publicly listed company, depending upon the amount of total company assets, either at least one full-time statutory auditor or an audit committee (감사위원회) is required.

2. Appointment and Removal of Auditor

The statutory auditor is elected at the shareholders meeting by an ordinary resolution and can only be removed by the shareholders by a special resolution which is the affirmative votes of at least two thirds of the voting rights of the shareholders present at a general meeting of shareholders and of at least one third of the total number of issued and outstanding shares.[412] Auditors may state their opinions on the removal of an auditor at a general meeting of shareholders.

However, no shareholder who holds more than three percent of the total number of issued and outstanding shares, exclusive of non-voting shares, may exercise his voting rights in respect of such excess shares beyond the above limit, in the appointment of auditors. The Articles of Incorporation may provide for a lower ratio than three percent of the total number of issued and outstanding shares. A company with total capital of less than KRW one billion may choose not to appoint auditors. Where a small company which has not appointed auditors files a lawsuit against a director or a director files a lawsuit against the small company, the company, director or any interested person must request a court to appoint a person to represent the company. Where no auditor has been appointed in a small company, an auditor in relevant provisions will be replaced and construed as a general meeting of shareholders.

The term of office of an auditor will expire upon the closing of an ordinary general meeting of shareholders convened in respect of the last period for the settlement of accounts within three years after his inauguration.[413] In addition, an

412) Article 409(1) of the Korean Commercial Act.

413) Article 410 of the Korean Commercial Act.

auditor may not concurrently hold the office of a director, a manager or an employee of the company or its subsidiary company.[414)]

3. Powers, Duties and Liabilities of Auditor

1) Duties and Power to Demand Reporting and to Inspect

Auditors must audit directors' performance of duties, and may, at any time, request a director to report on the relevant business and inspect the business affairs and financial conditions of a company.[415)] Auditors may seek assistance from professionals at the expense of the company. However, as the KCA does not specify details of such allowance, such as the scope of professionals or the limitation on costs and expenses, in case of a conflict between the interest of the statutory auditor and the company, a dispute may possibly arise.

If a director finds any fact that is likely to inflict a substantial loss on the company, he must immediately report such fact to its auditors.

2) Requests for Convening Shareholders' Meeting and Board of Directors' Meeting

An auditor may request the board of directors to convene an extraordinary general meeting of shareholders by presenting a written statement specifying the agenda of the meeting and the grounds for the convocation.[416)]

An auditor may also, if necessary, request convocation of a meeting of the board of directors by filing with directors a written request stating the agenda of the meeting and the reasons for which it is to be convened.[417)] In cases where there is a person eligible to convene the board, such person may request convocation of a meeting of the board of directors. After making a request by an auditor, if the directors fail to convene a meeting of the board of directors without delay, the auditor who has requested the convocation may convene such meeting.

---

414) Article 411 of the Korean Commercial Act.

415) Article 412(1) and (2) of the Korean Commercial Act.

416) Article 412-3(1) of the Korean Commercial Act.

417) Article 412-4(1) of the Korean Commercial Act.

3) Power to Inspect Subsidiary Company

An auditor of a parent company may request its subsidiary company to report on its business, if it is necessary, for performing his duties.[418] If, in such cases, a subsidiary company fails to make a report without delay or it is required to verify the contents of such reports, an auditor of the parent company may inspect the business affairs of the subsidiary company and the status of its property.

A subsidiary company may not refuse reporting to such auditor or inspection by such auditor, unless there exist good cause to the contrary.

4) Duty to Examine and Report

Auditors must examine the agenda items and documents to be submitted by directors to a general meeting of shareholders and, at the general meeting shareholders, must state their opinions as to whether such agenda items or documents include any matter contrary to any statute or the Articles of Incorporation of a company or any considerably unreasonable matter.[419]

5) Duty to Prepare Audit Records

Auditors must prepare a record pertaining to the audit, and a summary of audit process and the outcomes thereof must be recorded in the audit record and auditors who have conducted the audit must write their names and affix their seals, or shall affix their signatures, thereon.[420]

6) Liabilities of Auditor

If an auditor has neglected any of his duties, he must be jointly and severally liable for damages suffered by the company.[421] If an auditor has neglected his duties in bad faith or by gross negligence, he must be also jointly and severally liable for damages suffered by a third party.

---

418) Article 412-5(1) of the Korean Commercial Act.
419) Article 413(1) of the Korean Commercial Act.
420) Article 413-2(1) of the Korean Commercial Act.
421) Article 414(1) of the Korean Commercial Act.

In cases where an auditor is liable for damages suffered either by the company or a third party, if a director is likewise liable therefor, the auditor and the director must be jointly and severally liable for the damages.

4. Audit Committee

1) Audit Committee under the KCA

(1) General Audit Committee

A company may establish an audit committee (감사위원회) constituted by a committee within the board of directors, in lieu of auditors, as prescribed by the Articles of Incorporation. Once an audit committee has been established, there must not be an auditor.[422] The audit committee must consist of at least three directors and the ratio of outside directors must exceed two thirds of the total number of members. A resolution of the board of directors on the dismissal of a member of the audit committee must require the concurrent vote of at least two thirds of the total number of directors.[423] The audit committee must, from among its members, elect a member to represent the committee. In such cases, more than one member may be elected to jointly represent the committee. The audit committee may obtain professional assistance at the expense of the company.

While the board committee must notify each director of the resolutions it has adopted, and in such cases, any of the directors may request the convocation of a meeting of the board of directors and the board of directors may adopt, once again, the resolutions of the committee, however, this requirement does not apply to the audit committee.

(2) Mandatory Audit Committee

In case of a listed company, it, in light of the scale of assets, etc. must establish an audit committee.[424] The audit committee of a listed company must meet the requirements for a general audit committee of the Article 415-2(2)

422) Article 415-2(1) of the Korean Commercial Act.
423) Article 415-2(3) of the Korean Commercial Act.
424) Article 542-11(1) of the Korean Commercial Act.

mentioned just above and the followings:

(i) At least one member of the committee must be an accounting or financing expert, and

(ii) The representative of the committee must be an outside director.

Any person who falls under any cases of the Article 542-10(2)[425] may not be a member of the audit committee who is not an outside director of a listed company, and he must be removed from office when falling under any of such cases. Where the number of outside directors fails to meet the quorum required for the establishment of an audit committee due to any cause such as resignation or death of any outside director as member of the audit committee, a listed company must ensure that the requirements are met at the first general meeting of shareholders convened after such cause has occurred.

In cases of a listed company, a general meeting of shareholders must have the authority to appoint or dismiss members of an audit committee.[426] A listed company must appoint members of its audit committee from among directors appointed by a general meeting of shareholders.

Where the total amount of voting stocks of a listed company held by the largest shareholder, his specially related persons, and other persons determined by

---

425) The Article 542-10(2) of the Korean Commercial Act provides that any of the following persons must be a full-time auditor for a listed company, and he must be removed from his position as full-time auditor in any of the following cases:

(i) A minor, person under adult guardianship, or person under limited guardianship,

(ii) A person declared bankrupt and not yet reinstated,

(iii) A person for whom two years have not elapsed since his or her imprisonment without labor or greater punishment declared by a court was completely executed or exempted,

(iv) A person for whom two years have not elapsed since he was dismissed or removed from office after violating an Act separately prescribed by Presidential Decree,

(v) A major shareholder who owns more than 10 percent of the total number of issued and outstanding shares other than nonvoting shares on his or her own account regardless of in whose name the shares are held, or exerts de facto influence on important matters related to the management of the listed company, including the appointment and dismissal of directors, executive directors or auditors, and his or her spouse, lineal ascendants and lineal descendants,

(vi) Directors, executive directors, and employees who are engaged in the regular business of the relevant company, or directors, executive directors, and employees who have engaged in the regular business of the relevant company within two years. However, the directors who hold office or have had office as members of the audit committee will be excluded, or

(vii) A person determined by Presidential Decree who may have an influence on the management of the company.

426) Article 542-12(1) of the Korean Commercial Act.

Presidential Decree exceeds three percent of the total number of shares issued and outstanding, excluding nonvoting stocks, such shareholder may not exercise his voting rights on the stocks in excess when appointing or dismissing auditors or members of the audit committee who are not outside directors.[427] A lower ratio of holding shares may be determined in the Articles of Incorporation of a listed company.

Any shareholder who has stocks in excess of three percent of the total number of issued stocks other than nonvoting rights of a listed company, may not exercise his voting rights on the stocks in excess when appointing members of the audit committee as outside directors. A lower ratio of holding shares may also be determined in the Articles of Incorporation. When a listed company intends to submit a proposal on appointment or remuneration of auditors as an agenda item for a general meeting of shareholders, the company must propose and resolve the proposal separately from a proposal on appointment or remuneration of directors. Any auditor of a listed company and an audit committee may submit an audit and inspection report to directors at least one week prior to the date set for a general meeting of shareholders.

2) Other Considerations

Under the KCA, an audit committee is classified into two categories: a general audit committee and a mandatory audit committee. A general audit committee is an audit committee established in lieu of a statutory auditor in accordance with a company's Articles of Incorporation and a mandatory audit committee is an audit committee that is required to be established for a large listed company with total assets of KRW two trillion or more.

With respect to the composition of a mandatory audit committee, the so-called 'three percent rule or 3% rule' applies, which is a rule established to prevent a shareholder holding more than three percent of the voting shares from exercising its voting rights in respect of decisions relating to the appointment of a member of an audit committee. With respect to the composition of a general audit committee, the 'three percent rule' does not apply.

427) Article 542-12(3) of the Korean Commercial Act.

Meanwhile, under the KCA, although a small listed company with total assets of KRW one hundred billion or more but less than KRW two trillion is required to appoint one or more statutory auditors, an exception exists 'in the case an audit committee is established pursuant to the KCA or other applicable laws.' Based on the interpretation of the foregoing statutory provision, as small listed companies are exempt from the legal requirement to appoint a statutory auditor by establishing either a mandatory audit committee or a general audit committee, In corporate practice, small listed companies have avoided the requirement to appoint a statutory auditor by establishing a general audit committee which is exempt from the application of the three percent rule.

The legislative intent of the KCA with respect to an audit committee is to limit the application of the exception to the legal requirement to appoint a statutory auditor only to the case where 'establishment of a mandatory audit committee or the establishment of an audit committee pursuant to other laws.' Consequently, the establishment of a general audit committee in lieu of an auditor for the purpose of avoiding the '3 percent rule' is prohibited. As such, small listed companies must either (i) appoint a statutory auditor or (ii) in lieu of a statutory auditor, establish a mandatory audit committee, and the application of the three percent rule will be unavoidable.

VI. Case Study on Director, Board of Directors and Auditor

1. Case Study on Minutes of Board of Directors[428)]

1) Main Issues and Holdings

(1) The standard to determine whether it is unjust for a shareholder to exercise one's right to inspect and copy the minutes of board of directors' meeting, or the accounting ledgers, and related documents.

(2) Where an inspection and copying of the minutes of Board of Directors' meeting is deemed necessary for the exercise of shareholder's rights, whether the

428) Supreme Court Order 2013Ma657, decided on July 21, 2014. *See* also Supreme Court Order 2003Ma1575, decided on December 24, 2004.

shareholder's request to inspect and copy the minutes can be deemed unjust merely because the petitioning shareholder is seeking a hostile merger and acquisition of the company in question (negative in principle). Where an inspection and copying request demanded by a shareholder who seeks hostile merger and acquisition is deemed just.

(3) In a case where a foreign corporation 'B,' which increased its equity share by heavily purchasing 'A' company's shares with a view to acquiring A's elevator business unit, requested to inspect and copy the meeting minutes of A company's board of directors as taking issues of legitimacy of derivative contracts that A signed, there was an error of misapprehending the legal principles when the court below rendered the request unjust for lack of legitimate purpose.

(4) Whether the related documents submitted to the board of directors for purposes of Board resolution, etc. are subject to a request to inspect and copy the minutes of Board of Directors' meeting.

2) Summary of Order

(1) In case where a shareholder requests to inspect and copy meeting minutes of the board of directors, or accounting ledgers, journals, and relevant documents, under the Articles 391-3(3) and 466(1) of the KCA, the company may reject such request by proving it to be unjust. Whether it is unjust for a shareholder to exercise one's right to inspect and copy the documents should be determined by considering the totality of the circumstances, including how one came to exercise the rights, the purpose of the exercise of rights, and the existence of any ill will.

In particular, shareholder's exercise of rights should be viewed as unjust for lack of legitimate purpose if it harms the business operation or shareholders' collective interest, if there is a concern that the shareholder might use the acquired information in competitive practice or might exercise the right at the time when it is excessively disadvantageous for the company.

(2) Even if the request to inspect and copy is made by a shareholder seeking a hostile merger and acquisition (M&A) of the company in question, it should be granted if its purpose is not simply to put pressure on the company, but to

protect the company and shareholder interests by overseeing the company's management. In case where it is acknowledged that a shareholder needs to inspect and copy the minutes of board of directors' meeting in order to exercise shareholder's rights by, for instance, holding the director(s) accountable via derivative suits, filing for injunction, or filing for removal from office, the request - barring any extraordinary circumstances - should be deemed to protect the company and shareholder interests by overseeing the company's management, and thus, the mere circumstance that the petitioning shareholder seeks a hostile M&A cannot by itself be a reason to view the request as unjust for lack of legitimate purpose. A shareholder's inspection and copying request should be allowed, unless there is a concern that the shareholder might use the acquired information for competitive practice or might exercise the right at the time when it is excessively disadvantageous for the company.

(3) In a case where a foreign corporation 'B,' which increased its equity share by heavily purchasing 'A' company's shares with a view to acquiring A company's elevator business unit, demanded to inspect and copy the minutes of A company's board of directors' meeting, taking issues with, among others, the legitimacy of the derivative contract that A company signed, this Court holds that the court below, in rejecting the above demand on grounds of impropriety for lack of legitimate purposes, erred by misapprehending the legal principles regarding the exercise of shareholder's rights to inspect and copy the minutes of board of directors' meeting, as it cannot be said that B corporation's request to inspect and copy was unjust for lack of legitimate purpose on the ground that it was exercised solely for the purpose of pressuring A company, irrelevant from the motive to protect A company's and its shareholders' interests by overseeing A company's management, in light of all the circumstances including:

(a) that it is acknowledged that B corporation needs to inspect and copy the minutes of board of directors' meeting in order to exercise its shareholder rights, such as holding A company's director(s) accountable via derivative suit; and

(b) that it can be said neither that there is a concern for B corporation's use of the acquired information for competitive practice, nor that B corporation's timing of its rights exercise was so chosen as to make it excessively disadvantageous for A company.

(4) Had the related documents not been appended to the meeting minutes of board of directors even when they were submitted to the board of directors for resolution, it would be justified to consider those related documents not subject to the request for inspection and copy, but if those appended documents were directly cited in the meeting minutes of board of directors with words such as 'separately appended,' 'separate appendix,' or 'attached,' they should be deemed to constitute part of the meeting minutes of Board of Directors, and thus, subject to the request for inspection and copy.

3) Conclusion

Therefore, the court's orders on the parts pertaining to the Appendix List Items 1, 2, and 4 are reversed, and those parts are remanded to the court below for further review consistent with this Opinion. The remainder of the re-appeal is dismissed. It is so ordered as per Disposition by the assent of all participating Justices.

2. Case Study on Director and Auditor[429)]

1) Main Issues and Holdings

(1) Requirements for obtaining the status of director or auditor of a corporation (held: resolution of appointment at the general meeting of shareholders and consent of the appointee).

(2) Whether in such a case the appointee has to enter into a separate employment contract with the chief executive (negative).

2) Summary of Decision

To view that the status of director and auditor is only recognized when they enter into an employment contract with the chief executive, separate and apart

---

429) Supreme Court en banc Decision 2016Da251215, decided on March 23, 2017. *See* also Supreme Court Order 2005Ma541, decided on November 8, 2005 (overruled) and Supreme Court Decision 2008Do9410, decided on January 15, 2009 (overruled).

from the resolution of appointment by the general meeting of shareholders, is contrary to the purport of the KCA stipulating the appointment of director and auditor as the exclusive prerogative of the general meeting of shareholders, subject to the shareholders' collective decision-making. Also under the KCA, while the chief executive represents the company and is authorized to engage in all judicial and extrajudicial acts pertaining to the company's business affairs (Articles 389(3) and 209(1)), the statutory language and text make it clear that the appointment of director and auditor is not encompassed by the authority. Therefore, it is reasonable to view that the status of director and auditor is obtained insofar as there is a resolution of appointment by the general meeting of shareholders and the consent of the appointee.

Under the KCA, (a) a director, as a member of the board of directors, is authorized to take part in the company's decision-making on the administration of its affairs (Article 393(1)), (b) the Civil Act provisions on the delegation of mandate are applied mutatis mutandis to the relationship between the company and its directors (Article 382(2)), (c) a director is obligated to faithfully carry out his/her duties for the company pursuant to the laws and regulations and the articles of incorporation (Article 382-3), and (d) director's remuneration, when not determined under the articles of incorporation, shall be set by the resolution of the general meeting of shareholders (Article 388).

In light of the content and purport of these provisions as well, the status of director features the characteristics governed by the laws of organizations, rather than being grounded in the contract entered into between the director-appointee and the chief executive. In addition, the resolution by the general meeting of shareholders to appoint a new director often signifies the shareholders' decision to replace the management. In view of this, it would be problematic if it were to be deemed that a director- appointee does not obtain the director status notwithstanding the resolution of appointment, unless the outgoing chief executive agrees to sign an employment contract with the appointee, as this would deprive the shareholders of an effective remedy.

Meanwhile, an auditor is a necessary and permanent organ of a corporation to audit the directors' performance of their duties (Article 412(1)). Many of the KCA provisions on directors are applied mutatis mutandis to the relationship between the company and the auditor (Articles 415, 382(2), and 388). Unlike the appointment of directors, the Article 409(2) of the KCA specifically provides, regarding the appointment of an auditor, "No shareholder who holds more than three percent of the total shares issued and outstanding, exclusive of non-voting shares, shall exercise his voting rights in respect of such excess shares beyond the above limit."

Therefore, it would be unfair to bar a person from obtaining the status of auditor, notwithstanding the resolution of appointment, for reasons of the chief executive's refusal to sign an employment contract with the appointee, as this would disregard the purport of limiting the majority shareholders' voting rights on auditor appointment under the provision. Moreover, it goes without saying that it would be an anomaly in light of the nature of the laws of organizations to assign the decision whether to appoint an auditor, whose job it is to audit the directors' performance of their duties, to the very chief executive who is subject to audit.

In conclusion, in the event of appointing a director or auditor at a general meeting of shareholders, the appointee obtains the status of director or auditor inasmuch as there are the appointment resolution and the appointee's consent, regardless of whether the appointee entered into a separate employment contract with the chief executive.

3) Conclusion

Therefore, without having to decide on the Defendant's grounds of appeal on the instant ancillary claim No. 2, we decide to reverse the lower judgment in its entirety, and remand the case to the lower court for further proceedings consistent with this Opinion. It is so decided as per Disposition by the assent of all participating Justices on the bench.

Related Legal Issues and Questions:

1. What is a director in a stock company?
2. What are duties and liabilities of directors? What is a director's right?
3. What is the power and liability of a representative director?
4. What is the power and liability of an auditor?
5. How is an audit committee composed in a unlisted and a listed company?
6. What is the '3 percent rule' in the appointment of auditors or members of an audit committee?
7. What is the audit system for a company in Korea?

CHAPTER 9
ISSUANCE OF NEW SHARES

A stock company may increase or decrease its capital at any time. While the decrease of a company's capital is very restricted with strong requirements to protect creditors and third interested persons, the increase of a company's capital may be determined by the board of directors through the issuance of new shares. The matters relating to the issuance of new shares such as type and number of shares, par value per share and subscription payment date are determined by the board of directors with some requirements and procedures. In this Chapter, it is important to understand how a company may issue new shares and what requirements of the issuance of new shares are under the Korean Commercial Act.

I. Introduction to New Shares

The KCA provides flexible options for investors and companies to increase a company's capital by issuing new shares (신주). Then how does a company issue new shares under the KCA? In relating to the issuance of new shares, the KCA may answer even to other important issues: May the board be permitted to issue new shares without shareholder approval? Do shareholders have pre-emptive rights to acquire newly issued shares?

Unless otherwise specified in the Articles of Incorporation, matters relating to the issuance of new shares such as type and number of shares, par value per share and subscription payment date are determined by the board of directors, within the limit of the authorized capital. In principle, upon issuance of new shares, a shareholder has the right to be allocated shares in proportion to his shareholding percentage. However, as specifically provided for in the Articles of Incorporation, new shares may be allocated to parties other than the shareholders when deemed necessary to achieve the objectives of the company's management, including, without limitation, introduction of new technologies and improvement of the financial structure of the company.

II. Issuance of New Shares - Capital Increase

1. Determination for Issuance of New Shares

In cases where a company issues shares after its incorporation, the following matters, which are not provided for in the Articles of Incorporation, must be determined by the board of directors.

However, where it is otherwise provided for by the KCA or the Articles of Incorporation, they may be determined at a general meeting of shareholders:[430)]

(i) The classes and number of new shares,

(ii) The issuance price of new shares and the date set for the payment thereof,

(iii) In cases of no par value shares, the amount to be included in the paid-up capital out of the issuance price of new shares,

(iv) The method of subscribing to new shares,

(v) The name of a person who is to make an investment in kind and the class, quantity, and value of such property, and the class and number of shares to be given therefor,

(vi) Matters related to transferability of the shareholder's preemptive right to new shares, and

(vii) An intent that a certificate for preemptive right to new shares is to be issued only upon request of the shareholder and the period within which such request may be made.

A company may issue new shares at the price below par value. In cases where a company issues shares after two years have elapsed since its incorporation, the company may issue shares at a price below the par value by a special resolution adopted at a general meeting of shareholders which is the affirmative votes of at least two thirds of the voting rights of the shareholders present at a general

430) Article 416 of the Korean Commercial Act.

meeting of shareholders and of at least one third of the total number of issued and outstanding shares, and with the authorization of the court.[431] The minimum issue price of shares must be determined by a special resolution adopted at a general meeting of shareholders.

The court may grant authorization after altering the minimum issue price by taking into account the present conditions of the company and all the other circumstances. In such cases, the court may appoint an inspector to investigate the status of the company's assets and any other necessary matters. Shares at the price below par value must be issued within one month from the date of obtaining the authorization of the court. The court may extend the above period in its authorization.

If shares are issued at the price below par value, the registration of an alteration resulting therefrom must contain the amount unamortized.[432]

2. Preemptive Right

Each shareholder is entitled to the allotment of new shares in proportion to the number of shares which he holds.[433] A company may make an allotment of new shares to other persons than shareholders, as provided for in the Articles of Incorporation. In such cases, it must be limited to cases necessary for the achievement of the company's operational objectives, such as introduction of new technology, improvement of financial structures, etc. In cases where a company makes an allotment of new shares to other persons than its shareholders, the company must notify the shareholders of the matters on determination of particulars for issuance of new shares by no later than two weeks before the date of payment of the subscription price, or must publicly notify the same. By mandating the company to notify existing shareholders of the newly issued shares, the underlying purpose of the KCA provides existing shareholders a fair opportunity to protect their interests against the newly issued shares.

A company must fix a record date and must, at least two weeks before such record date, give a public notice to the effect that shareholders entered in the register of shareholders as of such record date would be entitled to the

431) Article 417(1) of the Korean Commercial Act.
432) Article 426 of the Korean Commercial Act.
433) Article 418(1) of the Korean Commercial Act.

preemptive rights for new shares and that such preemptive rights are transferable, if applicable. If the above record date is within the period of closure of register of shareholders and record date under the Article 354(1) of the KCA, the public notice must be given at least two weeks before the first day of such period.

A company must notify the holders of preemptive rights of the classes and number of shares subject to such preemptive rights and that their rights would be forfeited if they fail to apply for subscription to new shares on or before a fixed date.[434] Such notice must be given at least two weeks before the date for subscription to new shares above. In cases where a holder of preemptive rights fails to apply for subscription to new shares on or before the specified date after a notice is given, his rights will be forfeited.

3. Share Subscription Form and Certificate of Preemptive Right

1) Directors must prepare a share subscription form containing the following matters:[435]

(i) Matters on trade name, the total number of shares authorized to be issued and par value per share where par value shares are issued,

(ii) Matters on retirement of shares out of profits to be distributed to shareholders if so determined, the bank and any other financial institutions in charge of the payment of the subscription price and the place for payment and the name, address and business office of a transfer agent, if any,

(iii) Matters on the classes and number of new shares, the issuance price of new shares and the date set for the payment thereof, in cases of no par value shares the amount to be included in the paid-up capital out of the issuance price of new shares, the method of subscribing to new share and the name of a person who is to make an investment in kind and the class, quantity, and value of such property, and the class and number of shares to be given therefor,

(iv) Where the company issues shares at price below par, the conditions of such issuance and the amount yet to be amortized,

(v) Restrictions on the preemptive rights of shareholders or a provision that the preemptive rights are to be given to a particular third party, if applicable, and

(vi) Date of the resolution on the issuance of shares.

---

434) Article 419 of the Korean Commercial Act.

435) Article 420 of the Korean Commercial Act.

2) In cases where a company has provided for matters related to transferability of the shareholder's preemptive right to new shares, the company must issue certificates of preemptive rights when a certificate for preemptive right to new shares is to be issued only upon request of the shareholder and the period within which such request may be made, if applicable, or issue them at least two weeks prior to the fixed date for subscription to new shares, as the case may be.[436)]Each certificate of preemptive right must contain a serial number in addition to the following and the directors must write their names and affix their seals, or must affix their signatures, thereon:

(i) A statement to the effect that it is a preemptive right,

(ii) Matters contained in share subscription forms,

(iii) The class and number of shares subject to the preemptive right, and

(iv) A statement to the effect that the right would be forfeited if subscription to shares is not applied for on or before the specified date.

3) A preemptive right must be transferred only by the delivery of the certificate thereof.[437)] If a certificate of preemptive right has been issued, subscription to shares must be applied for by the certificate. A person who has lost a certificate of preemptive right may apply for subscription to shares by the share subscription form. However, such offer by the share subscription form will become ineffective if the application for subscription to shares is made by a certificate of preemptive right.[438)]

4) There is also one exception to the issuance of certificates of preemptive rights and the electronic registration of preemptive rights is available under the KCA. As prescribed in the Articles of Incorporation, a company may register preemptive rights with the electronic registration ledger of an electronic registration agency, in lieu of issuing certificates of preemptive rights. In such cases, the same matters discussed before in the electronic registration of shares under the Article 356-2 will apply mutatis mutandis.[439)]

In turn, in the electronic registration of preemptive rights, transfer or pledge of

---

436) Article 420-2(1) of the Korean Commercial Act.

437) Article 420-3(1) of the Korean Commercial Act.

438) Article 420-5(2) of the Korean Commercial Act.

439) Article 420-4 of the Korean Commercial Act.

preemptive rights registered with the electronic registration ledger will become effective when the transfer or pledge is registered with the electronic registration ledger. Also, a person who has registered preemptive rights with the electronic registration ledger is deemed to legitimately have the right to the registered preemptive rights, and the person who has relied on such electronic registration ledger in good faith and without gross negligence and thereby acquired the right pursuant to registration will validly acquire such right. Additionally, matters necessary for the procedures, methods and effects of electronic registration, supervision of an electronic registration authority, and other matters on electronic registration of preemptive rights will be applied by separately prescribed other Acts.[440)]

4. Payment for New Shares

1) Directors must cause persons who have subscribed to new shares to pay the full subscription price with respect to each share allotted to them on or before the date set for such payment.[441)]

2) Person who has subscribed to new shares may not, without the consent of the company, offset his liability for the payment of subscription price with his creditor's rights against the stock company.[442)] This is a debt-equity swap which requires the company's permission on a set-off against payment of the subscription price. Under the old rules of the KCA, a shareholder could not assert a set-off against the company as regards to payment of the subscription price for shares.

However, this old rule had been controversial, as its purpose and extent was unclear. For instance, let's suppose a company is currently restructuring. As a process of restructuring, it proceeds to execute a debt-equity swap where the creditors become shareholders and the company determines the issuance of new shares and agrees with the creditors to set off the payment of the subscription price for shares with receivables owed by the company. It was unclear whether the foregoing set-off was actually permitted under the old rule of the KCA. In reality, debt-equity swaps were limited to the use of companies under rehabilitation

440) Article 356-2(2), (3) and (4) of the Korean Commercial Act.

441) Article 421(1) of the Korean Commercial Act.

442) Article 421(2) of the Korean Commercial Act.

procedures or work-out companies that were defined under the Corporate Restructuring Promotion Act (기업구조조정촉진법). As a result, the issue of allowing debt-equity swaps beyond just work-out companies was raised and many deemed it necessary to permit other general companies to take advantage of investment conversions.

By the amendment of the KCA, it now provides that the purchaser of the newly issued shares may not be permitted to set off the payment of the subscription price with receivables owed by the company without the consent of the company. If the company, however, provides consent, the shareholder may set off its receivables owed by the company with its payment for the newly issued shares. Therefore, under the KCA, debt-equity swaps can be performed even if the company is not a work-out company or undergoing rehabilitation.

3) In cases of an investment in kind, directors must request the court to appoint an inspector who is to inspect the particulars such as the name of a person who is to make an investment in kind, the class, quantity, and value of such property, and the class and number of shares to be given therefor.[443] In such cases, an appraisal by a certified appraiser may be conducted in lieu of the inspection by an inspector.

However, inspector investigations and court reports may be criticized for causing uncertainty and contributing to unnecessarily long deal times and deal expenses. In this regard, the KCA seeks to loosen the standards by approving exceptions in certain situations and provides an exemption to the inspection. In turn, in any of the following cases, such appointment of an inspector for an investment in kind is not required:

(i) If the value of assets subject to an investment in kind does not exceed one fifth of the capital and not exceed the amount determined by Presidential Decree,

(ii) If assets subject to an investment in kind are securities having exchange quotation, in which case the price does not exceed the market value calculated by the method determined by Presidential Decree,

(iii) When a pecuniary claim which has become due against the company is to be contributed, in which case the value of the pecuniary claim does not exceed the value stated in the company's ledger,

(iv) Other cases determined by Presidential Decree, which are equivalent to

443) Article 422(1) of the Korean Commercial Act.

those described in (i) through (iii) above.

If the court acknowledges the particulars of an investment in kind to be improper after examining a report on investigation prepared by an inspector or the outcomes of appraisal conducted by an appraiser, it may make a necessary modification and inform directors and the person who has made the investment in kind, of such modification. If a person who has made an investment in kind objects to such modification, he may cancel his subscription to shares. If a person who has made an investment in kind does not cancel his subscription to shares within two weeks after the court informed him of alteration, the particulars of an investment in kind are deemed to have been modified accordingly.

5. Date of Becoming Shareholders and Effects of Failing to Make Payment

If a person who has subscribed to new shares pays the subscription price or makes an investment in kind, he will have the rights and obligations of a shareholder from the day immediately after the date set for the payment.444)

If a person who has subscribed to new shares fails to pay the subscription price or makes an investment in kind on or before the date set for the payment, his right will be forfeited. This will not affect any claim for damages against a person who has subscribed to new shares.

III. Actions and Liabilities in Issuance of New Shares

1. Rights to Injunction

If a company issues shares in violation of a statute or the Articles of Incorporation of a company or in a substantially unfair manner and shareholders are likely to suffer disadvantages thereby, the shareholders may request the company to cease such issuance.445)

444) Article 423(1) of the Korean Commercial Act.

445) Article 424 of the Korean Commercial Act.

2. Liability of Persons who have Subscribed to Shares at Unfair Prices

A person who has subscribed to shares at a substantially unfair issuance price in collusion with directors is liable to pay to the company the amount equivalent to the difference between such issuance price and the fair issuance price.[446] This does not affect the directors' liability to compensate for damages incurred by the company or shareholders.

3. Limitation on Assertion of Nullification or Revocation of Subscriptions

After one year has elapsed from the date of registration of an alteration due to the issuance of new shares, person who has subscribed to the new shares may not assert the nullification of his subscription by reason of defects in the requirements as to the share subscription form or certificate of preemptive right, or cancel his subscription on the ground of fraud, duress or mistake.[447] The same will apply where he has exercised his rights in respect to such shares.

4. Directors' Liability to Secure Subscription

In cases where shares have yet to be subscribed to or the subscription of shares has been canceled after the registration of alteration due to the issuance of new shares was made, the directors are deemed to have jointly subscribed to such shares.[448] This will not affect any claim for damages against directors.

As a result in such cases, the directors must pay for the shares subscribed by them.

5. Lawsuits for Nullification of Issuance of New Shares

Nullification of the issuance of new shares can be asserted only by a lawsuit filed by a shareholder, a director, or an auditor within six months from the date

446) Article 424-2(1) of the Korean Commercial Act.
447) Article 427 of the Korean Commercial Act.
448) Article 428(1) of the Korean Commercial Act.

of the issuance of such new shares.

When a judgment nullifying issuance of new shares becomes final and conclusive, such new shares will be invalidated in the future.[449] In such cases, the company must without delay give a public notice to the effect that certificates of new shares must be submitted to the company within a fixed period and must separately notify each shareholder and pledgee recorded in the register of shareholders of the same. Such period must exceed three months.

When a judgment nullifying issuance of new shares becomes final and conclusive, the company must refund to each shareholder the amount paid by him for new shares.[450] If such amount is considerably unreasonable in view of the status of the company's assets as at the time a judgment nullifying issuance of new shares becomes final and conclusive, the court may order either an increase or decrease in such amount, upon request of the company or of such shareholder.

IV. Capital Reduction

1. Introduction to Capital Reduction

A capital reduction means, as it says, reduction of capital of a stock company. A capital reduction may be categorized into a real capital reduction or a nominal capital reduction, depending on whether or not the amount of the net assets of the company is reduced.

In a real capital reduction, the proceeds from the capital reduction are distributed to the shareholders in accordance with their shareholding ratio. Since the shareholders are compensated or repaid, a real capital reduction is sometimes referred to as a capital reduction with consideration. A real capital reduction is often used as a method to reduce the size of the company in order to facilitate a sale or merger of the company or to collect the investment amount.

In a nominal capital reduction, on the contrary, although the nominal amount of capital will be reduced, there would be no change to the total amount of assets of the company. In other words, no proceeds are distributed to the shareholders as a compensation or repayment of their investment. In this regard,

449) Article 431(1) of the Korean Commercial Act.

450) Article 432(1) of the Korean Commercial Act.

it is sometimes referred to as capital reduction without consideration. A nominal capital reduction is often used by a troubled company to reduce book losses by reducing the book capital in order to close in the gap between the capital and net assets

The old rule of the KCA did not differentiate between the two different concepts of a real capital reduction and a nominal capital reduction, and required a special resolution of the shareholders meeting and a creditor protection procedure for all types of capital reductions. However, under the KCA by the amendment, a nominal capital reduction to compensate for capital deficiency may be conducted by obtaining an ordinary shareholders resolution without creditor protection procedure.

2. Requirements and Procedures of Capital Reduction

1) Resolutions for Capital Reduction

(1) In order to reduce capital, a special resolution is required.[451] A special resolution must be adopted by the affirmative votes of at least two thirds of the voting rights of the shareholders present at a general meeting of shareholders and of at least one third of the total number of issued and outstanding shares. However, any capital reduction for recovery from deficit must be made by an ordinary resolution.[452] A ordinary resolution must be adopted at a general meeting of shareholders by affirmative votes of a majority of the voting rights of shareholders present thereat and representing at least a quarter of the total number of issued and outstanding shares.

(2) In a resolution to reduce capital, methods of making such reduction must be determined.[453] In such cases, within two weeks after the date of the resolution for a capital reduction, the company must make public notice to the effect that the company's creditors with objections to the capital reduction, if any, submit such objections within a specified period of time and must give peremptory notice to respective creditors known to the company. In such cases,

---

451) Article 438(1) of the Korean Commercial Act.
452) Article 438(2) of the Korean Commercial Act.
453) Article 439(1) of the Korean Commercial Act.

the said period must not be less than one month. A creditor who fails to raise an objection within the such period is deemed to have approved the capital reduction. If a creditor has raised an objection, the company must make repayment to the creditor or furnish adequate security, or entrust assets of reasonable value to a trust company for the purpose of repaying the creditor.

(3) The requirement to conduct a creditor protection procedure even in the case of a capital reduction without consideration has been a hot topic subject to continuous criticism by the scholars who viewed such requirement as unnecessary and only causing waste of money and time, in light of the fact that no creditor's rights are directly infringed in a capital reduction without consideration. The KCA reflects such opinion of the scholars and includes a provision on exemption of a creditor protection procedure in case of a capital reduction without consideration conducted by a company to compensate for its capital deficiency. Accordingly, Such creditor protection procedure is not required where the capital reduction is made for deficit recovery.[454] As a result, it would enable a company to easily conduct capital reduction without consideration notwithstanding dissenting shareholders.

(4) A bondholder may raise an objection subject to a resolution passed by a meeting of bondholders. In such cases, upon request by any interested person, the court may extend in favor of the bondholder the period for raising such objection.

2) Consolidation of Shares

If shares are to be consolidated, a company must determine a period of not less than one month and must give a public notice to the effect that shares would be consolidated and that share certificates must be submitted to the company within such period and must separately give a notice to such effect to each of the shareholders and the pledgees recorded in the register of shareholders.[455] A consolidation of shares will take effect upon the expiration of the such period.[456] However, if the creditor protection procedures have yet to be completed, it will take effect upon the completion of such procedures.

454) Article 439(2) of the Korean Commercial Act.
455) Article 440 of the Korean Commercial Act.
456) Article 441 of the Korean Commercial Act.

If, in cases of a consolidation of shares, a person cannot submit his old share certificates, the company may, upon a request by such person, determine a period of no less than three months and give a public notice to the effect that any interested person must raise an objection, if any, on such certificates within such period and may deliver new share certificates to such person after the lapse of such period.[457] Expenses incurred in giving such public notice will be borne by the requester.

If shares, the number of which is unfit for a consolidation, exist, new shares issued for such portion unfit for the consolidation must be sold by means of auction and the proceeds from which must be delivered to the former shareholders in proportion to the number of shares they formerly held. Shares for which there is an exchange based market may be sold through such exchange and shares without an exchange quotation may be sold in a manner other than auction with the permission of the court.[458]

3) Lawsuits to Nullify Capital Reduction

Nullification of capital reduction can be asserted only by a lawsuit filed only by a shareholder, director, auditor, liquidator, bankruptcy trustee or creditor disapproving such capital reduction, within six months from the date the registration of alteration due to such capital reduction has been made.[459]

V. Case Study on New Shares[460]

1. Determination by Board of Directors

Under the Article 416 of the KCA, in cases where a company issues shares

457) Article 442(1) of the Korean Commercial Act.

458) Article 443(1) of the Korean Commercial Act.

459) Article 445 of the Korean Commercial Act.

460) Supreme Court Decision 2014Da53745, decided on August 29, 2016. *See* also Supreme Court Decision 2010Da49380, decided on November 15, 2012, Supreme Court Decision 2008Da96963, decided on February 25, 2010, Supreme Court Decision 2008Do9436, decided on May 29, 2009, Supreme Court Decision 2008GaHap6916, decided on January 23, 2009, and Supreme Court Decision 2000Da42786, decided on February 26, 2003.

after its incorporation, the following matters, which are not provided for in the Articles of Incorporation of a company, must be determined by the board of directors: (i) the classes and number of new shares, (ii) the issuance price of new shares and the date set for the payment thereof, (iii) in cases of no par value shares, the amount to be included in the paid-up capital out of the issuance price of new shares, (iv) the method of subscribing to new shares, (v) the name of a person who is to make an investment in kind and the class, quantity, and value of such property, and the class and number of shares to be given therefor, (vi) matters related to transferability of the shareholder's preemptive right to new shares, and (vii) an intent that a certificate for preemptive right to new shares is to be issued only upon request of the shareholder and the period within which such request may be made.

2. Determination by Shareholders' Meeting

However, these requirements may not apply where it is otherwise provided for by the KCA or the Articles of Incorporation provide that they must be determined at a general meeting of shareholders.

Related Legal Issues and Questions:

1. What requirements and procedures are necessary for the issuance of new shares under the Korean Commercial Act?
2. What requirements and procedures are necessary for the capital reduction under the Korean Commercial Act?

CHAPTER 10
ACCOUNTING AND DIVIDENDS

The accounting of a company, other than that provided for in the KCA, must be conducted in accordance with generally accepted fair and proper accounting practices. The dividend distribution must be determined by resolution of a general meeting of shareholders, or by resolution of the board of directors in cases where the board of directors approves financial statements. Further, a company may pay dividends by issuing new shares, by interim dividend or with assets other than money. In this Chapter, it is important to understand what the principles on accounting and dividend distribution are and how a company may distribute dividends under the Korean Commercial Act.

I. Accounting in Principle

The KCA by the Amendment in 2011 which took effect on April 15, 2012, changed a lot corporate accounting provisions: It (i) gives the board of directors the final authority to approve financial statements and decide to distribute dividends, (ii) explicitly excludes certain unrealized profits from the scope of distributable profits, and (iii) allows in-kind dividend distribution.

The accounting of a company, other than that provided for in the KCA and Presidential Decree, must be conducted in accordance with generally accepted fair and proper accounting practices. The important matters on the accounting of a company are as follow:

1. In each period for the settlement of accounts, directors must prepare the following documents and the supplementary schedules and obtain approval therefor from the board of directors:[461]

461) Article 447(1) of the Korean Commercial Act.

(i) balance sheets,

(ii) income statements, and

(iii) other documents prescribed by Presidential Decree, indicating the financial status and management performance of the company, and must prepare a business report and must obtain approval therefor from the board of directors.[462)]

2. Directors must submit to auditors the documents on such financial statements and business report six weeks prior to the date of an ordinary general meeting of shareholders.[463)]

3. Auditors must submit to directors an audit report within four weeks of receipt of the documents on such financial statements and business report.[464)] In cases where an auditor is unable to conduct an investigation necessary for an audit, the audit report must include a statement to that effect and the grounds therefor.

4. Directors must retain the documents on such financial statements and business report as well as an audit report at the principal office of the company for five years and must retain the copies thereof at the branch offices for three years, from one week prior to the date of an ordinary general meeting of shareholders.[465)] Any shareholder or creditor of a company may, at any time during its business hours, inspect such documents and request the copying of such documents or an extract thereof, with payment of fees determined by the company.

5. Directors must submit the documents on financial statements to an ordinary general meeting of shareholders and must obtain approval therefor.[466)] Directors must submit the documents on business reports to an ordinary general meeting of shareholders and must report the details thereof. If directors have obtained approval from a general meeting of shareholders for the such documents, they must give, without delay, public notice of the balance sheets.

462) Article 447-2(1) of the Korean Commercial Act.
463) Article 447-3 of the Korean Commercial Act.
464) Article 447-4(1) of the Korean Commercial Act.
465) Article 448(1) of the Korean Commercial Act.
466) Article 449(1) of the Korean Commercial Act.

However, a company may approve the documents on financial statements by a resolution of the board of directors as determined by its Articles of Incorporation, if an external auditor presents an opinion that each of the documents on financial statements appropriately represents the company's financial conditions and performance of management in accordance with statutes and the Articles of Incorporation and all the auditors or the members of the audit committee give consent thereto.[467] In cases where a board of directors gives approval such financial statements, directors must report the details of each document on financial statements to a general meeting of shareholders.

6. If no contrary resolution has been adopted within two years after an ordinary general meeting of shareholders, during which an approval on financial statements was given, the company is deemed to have discharged the directors and auditors from liability.[468]

II. Dividend Distribution

1. Dividend

(1) A dividend (배당) is a distribution of profits by a company to its shareholders. A company may distribute dividends within the limit of the value of net assets stated on the balance sheets after deducting the followings:[469] (i) the amount of capital, (ii) the total amount of the capital reserve and the earned surplus reserve accumulated until the pertinent period for the settlement of accounts of the company, (iii) the amount to be accumulated for the pertinent period for the settlement of accounts of the company, and (iv) unrealized profits determined by Presidential Decree. Each payment of dividends must be determined by resolution of a general meeting of shareholders.[470]

However, the same may be determined by resolution of the board of directors

467) Article 449-2(1) of the Korean Commercial Act.

468) Article 450 of the Korean Commercial Act.

469) Article 462(1) of the Korean Commercial Act.

470) Kwan Hoon Kwak, “The Study on Possibilities, Limitations and Improvement of the Use of Dividend in Kind (in Korean),” Commercial Law Review, Vol. 33 No.1, 2014, p.105.

in cases where the board of directors approves financial statements. In cases where dividends have been paid in violation of requirements and procedures mentioned above, any creditor of the company may claim a refund of such dividends to the company. There can be advantages to the board of directors' having final authority for dividend distribution. On the other hand, the KCA might increase director's liability, because it is not entirely clear about exemption of director's liability for their decision on dividend distribution.

(2) The Article 450 of the KCA provides that the directors and auditors are deemed exempted from liability for their decision on financial statements, unless any shareholder resolution is otherwise passed within two years after the financial statements are approved at the general meeting of shareholders. However, the KCA provisions relating to the board's final approval authority are silent on such exemption and thus, the Article 450 would not likely be applicable to a board's approval of financial statements. A further amendment to the KCA or the ruling by a authority seems necessary to clarify the ambiguity.

Distribution of profits must be made in proportion to the number of shares held by each shareholder. However, this may not apply in cases of different classes of shares.[471)]

(3) A company must pay dividends within one month from the date of adopting a resolution at a general meeting of shareholders or by the board of directors, or from the date of adopting a resolution on interim dividends.[472)] However, this may not apply where the date of the payment of dividends is determined otherwise by a general meeting of shareholders or the board of directors. The statute of limitations for a claim for such payment of dividends will expire, if it is not exercised for five years.

(4) Almost all Korean companies pay cash dividends only once a year at the end of their fiscal year, with a very few companies paying mid-year cash dividends. Majority of Korean companies have their fiscal year end in December and dividends are usually distributed around March of the following year.[473)]

471) Article 464 of the Korean Commercial Act.

472) Article 464-2(1) of the Korean Commercial Act.

473) Cheol Park, Soo Cheol Park, "The Behavior of Stock Prices on Ex-Dividend Day in Korea," Korean Journal of Financial Management, Vol. 26 No. 1, March 2009,

2. Stock Dividend

A company may pay dividends by issuing new shares by a resolution adopted at a general meeting of shareholders. Such stock dividends (주식배당) may not exceed the amount equivalent to half of the total amount of dividends.[474] Stock dividends must be paid based on the par value of shares and if the company have issued different classes of shares, such dividends may be paid in the same classes of shares, respectively.

A shareholder who has received stock dividends shall become a shareholder of new shares from the time of closing of the general meeting of shareholders at which a resolution on stock dividends is adopted. Where a resolution on stock dividends has been adopted, directors must notify, without delay, the shareholders entitled to receive the stock dividends and the pledgees entered on the register of shareholders, of the classes and number of shares to be allocated to the shareholders. The right of a pledgee will extend to shares to be distributed to a shareholder pursuant to stock dividends.

3. Interim Dividend

A company which has a period for the settlement of accounts once per year may determine in its Articles of Incorporation that the company may pay dividends (interim dividend, 중간배당) on a specified date set by a resolution of the board of directors to the shareholders on such date only one time during a business year.[475]

Interim dividends must be paid within the limit of the amount calculated by deducting the following amounts from the value of net assets on the balance sheets in the immediately preceding period for the settlement of accounts: (i) the amount of capital in the immediately preceding period for the settlement of accounts, (ii) the total amount of the capital reserve and earned surplus reserve accumulated until the immediately preceding period for the settlement of accounts, (iii) the amount which is to be distributed as a profit or paid at an ordinary general meeting of shareholders in the immediately preceding period for the

p.225.

474) Article 462-2(1) of the Korean Commercial Act.

475) Article 462-3 (1) of the Korean Commercial Act.

settlement of accounts, and (iv) the earned surplus reserve which is to be accumulated in the relevant period for the settlement of accounts for the payment of interim dividends.

If the value of net assets on the balance sheets in the relevant period for the settlement of accounts is deemed unlikely to amount to the total sum of amounts listed in the Article 462(1), the company must not pay interim dividends. Where, even if the value of net assets on the balance sheets in the relevant period for the settlement of accounts fails to amount to the total sum of the amounts listed in the Article 462(1), payment of interim dividends is made, directors must be jointly and severally liable to compensate for the difference to the company. Where the amount of dividend is less than such difference, the amount of dividend must be compensated. However, The same may not apply where the directors prove that they have not been negligent in rendering judgment that the situation failed to amount to the total sum of the amounts listed in the Article 462(1) is not likely to occur.

4. Dividend in Kind

A company may determine in its Articles of Incorporation that it may pay dividends with assets (dividend in kind, 현물배당) other than money.[476)]

A company that has determined payment of dividends with assets other than money may further determine the following: (i)w here the company determines that a shareholder may claim payment of money in lieu of a dividend in kind, such amount of money and the period set for such claim, (ii) where the company determines that it will pay money to the shareholders who have less than a certain number of stocks, in lieu of a dividend in kind, such number of stocks and the amount of money.

476) Article 462-4(1) of the Korean Commercial Act.

III. Case Study on Dividend Distribution in Practice[477)]

1. Practical Dividend Market

Korea presents a whole different environment when it comes to dividends. The ex-date, which is fixed to be the second last business day of each fiscal quarter by the exchange rule, always comes before the companies' dividend announcement dates. Unlike Japan where a similar ex-date rule is shared and the majority of companies provide a one year forward shareholder return plan to reduce uncertainty associated with payout amount, Korean companies rarely guide their upcoming dividends. In other words, shareholders are expected to hold their shares through ex-dates without having sufficient visibility on how much dividend would be distributed to them. A relatively high level of earnings volatility and opacity in dividend policy add on to the dividend risk unique to Korea.

However, this does not necessarily mean that Korea is not an attractive investment destination in terms of dividends. Key takeaways for 2022 dividends are as follows:

(i) Dividend ex-date falls before announcement date in Korea. Shareholders are presented with a unique set of risk and opportunity as they are expected to hold their share through ex-date without knowing how much dividend will be distributed.

(ii) The pro-dividend culture advocated by National Pension Service (NPS) of Korea rendered corporates to enhance shareholder return policies in the mid/long-term.

(iii) The analysis shows that KRX-IHS Markit Dividend Forecast Yield Top 50 index significantly outperformed KOSPI 200 during bear market when interest rate hikes took place. It is expected of this historical pattern to repeat in the second half of the year.

(iv) KOSPI 200 aggregate dividend will grow a solid 4% in FY 2022. Technology, banks, and automobile and parts will remain as the largest paying sectors. Oil refineries' dividends will growth at unprecedented rate while COVID-19 re-opening related stocks are showing varied rates of dividend recovery.

---

477) Stella Lim, Pedro Choi, "South Korea Dividends More to be Discovered," APAC Thematic Report, S&P Global Market Intelligence, June 17 2022.

2. Korea's Unique Dividend Timeline

Korea presents a whole different environment when it comes to dividends. Ex-date that falls before announcement poses risk that is unique to Korea.

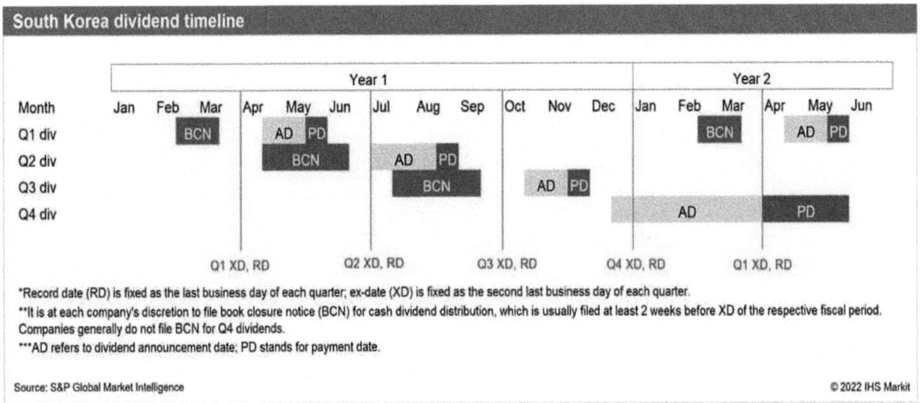

3. Dividend Growth Trend

The National Pension Service has increasingly been involved to cultivate a culture of emphasis on shareholder return among companies.

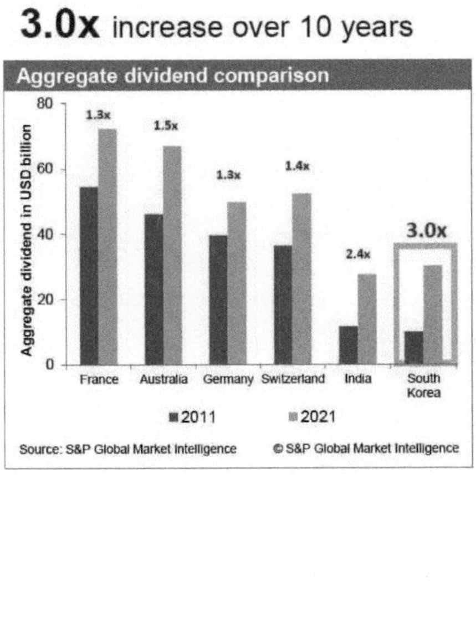

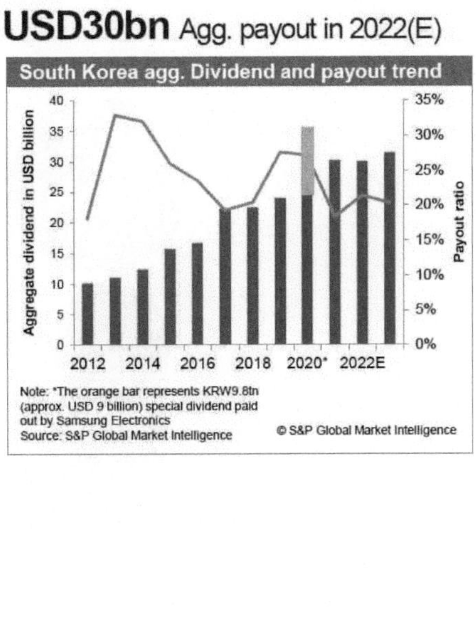

4. Dividend Stock Analysis

There was 74% chance Korean dividend stocks outperforming the market during bear period.

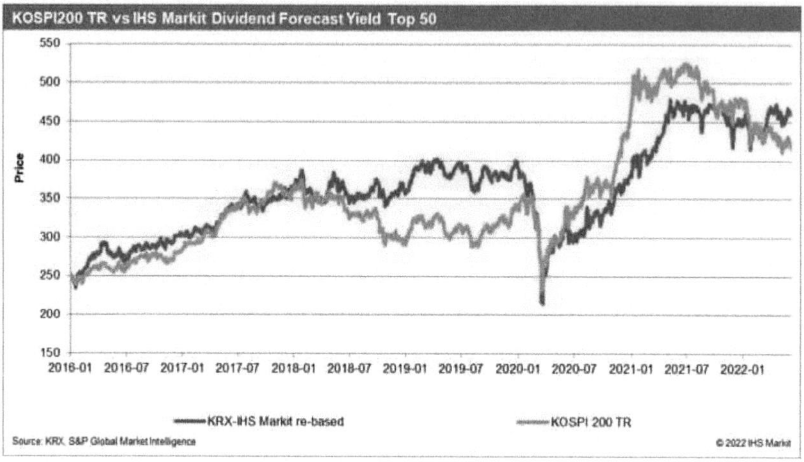

5. Sector by Sector Analysis Covering

During 2022, the top major sectors for a dividend distribution are technology, banks, automobile, covid re-opening and oil refinery.

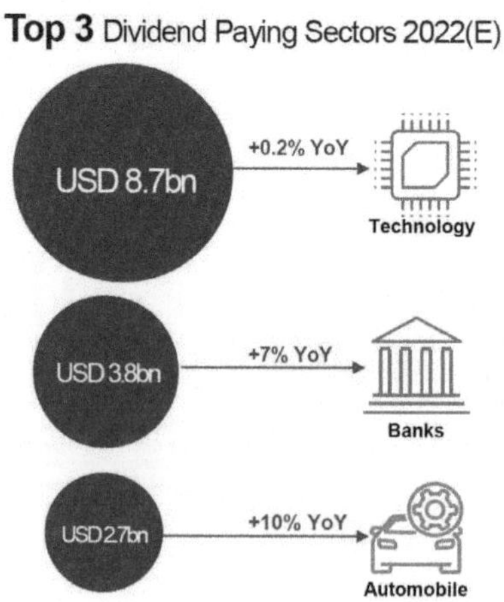

Related Legal Issues and Questions:

1. What are requirements and procedures for a dividend distribution?
2. What kinds of dividends are available under the Korean Commercial Act?
3. Does Korea accept a dividend in kind for a dividend distribution?

CHAPTER 11
CORPORATE BONDS

A corporate bond is a bond issued by a company in order to raise financing for a variety of reasons. A stock company may issue corporate bonds for subscription by a resolution of the board of directors. In cases of issuing bonds, a company may designate a bond administration company and entrust affairs to it. A meeting of bondholders may adopt resolutions with respect to matters provided for in the Korean Commercial Act and matters that may affect the interests of bondholders. In this Chapter, it is important to understand how corporate bonds may be issued and what kinds of corporate bonds can be issued by a company under the Korean Commercial Act.

I. Introduction to Corporate Bonds

A corporate bond (사채) is a bond issued by a company in order to raise financing for a variety of reasons such as to ongoing operations, M&A, or to expand business.[478] Under the Korean Commercial Act (KCA), corporate bonds may be issued by the decision of the board of directors. Bondholders are eligible for the principal and interest determined in the bonds by a company. The statute of limitations for the right to claim redemption of bonds will expire, if not exercised for ten years.[479] The statute of limitations for the right to claim payment of interest accrued on bonds will expire, if not exercised for five years.

A distinctive feature to corporate bonds section of the KCA has come out of the amendment to the KCA on April 14, 2011, which is the first amendment of this section since the KCA's enactment. Prior to this amendment, the KCA only

478) O'Sullivan, Arthur & Sheffrin, Steven M. "Economics: Principles in Action," Upper Saddle River, N.J.: Pearson Prentice Hall, 2003, p.281.

479) Article 487(1) of the Korean Commercial Act.

contained express provisions for issuances of ordinary corporate bonds, convertible bonds and bonds with warrants, sparking debate over whether issuances of other types of corporate bonds were permitted under the KCA. Since the KCA provisions now expressly provide for issuances of more varied types of corporate bonds and are specified as illustrative provisions, the debate has been put to rest. The relevant provisions of the KCA are examined in more detail below.

II. Issuance of Corporate Bonds

1. Bond Offering

A company may issue bonds for subscription by a resolution of the board of directors.[480] As prescribed by the Articles of Incorporation, the board of directors may determine the amount and type of bonds and entrust the representative director with the issuance of such bonds within a period not exceeding one year.

The following bonds must be included in the bonds mentioned above:

(i) bonds entitling its holders to dividends,

(ii) bonds that can be exchanged or redeemed with stocks or other securities, and

(iii) bonds the redemption or payment amount of which is determined by the pre-determined methods that are linked to the fluctuation of such things as securities, currencies, or other assets or indexes determined by Presidential Decree.[481]

A person who intends to subscribe to bonds shall prepare a subscription form in duplicate, stating the number of bonds to which he intends to subscribe and his address, and must write his name and affix his seal, or affix his signature, thereon.[482] A bond subscription form must be prepared by directors and contain the important matters on bonds.[483] In cases where the minimum issuance price

---

480) Article 469(1) of the Korean Commercial Act.

481) Chung, Joon-Woo, "The Critical Review of Offering and Administration of Corporate Bonds under the Commercial Law (in Korean)," Korea Economic Law Review, Vol. 13 No. 1, 2014, p.313.

482) Article 474(1) of the Korean Commercial Act.

483) A bond subscription form must contain the followings under the Article 474(2) of the Korean Commercial Act:

(i) The trade name of the company,

(ii) The total amount of capital and reserve,

(iii) The value of the net assets of the company indicated in the latest balance sheet,

has been determined, a bond subscriber must state in the subscription form the amount at which he intends to subscribe to. The provisions of a public offering above may not apply where total subscription to bonds is made under a contract. The same may apply to the portion of bonds subscribed for by a company commissioned to offer bonds for subscription.

When subscription to bonds is complete, directors must, without delay, cause bond subscribers to make the full payment or the first instalment payment on each bond.[484] A company commissioned to offer bonds for subscription may, in its own name, perform such acts on behalf of the company.

No certificate may be issued for a bond until its full amount has been paid up.[485] Instead of issuing bonds, a company may register bonds in the electronic registration ledger of an electronic registration agency, as prescribed by the Articles of Incorporation of a company.

A company must prepare a bond register, stating the following particulars:[486]

(i) The name and address of each bondholder, excluding bondholders of bonds regarding which bearer bonds have been issued,

---

(iv) The total amount of the bonds,
(v) The face amount of each bond,
(vi) The issue price or minimum issue price of each bond,
(vii) The rate of interest payable on each bond,
(viii) Methods and timing for the redemption of bonds and for the payment of interest,
(ix) The amount of and timing for each payment of the subscription price of the bonds, if payment is to be made in installments,
(x) If a decision has been made to restrict the bonds certificates either in bearer form or in registered form, a statement to that effect,
(xi) If the right of a bond holder has been registered in the electronic registration ledger of an electronic registration agency, in lieu of issuing bond certificates, a statement to that effect,
(xii) If bonds have been previously issued, the amount yet to be redeemed,
(xiii) If there exists a company commissioned to offer bonds for subscription, the trade name and address of such company,
(xiv) If there exists a bond administration company, the name and address of such bond administration company,
(xv) If it has been determined that a bond administration company may conduct an act set forth in the Article 484(4)(b) without obtaining a resolution at a meeting of bondholders, a statement to that effect,
(xvi) If a company commissioned to offer bonds for subscription has undertaken to subscribe to any portion of the total amount of bonds which have not been subscribed for through the public offering, a statement to that effect, and
(xvii) If a transfer agent has been designated, his full name, address and business office.

484) Article 476(1) of the Korean Commercial Act.

485) Article 478(1) of the Korean Commercial Act.

486) Article 488 of the Korean Commercial Act.

(ii) The serial number of each bond certificate,

(iii) Matters prescribed in Articles 474(2)(d), (e), (g) through (i), (m), (m-2), and (m-3),

(iv) The amount paid for each bond and the date of each payment,

(v) The date of issuing the bond, or in cases of registering a bondholder's right in the electronic registration ledger of an electronic registration agency in lieu of issuing a bond certificate, a statement to that effect,

(vi) The date of acquiring each bond, and

(vii) In cases of issuing a bearer bond, the class, number and serial number thereof, and the date of issuance.

2. Transfer of Registered Bonds

The effect of transfer of registered bonds may not be asserted against a company or a third party unless the name and address of the transferee have been entered in the bond register and his name has been entered in the bond certificates.[487)]

A bondholder may, at any time, request a company to change a registered bond certificate into a bearer certificate or vice versa. However, this must not apply where the form of a bond certificate is restricted in either registered or bearer form.[488)]

3. Bond Administration Company

1) Designation and Entrustment of Bond Administration Company

In cases of issuing bonds, a company may designate a bond administration company and entrust affairs, such as collecting redemption, preserving bonds and other administration of bonds.[489)]

In such cases, only a bank, trust company, and another person determined by Presidential Decree may become a bond administration company.[490)] A bond

487) Article 479(1) of the Korean Commercial Act.
488) Article 480 of the Korean Commercial Act.
489) Article 480-2 of the Korean Commercial Act.
490) Article 480-3(1) of the Korean Commercial Act.

underwriter may not become a bond administration company of the relevant bond. A person having special interests, who is determined by Presidential Decree, may not become a bond administration company.

A bond administration company may resign with the consent of the issuing company and of a meeting of bondholders. It may do so with the permission of the court where there exist unavoidable grounds therefor.[491] If a bond administration company is unfit to handle relevant administrative affairs or if there is good cause, the court may remove such company from office at the request of the issuing company or of a meeting of bondholders.[492] Where a bond administration company ceases to exist due to resignation or removal of the bond administration company, the company which has issued bonds must designate another bond administration company to succeed to the affairs and must entrust the company with affairs regarding bond administration for the bond holders.[493] In such cases, the company must, without delay, convene a meeting of bondholders and obtain consent thereto. If there exists any unavoidable cause, any interested person may request the court to appoint a successor to affairs regarding bond administration.

2) Powers and Duties of Bond Administration Company

(1) Powers of Bond Administration Company

A bond administration company may have the powers to do on behalf of the bondholders all judicial or extra-judicial acts necessary for collecting redemption concerning the bonds or for preservative measures to materialize the bonds.[494] When a bond administration company collects redemption, it must without delay give a public notice thereof and give separate notice to each bondholder known to the company. In such cases, a bondholder may claim payment of the relevant redemption amount and the interest accrued thereon against the bond administration company. In such cases, when the bond certificate has been issued, the claim for payment of the relevant redemption amount must be made in

491) Article 481(1) of the Korean Commercial Act.
492) Article 482 of the Korean Commercial Act.
493) Article 483(1) of the Korean Commercial Act.
494) Article 484(1) of the Korean Commercial Act.

exchange for the bondholder's bond certificate, and of the interest accrued thereon, in exchange for the coupon, respectively.

In cases where a bond administration company does any of the following acts, excluding acts necessary for collecting redemption concerning bonds or for preservative measures to materialize bonds, a resolution by a meeting of bondholders is required:

(i) Deferring of payment with respect to all the relevant bonds, or exoneration from or settlement of the liability accrued due to nonperformance of an obligation, and

(ii) A legal action with respect to all the relevant bonds, or an act falling under the procedures concerning debtor rehabilitation and bankruptcy.

However, a bond-issuing company may determine that an act under (ii) above may be done by a bond administration company without a resolution adopted by a meeting of bondholders. When a bond administration company has done an act under (ii) above without a resolution by a meeting of bondholders, it must without delay give a public notice thereof and give separate notice to each bondholder known to the company. Such public notification must be made in the same manner as public notification used by the company which has issued bonds. With respect to bonds, the administration of which has been commissioned to a bond administration company, the bond administration company may investigate the affairs and financial conditions of the bond-issuer company with the permission of the court, if necessary for conducting the acts for bond administration.

(2) Duties of Bond Administration Company

A bond administration company must fairly and sincerely administer bonds for and on behalf of bondholders.[495] A bond administration company must administer bonds for bondholders in good faith with the care of a good manager. When a bond administration company has done an act in violation of the KCA or a resolution by a meeting of bondholders, the company must be jointly and severally liable to the bondholders to compensate for the damage sustained due to the said violation.

495) Article 484-2(1) of the Korean Commercial Act.

If there exist two or more bond administration companies, all acts falling within the scope of their power must be jointly performed.[496] In such cases, when a bond administration company collects redemption, the company must be jointly and severally liable to the bondholders to pay the redemption amount.

If payment, settlement or any other process made by a company to a certain bondholder is considerably unfair, a bond administration company may demand the revocation thereof, only by lawsuits.[497] Such lawsuit must be filed within six months from the date a ground for revocation has been brought to the attention of the bond administration company, and within one year from the date such act was committed. When a resolution has been adopted by a meeting of bondholders, any representative of a meeting or implementer of a resolution may also file such lawsuit. However, such lawsuit must be filed within one year from the date such act was committed.[498]

3) Remuneration and Expenses for Bond Administration Company

Unless otherwise provided for in a contract concluded with the issuer company, any remuneration payable to a bond administration company, representatives, or implementers or any expenses incurred in the performance of their duties may be borne by the said issuer company, with the permission of court.[499] A bond administration company, representative or implementer may receive remuneration and expenses out of the amount of debt repaid, in preference to bondholders.

III. Meeting of Bondholders

1. Requirements and Procedures for Meeting of Bondholders

A meeting of bondholders (사채권자집회) may adopt resolutions with respect to matters provided for in the KCA and matters that may affect the interests of bondholders.[500] If at least two classes of bonds have been issued, a meeting of

---

496) Article 485(1) of the Korean Commercial Act.
497) Article 511(1) of the Korean Commercial Act.
498) Article 512 of the Korean Commercial Act.
499) Article 507(1) of the Korean Commercial Act.

bondholders must be convened for each class of bonds.[501)]

A meeting of bondholders must be convened by the company which has issued bonds or by a bond administration company.[502)] A bondholder who has each class of bonds, representing at least one tenth of the total amount of corresponding class of bonds, excluding the amount redeemed, may demand convocation of a meeting of bondholders by submitting to the bond-issuer company or a bond administration company a written statement or an electronic document specifying the agenda for the meeting and the grounds for convening such meeting. The holder of bearer bond certificates may not exercise his rights for the meeting of bondholders unless he has deposited his bond certificates.

The requirements and procedures required for the notice of convocation in a general meeting of shareholders under the Article 363(1)(2) will apply mutatis mutandis to cases where a company convene a meeting of bondholders. Notwithstanding such application, where a company has issued bearer bonds, it must give a public notice of its intent to convene a meeting of bondholders and the agenda for the meeting three weeks, and two weeks in case of a company with total capital of less than KRW one billion prior to the date of the general meeting of shareholders.[503)]

A meeting of bondholders may elect one or more representatives from among the holders of bonds representing no less than 1/500 of the total amount of the corresponding class of bonds, excluding the amount repaid, and may delegate a decision concerning matters which are to be dealt with by its resolution to him or them.[504)] If two or more representatives have been appointed, a decision must be made by a majority of their votes. A meeting of bondholders may adopt a resolution at any time to remove from office any representative of the meeting or implementer of the resolution and may alter details of any matter delegated to such person.

Any expenses incurred in relation to meetings of bondholders must be borne by the issuer company.[505)] Any expenses incurred in relation to a request for authorization of resolutions under the Article 496 must be borne by the company.

---

500) Article 490 of the Korean Commercial Act.
501) Article 509 of the Korean Commercial Act.
502) Article 491(1) of the Korean Commercial Act.
503) Article 491-2(2) of the Korean Commercial Act.
504) Article 500(1) of the Korean Commercial Act.
505) Article 508(1) of the Korean Commercial Act.

The court may, however, upon the application of any interested person or ex officio, specially determine a person who will bear all or part of such expenses.

2. Voting Right and Resolution

Each bondholder will have the right to vote in proportion to the sum, excluding the amount redeemed, of the corresponding class of bonds he owns.[506) A holder of bearer bond certificates may not exercise his voting rights unless he has deposited his bond certificates at least one week prior to the date set for a meeting of bondholders.

The resolutions by a meeting of bondholders must be adopted by the affirmative votes of at least two thirds of the voting rights of the bondholders present at a meeting of bondholders and of at least one third of the total number of issued and outstanding bonds..[507) Any consent or request under the Articles 481 (resignation and removal of bond administration company) through 483 (successors to affairs of bond administration company) and 494 (requesting issuer company to cause its representative to attend) may, notwithstanding the special resolution above, be decided upon by a majority vote of the bondholders present. A bondholder not attending a meeting of bondholders may exercise his right to vote in writing. To exercise votes in writing, a bondholder must submit a written application specifying required entries to the convocator of the meeting by no later than the day immediately preceding the date set for the meeting of bondholders. The number of voting rights exercised in writing must be included in the number of votes present.

A person who has convened a meeting of bondholders must request that a court authorize a resolution within one week from the date of adoption of such resolution. A court may not authorize a resolution of a meeting of bondholders in the following cases:[508)

(i) If procedures for convening the meeting of bondholders or the manner of adopting the resolution are in contravention of any statute or of any statement contained in the prospectus for offering of bonds,

---

506) Article 492 (1) of the Korean Commercial Act.

507) Article 495(1) of the Korean Commercial Act.

508) Article 497(1) of the Korean Commercial Act.

(ii) If the resolution is adopted in an improper manner,
(iii) If the resolution is considerably unfair, and
(iv) If the resolution is contrary to the general interests of the bondholders.

In cases falling under (i) or (ii) above, the court may authorize such a resolution by taking into account the details of the resolution and all other circumstances.

When a decision has been made either to authorize or not to authorize a resolution of a meeting of bondholders, the company which issued the bonds must, without delay, give a public notice thereof.[509]

A resolution of a meeting of bondholders must take effect by obtaining authorization of a court.[510] However, such authorization may not be required if the resolution is made with the consent of all holders of the class of bonds concerned. A resolution of a meeting of bondholders must be effective vis-a-vis all the bondholders who have the class of bonds concerned.

3. Implementation of Resolutions

A resolution of a meeting of bondholders must be implemented by a bond administration company and, in the absence of such company, by the representatives.[511] However, this may not apply where a person has been appointed to implement the resolution by a resolution of a meeting of bondholders.

IV. Classification of Corporate Bonds

1. Participating Bonds

By expressly providing that a company may issue corporate bonds to bondholders entitling them to participate in distributions of dividends,[512] the KCA

509) Article 499(1) of the Korean Commercial Act.
510) Article 498(1) of the Korean Commercial Act.
511) Article 501 of the Korean Commercial Act.
512) Article 469(2)(a) of the Korean Commercial Act.

establishes a clear basis for the issuance of ‘participating bonds’ (이익참가부사채). A shareholder who has the subscription right for participating bonds is entitled to acquire the participating bonds allocated in proportion to the number of shares held by him. A company must set a specific date and publicly announce that shareholders recorded on the register of shareholders as of the date is entitled to acquire the participating bonds allocated, at least two weeks before the set date. If shareholders have the right to acquire participating bonds, each shareholder must be notified of the amount and issue price of participating bonds, conditions for participation in the distribution of dividends, and the purport that he will forfeit the right to acquire participating bonds if he fails to subscribe for the participating bonds by the specified deadline.

When a company intends to issue participating bonds, its board of directors must determine the following matters, if its Articles of Incorporation do not provide for the matters:[513)]

(i) Total amount of participating bonds,

(ii) Conditions for and details of participation in the distribution of dividends, and

(iii) A statement that shareholders will be granted the right to subscribe for participating bonds and the amount of participating bonds subject to the right of subscription.

However, the foregoing will not apply where the Articles of Incorporation provide that such matters will be determined at a general meeting of shareholders.

When a company intends to issue participating bonds to any person other than shareholders, the value of participating bonds that the company is authorized to issue and the details of participation in the distribution of dividends must be determined by a special resolution adopted at a general meeting of shareholders under the Article 434 of the KCA, if its Articles of Incorporation do not provide otherwise for such matters.[514)]

When a company issues participating bonds, it must register the following matters with the registry having jurisdiction over its main office within two

513) Article 21(1) of the Enforcement Decree of the Korean Commercial Act.
514) Article 21(2) of the Enforcement Decree of the Korean Commercial Act.

weeks after payment is fully made:[515)]

(i) The total amount of participating bonds,

(ii) The amount of each participating bond,

(iii) The amount paid for each participating bond, and

(iv) A statement that the bond holder is entitled to participate in the distribution of dividends, and the conditions for and details of participation in the distribution of dividends.

2. Exchangeable Bonds

As with participating bonds, the KCA establishes a basis for the issuance of 'exchangeable bonds' (교환사채) by expressly providing that a company may issue exchangeable bonds.[516)]

When a company intends to issue exchangeable bonds the holder of which may exchange them with shares or any other securities held by the company, the following matters must be determined by a resolution of its board of directors:[517)]

(i) Classes and details of the shares or securities subject to exchange,

(ii) Conditions for exchange, and

(iii) The period during which exchange may be requested.

When a company intends to issue bonds exchangeable with the issuer's treasury stock, to any person other than a shareholder, matters concerning the party to whom the bonds may be issued must be determined by its board of directors, if its Articles of Incorporation do not provide for such matters. A company that issues exchangeable bonds must deposit shares or securities necessary for exchange in the Korea Securities Depository until the bond holder requests exchange or the end of the period for request for exchange of the bonds, or must electronically register such shares or securities with an electronic registry. In such cases, the Korea Securities Depository or an electronic registry must earmark and manage the shares or securities as trust property.

A person who requests the exchange of bonds must submit two sets of written requests to the company, along with the bond certificates. Such written requests

---

515) Article 21(10) of the Enforcement Decree of the Korean Commercial Act.

516) Article 469(2)(b) of the Korean Commercial Act.

517) Article 22(1) of the Enforcement Decree of the Korean Commercial Act.

must include the class, descriptions, and number of shares or securities subject to exchange and the date of request, and must be affixed with the seal or signature of the requesting person.

3. Redeemable Bonds

The KCA puts an end to debates over whether 'redeemable bonds' (상환사채) may be issued by expressly providing that a company may issue bonds which can be redeemed for shares or other securities.[518] A company issuing redeemable bonds may redeem such bonds and, at its option, repay their principal amount in cash, shares or other securities.

When a company intends to issue bonds redeemable for shares or other securities held by it, the following matters must be determined by its board of directors:[519]

(i) The class and descriptions of the shares or securities with which the bonds are to be redeemed,

(ii) Conditions for redemption,

(iii) A statement that the bonds shall be redeemed in exchange for shares or other securities at the company's option or upon the fulfillment of a certain condition or at maturity.

Where a company intends to issue bonds that may be redeemed in exchange for the issuer's treasury stock, to any person other than a shareholder, matters concerning the party to whom such bonds may be issued must be determined by its board of directors, if its Articles of Incorporation do not provide for such matters. A company that issues bonds redeemable upon fulfillment of a certain condition or at maturity must deposit shares or securities necessary for redemption in the Korea Securities Depository or electronically register such shares or securities with an electronic registry before the fulfillment of a certain condition or the maturity. In such cases, the Korea Securities Depository or an electronic registry must earmark and manage the shares or securities as trust property.

518) Article 469(2)(b) of the Korean Commercial Act.
519) Article 23(1) of the Enforcement Decree of the Korean Commercial Act.

4. Derivative-Linked Bonds

The KCA also establishes a basis for the issuance of bonds for which the redemption or payment amounts are determined according to a pre-determined formula linked to changes in prices of securities, currencies or other assets or indexes designated.[520] This definition and legal basis for 'derivative-linked bonds' (파생결합사채) in the KCA is a citation of the relevant definition for derivative bonds provided under the Article 4(7) of the Financial Investment Services and Capital Markets Act (FISCMA). When a company intends to issue bonds, the value of which redeemable or payable is determined by the predetermined methods linked to the fluctuation of such things as securities, currencies, or other assets or indexes, the following matters must be determined by its board of directors:[521]

(i) The securities, currencies, or other assets or indexes to be linked for determining the amount redeemable or payable, and

(ii) The method for determining the amount redeemable or payable in link with the assets or indexes.

As the language of the aforesaid provision in the KCA places no restriction on the types of underlying assets for the bonds, or the transaction structure or trading venue of the derivatives, it allows a company greater discretion in determining the terms and conditions and the structuring of its derivative-linked bond issuance. However, it must be noted that the Article 469(3) of the KCA provides that specific matters regarding the terms and conditions, the method of issuance and other like matters regarding bonds may be determined by the Enforcement Decree of the KCA. As such, certain restrictions may later be imposed by amendments to the Enforcement Decree of the KCA.

5. Convertible Bonds

A company may issue 'convertible bonds' (전환사채).[522] In such cases, any of the following matters not provided for in the Articles of Incorporation must be

520) Article 469(2)(c) of the Korean Commercial Act.

521) Article 24 of the Enforcement Decree of the Korean Commercial Act.

522) Article 513(1) of the Korean Commercial Act.

determined by the board of directors, unless the Articles of Incorporation provide that it will be determined by a general meeting of shareholders:[523)]

(i) The total amount of convertible bonds,

(ii) Conversion conditions,

(iii) Details on shares to be issued upon conversion,

(iv) The period within which conversion may be requested,

(v) Details on the preemptive rights of shareholders to subscribe to convertible bonds, and the amount of convertible bonds subject to such rights, and

(vi) Details on issuance of convertible bonds to persons other than shareholders, and the amount of such convertible bonds to be issued.

Any shareholder who has the right to subscribe to convertible bonds is entitled to allocation of bonds in proportion to the number of shares that he holds.[524)] In cases where convertible bonds are issued to those who are not the shareholders of a company, if the Articles of Incorporation do not specify the amount of convertible bonds to be issued, conditions of conversion, details of the shares to be issued upon conversion and the period during which the conversion may be requested, such matters must be determined by the special resolution of a shareholders' meeting.

6. Bonds with Warrants

A company may issue 'bonds with warrants' (신주인수권부사채) to subscribe to new shares.[525)] In such cases, any of the following matters that are not provided for in the Articles of Incorporation must be determined by the board of directors, unless the Articles of Incorporation provide that it be determined by a general meeting of shareholders:[526)]

(i) The total amount of bonds with warrants,

(ii) Details of warrants vested to such bonds,

(iii) The period during which the warrants can be exercised,

(iv) A statement on the transferability of the warrants only,

523) Article 513(2) of the Korean Commercial Act.

524) Article 513-2 of the Korean Commercial Act.

525) Article 516-2(1) of the Korean Commercial Act.

526) Article 516-2(2) of the Korean Commercial Act.

(v) A statement to the effect that, upon request of a person who intends to exercise his preemptive right to new stocks, payment of the issuance price of bonds with warrants is deemed made, instead of the redemption of such bonds,

(vi) Details on the preemptive rights to subscribe to bonds with warrants and the amount of bonds subject to such rights, and

(vii) Details on issuance of bonds with warrants to persons other than shareholders and the amount of such bonds with warrants to be issued.

The total issuance price of shares to be issued upon exercise of preemptive right to new stocks vested to each bonds must not exceed the total amount of such bonds with warrant. If, in cases where bonds with warrants are issued to those who are not shareholders, the Articles of Incorporation do not specify the amount of such bonds, the particulars of the preemptive rights to new stocks, and the period during which the preemptive rights to new stocks are to be exercised, these matters must be determined by the special resolution of a shareholders' meeting.

7. Contingent Capital Securities

The FISCMA provides that a listed company may issue so-called 'contingent capital securities' (조건부자본증권).[527] To be more exact, the Article 165-11(1) of the FISCMA provides that a listed company may, by a resolution passed by the board of directors, as prescribed by its Articles of Incorporation, issue bonds with an option to be converted into stocks, or to mitigate the obligations to redeem and to pay interest, upon the occurrence of a trigger event pre-specified based on the objective and reasonable criteria as at the time of issuance of the bonds.

1) Convertible Contingent Capital Securities

A listed company that intends to issue bonds which will be converted to stocks on condition that any ground preliminarily prescribed in accordance with objective and reasonable standards occurs when the relevant bonds are issued

527) Article 165-11 of the Financial Investment Services and Capital Markets Act and the Article 176-12 of its Enforcement Decree.

(convertible contingent capital securities, 전환형 조건부자본증권) must prescribe the following matters in its Articles of Incorporation:[528)]

(i) The purport that it may issue convertible contingent capital securities,

(ii) Total amount of convertible contingent capital securities,

(iii) Conditions of conversion,

(iv) Types and contents of stocks to be issued by conversion,

(v) The purport that the preemptive rights of convertible contingent capital securities shall be given to shareholders, and the amount of convertible contingent capital securities which are the subject-matter of the preemptive rights, and

(vi) Matters concerning the issuance of convertible contingent capital securities to persons other than shareholders, and the amount of convertible contingent capital securities issued for them.

Where any convertible contingent capital securities are issued, the grounds for the conversion of the relevant convertible contingent capital securities to stocks will be those that can be indicated by the price, indicator, unit or index that can be computed or observed by a reasonable method or incidents such as timely corrective measures,[529)] and such grounds, etc. must fulfill all of the following guidelines:

(i) The grounds, etc. must be highly unlikely to be changed or occur by usual efforts of a person related to the issuance of convertible contingent capital securities, such as the issuer and any shareholder or investor of the issuer, and shall comply with the requirements prescribed and publicly notified by the FSC,

(ii) The grounds, etc. must be sufficiently notified or announced to the public through the securities market, etc. in accordance with the guidelines and methods prescribed and publicly notified by the FSC.

In issuing any convertible contingent capital securities, a listed company must register them at the registrar for the issuance. A bond subscription form and a bond register of convertible contingent capital securities must specify the following:

(i) The purport that the convertible contingent capital securities may be converted

---

528) Article 176-12(1) of the Enforcement Decree of the Financial Investment Services and Capital Markets Act.

529) This is defined in detail by the Article 10(1) of the Act on the Structural Improvement of the Financial Industry.

to stocks,

(ii) Grounds for and conditions of conversion, and

(iii) Types and contents of stocks to be issued by conversion.

The conversion of convertible contingent capital securities to stocks takes effect on the third business day from the date any ground for conversion occurs. Where a listed company issues any convertible contingent capital securities, it must register the following matters at the location of its head office within two weeks from the date the payment is completed:[530)]

(i) Total amount of convertible contingent capital securities,

(ii) Amount of each convertible contingent capital securities,

(iii) Payment amount of each convertible contingent capital securities, and

(iv) Matters referred to in a bond subscription form and a bond register above, such as the purport that the convertible contingent capital securities may be converted to stocks, grounds for and conditions of conversion, and types and contents of stocks to be issued by conversion.

2) Bail-In Contingent Capital Securities

A listed company that intends to issue bonds with conditions that the obligation to redeem the bonds and to pay the interests thereof must be mitigated upon the occurrence of any trigger event specified in accordance with objective and reasonable standards when the relevant bonds are issued (bail-in contingent capital securities, 상각형 조건부자본증권) must prescribe the following matters in its Articles of Incorporation:[531)]

(i) The purport that it may issue bail-in contingent capital securities,

(ii) Total amount of bail-in contingent capital securities,

(iii) Conditions of mitigation of the obligation to redeem bonds and pay interests thereof (debt readjustment),

(iv) Contents of bail-in contingent capital securities to be changed due to debt readjustment.

---

530) Article 176-12(6) of the Enforcement Decree of the Financial Investment Services and Capital Markets Act.

531) Article 176-13(1) of the Enforcement Decree of the Financial Investment Services and Capital Markets Act.

A bond subscription form and a bond register of bail-in contingent capital securities must specify the following:[532)]

(i) The purport that the bail-in contingent capital securities may be subject to debt adjustment,

(ii) Grounds for and conditions of debt adjustment, and

(iii) Contents of bail-in contingent capital securities to be changed due to debt adjustment.

The debt adjustment of bail-in convertible contingent capital securities to stocks takes effect on the third business day from the date any ground for debt adjustment occurs.

V. Other Considerations

1. Prior to the rounds of amendments to the KCA, there was debate over whether the KCA provisions regarding corporate bonds should be read as restrictive or illustrative provisions.[533)] Regulators often took the view that the relevant KCA provisions were restrictive provisions that specifically list the types of corporate bonds permitted for issuance, interpreting the provisions to mean that issuances of any types of corporate bonds not so specified are not permitted. Such views were also criticized for hampering the ability of companies to obtain more varied and expedient funding options. For example, companies had found it difficult to issue newer types of financial instruments having the nature of corporate bonds that had emerged with the continuous development of capital markets. However, after the amendments to the KCA, it now specifies that the provisions enumerating the types of corporate bonds that may be issued are illustrative provisions, by stating that the term 'bonds' includes the bonds listed under the Article 469(2) of the KCA.

2. As exemplified by the aggregate amount of non-guaranteed bonds issued in the Korean capital markets, there is growing demand for the use of corporate

---

532) Article 176-13(2) of the Enforcement Decree of the Financial Investment Services and Capital Markets Act.

533) Chung Chan-Hyung, *op. cit.*, p.1265; Choi Junesun, *op. cit.*, p.675.

bonds as a means of corporate financing. Since the KCA establishes a legal basis for the issuance of various types of corporate bonds, an increased use of corporate bonds as funding methods can be expected, as well as an expanded scope of the types of corporate bonds, due to offerings of new financial products. Further, since the emergence of new types of corporate bonds in the capital markets will give rise to legal issues, including how to coordinate the interests of concerned parties such as shareholders, and legal issues and needs associated with the introduction of a new regulation system, companies need to proceed the issuance of corporate bonds with the assurance of legal issues when considering the use of various types of corporate bonds as funding methods or as offerings of new financial products.

VI. Case Study on Issuance of Convertible Bonds[534)]

1. Main Issues

(1) Whether a right of action for nullification of the issuance of convertible bonds is available under the KCA (affirmative) and how the grounds for nullification are determined.

(2) When convertible bonds are issued to persons other than stockholders, what degree of specificity is needed in conversion conditions stated in the Articles of Incorporation, by which a requirement of a special resolution by a general meeting of stockholders is overridden.

(3) The case holding that the issuance of convertible bonds cannot be nullified since it satisfies the minimum requirements under the Article 513(3) of the former KCA where the Articles of Incorporation specifies the issuance of convertible bonds that "the board of directors shall determine the conversion price at or above the face value of a stock at the time of issuance of bonds."

(4) Whether a new ground for nullification may be added after the time limit for bringing an action for nullification of the issuance of new stocks (negative)

---

534) Supreme Court Decision 2000Da37326, decided on June 25, 2004.

and whether the same legal principle is applicable to the claim for nullification of the issuance of convertible bonds (affirmative).

(5) The grounds for nullification in the claim for nullification of the issuance of convertible bonds.

(6) The case holding that outstanding convertible bonds or shares issued by the exercise of convertible rights cannot be nullified just because subscribers of convertible bonds have special relationships with dominant stockholder of the company, or the conversion price is relatively low when compared to the stock price at the time of issuance.

2. Summary of Decision

1) The Article 516(1) of the KCA provides that the Article 424 pertaining to the right to enjoin for the issuance of new stocks and the Article 424(2) pertaining to the liability of subscribers of stocks at unfair prices, etc. shall apply mutatis mutandis to the issuance of convertible bonds (CBs). However, the KCA does not take any position as to the applicability of the Article 429 pertaining to an action for nullification of the issuance of new stock to the issuance of convertible bonds. However, since the issuance of CBs, the bond with the right to convert into stocks in the future by the exercise of convertible rights, affects material resources of a stock company and economic relationships among preexisting stockholders, it is similar to the issuance of new stocks and thus, the Article 429 pertaining to action for nullification of the issuance of new stocks of the KCA shall be deemed to apply to the issuance of CBs by analogy. Under that circumstance, a specific cause for nullification as a means for an individual right of action, alleged by the parties, cannot but be decided on the basis of its individual nature. However, since the fact that there are grounds for nullification of the issuance of CBs itself constitutes one cause of action, multiple unlawful factors mentioned as grounds for nullification of the issuance of CBs should be considered holistically in the determination as to whether the issuance of CBs is void.

2) The Article 513(3) of the former KCA (amended by Act No. 6488 of July 24, 2001) provides that if the Articles of Incorporation does not provide for the

amount of CBs to be issued, its condition, stocks to be issued by conversion, the conversion period for the issuance of CBs to persons other than stockholder, then they shall be determined by resolution pursuant to the Article 434 of the KCA. Thus, in order to issue CBs without a special resolution of the general meeting of stockholders on the ground that the conversion conditions are already stated in the Articles of Incorporation, the conversion conditions must be stated specifically in the Articles of Incorporation. However, in case a stock company chooses, among various means of financing, to issue CBs to persons other than stockholders to raise funds so as to meet its capital needs, it is more desirable for the stock company to determine the conversion conditions such as the conversion price flexibly, depending on the amount of necessary funds and how urgently they are needed, the market price of the issuing company's stock, and concrete economic circumstances including the interest rate and market conditions. Thus, the same and conclusive conversion conditions need not be stipulated, beforehand, in the Articles of Incorporation for all occasions, since the provisions in the Articles of Incorporation could be amended only by the special resolution of the general meeting of stockholders. Accordingly, the delegation method is permissible, such that a specific conversion condition is determined by the board of directors within the limit prescribed in the Articles of Incorporation at each issuance of CBs with the general standards of conversion set forth in the Articles of Incorporation.

3) The case holding that the issuance of convertible bonds cannot be nullified on the ground that the criterion or delegation method is too abstract or broad, considering special factors related to determination of conversion conditions such as the conversion price, since it satisfies the minimum requirements under the Article 513(3) of the former KCA (amended by Act No. 6488 of July 24, 2001), where the Articles of Incorporation specifies as to the issuance of convertible bonds that “the board of directors shall determine the conversion price at or above the face value of a stock at the time of issuance of bonds” and such provision delegates the determination of specific conversion price at each time of issuance of CBs to the board of directors with the general criterion of “same as or above the face value of a share” as to the conversion price among other conditions specified in the Articles of a corporation as required under the Article 513(3) of the same KCA.

4) Under the Article 429 of the KCA, only stockholders, a director or an auditor can file an action for the nullification of the issuance of new stocks and they can do so only by filing a legal action within 6 months from the issuance of new stocks. This provision purports to stabilize complex juristic relations accompanying the issuance of new stocks in the early stage. If a new ground for an action for the nullification of the issuance of new stocks were allowed after the time limit for bringing an action, the purpose of the above provision would be ineffective since the juristic relation remains unstable. For that reason, the above provision restricts the right to bring a new ground for an action. On the other hand, the application of the Article 429 of the KCA, by analogy, allows a legal action for the nullification of the issuance of CBs. Thus, the requirement of filing within 6 months applies to such cause of action as to CBs and as a consequence, a new ground of asserting the nullification of the issuance of CBs cannot be added after the lapse of the six month time limit for bringing an action.

5) The Article 429 of the KCA, governing an action for nullification of the issuance of new stocks does not specify grounds for the nullification. On the other hand, since the Article 424 of the KCA, applicable mutatis mutandis, to the issuance of CBs provides "the issuance of stocks against the rules of law or the Articles of Incorporation or by conspicuously unfair methods" as an element for the injunction for issuance of new stocks, such element may be considered as a ground for the nullification of the issuance of CBs. However, once CBs are issued, subscribers' interests need protection, and since CBs or stocks converted from CBs circulate as securities, of the transactions need to be safely protected. Compared with the right to enjoin the issuance of CBs as a preventive remedy against an unlawful issuance, the grounds for claiming a nullification of the issuance of CBs must be interpreted as strictly as possible since the nullification after the issuance poses a threat to the stability of transactions and the rule of law. As a consequence, the issuance of CBs or issuance of stocks by the exercise of convertible rights shall be nullified only if the case involves circumstances where severe violations of law or the Articles of Incorporation and conspicuous unfairness goes against the essential characteristics of a stock company or the basic principles underlying corporate law, or affects preexisting stockholders' interests and management control rights over the company and the

extent of such circumstance can hardly be tolerated as overriding the concerns over transaction stability as to CBs or interests of stockholders or other persons concerned. Therefore, the grounds for nullification should not be limited only to the circumstance where it is objectively clear that CBs are issued solely for the purpose of causing a change in management rights or preventing such change, including currently pending or imminent disputes over the right of management.

6) The case holding that already issued convertible bonds or stocks issued by the exercise of convertible rights cannot be nullified just because subscribers of convertible bonds have special relationships with dominant stockholders of the company, or the conversion price is relatively lower when compared to the stock price at the time of issuance.

3. Conclusion

Therefore, the appeal shall be dismissed, and all costs of the appeal shall be assessed against the losing party. This decision is delivered with the assent of all justices who reviewed the appeal.

Related Legal Issues and Questions:

1. What kinds of corporate bonds are available under the Korean Commercial Act in Korea?
2. How can a company issue corporate bonds?
3. What is the legal requirements and procedures for issuing corporate bonds?

CHAPTER 12

BANKING AND FINANCE LAW

The 1997 and 2008 financial crises of Korea have resulted in significant reforms for the financial and banking sectors. Law based reforms have covered all of banking and financial institutions and created a competitive, safe and sound banking and financial system. Meanwhile, even though traditional and commercial banks are providing internet banking services as one of additional services, Korea's new internet-only banking system attracts public attention for the better banking service and the more profitable business than an existing internet banking. In this Chapter, it is important to understand what regulations of banks and internet-only banks must be considered, and what are different each other.

I. Introduction to Banking and Finance Law[535)]

The late 1997 financial crisis of Korea have resulted in significant reforms for the financial and banking sectors, including new banking regulatory framework. Korea suffered the serious turmoil in 1997 both as to individual financial institutions and the Korean banking and financial system in general. Since then, Korea has implemented more actively law-based financial reforms. One of more distinctive reforms has been for financial institutions to be consistent with international financial standards or best practices in their regulations. Nevertheless, Korea suffered another serious financial crisis along with the 2007-2008 subprime mortgage crisis of the U.S., revealing its susceptibility to international financial crises. The 2008 financial crisis has also caused another reform in Korea's ongoing financial and banking regulations.

535) This Chapter has been updated from my publication as "The Current Banking Regulations in Korea on the Legal Perspective, Sungkyunkwan Journal of Science & Technology Law, VOL. 6 No. 2, Fall 2012."

A look back on the history of the financial sector reforms in Korea shows that the Government's financial reforms since the early 1990s have focused primarily on financial deregulation and financial market liberalization.[536] Financial reform measures concerned with deregulation have covered interest rate deregulation, expansion of powers of financial institutions and of their sources of funds, managerial autonomy of financial institutions, realignment of business scope, and lowering of entry barriers for domestic and international institutions. Under these financial reform measures, Korea has been prudently attempting to strengthen its financial regulations, particularly since the turn of the 1990s. These financial reforms since the 1990s, especially after the 1997 financial and banking sector reforms, marked the beginning of a new banking system and bank structure quite different from anything Korea had ever had before.[537]

This Chapter is concerned mainly with these recent law-based banking reforms and current banking regulations out of financial and corporate reforms effected through the banking sector in Korea. In order to get through the banking sector regulations in Korea, it is important to understand the Banking Act (은행법) of Korea, which is the most important law for the regulation and operation of the general commercial banks and the foreign banks in Korea. The Banking Act of Korea, which generally governs regulations for banking activities and foreign banks, has been amended up to now to provide bank restructuring, and better bank management and operation of general commercial banks. Amendments to the Banking Act and other relevant legislations have been mainly concerned with overcoming the then-exiting financial crisis and problems, making Korea's banking and financial institutions safe, sound and competitive, and adopting internationally accepted standards of bank supervision. These amendments have strengthened the responsible bank management system through re-regulation of bank ownership and of the non-executive director ratio. The Banking Act provides for the annulment of an approval system in regard to the opening, closing and moving of a bank branch.[538] It also directly regulates the branches and representative offices of foreign banks.

---

536) Sang Hwan Lee & Chan Moon Park, "Korea," Banking Regulatory Review, Law Business Research, 2010, p.179.

537) Byung-Tae Kim, Korea's Banking Law Reform: Post Asian Crisis, Kluwer Law International, 2003, p.22.

538) Young Shim, Korean Bank Regulation and Supervision: Crisis and Reform, Kluwer Law International, 2000, pp.11-14.

In turn, some core issues for enhancing competitiveness of banking institutions and for promoting sound and safe bank regulations are dealt with as the main subjects in the Banking Act of Korea, which will be also reviewed separately below.

II. Korean Banking and Financial System in General

1. General Regulations on Banking and Finance

The Korean banking system has been modernized and developed along with other diversified financial systems for non-banking institutions since the 1950s, and it has been positioned on and regulated by the gradually united financial system of Korea in relation to all the Korean financial institutions including non-banking financial and foreign financial institutions. Historically, the modern banking system of Korea and the creation of a viable banking sector started when the National Assembly approved the drafts for the Bank of Korea Act and the Banking Act in April 1950. At that time, a new central bank, the Bank of Korea, came into being on June 12, 1950, and the commercial banks began to be reorganized under the Banking Act.[539)]

Under this evolving modern banking system, banking institutions of Korea have been developed and liberalized according to the implementation of Government steered economic development plans. Since the early 1980s, however, the Korean Government has pursued a policy of deregulation designed to increase the efficiency of the local financial industry and to cope with the ongoing internationalization of the domestic financial markets.[540)] As a result of various economic and political changes, the banking system has been undergoing a slow transition from a central control to a more market-driven order. Keeping in step with the previous financial and banking reforms, the consecutive reform measures

---

539) Bang-Shik Lee, Central Banking System (in Korean), July 1994, p.67. In history, there were several old style financial institutions (*e.g.*, *Kaegju*, *Yeokaeg*, or *Kae* in Korean language) in Korea before its modern banking and financial system. In 1878, the First National Bank, a Japanese bank, was established, and it engaged in modern banking practices including the issuance of bank notes. Also, a bank called the Bank of Korea was founded in 1909 to function as a central bank under Japan's domination *(id.,* p.68). However, they were all Japanese banks, not Korean ones.

540) Tae Hee Lee, "Special Report," Special Supplement of the International Financial Law Review, September 1991, p.128.

have focused on the banking restructuring and the new bank supervisory system, especially trying to avoid further difficulties in the banking and financial sectors.

In general, financial institutions in Korea consist of six categories:
(i) banks (*e.g.*, commercial banks and specialized banks),
(ii) non-bank depository institutions (*e.g.*, mutual savings banks, credit cooperatives including credit unions, community credit cooperatives and mutual banking entities, merchant banks, and the postal savings),
(iii) financial investment business entities (*e.g.*, securities and futures companies, collective investment business entities, investment advisory and discretionary investment business entities, and trust business entities),
(iv) insurance companies,
(v) other financial institutions (*e.g.*, financial holding companies, credit specialized financial companies, venture capital companies, securities finance companies, public financial institutions, and others), and
(vi) financial auxiliary institutions.[541)]

Banking institutions are further divided into two types according to the objectives and governing laws of each type (i) the commercial banks which consist of the commercial nationwide banks, the commercial local banks, and foreign bank branches, and (ii) the specialized banks. The principal legal difference between a commercial nationwide bank and a local bank is its geographic business scope (*i.e.*, a nationwide bank having a nationwide operation and a local bank not having a nationwide operation) and its minimum capital (*i.e.*, KRW one hundred billion for a nationwide bank and KRW twenty-five billion for a local bank).[542)] The principal practical difference is that a nationwide bank is normally more efficient than a local bank in scale of operations and level of profitability. Also, a nationwide bank is more active in foreign exchange business, whereas a local bank relies much more heavily on investment in domestic securities for revenues.

A foreign bank in Korea including its branch and representative office would be covered under one of the commercial bank categories. A foreign bank in Korea is chartered under the Banking Act, and its activities are primarily

541) Bank of Korea, "Financial Institutions in Korea as of December 2015," December 2015.
542) Article 8(2) of the Banking Act.

approved under this Act.[543] For commercial banks, including foreign banks, the formation of new domestic banks or foreign bank branches is subject to the Financial Services Commission (FSC, 금융위원회) approval under the Banking Act.[544] Additional banking business such as foreign exchange and trust activities by banks may need another approval by the Ministry of Economy and Finance (MOEF) under the Foreign Exchange Transactions Act and under the Trust Business Act.

In the Korean banking system, the Bank of Korea (BOK, 한국은행) acts as a central bank in Korea. It performs the usual functions of a central bank, serving as an issuer of bank notes and coins, banker to the banking sector, banker to the Government and controller of the money supply. Under the Bank of Korea Act, the BOK consists of three key bodies,[545] which are (i) the Monetary Policy Committee, (ii) the Governor of the BOK, and (iii) the Auditor.[546] However, the BOK, a central bank in Korea, has been reshaped by such financial reforms since 1998.

Most importantly with regard to the structure of the BOK, the Bank Supervisory Board, one of the BOK's bodies responsible for the bank supervision under the old Bank of Korea Act, was removed from the BOK and transferred to the newly established the FSC which merged all financial supervisory functions for bank, securities and insurance sectors.[547] Before the financial reforms to the 1997 crisis were carried out, the Bank Supervisory Board of the BOK, which was subject to the instructions of the Monetary Board, was in charge of the supervision and regular examination of banking institutions according to the old

543) Article 58 and 59 of the Banking Act.

544) Article 8(1) and 58 of the Banking Act.

545) Article 12, 33 and 43 of the Bank of Korea Act.

546) Prior to the financial crisis of 1997, the Bank of Korea consisted of four important bodies under the old Bank of Korea Act, which were (i) the Monetary Board, (ii) the Governor of the Bank of Korea, (iii) the Bank Supervisory Board, and (iv) the Auditor. Under the old Bank of Korea Act, the Monetary Board initially formulated monetary and credit policies, exercised other functions and powers explicitly granted to it, and was responsible for the general direction and supervision of the operation, management and administration of the Bank of Korea. The Bank Supervisory Board was, under instructions from the Monetary Board, responsible for the supervision and periodic examination of banking institutions. The supervision for non-banking financial institutions such as securities companies and insurance companies was executed by a separate Board which was the Security Supervisory Board and the Insurance Supervisory Board according to each of its own Acts. *See* Bang-Shik Lee, *id.*, p.68.

547) Article 3 of the Act Concerning Establishment of Financial Supervisory Organizations.

Bank of Korea Act. However, under the financial reform of December 1997, the FSC, a newly established committee is now in charge of the supervision and regular examination of banking institutions since April 1998.

[Korean Banking and Financial Sectors as of June 2022][548)]

Financial Sectors		**No.**
Bank Supervisory Entity	Financial Services Commission (FSC) and Financial Supervisory Service (FSS)	
Central Bank	Bank of Korea (BOK)	
Banks	Domestic Banks	20
	Foreign Bank Branches	35
Insurers	Life Insurance Companies	23
	Non-life Insurance Companies	29
Investment Companies	Securities Companies	58
	Futures Companies	4
	Asset Management Companies	382
	Investment Advisory Companies	342
	Real Estate Trust Companies	14
	Merchant Banks	1
Credit-specialized Financial Companies	Credit Card Companies	8
	Leasing Companies	26
	Installment Finance Companies	23
	New Technology Venture Capital Companies	82
Mutual Savings		79
Credit Union and Cooperatives	Credit Union	873
	Agriculture Cooperatives	1,115
	Fisheries Cooperative	91
	Forestry Cooperatives	142
Financial Holding Companies		10

548) Financial Statistics Information System (FISIS), "Number of Companies by Financial Sector," at <https://efisis.fss.or.kr>.

The Korean banking system had basically followed the historic US Glass-Steagall Act[549)] model with respect to separation of commercial investment banking functions. Commercial banks accepted deposits, issue loans and guarantees, administered trusts and performed limited money management and exchange risk-hedging services, but their ability to market bonds and commercial paper was restricted.[550)] However, since Korea legislated the Financial Holding Company Act (FHCA, Law No. 6274, 금융지주회사법)[551)] in October 23, 2000 which has a legal affiliation among bank holding companies, securities firms, and insurance companies, Korea now has new and different regulations about commercial banking business functions under the new FHCA.[552)]

On the surface, the Korean banking system resembles that of many OECD countries; but behind the scene Government intervention through so-called window guidance and other informal channels has remained important and necessary for the development of the country's economy. Traditionally, the Korean Government was involved directly or indirectly in the banking system through the MOFE (now MOEF) and the BOK. Even though the BOK, the primary regulatory agency, sought, in recent years, greater autonomy to become a central bank, the MOFE still had the strongest voice over the functions of the BOK and the banking system. For example, prior to the financial crisis of 1997, the Minister

---

549) Under the historic Glass-Steagall Act of the U.S., banks had limited securities powers. Banks could only underwrite Government debt, but they could do brokerage. Banking affiliates (non-bank subs of BHCs) could do more. For example, they could underwrite corporate debt and equity securities through so called 20 subsidiaries, so long as they were not engaged principally in these activities. However, the Gramm-Leach-Bliley Act (GLBA) enacted in November 1999 expressly repealed of the Glass-Steagall Act, which formerly imposed substantive restrictions on bank affiliations with securities firms. In turn, the US now has a legal affiliation among bank holding companies, securities firms, and insurance companies. For a more detailed discussion of the GLBA, *see* Joseph J. Norton, "Gramm-Leach-Bliley Act of November 1999: Overview of Selective Legislative and Regulatory Issues," Essay in International Financial and Economic Law, CCLS-London, 2000 and *see* also Hal S. Scott & Philip A. Wellons, International Finance Transactions, Policy and Regulation (7th edition), 2000, pp.95 and 100.

550) Byoung Kook Min, Chang Hee Lee and James M. West, "Special Report," International Financial Law Review: Special Supplement, September 1992, p.76.

551) For reference, the U.S. Bank Holding Company Act (BHCA) of 1956 defines the Bank Holding Company as the company that owns or controls one or more banks or other bank holding companies. In the US, such companies must register with the Board of Governors of the Federal Reserve System. Bank Holding Companies can do activities closely related to banking under the Article (4)(c)(8) of the BHCA (Hal S. Scott & Philip A. Wellons, *op. cit.,* p.138).

552) Bank Department of the Bank of Korea, "Study on the Introduction of the Financial Holding Company," April 2000.

of Finance and Economy presided over the Monetary Board of the BOK which determined monetary policy.[553] It is worth noting, however, that this historically distinctive feature of the Korean Government's intervention and practical control over banks was also important for a Governmentally receptive bank supervision and management. The Korean Government controlled many parts of banking activities through the holding of bank stocks or by the appointment of presidents of banks.

However, there were fundamental changes in the central banking system since the new Korean financial reform which was passed at the end of 1997. These changes included reforms for a more sound and competitive banking and financial system and for the liberalization and internationalization of the financial system, focusing on independence for the central bank. According to the new Bank of Korea Act regarding the independence of the BOK and the Monetary Policy Committee (MPC), the governor of the BOK serves concurrently as the chairman of the MPC, excluding the Governmental intervention by the MOFE (now MOEF). Moreover, in a major effort to liberalize the banking sector, the Government has turned over the ownership of major national commercial banks to private hands. Along with the denationalization of commercial banks, the Banking Act has been revised several times so far to provide banks a freer hand in dealing with their own managerial affairs in order to boost their public accountability by setting upper limits on the ownership of bank stocks per shareholder.

Moreover, at the end of 1995, Korea legislated a new law, the Depositor Protection Act (DPA, 예금자보호법, Law No. 5042) for a stronger bank deposit insurance scheme.[554] In turn, under the DPA, bank depositors have been protected by a new bank deposit insurance system from January 1, 1997 in the case of any bank bankruptcies. This bank deposit insurance system, in large, still makes the banking system of Korea safe and sound and even stronger.

In addition, in order to reorganize the regulations on the capital markets and financial investment sector, six existing laws addressing the capital markets, including the Securities and Exchange Act, the Indirect Investment Asset

---

553) Article 39 of the old Bank of Korea Act.

554) In fact, whenever banks carried large bad loans and had financial problems in the past, the Government and the BOK had consistently bailed them out without any special insurance fund to pay for the bail-outs.

Management Business Act and the Trust Business Act, were bundled into the Financial Investment Services and Capital Markets Act (FISCMA) in August 2007 and enforced in February 2009, By encouraging financial innovation and competition through the reorganization of regulations on the capital markets and financial investment companies, as well as expanding the direct financing market through measures such as the cultivation of large-scale investment banks and revitalization of the capital markets, the FISCMA aimed to create a foundation fostering harmony within the existing system of indirect financing centered around banks.[555] This expansion and systemic reorganization of the capital markets since the mid-2000s has led to a remarkable growth in new securities related institutions.

2. Recent Reforms for Banking and Financial Regulations

Over the past 25 years since the financial crisis in late 1997, Korea has implemented a series of law-based banking and financial reforms in order to secure safe and sound domestic financial markets and institutions. A most recent part of these series of financial sector reforms has been the amendments of a major law, the Banking Act, with respect to the prudential supervision and regulations for banks.

The Banking Act (은행법) was enacted on May 5, 1950 (Act No. 911) in order to contribute to stability of the financial markets and development of the national economy by ensuring the sound operation of banks, by elevating the efficiency of their financial intermediary functions, by protecting the depositors, and by maintaining an order in credit transactions. This Act was greatly amended on January 13, 1998 (Act No. 5499) right after the Korea's 1997 financial crisis and then has arrived at its present form as the result of being amended many times. The latest amendment was on April 20, 2021, Act No. 18128.[556]

The Banking Act is an act that ensures the sound operation of financial institutions, the efficiency of the fund brokerage functions, consumer protection and maintenance of the order of credit. The Act covers various kinds of financial institutions except the Bank of Korea, which are engaged in lending funds raised

555) Bank of Korea, Financial System in Korea, December 2018, p.13.

556) Even though the Banking Act has been also amended even more times in order to be arranged by other law amendments, minor changes could be relatively disregarded since other laws' amendments are not the Banking Act's own changes.

by bearing debts from many unspecified persons through the receipt of deposits and issuance of securities and other bonds.[557] The Banking Act consists of 12 Chapters and 69 Articles.

After the 1997 financial crisis and the IMF arrangement, and the 2008 another financial crisis, there have been several amendments to the Banking Act, in particular, distinctive recent amendments on April 27, 2002 (Act No. 6691), May 17, 2010 (Act No. 10303), March 29, 1016 (Act No. 14129) and December 7, 2021 (Act No. 18573).

III. Distinctive Issues on Bank Regulations

1. Bank Supervision

In Korea during the 1997 financial crisis, it was necessary to set up a strong and independent supervisory institution, strengthen and consolidate prudential supervision, and increase transparency in order to overcome the crisis. In turn, the bank supervision system greatly changed during the 1997 financial crisis, and the new Act Concerning the Establishment of a Financial Supervisory Body was legislated in December 29, 1997 for this purpose. Based on this Act, the new financial system brought together financial supervisory functions which were distributed among the MOFE (now MOEF), the BOK, the Securities Supervisory and the Insurance Supervisory Board, establishing a separate financial supervisory institution (i.e., the FSC) for all of them.

Why is this single watchdog for financial supervision necessary in the Korean financial situation? First of all, under the previous complicated supervisory system, it was difficult for supervisors to investigate fully the details of financial scandals occurring among different financial sectors and to resolve problems arising from them.[558] Looking back at the then-experience with financial supervision, there were many mistakes in supervising each financial institution by a separate supervisory body, and there had been many corporate and bank

557) Article 2(1) of the Banking Act.

558) Research Department of the Bank of Korea, "The Main Points of Reshaping the Central Banking and Financial Supervision System in Korea," January 1998.

bankruptcies. Also, as the global economy tended toward universal banking and the development of complex financial products like financial derivatives, it was necessary to establish an agency which could supervise and examine all financial institutions of which functions and products are different from each other.[559)]

Under these circumstances, Korea adopted a new bank supervision system. The new bank supervision system means a change of the supervisory entity for banks. Before the new financial reform of 1997 became effective, supervisory powers were distributed among the MOFE, the BOK, the Securities and Exchange Commission, the Securities Supervisory Board and the Insurance Supervisory Board. However, under the Act Concerning the Establishment of a Financial Supervisory Body in effect, a new financial supervisory entity, the Financial Services Commission (FSC, 금융위원회), was established under the Prime Minister and merged three supervisory offices of banks, securities companies and insurance companies.[560)] In turn, the Office of Bank Supervision (OBS) of the BOK was merged into the Financial Supervisory Service (FSS, 금융감독원) of the FSC, which was established in 1999 as prescribed by the Presidential Decree.[561)]

Under the new Act, the FSC consists of nine members. Three of them are ex-officio members: the Vice Minister of Finance and Economy, the Deputy Governor of the BOK, and the President of the Korea Deposit Insurance Corporation (KDIC, 예금보험공사).[562)] The other six members consist of the Chairman and Vice Chairman of the FSC[563)] who are appointed by the President, and four general members who are appointed by the President on the recommendation of the each of the pertinent organizations. The duties of the newly established FSC are to deliberate and resolve the main aspects of financial supervision, such as enactment and revision of regulations concerning supervision

---

559) Bank of Korea, *op. cit.* and Young Shim, *op. cit.*, pp. 84-86.

560) Article 3 of the Act Concerning the Establishment of a Financial Supervisory Body. The issue where the FSC should be positioned was in high debate when it was legislated. After a long discussion, it was decided that it should be established under the Prime Minister because the Government is the last entity responsible for the financial supervision.

561) From April 1, 1998 on which the Act was in effect for an interim period until the FSS was established, the Office of Bank Supervision had been separated from the BOK and established as a special juridical person with no capital.

562) Article 4 of the Act Concerning the Establishment of a Financial Supervisory Body.

563) The Chairman is appointed by the President on the deliberation of the State Council, and the Vice Chairman is appointed by the President on the recommendation of the MOEF. *See* Article 4 of the Act Concerning the Establishment of a Financial Supervisory Body.

of financial institutions, securities and futures market, and authorization of business-related matters of financial institutions. The FSC also directs and supervises the operations, administration and management of the FSS.[564)]

On the one hand, the FSS of the FSC is a special juridical person with no capital and performs directly the examination and supervision of financial institutions under the direction of the FSC and the Securities and Futures Commission.[565)] Until the establishment of the FSS, its function had been performed by four supervisory bodies (the OBS of the BOK for commercial banks, the Securities Supervisory Board for securities companies, the Insurance Supervisory Board for insurance companies and the Credit Management Fund for other non-bank financial institutions).[566)] The FSS has as its executive officers one Superintendent, four Deputy Superintendents, nine Assistant Superintendents and one Auditor.[567)] The Chairman of the FSC serves concurrently as the Superintendent of the FSS.

After such restructuring of a single supervision system even since 1998, it is noted that there have still been many arguments regarding the BOK's potential role for bank supervision which is completely transferred to the FSC and the FSS.

2. Bank Ownership Regulation

1) Restrictions on Bank Ownership under the Banking Act

Through the recent banking and financial reforms including bank restructuring and mergers since the financial crisis of 1997, the bank ownership and structure

---

564) Financial Supervisory Commission and Financial Supervisory Service, Financial Reform and Supervision: 2001, June 2001, pp.23 and 24, and *see* also the Articles 3, 17 and 18 of the Act Concerning the Establishment of a Financial Supervisory Body.

565) The Securities and Futures Commission (SFC) was established in the FSC and is in charge of investigation of unfair trading in securities and futures market, and the pre-deliberation of matters concerning the supervision of securities and futures market before the deliberation and resolution by the FSC.

566) However, the Office of Bank Supervision (OBS) of the BOK had been split off from the BOK and established on April 1, 1998 as a special juridical person (Research Department of the Bank of Korea, *op. cit.*). The OBS performed the examination and supervision of the banks for a temporary period under the direction of the FSC.

567) Article 29 of the Act Concerning the Establishment of a Financial Supervisory Body.

have greatly changed, and the ownership limitations have been re-arranged. As a result, while anyone intending to become the largest shareholder of a bank or the largest shareholder intending to relinquish this status had to obtain approval from the FSC under the old Banking Act until 1999, this provision was deleted under the new Banking Act. With respect to the holding limits of a banking institution's stocks, the Banking Act now provides only for the stockholding limit by the same person, and any stock hold beyond that limit is subject to approval by the FSC.

Under the main rule of the stockholding limit of a bank, one stockholder and a person in a special relationship with him (same person) cannot hold or actually control more than 10/100 (15/100 in case of a local bank) of the total number of the issued voting stocks of a bank.[568)] This rule includes a holding by the same person in his own or another's name, or the exercise of the voting right in collusion.

However, there are several important exceptions to the ten percent main rule (10% rule). The 10% rule does not apply to cases falling under any of the following, and the report to the FSC or the approval by the FSC is required for these exceptions:[569)]

(i) Where the Government and the KDIC hold stocks of the banks and where the holding is less than 15/100 of the total number of the issued voting stocks of a local bank.

(ii) The same person may hold stocks of a bank by obtaining approval from the FSC, whenever the limits are exceeded. However, the FSC may grant approval by setting the separate limits of stockholdings, only where it is deemed necessary in view of the possibility to contribute to the efficiency and soundness of banking business, the stock distribution of stockholders of the relevant bank, etc., and if the same person intends to hold stocks in excess of the approved limit, he must obtain approval again from the FSC: 10/100, 25/100, or 33/100 of the total number of issued voting stocks of the relevant bank.

(iii) Where a non-financial business investor intends to hold the stocks of a bank in excess of 4/100 of the total number of issued voting stocks of a bank, and he becomes the largest stockholder of a bank (excluding a local bank) or

568) Article 15(1) of the Banking Act.

569) Articles 15(1) through (4) of the Banking Act.

participates in the management of the relevant bank by appointing or dismissing its executives, he must obtain approval from the FSC.[570] Otherwise, no non-financial business investor may hold more than 4/100 of the total number of issued voting stocks of a bank (15/100 in cases of a local bank), notwithstanding the Article 15(1) of the Banking Act.[571]

Nevertheless, the 10% rule and its exceptions of the Articles 15(1) and (3) of the Banking Act will apply to any of the following non-financial business investors, where (i) a non-financial business investor who has submitted to the FSC a plan for converting itself into a person who is not a non-financial business investor within two years and has obtained approval therefor, (ii) a non-financial business investor who holds stocks within the scope of the stockholding ratio of a bank by a foreigner under the Foreign Investment Promotion Act, or (iii) a non-financial business investor who has obtained approval from the FSC by satisfying the certain requirements as a fund under the Article 5 of the National Finance Act or a juristic person managing and operating the fund.[572]

In particular for foreign banks, there is one special provision in the Article 16-5(1) of the Banking Act. When judging whether a company mainly conducting banking business overseas or the same person including a holding company of the relevant juristic person, the stocks or stakes of which are held directly or indirectly by the relevant foreign bank, etc. may be excluded from the scope of the same person.[573]

For any exceptions above, the FSC has the authority to review and reject any proposals to transfer significant ownership or controlling interests in existing banks to other parties. Where the FSC refuses to accept a report or does not grant approval with respect to the exceptional stockholding of a banking institution, it must specify and notify such causes to the applicant within the period of 60 days.[574] The qualifications for any person capable of holding stocks of the banks, the requirements and procedures for the report or the approval related to stockholding and other necessary matters are determined in detail by

570) Article 15-2 of the Banking Act.

571) Article 16-2(1) of the Banking Act.

572) Article 16-2 of the Banking Act.

573) Article 16-5(1) of the Banking Act.

574) Article 15(4) of the Banking Act.

the Presidential Decree in consideration of the propriety of the size of assets and financial status, the size of loans from the relevant financial institution, and the possible contribution to the efficiency and soundness of the banking business.

The FSC has also power to order the person holding stocks of banking institutions beyond the stockholding limit to dispose of such stocks beyond the relevant limit within a specified period of not more than six months.[575)]

2) Distinguished Feature of Bank Ownership Regulation

The bank ownership limit for a single person has been relaxed since the 2002 amendment to the Banking Act. The bank ownership limit for a shareholder and any associate(s) who has a special relationship with such shareholder has been raised to ten percent from previous four percent. The old Banking Act put the bank ownership ceiling at four percent for domestic investors, compared with ten percent for foreign investors. Such different treatment has drawn criticism from domestic investors who insisted that the previous Banking Act discriminated against local investors.[576)] The Banking Act also now allows any shareholder and his associate(s) who has a special relationship with such shareholder to own stocks of a bank in excess of 10 percent of the total voting stocks of the banking institution concerned upon the approval of the FSC.

The bank ownership limit for a business conglomerate has been especially and separately regulated. Under the Banking Act, business conglomerates or industrial corporations known as *Chaebols* in Korean are prohibited to own stocks of a bank in excess of four percent of the total voting stocks of the bank concerned (in excess of fifteen percent in case of local banks). However, they may own up to ten percent of the capital stock of a bank upon the approval of the FSC, provided that they do not exercise their voting rights for shares exceeding the four percent ceiling. This is to prevent business conglomerates from using banking institutions as their private coffers.[577)]

Despite previous amendments to the Banking Act, Korea has never altered its position that industrial companies, especially as to the top business conglomerates (*i.e.*, *Chaebols*), should not own commercial banks. If industrial companies were

---

575) Article 16(3) of the Banking Act.
576) Byung-Tae Kim, Korea's Banking Law Reform: Post Asian Crisis, *op. cit.*, p.183.
577) *Id.*, p.184.

to control banks, they might exploit the bank assets recklessly, as if from their private vaults. They could also restrict the operating activities of rival companies through the control of the banks. For these reasons, bank ownership by industrial companies had never been allowed. However, the previously existing limitation on bank ownership had a tendency to suppress the participation of all domestic capital rigidly, not just industrial capital, in bank management.[578] Currently, there is one important exception to the holding limit of four percent for business conglomerates or industrial corporations. Those companies can now hold up to thirty four percent in the cases of internet-only banks, which will be discussed separately below in detail.

The FSC's active regulations on stocks exceeding the ceiling have been provided for in the Banking Act. The Banking Act requires the FSC to examine any shareholders who secure ten percent ownership of a bank or higher. When they fail to comply with the holding requirements of stocks exceeding the ceiling, the FSC may order them to dispose of the stocks in excess of the ceiling.

In relating to bank ownership regulations in the past, there were some dishonorable cases which could be very arguable between interested parties due to unclear and unfair bank regulations. For example, they are the cases of the Newbridge Capital's holding stocks of the Cheil Bank and the Lone Star Funds' holding stocks of the Foreign Exchange Bank of Korea.[579] In particular, the Lone Star Funds case has raised whether it was a non-financial business investor under the Article 16-2 of the Banking Act or not since our old banking act was not clear on this issue, and the FSC's approval of the excessive holding of bank stocks by the Lone Star Fund has been also criticized by many professional. On August 2022, the International Center for Settlement of Investment Disputes (ICSID) made its final decision in an investment-state dispute (ISD) between the Korean Government and Lone Star Funds and Korea lost the case.[580]

---

578) As a result, by the amendment to the Banking Act in April 2002, Korea expanded the cap on bank shareholdings to nine percent from the previous four percent. Nevertheless, industrial capital was not allowed to exercise voting rights on shares exceeding the four percent level. However, the ownership ceiling on local banks remained at the current level of fifteen percent. After that, the next another amendment to the Banking Act returned nine percent back to four percent ceiling.

579) Dong-Wook Won, "The Situation and Future Tasks of the Korean Banking Law (in Korean)," The Korean Journal of Financial Law, Vol. 8 No. 1, 2011, p.312.

580) Korea Times, "Korea ordered to pay Lone Star $216.5 mil. in investor-state suit," August 31, 2022. The ICSID has ordered Korea to pay $216.5 million to the

3. Corporate Governance for a Bank

Corporate governance structures for a bank have been undergoing large scale transformations in the past decade with the introduction of outside directors, audit committees and compliance officers. As a corporate governance of a bank, the Banking Act had regulated the qualification of executives of a bank, restriction on concurrent posts held by executives, prohibition on divulgence of confidential information, composition and powers of the board of directors, establishment of audit committees, internal control standards and internal regulations on controlling structure of a bank, etc., but most provisions on a governance by the Banking Act has moved to the Act on Corporate Governance of Financial Companies (ACGFC, 금융회사의 지배구조에 관한 법률) since the ACGFC was enacted on July 31, 2015 (Act No. 13453).

The executives of a bank are important persons to operate and manage a bank and to be able to protect consumers. They have to be persons who have experience and knowledge in finance and who are unlikely to impede the public interest, sound management and order of credit of the bank. In turn, no person falling under any of the followings cannot be an executive of any bank, and if he falls hereunder after becoming one, he must relinquish such office:[581)]

(i) A minor, a person under adult guardianship, or a person under limited guardianship,

(ii) A person declared bankrupt but not yet reinstated,

(iii) A person in whose case five years have not passed yet since imprisonment without labor or heavier punishment to which he was sentenced was completely executed (or is deemed to have been completely executed) or was remitted,

(iv) A person who was sentenced to the suspension of imprisonment without labor or heavier punishment, and is still in the period of suspension,

(v) A person in whose case five years have not passed yet since a fine or heavier punishment to which he was sentenced under the ACGFC or any other finance-related statutes was completely executed (or is deemed to have been completely executed) or was remitted,

---

Texas-based private equity firm Lone Star Funds, virtually putting an end to the decade-long legal battle.

581) Article 5 of the Act on Corporate Governance of Financial Companies.

(vi) A person who serves and served as an executive officer or an employee of a financial company in which case five years have not yet passed since any of the following measures was taken against the company (limited to persons specified by Presidential Decree as directly liable for the cause of such measures or those reasonably responsible for such measures):

(a) Revocation of permission or authorization for, or registration, etc. of, business under a finance-related statute,

(b) A measure of timely correction under the Article 10(1) of the Act on the Structural Improvement of the Financial Industry, and

(c) An administrative disposition under the Article 14(2) of the Act on the Structural Improvement of the Financial Industry,

(vii) A person in whose case the period specified by Presidential Decree not exceeding five years for each category of sanctions has not yet passed since a sanction (including a notice equivalent to the relevant measure, in cases of an executive officer or an employee who has already retired or resigned from office) was taken against him under any finance-related statute for his conduct as an executive officer or an employee, and

(viii) A person specified by Presidential Decree, by whom public interest and sound management of the relevant financial company or credit order are likely to be undermined.

A bank must appoint not less than three directors ('outside directors') who are not engaged in the general affairs of the board of directors. In such cases, the number of outside directors must be a majority of the total number of directors.[582] All directors must satisfy certain qualifications, including a standard known as the pit and proper test that generally examines directors' integrity and managerial ability.[583]

For the effectiveness of bank management, previous restrictions on concurrent posts held by bank officers have been released. Previously, no officer or employee of a bank could be an officer or employee of its subsidiary. The ACGFC now permits bank employees or officers to hold concurrent posts at such bank's subsidiaries.[584] However, previous restrictions on certain concurrent posts

582) Article 12(1) of the Act on Corporate Governance of Financial Companies.

583) Sang Hwan Lee & Chan Moon Park, *op. cit.*, p.182; Articles 5 and 6 of the Act on Corporate Governance of Financial Companies.

584) Article 10(3) of the Act on Corporate Governance of Financial Companies.

held by officers remain under the ACGFC: for example, no officer or employee of a bank may be an officer or employee of the Bank of Korea, other financial institutions or bank holding companies.[585] However, this rule does not apply to any of the exceptions under the Article 10 of the ACGFC.

On the other hand, any executives or employees (including those who were executives or employees) of a bank must neither divulge any confidential information or data that he became aware of in the course of his duty (including large stockholders of a bank or specially related persons with the relevant large stockholders) nor use them for the purposes other than a business purpose.[586]

As one of the most important changes in bank regulations, a bank must set fundamental procedures and standards which is called as 'Internal Control Standards' (내부통제기준) to be followed by its executives in performing their duties to observe laws and subordinate statutes, to ensure its sound management, and to protect its stockholders and depositors. A bank must appoint, as 'Compliance Officer,' (준법감시인) at least one person assigned to monitor whether the Internal Control Standards are observed and to investigate and report any violation of the Internal Control Standards to the audit committee.[587] A bank also must stipulate specific principles and procedures which is called as 'Internal Regulations on Corporate Governance' (지배구조내부규범) to be observed in connection with the operation of its board of directors in order to protect its stockholders and users.[588] For this purpose, all banks have been adopting the Standards of Internal Regulations on Corporate Governance which was established by the Korea Federation of Banks on January 26, 2015.[589]

Other matters on the corporate governance of financial companies including a bank are also regulated under the ACGFC and so it can be referred for the other regulations and further details.

---

585) Article 10(3) of the Act on Corporate Governance of Financial Companies.

586) Article 21-2 of the Banking Act.

587) Article 25(1) of the Act on Corporate Governance of Financial Companies.

588) Article 14(1) of the Act on Corporate Governance of Financial Companies.

589) *See* Korea Federation of Banks, Standards of Internal Regulations on Corporate Governance, January 26, 2015.

4. Banking Business Regulation

1) Scope of Banking Business

Under the Banking Act and its regulations, banks are permitted to engage in all services in banking business (은행업무) within the scope prescribed by the Banking Act and other related laws. Currently, there are 3 categories of banking business in which the banks may be engaged; (i) core banking business, (ii) incidental banking business, and (iii) concurrent banking business.

(1) First, as a core business (고유업무), a bank may be basically engaged in (i) receipt of deposits and saving deposits, and issuance of securities and other debentures; (ii) loans of funds or discount of notes; (iii) domestic and foreign exchange.[590)]

(2) Second, as an incidental business (부수업무), a bank may be engaged in all services incidental to banking services;[591)] (i) guarantee of debts or takeover of notes; (ii) mutual savings; (iii) factoring (referring to purchase and recovery of bonds on sales price of a company and affairs related thereto); (iv) safeguard deposits; (v) execution of collection and payment as an agent; (vi) credit depository of a local Government as an agent; (vii) execution of payment related to electronic commercial transactions as an agent; (viii) sale and lease of computer systems and software related to banking business; (ix) training on finance and publication of books and periodicals on finance; (x) investigations and research on finance; (xi) other incidental services to banking services (for example, lease of real estate for business purpose, sale of revenue stamps, lotteries, gift certificates, etc. as an agency, and advertisement utilizing physical facilities such as the Internet webpage, books, publications, computer facilities, etc. of a bank as an agency).[592)]

Where a bank intends to be engaged in incidental services, it has to file a report thereon with the FSC within seven days prior to the date on which it

---

590) Article 27(2) of the Banking Act. This Article was wholly amended by Act No. 10303, May 17, 2010.

591) Article 27-2 of the Banking Act. This Article was newly inserted by Act No. 10303 on May 17, 2010.

592) Article 18(1) of the Presidential Decree of the Banking Act.

intends to start such services. Such report must be accompanied by documents including business plans, documents on forecast profits and losses, etc.[593] Where such reported details fall under one of (i) where they undermine soundness in the management of the bank in question, (ii) where they cause hindrance to the protection of bank users, such as depositors, or (iii) where they undermine the stability of financial markets, the FSC may order the restriction or correction of the relevant incidental services.

(3) Third, as concurrent business (겸영업무), a bank may directly run the certain business other than banking business:[594] (i) Financial business prescribed by Presidential Decree among business requiring authorization, permission, or registration under finance-related acts and subordinate statutes prescribed by Presidential Decree. For example, sale, purchase and brokerage of derivatives; sale and purchase of derivatives-combined securities; underwriting and sale of state bonds, local Government bonds and special bonds; sale and purchase of state bonds, local Government bonds, special bond, and corporate bonds; brokerage of subscription and sale of state bonds, local Government bonds and special bonds; collective investment business; investment advisory business; trust business; investment brokerage business of collective investment securities; business of a general administrative company; business of a transfer agent; business of an insurance agency; business of a retirement pension business operator; credit card business; and trust business for secured bonds,[595] (ii) Finance-related business provided for in finance-related statutes that are permitted for a bank to run under the finance-related statutes,[596] and (iii) Financial business prescribed by Presidential Decree that has no risk of falling under any incidental businesses above even if a bank operates such businesses. For example, entrustment of the

593) Article 27-2(3) of the Banking Act. In detail, the following documents must be accompanied with the report: (i) An operational plan, (ii) An estimated statement on profits and losses, (iii) Articles of Incorporation, (iv) A copy of the minutes of the board of directors that has resolved on the operation of incidental services, and (v) Other documents determined and publicly notified by the FSC, related to the operation of incidental services (*see* Article 18(2) of the Presidential Decree of the Banking Act).

594) Article 28(1) the Banking Act. This Article was wholly amended by Act No. 10303 on May 17, 2010.

595) Article 28(1) the Banking Act and Article 18(2) of the Presidential Decree of the Banking Act.

596) Article 28(1) the Banking Act and Article 18(3) of the Presidential Decree of the Banking Act.

management of securitization assets and debt collection of a special purpose company; entrustment of the management of securitization assets and debt collection of a special purpose company for mortgage-backed bonds; brokerage, mediation, or agency services of the merger and acquisition of enterprises; counseling and support services concerning the management, corporate restructuring and finance of enterprises; investment and loan transactions of securities; sale of commercial bills and trade bills; sale of financial products of a person who runs the financial business pursuant to finance-related statutes and trade insurance as an agent; brokerage, intermediation, or agency for loans and for sale and purchase of loan claims; business affairs that can be conducted in accordance with the related statutes of a country in which an overseas branch is located (limited to cases where the relevant overseas branch conducts the business affairs); other business affairs determined and publicly notified by the FSC that are unlikely to fall under any incidental businesses above.[597)]

Where a bank intends to directly run concurrent business, it has to file a report thereon with the FSC. If the reported details undermine soundness in the management of the bank, cause hindrance to the protection of depositors, or undermine the stability of financial markets, the FSC may order the restriction or correction of the relevant concurrent businesses.

2) Regulatory Structure of Banking Business

Prior to the amendment of the Banking Act in 2010, the details of the scope of banking business were strangely regulated by the Banking Act, its Presidential Decree, and Guideline by MOSF (currently MOEF) and the FSC in separate format. While the core business and the concurrent business were regulated by the Banking Act and its Presidential Decree, the incidental business was regulated by MOSF and by FSC as a different format. Banks' incidental business were described in the Guideline of the Scope of Banks' Incidental Business proclaimed by the MOFE (the former MOSF and currently MOEF) since 1998,[598)] which had been previously described in the Directives by the BOK. This caused inefficient and unsound bank supervision and regulations. As a result, the power

---

597) Article 28(1) the Banking Act and Article 18(4) of the Presidential Decree of the Banking Act.

598) Dong-Won Ko, “Legal Review on Regulations on the Scope of Banking Business in Korea (in Korean),” The Korean Commercial Law Review, Vol 26 No.3, 2007, p.188.

of decision-making of the scope of incidental business was transferred from the MOFE to the financial supervisory authorities, the FSC.

Banks' incidental business was again regulated in the Guideline from 2008 since then by the FSC which had more access to market information. Finally, since the Banking Act was amended on November 15, 2010 and the Guideline of the FSC was abolished on November 16, 2010,[599] it is now regulated in the Banking Act and its Presidential Decree together with other core business and concurrent business. In turn, all banking businesses, no matter what they are, are now described at one place in the Banking Act and its Presidential Decree.

5. Prudential Regulation

A bank must ensure soundness in its management by making its equity capital solid and maintaining appropriate liquidity in running banking business. While the Banking Act empowers the FSC to set forth the management guidance regulations for matters concerning the adequacy of capital, the soundness of assets, the liquidity, and other matters necessary for securing the sound management of a bank in the FSC's determining the standards for management guidance, it requires the FSC also to reflect the principle of supervision as recommended by the BIS over the soundness of financial institutions.[600]

As for the adequacy of capital of a bank, Korea has adopted, since July 1992,[601] the capital adequacy ratio of the bank against risk-weighted assets based on the criteria of the International Convergence of Capital Measurement and Capital Standards (so-called 'Basel Capital Accord')[602] of July 1988 by the Basel Committee on Band Supervision (the 'Basel Committee'). The Basel Capital Accord of 1988 was amended in June 1999,[603] but the Basel Committee

599) FSC Announcement, No. 2010-40, November 16, 2010.

600) Article 34(2)(3) of the Banking Act.

601) In July 1992, Korea adopted the capital adequacy ratio of the Basel Capital Accord, and since late 1995 it has required banking institutions to have at least the ratio of 8%. *See* FSC, "BIS Ratio Rises Again, Approaches Advanced Standards," June 18, 2012.

602) For more discussion of the Basel Capital Accord of 1988, *see* Joseph J, Norton, Devising International Banking Supervisory Standards, Graham & Trotman / Martinus Nijhoff Publishers, 1996.

603) Basel Committee on Banking Supervision, "A New Capital Adequacy Framework," Basel Committee Publications No. 50, June 1999.

presented a more concrete proposal, reflecting the parties' comments and the results of ongoing dialogue with the industry and with supervisors worldwide. Through the new Basel Capital Accord (Basel II) of 2004,[604] the Basel Committee has issued the Basel III rules text in 2010, which presents the details of global regulatory standards on bank capital adequacy and liquidity agreed by the Governors and Heads of supervision, and endorsed by the G20 Leaders at their November Seoul summit.[605] The standard has been revised to address issues that the Basel Committee identified in the course of monitoring the implementation and impact of the framework. This final standard incorporates changes that were proposed in a March 2018 consultative document and has been informed by a quantitative impact based on data as of end-December 2017. After the post-crisis regulatory reforms, the Minimum Capital Requirements for Market Risk now replaces an earlier version of the standard as published in January 2016. The adjustments to the market risk framework were endorsed by the by the group of Central Bank governors and heads of supervision on January 14, 2019.[606] This revised standard came into effect on January 1, 2022. The revised standards will make banks more resilient and restore confidence in banking systems.

At present, through the amendments of the Banking Act and relevant Regulations of the FSC, Korea has incorporated market risks in calculating the capital adequacy ratio. The capital adequacy ratio of a bank in Korea must not be currently less than 8% against risk-weighted assets based on the criteria of the Basel Capital Accord.[607] In practice, the capital adequacy ratio of Korea's commercial banks has risen continuously since the financial crisis of 1997, and as of the September 2022, it stands at more than 13 percent.[608] This rise is attributed to the positive effects of continued restructuring and to financial institutions' larger profits and less loan loss provision due to the disposal of the non-performing loans. Reviewing it in detail, domestic banks' common equity

---

604) Basel Committee on Banking Supervision, “Overview of The New Basel Capital Accord,” Consultative document issued for comment by 31 May 2001, January 2001.

605) Bank for International Settlements (BIS), “Basel III: International framework for liquidity risk measurement, standards and monitoring,” Press Release, December 2010.

606) The Basel Committee, “Minimum Capital Requirements for Market Risk,” January 14, 2019.

607) Article 26(1) of the Rules of Bank Supervision of the FSC.

608) Financial Supervisory Service, “Capital Ratios of Banks and Bank Holding Companies, Third Quarter 2022,” Press Release, December 6, 2022.

Tier 1 (CET1) capital ratio stood at 12.26% as of end-September 2022. The Tier 1 capital ratio was seen at 13.51% and total capital ratio was 14.84%. Meanwhile, leverage ratio stood at 6.09%.[609] Though the domestic banks' capital ratios satisfy regulatory requirements, however, they should get prepared for more volatile financial markets and worse economic situations at home and abroad.

If the FSC finds that a bank is likely to seriously undermine soundness in its management, including a failure to meet such management guidelines, or that it is inevitable to maintain the soundness in management, it may request the bank to take necessary measures for improving business management, such as increasing capital, restricting dividends of income, securing assets with high liquidity, and issuing and holding a certain amount of contingent bonds under the Article 33(1)(b) through (d) of the Banking Act.[610]

Meanwhile, no bank can extend credit exceeding 25/100 of the relevant bank's equity capital to the same individual, corporation or person.[611] The Banking Act also prohibits a bank from extending loans to the large shareholder in excess of the credit ceiling within the limit of twenty five percent of such bank's total capital.[612] Where a bank wishes to extend loans in excess of the credit ceiling to the large shareholder, such bank is required to get the approval of its board members in order to do so. A bank's maximum purchasing limit of shares of a large shareholder has been set within one percent of a bank's capital.[613] The Banking Act blocks a bank from owning shares in its large shareholders worth more than one percent of the bank's capital. Previously, there was no such limit. Where a bank wishes to purchase shares in its large shareholders in excess of

---

609) [Banks' Capital Ratios, September 2022] (in percentage)

	Dec. 2019	Dec. 2020	Dec. 2021	Jun. 2022	Sep. 2022
CET1 capital ratio	11.46	12.45	12.99	12.71	12.26
Tier 1 capital ratio	12.30	13.47	14.18	13.95	13.51
Total capital ratio	13.91	15.00	15.53	15.30	14.84
Leverage ratio	6.42	6.41	6.50	6.24	6.09

[Source: Financial Supervisory Service, "Capital Ratios of Banks and Bank Holding Companies, Third Quarter 2022," *id.*]

610) Article 34(4) of the Banking Act and this was lastly amended on March 29, 2016.

611) Article 35(1) of the Banking Act.

612) Article 35-2 of the Banking Act.

613) Article 35-3 of the Banking Act.

the purchase ceiling, such bank is required to obtain the approval of its board members in advance to do it.

Additionally, a large stockholder of a bank must not perform any of the following acts with intent to make personal gain, contrary to the bank's interests:[614)]

(i) Requesting the bank to present its internal data or information not yet disclosed to the general public with intent to exercise any undue influence. However, this will not apply to the exercise of rights under the Article 33(6) of the ACGFC and the Article 466 of the KCA,

(ii) Exercising undue influence over personnel affairs or management of the bank in collusion with another stockholder on condition of providing any such consideration as economic gains, etc.,

(iii) Exercising influence over the management of bank, such as requesting it to make the early recovery of credit from a rival company with intent to interfere with the business activities of the rival company,

(iv) Credit granted from a bank in excess of the 25/100 credit granting limit for a large stockholder of a bank,

(v) Extending credit from another bank by causing a bank to violate the 25/100 credit granting limit for a large stockholder of a bank,

(vi) Extending credit by causing a bank to violate the prohibition of any extension of credit to support investment of a large stockholder of a bank in another company,

(vii) Causing a bank to violate the prohibition of any acts which gratuitously transfer its assets to a large stockholder of a bank, or trade or exchange its assets or extend credit to or with a bank under substantially unfavorable conditions compared with ordinary terms and conditions of transactions.

(viii) Causing a bank to possess stocks of its large stockholder in excess of the 1/100 acquisition limit on equity securities issued by a large stockholder, and

(ix) Other acts prescribed by Presidential Decree, equivalent to those defined in (i) through (iii) above.

---

614) Article 35-4 of the Banking Act and this was lastly amended on July 31, 2015.

6. Foreign Bank Regulation

1) Foreign Banks in General

Modern financial and banking institutions of Korea have been developed and liberalized according to the implementation of Government-steered economic development plans since they were created and reorganized with relevant laws and by the Government in the 1950s. Accordingly, foreign banks (외국은행) in Korea have been expanded directly in relation to such economic development and the Government's favorable rules and plans toward them.[615] The first foreign bank under the Korean modern banking system is the Korean branch of Chase Manhattan Bank of the U.S., which was established in Korea in 1967. Though there were several Japanese bank branches before the modern banking starting point of 1950, they were not regarded as real foreign bank branches in Korea's modern banking system.[616]

Before foreign banks were introduced in Korea, Korean domestic financial institutions were not ready to compete with foreign banks or in international financial markets. In turn, the Korean Government made policies to allow foreign banks to establish their branches in Korea, sometimes with some strong limitations or sometimes without limitations. In order to motivate domestic banks into improving their banking practices and managerial skills, the Government allowed additional foreign bank branches to open in Korea since 1981.

Since their arrival in Korea in 1967, foreign bank branches (외국은행 국내지점) have taken a large share of the domestic financial market and have realized high profits as a result of various privileges and of their competitive positions.[617] However, the continued relaxed and improved rules have eventually led to an altered environment and financial market in which Korean domestic banks and foreign bank branches could compete. These changes also improved existing unequal competitive conditions by reducing privileges for both domestic and foreign bank branches and relaxing cumbersome regulations.

---

615) Tae Hee Lee, *op. cit.*, p.128.

616) Seog Roon Lee and Jung Soo Lee, Korean Banking Institutions (in Korean), 1997, p.230.

617) Korea Development Bank, "KDB Data Plaza: Foreign Banks in Korea," available at <http://www.kol.co.kr/~kdbmst/ focus/for_bank.html>.

2) Regulations for Foreign Banks

Even before the new financial reforms after Korea's recent financial crisis, the Korean Government had implemented a detailed financial market open policy and had proceeded to allow foreign banks to do various kinds of businesses in Korea.[618] Compared with the past financial reforms, however, the Korean Government's recent reforms since December 1997 have been to pursue a stronger and sounder financial system, to follow international trends and to enhance the foreign bank regulation. Accordingly, while only branches and representative offices could be established under the old Banking Act,[619] the subsidiaries of foreign banks were allowed in the 1997 financial reform package under consultation with the IMF after the financial crisis in 1997.[620]

In fact, according to the ‘Government's Banking and Financial Market Open Schedule’ of 1996, the new form of a Korean subsidiary by a foreign banking institution was supposed to be allowed beginning in December 1998.[621] However, Korea's then-existing recent financial crisis caused this schedule to be decayed and to take effect beginning with the date of the new financial reform. According to the Letter of Intent by the Government of Korea, the Government announced that it would allow foreign financial institutions to purchase equity in domestic banks without any restrictions.[622] This meant that 100 percent ownership by foreign financial institutions could be allowed. Following the Government's foreign bank-related policies, the Banking Act was amended, on December 29, 1997, in order to allow subsidiaries or joint ventures by foreign banking and financial institutions.

In addition, based on the 1997 Agreement with the IMF, the Government has

---

618) Dong-Won Ko, *op. cit.*, p.12.

619) Under the old Banking Act which was effective until the financial reform of 1997, foreign banking institutions could enter into Korea in the form of a branch or representative office. That is, the old Banking Act and the Foreign Capital Inducement Act operated to bar foreign banks from either acquiring a controlling interest in national banks or establishing their subsidiaries. Therefore, a subsidiary or any other form was not allowed until the new financial reform was put into practice at the end of 1997. However, there was one exception for the limited forms of foreign banks in Korea. In 1983, the KorAm Bank was formed as a joint-venture bank between Bank of America of the U.S. and several Korea's most renowned companies. *See* Byoung Kook Min, Chang Hee Lee and James M. West, *op. cit.,* p.38.

620) Government of Korea, “Letter of Intent of the Government of Korea,” December 3, 1997, available at <http://www.imf.org/external/np/loi/120397.htm>.

621) Ministry of Finance and Economy(MOFE), “Effect of OECD Membership and Future Tasks,” October 1996, p.38.

622) Government of Korea, *op. cit.*

been rapidly removing restrictions on M&A activity in the financial sector to facilitate troubled banks. In reality, there were many M&A cases among banks during the implementation of the recent financial reforms. According to this policy and relevant law amendments, foreign banking institutions could merge with domestic banks.

By the restructure of the Korean banking system and banking sector which referred to foreign banks, most banking rules and policies may also be now applied directly to foreign banks. For example, foreign banks in Korea, like other domestic banks, are now supervised by a single watchdog, the FSC and are insured by the KDIC subject to the compulsory bank deposit insurance system. Even though foreign banks had been treated unequally in certain cases compared with domestic banks and may have had some privileges or some restrictions,[623] they are now basically regarded as financial institutions under the Banking Act, and foreign bank branches in Korea are treated equally with domestic banks once foreign bank branches are established in Korea.[624] Therefore, through Korea's several reforms for foreign banks, especially the 1997 financial reform, their national treatment in Korea has been getting stronger according to international standards.

Relating to the foreign bank supervision, however, the legal status of a foreign bank branch or representative office in Korea for the supervision purpose is not clear. This problem is whether or not a foreign bank branch (or representative office) is an entity which is legally separate from its parent bank and whether or not the parent bank is liable on a deposit placed in its foreign branch.[625] A foreign bank branch is an integral part of the foreign banking institution and acts as a legal and functional extension of such parent bank.[626] A branch does not have a legal personality separate from that of the parent bank.[627] However, in the common law world, the separate entity doctrine has been accepted, implying

---

623) Lee Ik Joo, "Foreign Banks in Korea (in Korean)," Monthly Review of the Korea Exchange Bank, Vol XXV No.7, July 1991.

624) Article 59(1) of the Banking Act.

625) This legal status problem is raised only in a foreign bank branch or representative office, but mainly in a foreign bank branch. Another form such as a subsidiary has no such problem because a subsidiary is separately capitalized in the host country and is legally liable for the deposit at its own risk.

626) Edward L. Symons and James J. White, Banking Law (3rd edition), West Publishing Co., 1995, p.737.

627) *See* Committee on Banking Regulations and Supervisory Practices, Revised Basle Concordat on Principles for the Supervision of Bank's Foreign Establishments, May 1983, p.2. It defines branches as operating entities that do not have a separate legal status and are thus integral parts of the foreign parent bank.

that the deposit would be legally payable only at the foreign branch.[628]

In the United States, one common thread running through relevant New York cases holds that in regard to business transactions between a parent and its foreign branch, the branch must be considered a separate entity.[629] However, recent decisions explicitly reject a separate entity principle, emphasizing that there is a general banking principle that the parent bank is ultimately liable on a deposit placed in its foreign branch.[630]

In Korea, even though there is no clear-cut guideline about the legal status of a foreign bank branch in Korea, the Banking Act provides that any branch office of a foreign bank must hold the whole or part of its assets in Korea under the conditions as prescribed in the relevant Presidential Decree.[631] In addition, if a branch office of a foreign bank is liquidated or becomes bankrupt, its assets, capital, reserve funds and other surplus must be appropriated preferentially for performance of obligations held by citizens of Korea and by foreigners who are domiciled or resident in Korea.[632] In this case, since the provisions of the Banking Act concerning the capital of banking institutions is applied to foreign bank branches, a branch's operating funds are deemed as its own capital.[633] With respect to a foreign bank's branch, the following operating funds are deemed as a branch's capital: (i) Funds in Korean currency supplied for a branch of a foreign bank by selling funds in foreign currency by its head office to the BOK for the establishment of the branch and business activities, (ii) Funds transferred from the reserves by a branch of a foreign bank, (iii) Funds transferred from earned surplus carried forward by a branch of a foreign bank already established in Korea to establish an additional branch of the foreign bank, (iv) Funds in Korean currency raised by selling funds in foreign

628) Edward L. Symons and James J. White, *op. cit.,* p.774.

629) Pan-American Bank & Trust Co. *v.* National City Bank, 6 F.2d 762 (1925) 269 U.S. 554, 46 S.Ct. 18, 70 L.Ed.408. Also, the International Banking Act of 1978 treats branches of foreign banks in the U.S. as separate entities for many purposes. *See* 12 U.S.C.A. 3102.

630) In Sokoloff *v.* National City Bank of New York, 130 Misc, 66, 224 N.Y.S. 102 (1927), affirmed 223 A.D. 754, 227 N.Y.S. 907 (1928), affirmed 250 N.Y. 69, 164 N.E. 745, the court found that although a branch is a separate entity in the sense that it maintains its own books and repays deposits only at its own office, the overall relationship of a parent to its branch is not one of independence and that [u]ltimate liability for a debt of a branch would rest upon the parent. *Cf.* United States v. First National City Bank, 379 U.S. 378, 85 S.Ct. 528, 13 L.Ed.2d 365 (1965).

631) Article 62 (1) of the Banking Act.

632) Article 62 (2) of the Banking Act.

633) Article 63 of the Banking Act.

currency by a branch of a foreign bank to the BOK, and (v) Funds operated in Korea, among those borrowed from the head office or overseas branch of a foreign bank with a maturity of more than one year.[634)]

In other case, the single customer loan limit constrains foreign branches' operations in twenty or twenty five percent of the branches' capital rather than of the parent bank's capital.[635)] In this regard, the Banking Act treats foreign bank branches in Korea as separate entities from their parent banks for many purposes.

7. Implication to the Regulations on Banking and Financial Institutions

As a result of financial reforms after the recent 1997 and 2008 financial crises, there have been great changes in both Korea's financial system and banking sector regulations. There have been desperate efforts in Korea to develop the Banking Act through its amendments for the efficient and sound banking sector in Korea. Bank supervision is now governed by a single committee, the FSC, over banks, securities companies and insurance companies since the Government has established a unified financial regulatory agency with operational and financial autonomy. The bank deposit insurance scheme has been strengthened to protect depositors against recent bank bankruptcies or mergers. Even foreign banks can now establish their subsidiaries as well as participate in joint venture banks with Korean partners because regulations for the foreign financial institutions have been favorably changed.

However, there are still very arguable controversies and conflicts for Korea's bank regulations. For example, there are still many controversies between the BOK and the FSC regarding the role for the efficient bank supervision. Also, despite of the regulation of an outside director of a bank under the Banking Act, it is reported that in practice, outside directors of a bank are unaware of the role to be successful. In particular, since there were unclear reform package and emergency measures during the financial reforms, the dishonorable case of Lone Star Funds[636)] has raised a fundamental legal leak and weakness, and, fortunately,

---

634) Article 26 of the Presidential Decree of the Banking Act.

635) Article 35 of the Banking Act.

636) For more information on the case of the Lone Star Funds in Korea, *see* National Assembly Research Service, "Sale of Stocks by the Lone Star Fund and Non-financial Business Operators or Not? (in Korean)," Issue & Point, No. 325, November 17, 2011 and Korea Times, *op. cit.*, August 31, 2022.

more prudent and clear provisions of the bank ownership regulation have been realized in the Banking Act.

In addition, while it goes without saying that Korea keeps putting more efforts making sound and safe banking and financial system and regulations on the national level, it is also important to cope with the repeated financial crisis on the world, which could be affecting Korea's financial market and banking regulations. The contagion effects of one country's financial crisis could be affecting financial and currency markets in neighbor countries and eventually all over the world, and magnifying fundamental political, financial and economic problems. This may not be a story only for Korea and its financial market, but applicable to all countries and their economies. Despite generally improved economic conditions and a long period of healing after the failure of Lehman Brothers, progress toward global financial stability has recently experienced a setback. This is why in recent years, there has been an explosion in both international banking and financial activity and the need for international rules as to how the business of international banking and finance should be conducted and regulated. Based on this reality, an international consensus on the requirements for a sound financial system has been developed due to the growth of international co-operation and the necessity for the establishment of minimum standards, and the realization of the importance of domestic financial stability.

Lastly, Korea should continue to suffer the ordeal of financial reform and bank restructuring in order to provide the impetus for building an internationally competitive advanced economy even in the further centuries. As a goal and for the best results, law-based reforms on the national level including short term as well as long term reforms should be continued in line with international banking and financial standards and their further developments if any.

IV. Internet-only Banking System

1. Introduction[637)]

In many countries, internet banking is a fast-growing area of business, attracting

637) This part has been updated and revised from my paper published as "Korea's New Challenge to the Internet-only Banking System, Korean Journal of Banking and Financial Law, Vol. 8 No. 2, November 2015."

bank customers through convenience and cost-savings. Even though most traditional and commercial banks are currently providing internet banking services as one of additional services under the existing banking system, the new internet-only banking system attracts public attention for the better banking service and the more profitable business than an existing internet banking.

Internet-only banks[638] emerged in the 1990s in many countries with the advent of online banking technology. Such banks are ones that offer financial services online such as the usual savings, wiring and loan services without conventional brick-and-mortar branches.

Catching up with the new phase of international banking industry, the FSC which is a bank supervisory entity in Korea has announced the introduction plan for the internet-only banking system in Korea on June 19, 2015.[639] The FSC's announcement was for its detailed plan to introduce internet-only banks in Korea to enable financial consumers to use more convenient banking services at lower costs and to promote competition and innovation in the banking sector. The FSC's plan was not the first attempt but was strongly executing at that time especially to vitalize the so-called 'fintech' while previous plan in 2008 had been prepared just for new bank entry to build up market share and to make banking market competitive. The FSC's approach in relation to internet-only banks was not fairly conservative anymore and this was reflected in the FSC's plan published on June 19, 2015.

In line with the given purposes of the introduction of internet-only banks, the FSC would lower entry barriers and minimize ex-ante regulations to attract more players and encourage diverse and innovative business models under the internet-only banking system. According to the FSC's plan, the FSC took a two-track approach for internet-only banks at that time: (i) pilot operation of one or two internet-only banks under the current Banking Act, and (ii) additional licenses for more diverse companies after a revision to the Banking Act.[640] Anyhow, this has resulted in the new enactment of the 'Act on Special Cases

---

638) The other terms 'virtual bank,' 'internet primary bank,' 'internet bank,' and 'online bank' refer to the internet-only bank, and are used interchangeably. However, the term 'internet-only bank' only, which is used officially by the FSC, will be used hereinafter to avoid any confusion.

639) Financial Services Commission, "Plan To Introduce Internet-only Banks in Korea," Press Release, June 19, 2015.

640) For a general legal analysis on the internet-only banking system, *see* Byung-Tae Kim, "「Act on Special Cases concerning Internet-only Bank」 and Its Legal Issues (in Korean)," Advanced Commercial Law Review, Vol. 86, April, 2019.

concerning Establishment and Operation of Internet-only Banks' ('Internet Bank Act,' 인터넷전문은행 설립과 운영에 관한 특례법) in October 2018 for the internet-only banking system.[641]

2. Internet-only Banking System in Korea

1) What is an Internet-only Bank?

Internet-only banks (인터넷전문은행) are a result of the electronic banking phenomenon. Electronic banking, also known as electronic fund transfer, is the use of technological methods to provide financial services to consumers and businesses. It includes services such as automated teller machines (ATM), telephone banking, the use of debit and credit cards, smart cards, and internet banking. Internet-only banks are a species of electronic banking and have been the result of the importance and growth of electronic cash.

The internet-only banking system is a different concept from an internet banking currently operated by general commercial banks. The phrase internet-only bank, strictly speaking, means a bank which has no branches at all. Accordingly, it must be distinguished from the on-line services offered by traditional banks which use the Internet as an additional distribution channel.[642] Internet banking has now become a separate business, apart from its brick and mortar ancestors.

These new internet-only banks have some obvious advantages, such as no branch maintenance, fewer personnel costs, no paper, and no time and place limitations.[643] Internet-only banks may also offer various services at more economical costs to the bank customers because as a result, they either have no offline branches or have only a few if they have to. Internet-only banks are able to stay in business because of their amazing cost savings infrastructure or lack thereof. However, the most obvious drawback for internet-only banks is the fact that customers must deposit checks and cash through the mail (in case of the

---

641) *Id.*, p.89.

642) David Ellis, "Online Banking is Becoming the Most Popular Way to Bank," The Business of Surveillance: Balancing Concerns over Ubiquitous Technology, February 12, 2007, available at <http://iblsjournal.typepad.com/illinois_business_law_soc/2007/02/virtual_bank_re.html>.

643) Jennifer Maree, "Banking in the 21st Century: Cyberspace and Internet Banks - Redefining Compliance with the Community Reinvestment Act," Banking Law Journal, October 2002, p.797.

U.S.) or the ATM, which is an unacceptable feature for many people.[644]

Regardless of what the critics say, Korea attempted to change the banking system under the circumstances in order to introduce the new internet-only banking system in the country. However, there are still some legal issues to be solved for the sound and new banking system with internet-only banks. In particular, some legal perspectives for the internet-only banking system in Korea should be highlighted and reviewed; for example, such as bank entry conditions, commercial banks' ownership by companies mainly engaged in non-financial activities, real-name financial transaction system, scope of banking business, bank's minimum capital, etc.

2) FSC's Plan and Implementation

On June 19, 2015, the FSC announced the plan to introduce internet-only banks as part of its efforts to deregulate the local financial industry and foster the fast-growing financial technology sector. According to the FSC's announcement, the FSC took two steps to introduce the internet-only banking system in Korea. In the first step for a pilot operation, the FSC would grant preliminary licenses to one or two internet-only banks under the current Banking Act as pilot cases to test the viability of internet-only banking business. During this period, the current Banking Act thus applied for the approval of initial internet-only banks at the FSC's discretion. In the second step for the revision to the Banking Act, the FSC would push forward a revision to the Banking Act to ease the restriction on shareholding by non-financial companies to attract more diverse business providers into banking business. Then more internet-only banks if any were scheduled to be licensed by the FSC thereafter.

As scheduled, during 2 days of September 30 and October 1, 2015, the FSC started to receive preliminary applications from consortiums for a license to launch the country's first internet-only bank.[645] Given the purpose of the introduction of the internet-only banking system, in particular, the FSC's review

---

644) Christian N. Watson, "The Growth of Internet-Only Banks: Brick and Mortar Branches Are Feeling the 'Byte'," North Carolina Banking Institute, April 2000, p.350.

645) The Korea Times, "Regulator Starts Receiving Applications for Internet-only Banks," September 30, 2015. The FSC accepted bids and gave approval to operators while the FSC scrutinized all documents submitted by applicants and checked related qualifications, including their financial stability, shareholdings structure and customer service plan, before a final decision.

for approval was focused on the factors such as (i) innovativeness of business plan, (ii) stability of business model, (iii) consumer convenience, (iv) contribution to competitiveness of Korea's financial sector, and (v) possibility of global expansion. Supplementary criteria was considered to review whether it would have a proper response system in emergencies such as electronic failures or whether large shareholders have a proper plan to recapitalize in the case of liquidity crunch.[646]

At this time, the FSC encouraged an IT firm-led consortium to make a bid for the new banking business in order to attract industrial money to the financial sector. For this goal, the FSC was working hard for the intended initial launching of internet-only banking system on lowering legal entry barriers, including stake ownership limits, which had banned non-financial firms from owning more than four percent stake in a bank. It had already removed the requirements that all banks must have physical offices and face-to-face channels with customers.

After the FSC's plan was announced, four consortiums of banks, brokerages and tech firms were known to be competing in the bid: Kakao Bank, Interpark Grand Bank, KT Bank and 500V Bank consortia.[647] During the application period, however, only three consortiums except 500V finally applied for licenses from the financial regulator to run internet-only banks.[648] The Kakao Bank consortium comprised Kakao Corp., Korea Investment Holdings Co. and KB Kookmin Bank. The Interpark Bank Grand consortium involved 10 companies, including Interpark, SK Telecom, Industrial Bank of Korea, NH Investment and Securities, GS Home shopping, NHN Entertainment and Hyundai Marine & Fire Insurance Co. The KT consortium engaged twelve participants, including mobile carrier KT, Woori Bank, Hyundai Securities Co., Hanwha Life Insurance, KG Inicis, Danal, POSCO ICT and Ezwelfare Co.[649] They all included financial institutions including banks and ICT companies.

After all, the FSC granted preliminary approval on November 29, 2015 to two consortiums - one led by Kakao and the other by KT Corp. - out of three bidders to set up internet-only banks.[650] On December 14, 2016 the FSC granted

646) Financial Services Commission, *op. cit.*

647) The Korea Herald, "Applications for Internet-only Banks Begin," September 30, 2015.

648) The Korea Times, "KT, Kakao, Interpark Consortiums Apply for Internet-only Bank License," October 1, 2015. The 500V consortium, led by the venture firms' association and known as a potential applicant, withdrew its plan to join the competition, saying it would bid in the second round scheduled for next year.

649) Financial Services Commission, "The Results of Preliminary Applications for Internet-only Banks (Korean paper)," Press Release, October 1, 2015.

final approval for K-Bank, Korea's first internet-only bank. It is the first bank newly approved in 24 years since 1992, which will spur fresh competition in the banking sector.[651] The other internet-only bank, Kakao Bank, was granted for final approval in the end of 2016. In fact, both banks were approved with certain condition that the bank conducts the banking business by means of electronic financial transactions under the Banking Act.[652] And then the FSC granted Toss Bank, the third internet-only bank, a preliminary license to operate internet-only bank on December 16, 2019 after receiving and reviewing three applications.[653] In case of Toss Bank, it was approved under the Internet Bank Act.

V. Proper Regulations for Internet-only Banks

1. Bank Ownership Restrictions

1) Ownership Limitation in General

Korea has some restrictions on the bank ownership under the Banking Act. With respect to the holding limits of a banking institution's stocks, the Banking Act provides for the stockholding limit by the same person, and any stock holding beyond that limit is subject to the approval by the FSC. As the main rule of the stockholding limit of a bank, one stockholder and a person in a special relationship with him cannot hold or actually control more than 10/100 (15/100 in case of a local bank) of the total number of the issued voting stocks

650) Financial Services Commission, "Preliminary Approval Granted to Kakao and KT Consortiums for Internet-only Bank," November 29, 2015.

651) Financial Services Commission, "FSC approves Korea's 1st Internet-only bank," Press Release. December 14, 2016.

652) According to the Article 2 of the Addenda in the Act on Special Cases concerning Establishment and Operation of Internet-only Banks, a bank that the FSC authorized under the Banking Act before the Internet Bank Act enters into force is deemed an internet-only bank under the Internet Bank Act.

653) Financial Services Commission, "FSC Approves Internet-only Bank License for Toss Bank," December 16, 2019. For 'Toss Bank,' the evaluation committee concluded that its business plan showed a sufficient level of innovativeness, inclusiveness and stability. Meanwhile, the committee decided that the application by 'Soso Smart Bank' did not show a sufficient level of preparation in terms of its financing and business plans. One of the applicants, 'Familia Smart Bank,' submitted a notice for withdrawal prior to the review by the evaluation committee.

of a bank.[654] This main rule includes a holding by the same person in its own or another's name, or the exercise of the voting right in collusion. The Banking Act requires the FSC to examine any shareholders who secure ten percent ownership of a bank or higher. When they fail to comply with the holding requirements of stocks exceeding the ceiling, the FSC may order them to dispose of the stocks in excess of the ceiling.

However, there are also several important exceptions to the 10% main rule. The 10% rule does not apply to cases falling under any of the following, and the report to the FSC or the approval by the FSC is required for these exceptions:[655] (i) Where the Government and the KDIC hold stocks of a bank and where the holding is less than 15/100 of the total number of the issued voting stocks of a local bank, (ii) The same person may hold stocks of a bank by obtaining approval from the FSC, whenever the limits are exceeded, and the FSC may grant approval by setting the separate limits of stockholdings, only where it is deemed necessary in view of the possibility to contribute to the efficiency and soundness of banking business, the stock distribution of stockholders of the relevant bank, etc., and if the same person intends to hold stocks in excess of the approved limit, he must obtain approval again from the FSC: 10/100, 25/100, or 33/100 of the total number of issued voting stocks of the relevant bank, and (iii) Where a non-financial business investor intends to hold the stocks of a bank in excess of 4/100 of the total number of issued voting stocks of a bank, and he becomes the largest stockholder of a bank, excluding a local bank or participates in the management of the relevant bank by appointing or dismissing its executives, he must obtain approval from the FSC.[656]

Nevertheless, 10% rule and its exceptions of the Article 15(1) and (3) will apply to any of the following non-financial business investors, where (i) a non-financial business investor who has submitted to the FSC a plan for converting itself into a person who is not a non-financial business investor within two years and has obtained approval therefor, (ii) a non-financial business investor who holds stocks within the scope of the stockholding ratio of a bank by a foreigner under the Foreign Investment Promotion Act, or (iii) a non-financial

654) Article 15(1) of the Banking Act.

655) Article 15(1) through (8) of the Banking Act.

656) Article 16 of the Banking Act.

business investor who has obtained approval from the FSC by satisfying the certain requirements as a fund under the Article 5 of the National Finance Act or a juristic person managing and operating the fund.[657] In particular for overseas banks, there is one special provision in the Article 16-5(1). When judging whether a company is mainly conducting banking business overseas or the same person including a holding company of the relevant juristic person, the stocks or stakes of which are held directly or indirectly by the relevant foreign bank, etc. may be excluded from the scope of the same person.[658]

For the above any exceptions, the FSC has the authority to review and reject any proposals to transfer significant ownership or controlling interests in existing banks to other parties. Where the FSC refuses to accept a report or does not grant approval with respect to the exceptional stockholding of a banking institution, it must specify and notify such causes to the applicant within the period of 60 days.[659] The qualifications for any person capable of holding stocks of a bank, the requirements and procedures for the report or the approval related to stockholding and other necessary matters are determined in detail by the Presidential Decree in consideration of the propriety of the size of assets and financial status, the size of loans from the relevant financial institution, and the possible contribution to the efficiency and soundness of the banking business.

On the other hand, as discussed above, business conglomerates or industrial corporations known as *Chaebols* in Korea are prohibited under the Banking Act to own stocks of a bank in excess of four percent of the total voting stocks of the bank concerned (15/100 in case of a local bank).[660] However, they may own up to the limit set in the main sentence of Article 15(1) upon the approval of the FSC, provided that they do not exercise their voting rights for shares exceeding the four percent ceiling. This is to prevent business conglomerates from using banking institutions as their private coffers.[661]

The FSC's such active regulations on stocks exceeding the ceiling have been provided for in the Banking Act. Despite previous amendments to the Banking

---

657) Article 16-2(2) of the Banking Act.
658) Article 16-5(1) of the Banking Act.
659) Article 15(4) of the Banking Act.
660) Article 16-2(1) of the Banking Act.
661) Byung-Tae Kim, "Current Banking Regulations in Korea on the Legal Perspective," *op. cit.*, p.82.

Act, Korea has never altered its position that industrial companies, especially as to the top business conglomerates (i.e., *Chaebols*), must not own commercial banks. If industrial companies were to control banks, they might exploit the bank assets recklessly, as if from their private vaults. They could also restrict the operating activities of rival companies through the control of the banks. For these reasons, bank ownership by industrial companies had never been allowed. However, the previously existing limitation on bank ownership had a tendency to suppress the participation of all domestic capital rigidly, not just industrial capital, in bank management. Through the amendment to the Banking Act, Korea has expanded the cap on bank share holdings by the FSC's approval to ten percent from the previous four percent. Nevertheless, industrial capital is not allowed to exercise voting rights on shares exceeding the four percent level. However, the ownership ceiling on local banks remains at the current level of fifteen percent.

2) Ownership Limitation for Internet-only Banks

In relation to bank ownership regulations in commercial banks, there must be some different regulations for internet-only banks to induce ICT companies because those ICT companies are expected to be main partners for the purpose of the technical operations of internet-only banks.[662] However, the current Banking Act bans non-financial companies from holding more than four percent of shares in a bank under the Article 16-2 of the Banking Act. If this rule survives even in the regulations of internet-only banks, such restriction, of course, makes it impossible for ICT companies to enter an internet-only banking business.

Therefore, during the implementation by the FSC for the approval of the K Bank and the Kakao Bank under the Banking Act, it planned to ease the restriction on shareholding by non-financial companies, which are 'non-financial business investors' under the Article 2(9) of the Banking Act, from the four percent to fifty percent only for internet-only banks.[663] This could be applied only to internet-only banks, not to all commercial banks. However, even in internet-only banks, this rule was not expected to be applied to business conglomerates such as *Chaebols*.[664]

---

662) Finance & Economy Times, "People & Opinion: The Success of an Internet-only Bank depends on Prospective Regulations (in Korean)," July 13, 2015, p.11.

663) Financial Services Commission, "Plan to Introduce Internet-only Banks in Korea," *op. cit.*

Meanwhile, under the Banking Act, commercial banks can not extend credit exceeding 25/100 of the relevant bank's equity capital to the same individual, corporation or person.[665] The Banking Act also prohibits a bank from extending loans to the large shareholder in excess of the credit ceiling within the limit of twenty five percent of such bank's total capital.[666] Where a bank wishes to extend loans in excess of the credit ceiling to the large shareholder, such bank is required to get the approval of its board members in order to do so. A bank's maximum purchasing limit of shares of a large shareholder has been set within one percent of a bank's capital.[667] The Banking Act blocks a bank from owning shares in its large shareholders worth more than one percent of the bank's capital. Where a bank wishes to purchase shares in its large shareholders in excess of the purchase ceiling, such bank is required to obtain the approval of its board members in advance to do it.

In turn, with respect to the possible ownership limitation in internet-only banks, it is necessary that internet-only banks are subject to stricter regulations in regard with a large shareholder to avoid a conflict of interest, even though it is expected that the FSC would raise the ceiling of shareholding by non-financial companies to a fifty percent stake necessary for controlling power over management while keeping the cross-check by other shareholders.[668] As the FSC has already announced, the credit ceiling that a bank can provide its large shareholder would be required to be cut from the current twenty five percent of the bank's equity capital to ten percent. Internet-only banks should be also prohibited from acquiring shares issued by a large shareholder.

As a result, with the enactment of the Internet Bank Act in October 2018, all matters have been sorted out as follows:[669]

---

664) *Id.* The FSC had already announced that out of non-financial companies, business groups subject to cross-shareholding restrictions would be exempted from the eased shareholding regulation to prevent only a few conglomerates from exercising too much economic control. As of the end of 2014 when first applications for an internet-only bank were drafted and reviewed, 61 companies with assets more than KRW five trillion were designated as 'business groups subject to cross-shareholding restrictions.' Among them, those who were not deemed 'non-financial' were not subject to the four percent shareholding restriction under the Banking Act.

665) Article 35 (1) of the Banking Act.

666) Article 35-2 of the Banking Act.

667) Article 35-3 of the Banking Act.

668) Byung-Tae Kim, "Act on Special Cases concerning Internet-only Bank and Its Legal Issues," *op. cit.*, p.105.

669) Byung-Tae Kim, "Fit and Proper Test for Large Shareholders under the 'Act on

(i) Limits on Stockholding by Non-Financial Investor

A non-financial investor may hold not more than '34/100' of the total outstanding voting stocks of an internet-only bank.[670] The qualifications of a non-financial investor who can hold stocks of an internet-only bank, exceeding the limits specified in the main sentence of the Article 15(3) of the Banking Act, and requirements for approval related to holding of stocks thereof must be determined in consideration of (a) investment capability, financial status, and social credibility, (b) effect on concentration of economic power, (c) appropriateness of a plan for shareholder composition, (d) asset ratio of companies which engage in information and communications business, and (e) contribution plan for promotion of convergence between finance and information and communications technology, microfinance support, etc.

(ii) Credit Granting Limit on Same Person

An internet-only bank may not grant credit exceeding 20/100 of the equity capital of such internet-only bank to the same borrowers. However, this will not apply to cases falling under any of the followings:[671]

(a) Where it is necessary for the national economy or for an internet-only bank to promote effectiveness in securing claims, and

(b) Where an internet-only bank exceeds the limit specified in the main sentence due to changes in its equity capital or changes in the composition of the same borrowers although it did not grant further credit.

An internet-only bank may also not grant credit exceeding '15/100' of its equity capital to each same borrowers or corporations.[672]

Special Cases concerning Internet-only Bank' (in Korean)," Korean Journal of Banking and Financial Law, Vol. 13 No. 2, November 2020, pp.75-79.

670) Article 5 of the Act on Special Cases concerning Establishment and Operation of Internet-only Banks.

671) Article 7(1) of the Act on Special Cases concerning Establishment and Operation of Internet-only Banks.

672) Article 7(2) of the Act on Special Cases concerning Establishment and Operation of Internet-only Banks.

(iii) Prohibition against Credit Granting to Large Shareholders

An internet-only bank may not grant credit to its large shareholders. However, this will not apply where credit granted to a person not a large shareholder becomes credit granted to a large shareholder due to corporate merger, business transfer, change in the constitution of the same borrowers, etc. and where other extenuating circumstances exist as prescribed by Presidential Decree.[673] An internet-only bank must not make an exchange with other banks to grant credit to circumvent the prohibition against credit granting above. In addition, an internet-only bank must not gratuitously transfer its assets to its large shareholders or trade its assets under substantially unfavorable conditions compared with ordinary terms and conditions of transactions.

(iv) Acquisition of Equity Securities Issued by Large Shareholders

An internet-only bank may not acquire equity securities issued by its large shareholders. However, this will not apply where it is necessary to exercise a right such as a security right or whether other extenuating circumstances exist as prescribed by Presidential Decree.[674]

(v) Exercise of Unfair Influence by Large Shareholders

Large shareholders of an internet-only bank must not perform any of the following acts, contrary to the internet-only bank's interests:[675]

(a) Requesting the internet-only bank to present its internal data or information not yet disclosed to the general public,[676]

(b) Exercising unfair influence over personnel affairs or management of the internet-only bank in collusion with another shareholder on condition of providing any such consideration as economic gains, etc.,

---

673) Article 8(1) of the Act on Special Cases concerning Establishment and Operation of Internet-only Banks.

674) Article 9(1) of the Act on Special Cases concerning Establishment and Operation of Internet-only Banks.

675) Article 10 of the Act on Special Cases concerning Establishment and Operation of Internet-only Banks.

676) This will not apply to the exercise of rights under the Article 33(6) of the Act on Corporate Governance of Financial Companies and the Article 466 of the KCA.

(c) Exercising influence over the management of the internet-only bank, such as requesting it to make the early recovery of credit from a rival company in regard to the business activities of the rival company,

(d) Obtaining credit from the internet-only bank by causing it to violate the Article 8(1),

(e) Obtaining credit from another bank by causing the internet-only bank to violate the Article 8(2),

(f) Causing the internet-only bank to violate the Article 8(3) to gratuitously transfer its asset to or trade the asset with a large shareholder, and

(g) Causing the internet-only bank to violate the Article 9(1) to acquire equity securities issued by a large shareholder.

2. Scope of Banking Business

1) Banking Business in General

Under the Banking Act, banks are permitted to engage in all services in banking business within the scope prescribed by the Banking Act and its Presidential Decree. Currently, there are three possible categories of banking business in which the banks may be engaged; (a) core business, (b) incidental business, and (c) concurrent business. Meanwhile, where a bank intends to be engaged in incidental services or concurrent business, it has to file a report thereon with the FSC.

(i) As a core business, a bank may be basically engaged in (a) receipt of deposits and saving deposits, and issuance of securities and other debentures, (b) loans of funds or discount of notes, and (c) domestic and foreign exchange.[677)]

(ii) As an incidental business, a bank may be engaged in all services incidental to banking services[678)] and the details are stipulated in the Article 18(1) of the Presidential Decree of the Banking Act.

---

677) Article 27(2) of the Banking Act. More discussion and details can be referred from the part of the Regulations on Banking Business above.

678) Article 27-2 of the Banking Act. More discussion and details can be referred from the part of the Regulations on Banking Business above.

(iii) As a concurrent business, a bank may directly run the certain business other than banking business[679] and the details are stipulated in the Article 18-2(2) and (4) of the Presidential Decree of the Banking Act.

2) Regulatory Structure of Banking Business for Internet-only Banks

Under the FSC's plan, operations by internet-only banks would range from deposits, lending and credit cards to foreign exchange transactions, and their financial soundness would be regulated in the same way as that of other commercial banks. The FSC's plan said that Internet-only banks would also be allowed to engage in credit card business as a concurrent service.[680] That means that the FSC seemed to have the plan that internet-only banks would be allowed to engage in businesses same as commercial banks do under the Articles 27, 27-2 and 28 of the Banking Act.

However, if the FSC keeps insisting its plan to allow internet-only banks to engage in businesses same as commercial banks do, there would also be a serious conflict with its another new policy to lower the minimum equity capital for internet-only banks. This could produce undesired consequences that internet-only banks with a lowered capital might engage in businesses same as commercial banks do.

The Internet Bank Act enacted in October 2018 has followed the FSC's announcement and finally the issue on banking business for internet-only banks has been sorted out in the Article 6 of the Internet Bank Act. Internet-only banks are allowed to engage in businesses same as commercial banks do core and incidental businesses, but they may not provide credit to a corporation.[681] However, as an exception, they may provide credit to small and medium businesses under the Framework Act on Small and Medium Enterprises.

However, it should be noted that internet-only banks are not a replacement of commercial banks which are running their business in financial markets. This means that it should not be regarded as an additional bank entry for a limited

679) Article 28(1) the Banking Act. More discussion and details can be referred from the part of the Regulations on Banking Business above.

680) Financial Services Commission, "Plan to Introduce Internet-only Banks in Korea," *id.*

681) Article 6 of the Act on Special Cases concerning Establishment and Operation of Internet-only Banks.

banking market at where commercial banks have been struggling for the survivals. In contrast to the FSC's plan, and considering successful possibility of the internet-only banking system, the scope of banking business for internet-only banks needs to be limited to certain businesses such as FinTech related business, crowd funding or P2P loan in order to achieve their purposes and to improve the nation's finance industry with FinTech.

3. Prudential Regulations

1) Prudential Regulations in General

The Banking Act in Korea empowers the FSC to set forth the management guidance regulations for matters concerning the adequacy of capital, the soundness of assets, the liquidity, and other matters necessary for securing the sound management of a bank in the FSC's determining the standards for management guidance. It also requires the FSC to reflect the principle of supervision as recommended by the BIS over the soundness of financial institutions.[682]

As for the adequacy of capital of a bank, Korea has adopted, since July 1992,[683] the capital adequacy ratio of the bank against risk-weighted assets based on the criteria of the 'International Convergence of Capital Measurement and Capital Standards' (so-called 'Basel Capital Accord') of July 1988 by the Basel Committee on Bank Supervision (Basel Committee). The Basel Capital Accord of 1988 was amended in June 1999,[684] but the Basel Committee has presented a more concrete proposal, reflecting the parties' comments and the results of ongoing dialogue with the industry and with supervisors worldwide. Through the new Basel Capital Accord (Basel II) of 2004,[685] the Basel Committee issued the Basel III rules text in 2010, which presents the details of global regulatory standards on bank capital adequacy and liquidity agreed by the governors and

682) Article 34(2) and (3) of the Banking Act.

683) In July 1992, Korea adopted the capital adequacy ratio of the Basel Capital Accord, and since late 1995 it has required banking institutions to have at least the ratio of 8%. *See* Financial Services Commission, "BIS Ratio Rises Again, Approaches Advanced Standards," June 18, 2012.

684) Basel Committee on Banking Supervision, "A New Capital Adequacy Framework," Basel Committee Publications No. 50, June 1999.

685) Basel Committee on Banking Supervision, "Overview of the New Basel Capital Accord," Consultative document issued for comment by May 31, 2001, January 2001.

heads of supervision, and keeps working on the development of it.[686]

At present, through the amendment of the Banking Act and relevant Regulations of the FSC, Korea has incorporated market risks in calculating the capital adequacy ratio.[687] The capital adequacy ratio of a bank in Korea must not be currently less than 8 percent against risk-weighted assets based on the criteria of the Basel Capital Accord.[688] In practice, the capital adequacy ratio of Korean commercial banks has risen continuously since the financial crisis of 1997, and as of the end of 2021, it stands at more than 13 percent. If any bank is deemed possibly to cause serious damage to its sound management such as by failing to meet the capital adequacy, the FSC may require it to take measures necessary to improve the management such as by increasing the paid-in capital or restricting the profit sharing. securing assets with high liquidity, and issuing and holding a certain amount of contingent bonds.[689]

2) Prudential Regulations for Internet-only Banks

Even under the internet-only banking system, all banks including internet-only banks must ensure soundness in their management by making their equity capital solid and maintaining appropriate liquidity in running banking businesses. Therefore, an internet-only bank as one of commercial banks must be subject, in principle, to the same regulations on financial soundness and business operations as commercial banks.

However, at the initial launching stage, an internet-only bank needs to be granted a grace period for some regulations that could be excessive burden in the early stage of operation. Accordingly, as an exception, the Basel I standards are applied, according to the FSC's plan and in initial stage, to internet-only banks in regard with the BIS capital requirements, while the Basel III standards are applied to commercial banks.[690] Regarding liquidity coverage ratios, internet-only banks are also required to meet sixty percent, while commercial banks are required

686) More discussion and details can be referred from the part of the Regulation on Capital Adequacy above.

687) Article 20 of the Presidential Decree of the Banking Act.

688) Article 26(1) of the Rules of Bank Supervision of the FSC.

689) Article 34(4) of the Banking Act.

690) Financial Services Commission, "Plan To Introduce Internet-only Banks in Korea," *op. cit.*

to meet a hundred percent since 2019. After the grace period for internet-only banks, it is necessary that such regulations will be gradually strengthened to the levels of commercial banks.

4. Other Issues

1) Equity Capital Requirement

Under the Banking Act, a bank is required to have its minimum capital to get a banking business license from the FSC; *i.e.*, KRW one hundred billion for a nationwide bank and KRW twenty-five billion for a local bank.[691] However, if this principle still prevails over internet-only banks, there will be no possibility of potential stockholders from ICT companies.

In turn, the capital requirement for internet-only banks should be rearranged for the capability of such banks. In line with the new principle, the FSC has announced the minimum equity capital requirement would be lowered to KRW fifty billion for internet-only banks, half of the requirement for commercial banks under the Banking Act. At one time, a certain bill presented by the National Assembly for the amendment to the Banking Act in order to lower the minimum equity capital for internet-only banks to KRW twenty five billion was independently under the review at the National Assembly.[692]

Finally, the Internet Bank Act enacted in October 2018 has been sorted out for debates on the capital of an internet-only bank. It provides for that the capital of an internet-only bank may be at least KRW twenty five billion.[693] And also an internet-only bank must maintain the such amount of capital in conducting the banking business.

If necessary, the minimum capital requirement needs to be rearranged again after the review of initial business operations by internet-only banks once they run safe and sound businesses.[694]

---

691) Article 8(2) of the Banking Act.

692) Financial Services Commission, "The Results of Preliminary Applications for Internet-only Banks (in Korean)," *op. cit.*

693) Article 4(1) of the Act on Special Cases concerning Establishment and Operation of Internet-only Banks.

694) Byung-Tae Kim, "Act on Special Cases concerning Internet-only Bank and Its Legal Issues," *op. cit.*, p.96.

2) Non-face-to-face Identification

Korea has adopted the 'Act on Real Name Financial Transactions and Confidentiality' (금융실명거래 및 비밀보장에 관한 법률) in order to realize economic justice and to facilitate the sound development of national economy by implementing real name financial transactions and ensuring the confidentiality thereof through normalized financial transactions.[695] Under the Article 3(1) of this Act, financial companies, etc. must perform financial transactions with customers under their real names.

To this main principle, the FSC had already decided in May 2015 to loosen the strict requirement of the face-to-face identification to confirm customers' real names when they open new bank accounts by allowing alternative methods of the non-face-to-face identification.[696] As a result, all banks are now required to choose one of following alternative methods of non-face-to-face identification under the Electronic Financial Transactions Act (EFTA, 전자금융거래법); (i) ID card, (ii) Driver's License, (iii) Passport, (iv) Foreign Registration Card, (v) Mobile Phone, and (vi) other methods speculated by the FSC.[697] It is noted for sure that such eased identification rules will also facilitate the establishment of internet-only banks.

3) IT-related Risk Management and Facilities

In particular, internet-only banks are obviously more exposed to risks relating to the use of their technologies. If an internet-only bank's web-site goes down it will be unable to conduct its business. In turn, internet-only banks are required to take appropriate steps to reduce these risks.

The FSC should be concerned that internet-only banks are able to monitor the risks that apply to them in the same way as conventional banks. Even though the FSC's announcement has not yet shown on how to control IT-related risks in

695) Article 1 of the Act on Real Name Financial Transactions and Confidentiality.

696) When the internet-only banking system was introduced at the beginning, the FSC suggested several alternative methods of non-face-to-face identification such as (i) a copy of ID cards, (ii) video call, (iii) ID verification upon delivery of a debit card, or (iv) use of information on existing accounts (Financial Services Commission, "Plan To Introduce Internet-only Banks in Korea," *op. cit.*).

697) Article 6(4) of the Electronic Financial Transactions Act and Article 6(3) of its Enforcement Decree.

internet-only banks, it is required for the FSC to pay special attention on that even under the same way for conventional banks.

Meanwhile, internet-only banks need not to hold IT facilities by themselves for professional, technical and economic reasons as long as these facilities are safe and under their risk management. As the FSC announced, therefore, internet-only banks are allowed to outsource their IT facilities to IT companies to reduce initial costs.[698]

5. Implication to Better Regulations of Internet-only Banks

Before the FSC announced its plan for internet-only banks in 2015, it had been stringent enough to prevent any internet-only banks from entering the banking market in Korea. However, the FSC shifted its existing ground since it announced its plan in June 2015, and pushed for introducing the new type of bank for the first time in the country, saying it would transform banking business practices. In particular, an internet-only bank has been recently regarded as a key player of the so-called FinTech, a term describing the combination of finance and technology.[699] That is why the Korean Government has sought to improve the nation's finance industry with FinTech by making its services more convenient and accessible to customers.

The FSC's plan issued on June 2015 contained regulations dealing with these concerns and risks in particular. It is noted, however, that since internet-only banks are broadly one of commercial banks under the Banking Act, the same standards under the Banking Act and the 'Regulation on Supervision of Banking Business' by the FSS should be also basically applied to internet-only banks. As a result, it is now expected that internet-only banks may offer almost all the services that general banks provide from deposits and lending to foreign exchange through Web and mobile platforms.

However, some exceptions and different regulations should be necessary in order to achieve the purposes of the internet-only banking system. In particular, it seems to be desirable that the scope of business for internet-only banks is limited

698) Financial Services Commission, "Notice of Revision to 「Regulation on Financial Institutions' Outsourcing of Data Processing Business & IT Facilities」," Press Release, June 10, 2015.

699) The Korea Times, "KT, Kakao, Interpark Consortiums Apply for Internet-only Bank License," *op. cit.*

to certain businesses for their IT related and specific purposes. When asked if internet-only banks would be profitable, there is no clear answer yet to this. Instead, it is true that internet-only banks around the world are faltering. For example, the number of internet-only banks in the U.S. peaked 2001 and is now declining, while the number of brick-and-mortar branches is ever increasing.[700] Such decline in internet-only banks causes us to step back and seriously consider if there are inherent flaws in the proposition of internet-only banks. Therefore, there will be no necessity for conventional banks and internet-only banks to share same financial market together and to compete against each other. Both conventional and internet-only banks should go in different ways for their own profits and survivals. That is why they need to look for their own strong business pies, *i.e.,* different scope of businesses.

Meanwhile, Korea has its regulatory experiences with conventional banks, but not much experiences with internet-only banks yet. Though the legal issues anticipated in internet-only bank operations are similar, with some exceptions, to those already experienced by traditional banks offering internet banking services, it should be also noted that internet-only banks are banks in their own right.

It is also important, for more desirable and better regulations and supervision of internet-only banks in Korea, that Korea needs to consider and relies on the experiences of regulators in the other jurisdictions such as the U.S., Japan or Hong Kong.[701]

VI. Case Study on Banking and Finance Law

1. Lone Star v. Korean Government Case[702]

For the so called 'Lone Star Case', which was brought to the ICSID by the Lone Star in late 2012, a tribunal at the International Center for Settlement of Investment Disputes (ICSID) finally ruled on August 31, 2022 that the Korean

700) Sangche Lee, "Internet-only Banks: Uncertain Innovation," Economic Papers, Vol. 7 No. 1, 2015, p.161.

701) Byung-Tae Kim, "Act on Special Cases concerning Internet-only Bank and Its Legal Issues," *op. cit.*, p.114.

702) LSF-KEB Holdings SCA and others (Lone Star) *v.* Republic of Korea, ICSID Case No. ARB/12/37.

Government must pay the Lone Star US$216.5 million in compensation plus interest calculated after December 2011. It brings an end to a decadelong legal battle over the firm's claims it suffered massive losses due to the Korean Government's delay in approving a lucrative deal.[703] The ruling reflects the partial acceptance of the Lone Star's claim that it suffered damages due to the Korean Government's delaying of the controlling stake in the now-defunct Korea Exchange Bank (KEB) to the global banking giant HSBC in 2010-2012.

The Lone Star claimed the Korea Government deliberately delayed approval of the deal, and deprived the firm of fair and equitable treatment and other protections guaranteed in the investment treaty. Korea rejected the claims, arguing it treated the Lone Star equally and fairly, as in the case of domestic entities, in accordance with international laws and local regulations. In another issue, the Lone Star claimed local tax authorities applied inconsistent standards, seeking to reimburse the taxes it paid on the proceeds from selling off its assets because it is technically the subsidiaries based in either Belgium or Luxembourg that carried out the transactions. The Lone Star claims it should be exempt from taxes under investments treaties Korea has with the European nations. But Korea says the subsidiaries are paper companies and should not be protected by investment treaties.

It is a tragedy that the Lone Star, which made KRW 4.7 trillion in profits from the sale of its stake in the KEB, should be compensated for such 'damages.' The Lone Star, which owns over KRW 3 trillion worth of assets in the form of golf courses in Japan, was unable to own even a 10% stake of a Korean bank in the beginning. It is an immoral speculative fund that used deception to take control of the KEB. When the KEB merged with the KEB Card in late 2003, the Lone Star intentionally engaged in illegal activity to lower the stock price of the KEB Card by spreading false capital reduction rumors. After selling its shares in the KEB, the Lone Star filed a lawsuit against the Korean Government for damages totaling US$4.68 billion (around KRW 6.27 trillion) and even demanded the taxes it paid be reimbursed.

Throughout the years, the Lone Star has acted as if it considers the Korean financial market its own playground. The Korean Government countered the Lone

703) Meanwhile, the Korean Government has decided to actively review its options for applying for an annulment of the verdict due to its objection to the tribunal's decision. However, given that only about 10% of annulment applications are accepted, the ruling is unlikely to be overturned.

Star's claims by saying that the delay in the approval of the sale was because of audits, investigations and trials related to the US firm's eligibility as a major shareholder. Nevertheless, two of three judges at the tribunal rejected this argument. However, since the tribunal recognized the fact that the Lone Star had brought the investigation of stock price manipulation upon itself, the amount to be compensated was significantly reduced.

This entire incident stemmed from the ridiculous decision to sell the KEB to the Lone Star, which was a very unqualified buyer. It's a tragically painful case in which a speculative capital fund only made gains because Korea's financial supervision system failed to function properly. The issue of delaying the approval of the sale came from the Government's attempt to fix this mess. It's also worth pointing out that high-ranking officials are not free from responsibility concerning this case.[704] If the ICSID tribunal's ruling is finalized as it currently stands, those responsible should be clearly identified and, along with the exercise of the right to indemnity, those responsible must be held criminally liable.

Anyhow, it must be clear that the Lone Star's entry into and exit from Korea has been a target of criticism in Korea amid widespread public perceptions that the firm made huge profits by taking advantage of the country's economic difficulties in the wake of the Asian financial crisis in the late 1990s.[705]

For the details on the case of the LSF-KEB Holdings SCA and others (Lone Star) v. Republic of Korea (ICSID Case No. ARB/12/37), the original full text is available from the ICSID webpage.

2. Right to Bank Deposit[706]

1) Main Issues

(1) To whom rights to the bank deposit or its disposal belong to in the case where a joint account was established to deposit funds raised and shared by the

704) Hankyoreh, "[Editorial] Behind Lone Star Case is Failure of Korea's Financial Supervisory System," September 1, 2022; The Korea Times, "Lone Star Ruling regarded as '50% Defeat' for Korean Gov't," September 1, 2022.

705) Yonhap News Agency, "S. Korea Ordered to Pay Lone Star US$216.5 mln in Investor-state Suit," August 31, 2022.

706) Supreme Court Decision 2002Da55908, decided on October 14, 2004.

joint account for the purpose of prevention and supervision so that any of the joint account holders alone may not withdraw from the account until the specific purpose, except the general partnership funds deposit purpose, is accomplished.

(2) Whether the bank may set off a separately outstanding loan obligation of one of the joint account holders against his/her proportional equity in the whole joint account deposit (affirmative) and the elements for the transfer of the right to the equity of one of the joint account holders to another joint account holder in order for such transfer to hold against the set-off by the bank.

(3) The case holding that the bank may not set off separately outstanding loan obligation of one of the joint account holders who already lost his/her right to deposit due to an explicit or implicit agreement as to the belongings of rights to deposit in the bank between the joint account holders and the bank.

2) Summary of Decision

(1) In the case where the joint bank account, in the name of joint owners, is established with the condition that the rights to the account shall be exercised jointly, if the partnership funds are deposited in the name of joint owners, rights to the bank deposit are deemed to be in a quasi joint ownership relationship. However, if the joint account was established to deposit funds raised and shared by joint account holders for the specific purpose, except for the general partnership funds deposit purpose, as well as for the purpose of prevention and supervision so that any of the joint account holders alone may not withdraw from the account until the specific purpose leading to the establishment of such joint account is accomplished, then each joint account holder shares one whole claim to the bank deposit in common according to their equity ratio, and a right to dispose of each share of the bank deposit belongs to each one of joint account holders.

(2) The bank may set off separately outstanding loan obligations of one of the joint account holders against his/her proportional equity in the whole joint account deposit. As a consequence, in order for one of the joint account holders to defend against the bank's set-off contention, based on the fact that the other

joint account holder's proportional equity in the deposit transferred to himself/herself, the joint account holder must have a separate agreement as to the belonging of a right to the deposit with the bank, or must satisfy the elements for the transfer of a right to the equity of one of the joint account holders to another joint account holder in order for such transfer to hold against the set-off by the bank.

(3) The case holding that the bank may not set off separately outstanding loan obligations of one of the joint account holders who already lost his/her right to deposit due to an explicit or implicit agreement as to the belongings of rights to deposit in the bank between the joint account holders and the bank

3) Conclusion

Therefore, the late payment damages judgment as to 91,658,847 won against the Defendant is vacated, and since this part can be decided by this Court, we enter a judgment that the Defendant is obligated to pay to the Plaintiff late payment damages with an annual interest rate of 6% as provided under the KCA from March 18, 2001, which the record reveals obviously as the next day following the delivery of a copy of the complaint of this case, to May 31, 2003, and from the next day to the full payment date, with the annual interest rate of 20% as provided under the Special Act on the Expedition of Lawsuits, etc. Thus, the part of the judgment against the Defendant ordering late payment damages exceeding the above is reversed and the Plaintiff's claim as to this part is dismissed. The remaining grounds of appeal shall be dismissed as being without merit, and it is so decided as per Disposition by the assent of all Justices who reviewed the appeal.

Related Legal Issues and Questions:

1. Why and how did financial crises happen in 1997 and 2008 in Korea or other countries?
2. What regulations are applicable to banking institutions?
3. What were Korea's financial reform measures to overcome the financial crisis?
4. What kinds of banking are available in Korea?
5. What are different regulations over internet-only banks and conventional banks in Korea?

CHAPTER 13

OTHER FINANCIAL MATTERS - Fintech and Open Banking

A fintech refers to firms using new technology to compete with traditional financial methods in the delivery of financial services. There are many fintech related laws and regulations in Korea. One of financial businesses fintech firms can be involved is an open banking service. The so-called open banking system is a platform which invites users of fintech services and allows more people to enjoy simpler financial transactions. In this Chapter, it is important to understand what a fintech means and why it is important in financial system. Further, Regulations of a fintech and an open banking service must also be reviewed in this Chapter.

I. Introduction to Fintech

The term 'fintech' is the combination of finance and technology, and refers to firms using new technology to compete with traditional financial methods in the delivery of financial services.[707] It is an industry that uses series of technological innovations such as cloud computing and big data to allow technology to serve finance and greatly improve financial efficiency.

During recent years, there have been active developments of various fintech businesses in Korea. Fintech companies and many other major companies in Korea have been actively pursuing simple payment services, which are being provided in various ways both online and offline. The Financial Services Commission (FSC) has been working to develop its key policy plans for fintech and digital finance, which include advancing digital finance, promoting data economy, cultivating new fintech industry and services, working on regulatory

707) Rory Van Loo, "Making Innovation More Competitive: The Case of Fintech," UCLA Law Review. Vol. 65 No. 1, February 1, 2018, p.232.

reform in fintech and digital sectors, and strengthening the foundation for innovation.[708)]

On the other hand, the Fintech Center Korea was established on March 2015 to contribute to improve the benefits of financial consumers and develop the financial industry by creating the innovative financial ecosystem and activating fintech services in Korea. The Seoul FinTech Lab was also established in early 2018 to provide future entrepreneurs and early-stage startups with various support programs, from offices, mentoring and networking opportunities to demo-day and overseas IR events. It provides various supports and helps startups connect to a wide network of experts in order to accelerate the growth of fintech startups. The Blockchain Regulatory-Free Zone and U-Space BIFC of Busan is now actively developing new blockchain technologies without restriction in the following four areas: logistics, tourism, public safety and finance.[709)] While the COVID-19 pandemic has not had a significant impact on the fintech industry, it is expected that the move towards contact-free, rather than face-to-face, businesses is much favorable development for fintech companies.

On the other hand, in particular, a central bank digital currency (CBDC) is also drawing much attention from the public, as well as policy makers. However, the issuance of the CBDC would require a legal basis. Since the current central banking system is based on currency and reserves, the issuance of the CBDC as an electronic version of legal tender might not be consistent with the current Bank of Korea Act. In addition, it is unclear whether paying a positive or negative interest rate on the CBDC would be viable. Other legal issues, such as privacy and abuse of power, may arise since the central bank can collect personal information from daily transaction data.[710)]

---

708) Financial Services Committee, “Fintech and Digital Finance Policy for 2020,” Press Releases, February 26, 2020.

709) Not only that, but Busan offers the best conditions to commercialize the IT ecosystem. Indeed, Busan fosters making a cluster of financial technology firms. One example of such cluster is the ‘U(unicorn)-space BIFC),’ a space that currently houses 44 fintech, blockchain, financial big data and artificial intelligence-related companies.

710) Kwon, O., J. Park, and B. Kim. “Fintech, Cryptoassets, and Central Bank Digital Currency in the Republic of Korea,” ADBI Working Paper No. 1018, October 2019, p.8.

II. Fintech Businesses and Laws

1. Fintech Businesses in Korea

In Korea, the Government, the financial regulatory authority, and the financial industry are working closely together to promote the FinTech business. These efforts include designating FinTech as one of the nation's major growth engines, operating help centers to promote the business and easing regulations through the regulatory sandbox. As a leading digital city with a high internet penetration, financial literacy and acceptance rates, Korea offers numerous opportunities for the fintech business. Korea's fintech market saw a 20% increase in both the number of registered users (121 million) and the amount of daily transaction (USD 5.9 billion, as of 2019). Korea is also ranked 11th out of 27 countries in consumer fintech adoption rate (67%) with potential for further growth.[711]

According, there are no fintech businesses that are expressly prohibited at present. However, it seems that the Korean Government continues to maintain a negative view on businesses relating to virtual assets and has not withdrawn its policy to prohibit financing using virtual assets, such as initial coin offering (ICO), which it announced previously.[712]

In addition, according to the Specified Financial Information Act, the VASPs must report to the KFIU, and if they fail to comply with any duties of reporting, then the Commissioner of the KFIU may cancel the report or report on modification and may order them to suspend all or part of their operations for a period of up to six months.[713] Businesses that trade virtual assets in fiat currency such as KRW require a real-name verifiable bank account for such reporting purposes,[714] but in practice, banks have not been cooperative in providing such accounts. However, where fiat currency is not used and only exchange transactions between cryptocurrencies are supported, the KFIU report may be accepted even without a real-name verifiable bank account.[715]

711) Fn Hub Korea (International Financial Market Dept.), "Continuous Financial Innovation," available at <https://www.fss.or.kr/fhkeng/main/main.do>.

712) Kwon, O., J. Park, and B. Kim. *op. cit.*, p.5.

713) Articles 7(4) and (5), and 15(4) of the Act on Reporting and Using Specified Financial Transaction Information.

714) Articles 4(1) and 7(3) of the Act on Reporting and Using Specified Financial Transaction Information.

715) ICLG, "Fintech Laws and Regulations Korea 2022," Retrieved on January 5, 2023

The fintech industry in Korea has been growing steadily since the mid-2010s. Now, fintech is gradually spreading into payment and settlement services, and further into peer-to-peer lending, crowd funding, robot-advisors, etc.[716] However, compared to the U.S. or China, Korea's fintech industry still remains small. However, despite this, Korean fintech startups have shockingly snowballed in recent years, accounting for more than some 400 fintech companies.[717]

2. Fintech Laws and Regulations in Korea

1) Financial Regulations for Fintech

(1) During the past years, financial authorities in Korea have been trying to actively promote domestic fintech businesses through legislative reforms and the introduction of supportive policies. Among them, there are important and distinctive laws and regulations in Korea which must be considered for the fintech. First of all, the Electronic Financial Transactions Act (EFTA, 전자금융거래법), which is lastly amended on June 9, 2020, is for ensuring the safety and reliability of electronic financial transactions by clarifying their legal relations and to promote financial conveniences for people and contribute to national economic development by creating a foundation for the sound development of the electronic financial industry. Korean simple payment platforms such as Toss, Kakao Pay and Naver Pay are rooted in this law. It is now in the process of amending to comprehensively repair the regulatory system relating to the electronic financial market, including the simple payment service. The proposed amendment to the EFTA includes details regarding the granting of special exemptions relating to capital and registration requirements according to size, which is expected to revitalize the fintech industry and make it easier for technology companies to enter into the financial sector. In particular, the existing electronic financial business classification was reorganized by function, and a comprehensive payment settlement business license was newly established, which gives the licensed company the authority to open an account which was only granted to financial institutions such as banks previously. These changes will

---

form <<https://iclg.com/practice-areas/fintech-laws-and-regulations/korea>.

716) Kwon, O., J. Park, and B. Kim. *op. cit.*, p.1.

717) James, "The Future of Fintech in South Korea," the QARA, May 25, 2018.

promote the emergence of electronic finance companies which provide comprehensive payment and settlement services.

The Act on Online Investment Linked Finance Businesses and the Protection of Users (P2P Finance Act, 온라인투자연계금융업 및 이용자 보호에 관한 법률) enacted on November 26, 2019 (Act No.16656, enforced from August 27, 2020) is for promoting online investment-linked financial businesses to make them robust and to contribute to financial innovation and the development of the national economy by providing for matters necessary for the registration and supervision of online investment-linked financial businesses and matters concerning the protection of users thereof. It is expected to facilitate the development of the peer-to-peer lending (P2P lending) business, as it will bring P2P lending into the financial regulatory system and allow financial institutions to invest in P2P lending.

Furthermore, the Act on Reporting and Using Specified Financial Transaction Information (Specified Financial Information Act, 특정 금융거래정보의 보고 및 이용 등에 관한 법률), which was enacted on September 27, 2001 (Act No. 6516, lastly amended on December 28, 2021), is introducing the concept of virtual assets and virtual assets businesses. Under the Specified Financial Information Act, 'virtual assets' means electronic certificates including all rights thereto that have economic value and that can be traded or transferred electronically,[718] and virtual assets service providers (VASPs) must report to the Korea Financial Intelligence Unit (KFIU) in order to provide virtual assets services. In addition, as Korea's data privacy regime is expected to undergo considerable change due to recent amendments to Korea's three major data privacy laws, it is likely that new businesses utilizing personal or credit information will develop in the market. It also introduces reporting obligations on the parties engaging in cryptocurrency-related businesses and various regulations relating to AML/CFT (anti-money laundering and countering the financing of terrorism), thereby bringing an official regulatory system to the cryptocurrency industry. However, the FSC has expressly stated that the implementation of the Specified Financial

718) Article 2(c) of the Act on Reporting and Using Specified Financial Transaction Information. However, the followings are excluded from virtual assets: (i) Electronic certificates or information about such certificates that cannot be exchanged for money, goods, or services, etc., and the place and purpose of use of which is restricted by the issuer, (ii) Tangible and intangible products obtained through the use of game products, (iii) Electronic prepayment means and electronic currency, (iv) Electronically registered stocks, (v) Electronic bills, (vi) Electronic bills of lading, and (vii) Transactions prescribed by Presidential Decree taking into account the forms and characteristics of transactions.

Information Act does not mean the legitimization of the cryptocurrency industry as a whole and that it still intends to take strong actions against excessive speculation and other illegal activities related to virtual assets jointly with other relevant authorities.[719)]

The Special Act on Support for Financial Innovation (Financial Innovation Act, 금융혁신지원 특별법) was also enacted on December 31, 2018 (Act No. 16183, lastly amended on April 20, 2021) to contribute to the national economy by accelerating the development and advancement of financial services to increase the convenience and benefits for financial consumers and by creating jobs related to financial services. It has created financial regulatory sandboxes which temporarily exempt or suspend existing regulations for promising fintech startups to promote the development of innovative financial services. Such regulatory exemptions may apply to a wide range of laws and regulations affecting the financial sector and fintech businesses in general, including those related to the processing of personal data.[720)] After the Financial Innovation Act entered into force, the regulatory sandboxes where the existing regulations is not applied for a certain period have been introduced into the financial sector.[721)] Since the implementation of the system in April 2019, a total of 139 innovative financial services have been designated as of February 2021, providing opportunities for many small and medium-sized companies to enter the market for the first time. In addition, under the Financial Innovation Act, small and medium-sized companies with the relevant technology will be allowed to operate the part of the fintech business that existing financial companies want to operate via the 'designated agent' system.[722)] In principle, the financial regulations and sandbox options in Korea are basically applicable to companies established in Korea. Therefore, in order to enter into the fintech business in Korea, it would be necessary to establish an entity in Korea, obtain the required approvals and permissions, and procure relevant registration and approval for regulatory exemption where necessary.

---

719) Financial Services Commission, "Financial Measures to Curb Speculation in Cryptocurrency Trading," Press Release, January 23, 2018.

720) Articles 23 and 24 of the Special Act on Support for Financial Innovation.

721) Joon Young Kim, Samuel Yim, Gye-Jeong Kim and Ina Chung, "FinTech in South Korea: Overview," Kim & Chang, 2022.

722) Article 25 of the Special Act on Support for Financial Innovation.

(2) Financial regulators and policy-makers in Korea are receptive to fintech innovation and new, technology-driven entrants to regulated financial services markets.[723] The financial authority has announced that it intends to promote the development of fintech companies' innovative ideas by introducing a 'digital sandbox' that allows such companies to conduct experiments testing the innovativeness and business feasibility of such ideas based on actual data.[724]

As the fractional investments have recently expanded, new related issues have arisen. Fractional investment businesses can apply for a provisional exemption on certain rules pursuant to the Financial Innovation Act if they have to get an exemption from the application of certain financial regulations such as the Financial Investment Services and Capital Markets Act (FSCMA) to operate their businesses. A fractional investment is generally known as investing in a share of the ownership right for real-life assets. Indeed, most investors also perceive that they actually possess a piece or fraction of the ownership right through their investments. However, as opposed to such general awareness of investors, there has been a growing trend of fractional investment businesses engaged in issuing and distributing the right to profits generated from assets, not the ownership rights to assets. Therefore, the FSC has introduced the 'Guideline on Securities Business Dealing with Fractional Investment' in 2022 to inform about the applicability of the FSCMA on fractional investment business and matters to consider for investor protection. This guideline largely consists of the standards for deciding whether a fractional investment product qualifies as a financial security and the issues that fractional investment businesses should consider in relation to fractional investment products that are considered as securities.[725]

Furthermore, acceleration of digital transformation in financial services has been pushing up demand for new digital technologies such as cloud computing, big data analysis and artificial intelligence (AI). However, there have been continuous complaints from the industry that the current regulations on data security in the financial sector regarding cloud computing and network separation have been too strict, hindering the adoption and use of new digital technologies. In order to address this issue, the FSC has prepared the measures for improving regulations on the use of cloud computing and network separation to promote digital

723) ICLG, "Fintech Laws and Regulations Korea 2022," *op. cit.*

724) Fn Hub Korea, "Regulatory Update / Latest Buzz," Monthly Newsletter of Fn Hub Korea by the FSS, Vol 131, April 2022.

725) *Id.*

innovation in the financial industry after considering various opinions from experts and related parties. Such measures will include the revision of the Enforcement Decree of the EFTA and its supervisory regulation in 2022, and the revision to the 'Guideline on the Use of Cloud Computing Service in the Financial Sector' in 2022.[726)]

2) Non-Financial Regulations for Fintech

(1) In Korea, the processing (*e.g.*, collection, use or transmission) of personal data is regulated by the three major data privacy laws: the Personal Information Protection Act (PIPA), the Act on the Promotion of Information and Communications Network Utilization and Information Protection (Network Act), and the Credit Information Use and Protection Act (Credit Information Act). Under these laws, the explicit prior consent of data subjects is required, in principle, to process personal data and this consent requirement is strictly enforced in comparison to the data privacy laws of other jurisdictions. These three laws were recently amended to promote the utilization of data and the development of the Data Economy. In particular, the amendments introduce the concepts of pseudonymized information, data portability and Mydata, which are similar to the respective concepts under other data privacy laws such as the EU's GDPR and PSD2.[727)] The foregoing amendments are expected to have far-reaching implications for the fintech industry as well as many fintech businesses that rely on the collection and analysis of personal data in order to provide their services. These data privacy laws prescribe various administrative sanctions (*e.g.,* administrative fines, penalty surcharges or corrective orders) and criminal penalties (*e.g.*, fines or imprisonment) depending on the nature and severity of the data privacy violation.

(2) Under Korean data privacy laws for data privacy regulations, the consent of data subjects is required, in principle, to conduct cross-border transfers of personal data from Korea. In addition, data privacy laws in Korea have a special provision regarding their extraterritorial application. For example, the Network Act

---

726) *Id.*

727) ICLG, "Fintech Laws and Regulations Korea 2022," *op. cit.*; Chloe Jung-Myung LEE and Ross Harman, "Introduction to FinTech Laws and Regulations in South Korea," Lee & Ko, October 18, 2022.

stipulates that it will apply to any act done overseas if such conduct affects the domestic market or users in the market.[728] Accordingly, If any companies are processing the personal data of Korean data subjects, then Korean data privacy laws will technically apply even if such companies are located abroad. For the reference, a lower Korean court has previously ruled that Google Inc. located in the U.S. was subject to the Network Act because, among other reasons, it provided Korean-language services targeting Korean users through a website using a Korean domain, and it generated revenue by providing such services.[729] Although the foregoing court decision is awaiting review by the Supreme Court and its final outcome appears uncertain, in practice, however, that data protection authorities in Korea are likely to consider the above mentioned factors when determining the extraterritorial applicability of Korean data privacy laws.

(3) With respect to cyber security laws, there are no such kinds of cyber security laws or regulations in Korea that apply specifically to fintech businesses. Nevertheless, they are required to comply with the 'Standards of Technical and Managerial Security Measures for Personal (Credit) Information' which are the implementing regulations issued under the Credit Information Act if they process any personal or credit information.[730] In addition, any fintech businesses that have obtained licenses or permits in order to conduct business in the financial sector are be required to comply with the EFTA and various regulations issued thereunder.

(4) From July 1, 2019, AML obligations which was previously applied only to financial companies also became applicable to fintech businesses that qualified as electronic financial business operators. Under the Specified Financial Information Act, it also apply to VASPs which conduct any activities in relation to virtual assets[731] Consequently, fintech businesses that have registered as electronic financial business operators under the EFTA are also subject to KYC (know your customer), CDD (customer due diligence) and other AML (anti money laundering) obligations. Additionally, as mentioned above, VASPs also bear AML obligations

728) Article 5-2 of the Promotion of Information and Communications Network Utilization and Information Protection. This provision was newly inserted on June 9, 2020.

729) Seoul Central Court Decision 2014GaHap38116, decided on October, 16, 2015.

730) ICLG, "Fintech Laws and Regulations Korea 2022," *op. cit.*

731) Article 2(i) of the Act on Reporting and Using Specified Financial Transaction Information.

due to the Specified Financial Information Act.

(5) Although lacking legally binding force, financial authorities in Korea including the FSC have also issued a number of regulatory guidelines which financial companies are recommended to comply with. Therefore, fintech businesses must also closely follow the drafting and publication of such regulatory guidelines in addition to changes to relevant laws and regulations. Such regulatory guidelines not only aim to clarify legal requirements applicable to financial companies (*e.g.*, AML obligations for cryptocurrency transactions) but also have the effect of stimulating industrial development by promoting investments into fintech businesses by financial companies.[732)] Furthermore, the financial authority announced that it will lay a legal foundation for promoting finance-IT convergence through fintech investment by financial companies as well as the comprehensive and systematic development of fintech.

III. Funding and Investment to Fintech

1. Regulations on Fintech Funding and Investment

In Korea, there are various funding measures available depending on the size and purpose of business. If it is not much huge, it is possible to procure funding for new businesses and new technology businesses via venture capital. In the past, there were other various funds such as the new Business Investment Union and the Korea Venture Investment Union under the Support for Small and Medium Enterprise Establishment Act and the Act on Special Measures for the Promotion of Venture Businesses. However, the Venture Investment Promotion Act (벤처투자 촉진에 관한 법률), which was enacted on February 11, 2020 (Act No. 16998, effective from August 12, 2020) unified the scattered venture investment system into the 'Venture Investment Union' system and easing the regulatory atmosphere.[733)] This can help vitalize investment and funding into startup and venture companies.

On the other hand, venture companies may receive loans at a low interest rate,

732) ICLG, "Fintech Laws and Regulations Korea 2022," *op. cit.*

733) Article 50 of the Venture Investment Promotion Act.

within the scope of KRW six billion to ten billion, from the 'Small to Medium-sized Venture Company Establishment and Promotion Fund,' which is operated by the Korea SMEs and Startups Agency, pursuant to the Small and Medium Enterprises Promotion Act (중소기업진흥에 관한 법률).[734] In addition, there are various other fintech support businesses that provide financial technology available to fintech companies.

As other incentive schemes for investment in tech or fintech businesses, the FSC enacted the 'Guidelines on Financial Companies' Investment in Fintech Business' in 2019 to facilitate financial companies' investment in fintech business.[735] The guidelines allow banks, securities companies, insurance companies and credit card companies to apply for fast preliminary approval review and competition restriction review with regard to their investment in fintech companies and actively seek to exempt directors and officers of such institutions from restrictions relating to property damage due to investment failure if the actions of the directors did not involve gross negligence or an intentional act.

Additionally, there are tax privileges available to venture companies and small and medium startups such as reduced corporate tax or no taxation on capital gain by the founder. Moreover, the Restriction of Special Taxation Act provides for a 50 percent reduction on corporate tax for five years for small and medium startup ventures that engage in fintech business such as electronic financial business according to the EFTA, online small amount investment brokerage business according to the FISCMA, and small amount overseas remittance business according to the Foreign Exchange Transactions Act.

2. IPO Qualifications and Conditions

Specific requirements for initial public offering (IPO) will differ depending on in which stock market the IPO will transpire, but generally, the followings are required for the IPO: (i) quantitative requirements such as a record of business activities and results by the company and shareholder distribution, and (ii) qualitative requirements such as continuity, transparency, stability of business and

734) Articles 66 and 67 of the Small and Medium Enterprises Promotion Act.

735) Financial Services Commission, "Guidelines on Financial Companies' Investment in Fintech Business," September 4, 2019.

protection of investors.[736)]

However, the Korea Exchange (KRX, 한국거래소) applies relaxed quantitative requirements to companies that have technology and potential for growth such as fintech companies through various incentive programs, including: (i) no-profit company IPO (*i.e.*, Tesla requirement IPO) for companies that show potential for growth but have not yet realized any profit by applying a relaxed profit standard, (ii) technology test special IPO, which allows small-sized companies (with capital of no more than KRW 1 billion or market capital of KRW nine billion) that have obtained a certain technology rating through a review by a professional agency, and (iii) growth special IPO, as per the recommendation of an IPO facilitator.[737)]

In addition, the KRX gives preferential treatment to fintech companies with regard to the qualitative requirement review as reflected in a series of policies. Specifically, when conducting the qualitative requirement review: (i) innovation, technology and potential for growth are primarily considered to assess the continuity of the company, (ii) innovativeness of the fintech companies are highly regarded, and (iii) among the four areas of review (market attractiveness, feasibility of business structure, competitive advantage of business structure and business competitiveness), fintech companies are regarded as having greater feasibility and competitive advantage of business structure.[738)] It is expected that such special treatment for fintech companies will help various fintech companies to enter into the domestic stock market.

As an IPO example for fintech businesses, the Webcash, a B2B fintech company, was the first fintech company in Korea to be listed on KOSDAQ in early 2019. In addition to it, the Settlebank, which provides simple payment services and virtual account services, and the Aton, a fintech security solution and platform company, have successfully completed their respective IPOs and are currently being traded on the Korean stock market. As of 2022, more fintech companies such as overseas remittance service companies and foreign exchange service companies are preparing to proceed with IPOs in accordance with the Government's fintech preferential IPO policy.

---

736) ICLG, "Fintech Laws and Regulations Korea 2022," *op. cit.*

737) *See* Korea Exchange, "Listing Requirements for the KOSDAQ Market."

738) *Id.*

IV. Open Banking System

1. Introduction to Korean Open Banking

The open banking service has officially launched in Korea on December 18, 2019.[739] It allows bank customers to use any mobile application to access their bank accounts at any local bank and also to withdraw or transfer their savings from any bank account. Anyone could use the application of one local bank to access an account at a different bank and send money to or from any other account held.

As the IT and its related businesses had become more active, the Korean Government recognized that financial payment services and data sectors have a significant potential for innovation, and announced on February 25, 2019 its plan to establish an open banking system, which would allow fintech firms access to banks payment network through open API initiatives.[740]

Since its first launch in December 2019, the open banking in Korea has become widespread with the cumulative number of subscription reaching about 76.6 million with more than 138.5 million accounts registered as of April 25, 2021. In order to promote further development of the open banking, the FSC announced measures to expand participating institutions. As a result, about one hundred banks, fintech companies, mutual finance companies, savings banks, and securities firms have joined and are providing the open banking services as of April 25, 2021.[741]

2. Key Features

The authorities aim for the open banking system to serve as an infrastructure

---

739) Financial Services Commission, "Open Banking Service Launched for Banks and Fintech Businesses," Press Release, December 18, 2019. The open banking service was a pilot launched in Korea last on October 30, 2019 with participation by 10 banks (NH Bank, Shinhan Bank, Woori Bank, KEB Hana Bank, IBK, KB Kookmin Bank, Busan Bank, Jeju Bank, Jeonbuk Bank and BNK KyongnamBank). Since its pilot launch on October 30, 2019, more than 3 million people have registered more than 7 million accounts through open banking.

740) Financial Services Commission, "New Open Banking System in Korean Banking Sector," Press Release, October 30, 2019.

741) Financial Services Commission, "Open Banking Services Available from Savings Banks," Press Release, April 28, 2021.

open to all licensed fintech companies and banks to access the systems of other banks in Korea. A platform that allows trusted third parties to access to customer's financial data held by financial institutions through a secure and standardized way of open API.[742)]

[Basic Concept and Structure of Open Banking System][743)]

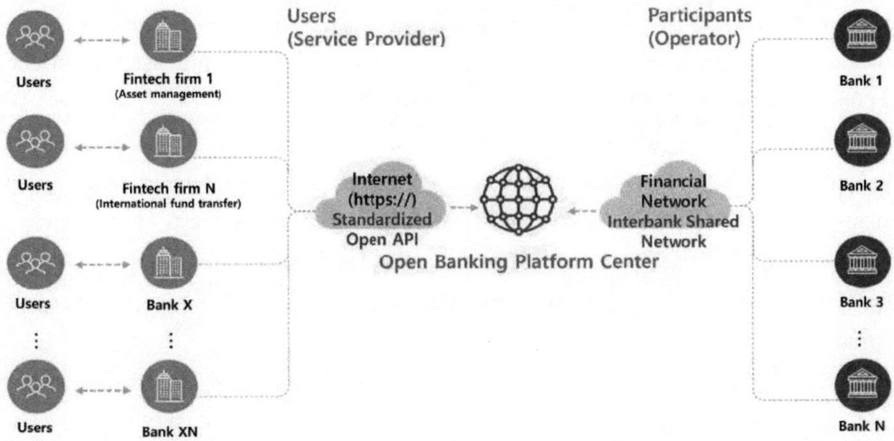

For end-users, the open banking system allows them to access nearly all banking services offered by any bank through a single smartphone application, including withdrawals and transfers. Bank customers can choose any mobile banking application to manage all their accounts in a single application without having to use separate applications for different banks.

Fintech firms attempting to participate in the open banking system are subject to a security check by the Financial Security Institute and a 24-hour Fraud Detective System will closely monitor fraudulent activities and automatically shut down suspicious transactions.

The open banking system may lower transaction fees and enhance user convenience. The current fee of KRW 400 to 500 per transaction may be lowered to about KRW 40 to 50 for large service providers, and KRW 20 to 30 for small and medium-sized firms.

---

742) *See* Yunjong Moon, "Introduction and Progress of Korean Open Banking," International Cooperation Center of the KFTC, December 17, 2020.

743) *Id.*

3. Implications and Expectation

The open banking services have become more than simply a payment system and has emerged as a key financial infrastructure, bringing tectonic shifts in the financial industry. The open banking service in Korea provides wire transfer functions in addition to the account checking function. As the Government expects, the open banking system will boost innovation and competitiveness in the financial sectors by introducing a comprehensive financial service platform, allowing fintech businesses to adopt open banking, and improving user experience for consumers.

The lowered entry barrier for fintech firms will lead to the provision and development of better services tailored to the needs of consumers at lower costs. Banks will be able to diversity and widen their customer base, and grow as comprehensive financial service platforms. For consumers, increased ability to choose between different financial services and enhanced control over personal information will lead to improved user experience.[744)]

The Government will ensure that the open banking system is operating in a stable and secure manner, and introduce new types of payment services, such as My Payment in order to encourage participation by more fintech businesses. In order to continue to promote innovative financial solutions through open banking, the Government needs to establish legal foundations through the revision of the EFTA while expanding the scope and function of the open banking service. In detail, it needs to push for the enactment of a legislative provision of the EFTA that requires banks to provide their money transfer function through open API.[745)]

V. Case Study on Sandbox for Fintech

1. Financial Regulatory Sandbox

The FSC has officially launched a financial regulatory sandbox on April 1,

---

744) Financial Services Commission, "Open Banking Service Launched for Banks and Fintech Businesses," Press Release, December 18, 2019.

745) Financial Services Committee, "Fintech and Digital Finance Policy for 2020," Press Releases, February 26, 2020.

2019 as the Special Act on Financial Innovation Support took effect.[746] Since the preliminary application period for financial regulatory sandbox was open last January 2019, the FSC received 105 applications. Among them, 19 applications were shortlisted for priority review by an evaluation committee, composed of Government officials and private experts. The evaluation committee held its first meeting today to discuss how to run the regulatory sandbox scheme.

The further shortlisted applications will be evaluated with focus on whether their technology and services would bring about innovativeness, inclusiveness and positive effect.

2. Case Example of Shinhan Credit Card Co.

The Shinhan Credit Card Co. was designated as one of cases from the financial regulatory sandbox program on November 2021, It is a credit card company in Korea with 22 million customers and overwhelming customer-transaction data infrastructure. The detailed information of the enterprises that have been designated under the financial regulatory sandbox program is as follows.[747]

1) Details and outcomes of sandbox designation

(i) Program type: Innovation financial service

(ii) Service name: Non-face-to-face real name verification service using facial recognition technology

(iii) Key details of the service: (i) Non-face-to-face real name verification using biometric information (facial information) based on biometric technology, and (ii) When issuing a card, proceed to the following procedure: ① Name verification by scanning ID ② Information extraction ③ ID verification ④ Facial Scan ⑤ Validation Check ⑥ Verification Complete.

---

746) Financial Services Commission, "Financial Regulatory Sandbox Launched," Press Release, April 1, 2019.

747) Fintech Center Korea, "Sandbox Case," available at <ttps://sandbox.fintech.or.kr/>.

2) Service flowchart

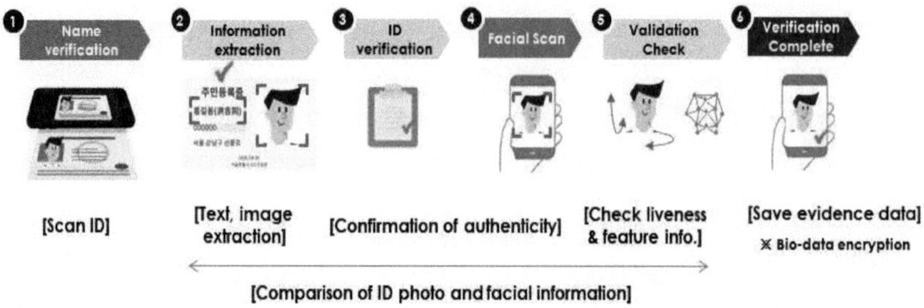

3) Related Regulations

(i) Article 6(2) of the Electronic Financial Transactions Act, and (ii) Article 34(c) of the Electronic Financial Supervision Regulations.

4) Main Additional Conditions

(i) Apply facial recognition technology only when it is confirmed that the ID is nor gorged through ID verification system, and (ii) Only for domestic individual customers over the age of 19.

5) Date of Designation and Service Launch

(i) Designation on November 12, 2021, and (ii) service launch date on 1Q, 2022.

Related Legal Issues and Questions:

1. How is the fintech business regulated in Korea?
2. How can we protect consumers in the means of regulations for the fintech.
3. Why do we need the open banking system?
4. How are fintech firms involved in the open banking system in Korea?

CHAPTER 14
INSURANCE LAW

An insurance law is the practice and regulation of law surrounding insurance and insurance companies, including insurance policies, contracts and claims. In Korea, there are various source of laws with respect an insurance and an insurance business. For example, the Korean Commercial Act and the Insurance Business Act including their subordinate regulations and decrees are the main source of laws for an insurance and an insurance business, and other various special laws, such as the Automobile Accident Compensation Act, the Act on the Indemnification for Fire-Caused Loss and the Purchase of Insurance Policies, the Depositor Protection Act, etc. also apply to each kind of insurance contracts. In addition, the Act on the Corporate Governance of Financial Companies and the Act on the Protection of Financial Consumers must also be considered for the regulations of an insurance and insurance business companies.

I. Introduction to Insurance Law

An insurance can be explained as a means of protection from financial loss in which, in exchange for a fee, a party agrees to compensate another party in the event of a certain loss, damage, or injury. It is a form of risk management, primarily used to hedge against the risk of a contingent or uncertain loss.[748] An entity which provides insurance is known as an insurer, insurance company, insurance carrier, or underwriter. A person or entity who buys insurance is known as a policyholder, while a person or entity covered under the policy is called an insured.

Meanwhile, an insurance law is the practice and regulation of law surrounding insurance and insurance companies, including insurance policies, contracts and

748) LS Sealy and BJA Hooley, *op. cit.*, p.1190.

claims. It can be broadly classified into following categories: regulation of the business of insurance, regulation of the content of insurance policies, especially with regard to consumer policies, regulation of claim handling wise, and regulation of the insurance contract.

In Korea, even during the global disaster due to COVID-19, Korea's insurance policy, contract and regulation are being highlighted. As at June 30 2022, there were 23 life insurers and 29 non-life insurers (14 domestic insurance companies and 23 foreign insurance companies) in Korea.[749] The net income of life insurers increases to KRW 805 billion for Q2 of 2022 from KRW 592 billion for the Q2 of 2021.[750] Total asset of life insurers at the end of the A2 of 2022 was KRW 942 trillion, decreased by 2.5 percent compared to the end of the Q1 of 2022. Return on equity (ROE) was 6.11 percent for the Q2 of 2022, fell by 0.65 percent compared to the Q2 of 2021. Total premiums of life insurers for the Q2 of 2022 was KRW 25.5 trillion, decreased by 9.1 percent compared to the Q2 of 2021.

The net income of non-life insurers increases to KRW 1,782 billion for Q2 of 2022 from KRW 1,213 billion for the Q2 of 2021.[751] Total asset of non-life insurers at the end of the A2 of 2022 was KRW 364 trillion, increased by 0.01 percent compared to the end of the Q1 of 2022. Return on equity (ROE) was 16.03 percent for the Q2 of 2022, rose by 5.08 percent compared to the Q2 of 2021. Total premiums of non-life insurers for the Q2 of 2022 rose to KRW 27.0 trillion, up by 8.2 percent compared to the Q2 of 2021.

The reinsurance market in Korea has stagnated after years of growth. However, as of the first half of 2021, domestic reinsurance revenue increased by 3.8% year-on-year, while overseas reinsurance revenue decreased by 7.3%. Meanwhile, the domestic life insurance market recently ranked eighth and the non-life insurance market ranked eleventh in the world in terms of revenue. Even though both life insurers and non-life insurers has experienced a difficult year around in 2018, the non-life insurance market is anticipating a positive year with higher auto insurance premiums and weaker competition while the life insurance market is still under pressure to inject more capital amid the adoption of the new

---

749) Financial Statistics Information System (FISIS), "Number of Companies by Financial Sector," available at <https://efisis.fss.or.kr>.

750) Korea Insurance Research Institute, "Korean Insurance Industry Trend 2Q 2022," June 2022.

751) Korea Insurance Research Institute, *op. cit.*

'International Financial Reporting Standard 17' (IFRS17). In preparation for the implementation of IFRS17, both life and non-life insurers are reorganizing their product portfolios to focus mainly on protection-type products.[752]

Now, let's dive into the regulations and developments of an insurance and an insurance business in Korea below.

II Insurance Regulations in Korea

1. Source of Laws for Insurance

Both the Korean Commercial Act (KCA, 상법) and the Insurance Business Act (IBA, 보험업법) including their subordinate regulations and decrees are the main source of laws for insurance and insurance business in Korea. They provide the statutory framework for the regulations of the insurance and reinsurance businesses, and the insurance and reinsurance contracts.

The IBA is a special Act in order to contribute to the sound development of insurance business and the balanced development of the national economy by ensuring the sound management of insurance business operators and by protecting rights and interests of policyholders, the insured and other interested persons.[753] While the IBA aims to promote the sound operation of insurers and reinsurers and to protect policyholders, it provides for license for insurance business, insurance companies, solicitation of insurance, asset management of insurance companies, supervision of insurance companies, dissolution and liquidation of insurance companies, etc.

The KCA provides the general legal framework for insurance and reinsurance contracts in its Part IV.[754] It includes regulations that cover insurance in general and its general provisions including party autonomy. In relation to insurance contracts, the KCA regulates the contractual provisions such as formation, effectiveness, reinstatement following lapse, nullification, amendment, and termination

752) Life insurers are reducing their savings-type insurance including annuity insurance while increasing death and health insurance. Non-life insurers are also focusing less on long-term savings insurance and more on protection-type insurance, especially personal insurance, resulting in higher proportions of accident and disease insurances.

753) Article 1 of the Insurance Business Act.

754) Articles 638 through 739-3 of the Korean Commercial Act.

of an insurance contract.

Various special laws for insurance, such as the Automobile Accident Compensation Act, the Act on the Indemnification for Fire-Caused Loss and the Purchase of Insurance Policies, the Depositor Protection Act, etc. apply to each kind of insurance contracts.

In addition, the Act on the Corporate Governance of Financial Companies (ACGFC, 금융회사의 지배구조에 관한 법률) applies to the insurance business companies. On August 1, 2016, the ACGFC became effective, which was enacted to strengthen regulations on corporate governance of financial companies including insurance companies. The ACGFC provides a set of uniform regulations on corporate governance issues (*e.g.* the ratio of outside directors to inside directors, qualification of officers, etc.) that were previously distinct for each financial sector. In particular, it introduced new rules on the periodic review of qualification of the major shareholders in the non-banking sector. The Act on the Protection of Financial Consumers (APFC, 금융소비자 보호에 관한 법률), which is a framework act intended to strengthen the protection of financial consumers, took effect from March 25, 2021. The APFC introduces, among other things, (i) the principle of suitability and appropriateness for certain insurance products, such as variable insurance, (ii) placing the burden of proof on insurers in cases involving breach the insurer's duty to explain its products, (iii) punitive surcharges, and (iv) authority for the FSC to issue sales suspension orders.

2. Regulatory Authorities for Insurance

The main regulators for insurance in Korea are the Financial Services Commission (FSC, 금융위원회) and the Financial Supervisory Service (FSS, 금융감독원) which regulate the insurance industry. The FSC prepares financial policies and systems (*i.e.*, it legislates and amends the development plans and regulations of insurance business), monitors, inspects and sanctions financial institutions, including insurance companies, and approves the establishment of financial institutions, including insurance companies. The FSC regulates insurance business in accordance with the IBA and the Insurance Supervision Regulations of the FSC. As the executive arm of the FSC, the FSS records the current status of insurance contracts and the financial status of insurance companies, monitors insurance companies' business operations, and sanctions insurance companies. It conducts day-to-day supervision and audit of the insurance and reinsurance industry. The FSS also directly inspects and supervises insurance companies and their employees, including insurance brokers. In case of foreign insurance company, the regulation of an insurance subsidiary in Korea does not extend to the foreign insurance group to which the subsidiary belongs.

III Regulations of Insurance Contract under the KCA

1. Type of Insurance Contract

The Part IV of the KCA classifies an insurance contract (보험계약) into two categories: (i) non-life insurance contract including fire insurance, transportation insurance, marine insurance, liability insurance, automobile insurance and guarantee insurance, and (ii) personal insurance contract including life insurance, accident insurance and sickness insurance.

It is common, in particular, for insurance companies to draft general conditions and standard contractual terms in advance, and to adopt the same when executing insurance contracts ('terms and conditions').[755)] The standard terms and conditions are binding on parties to insurance contracts, but if the parties agree otherwise on particular conditions, to the extent that those particular conditions apply, the standard terms and conditions would not apply.

2. Insurance Contract and Party's Duty

1) Under the KCA, an insurance contract will take effect when one of the parties pays the contractual premiums, and the other party promises to pay a certain amount of insurance coverage or other benefits upon occurrence of an uncertain event against the property, life, or body of the former.[756)] In general, the major elements of an insurance contract include the insurance money and insurance premium amounts, the risks covered by the insurance which will be the

755) LS Sealy and BJA Hooley, *op. cit.*, p.1192.

756) Article 638 of the Korean Commercial Act; Park Eungyoung, "Case Study on the Duty to Notify of the Alteration or Increase of Risks under the Korean Commercial Act (in Korean)," Law Review, Vol. 58, 2015, p.140. *See* also Supreme Court Decision 2013Da217108, decided on July 24, 2014.

grounds for payment of the insurance money, insurers' obligations, insurance periods, exclusion clauses and the governing law clauses.

When an insurer receives from a policyholder a payment of the whole or any part of the amount equivalent to the premium, as well as an application for an insurance contract, it must give him notice on whether it accepts the application or not within 30 days unless otherwise stipulated.[757] If the insured under a personal insurance contract is to undergo a physical examination, however, the period will run from the date of such physical examination. If the insurer neglects to give a notice on whether or not it accepts such application within the period 30 days, it is deemed to have accepted the application. Where the insurer receives from a policyholder the whole or any part of the amount equivalent to the premium, as well as an application for an insurance contract, if any event specified in the insurance contract has taken place before it accepts the application, it must assume contractual obligations unless it has any reason to reject the application. However, this will not apply where the insured of a personal insurance contract is to undergo a physical examination, but fails to do so.

When an insurer enters into an insurance contract, it must issue the terms and conditions of the insurance contract to a policyholder, and explain important terms and conditions.[758] In cases where the insurer's obligation of explaining and notifying the terms of the insurance policy is breached, the insurer cannot argue that those terms are included in the insurance contract. If the insurer violates his duty to issue and explain terms and conditions of the insurance contract, the policyholder may cancel the insurance contract within three months from the date the insurance contract takes effect. When an insurance contract has been made, the insurer must, without delay, prepare an insurance policy and deliver it to a policyholder, except where the policyholder fails to pay the whole premium or its first installment.[759]

2) If, at the time of making an insurance contract, a policyholder or the insured, due to bad faith or gross negligence, failed to disclose or misrepresented material facts, the insurer may terminate the contract within one month after it becomes aware of the non-disclosure or misrepresentation or within three years

757) Article 638-2(1) of the Korean Commercial Act.
758) Article 638-3 of the Korean Commercial Act.
759) Article 640 of the Korean Commercial Act.

after the contract was made:[760] However, this will not apply where at the time of making the insurance contract the insurer knew the non-disclosure or misrepresentation or failed to do so due to gross negligence.

Then what could be material facts? In such case, any fact about which the insurer asks in writing will be presumed to be material.[761] Generally, material facts or information refer to facts or information that have a grave impact on the insureds' interests such that, if made known to the insureds, it could influence their decision on whether or not to sign the contract. Examples of material facts or information include, for car insurance, facts or information about the main driver to be covered, a car's model and the purpose of the car, for fire insurance, the materials of an object, the structure of the object and the circumstances surrounding the object, for casualty insurance, exemption clauses for climbing and hand-gliding or other similarly dangerous activity, or exemption for driving without a license and for life insurance, an insured's gender, age and medical history.

A breach of the obligation to notify in an insurance contract is considered to be failure to notify or insufficient notice, committed intentionally or in gross negligence. Intentional breach by a person refers to a failure to notify when he is aware of the material facts that have not been notified or the notice was intentionally untruthful. Grossly negligent notice means that a person has failed to acknowledge the importance of the matter to be notified or he was unaware the matter was material. In cases where the obligation of notifying material facts is breached, an insurance contract may be terminated by an insurer and the burden of proof for establishing the breach rests with the insurer. However, if the policyholder can prove that the breach has no causal relationship with the occurrence of an insured accident, the insurance money can be claimed. In addition, in cases where an insurer knew about the material facts that were not notified or, through its own fault, was ignorant of the material facts, the insurer would not be permitted to terminate the insurance contract.

3) If, during the period of coverage, a policyholder or the insured becomes aware of the fact that the possibility of the occurrence of a peril insured against has been substantially changed or increased, he must give a notice thereof to the

760) Article 651 of the Korean Commercial Act.

761) Article 651-2 of the Korean Commercial Act.

insurer without delay.[762] If the policyholder or the insured has neglected to do so, the insurer may terminate a contract within one month after it becomes aware of such fact. When the insurer is informed of such alteration or increase of the risks, it may demand an increase in the premiums or rescind a contract within one month of being informed thereof.

When a policyholder, insured, or beneficiary becomes aware of the occurrence of a peril insured against, he must without delay give a notice thereof to an insurer.[763] If any loss caused by the policyholder, insured, or beneficiary increases due to his negligence of the duty to notify, the insurer may not be liable for compensation for such increased loss. An insurer must pay the insured amount to the insured or beneficiary, if there is an agreed period for such payment, within the agreed period, or if not, within ten days of the determination of the insured amount payable without delay, upon receipt of notification.[764] If a peril insured against has occurred due to bad faith or gross negligence of a policyholder, the insured or beneficiary, the insurer is not liable to pay the insured amount,[765] and also if a peril insured against has been caused by war or other public disturbances, the insurer is not liable to pay the insured amount, unless otherwise agreed by the parties.[766]

3. Interpretation of Insurance Contract

When interpreting an insurance contract and its standard terms and conditions, general contract principles under the Contract Law must be considered, and for the standard terms and conditions, the Act on the Regulation of Terms and Conditions (약관의 규제에 관한 법률) will apply. In principle, if there is a conflict between the standard terms and conditions and any particular conditions, the latter must prevail. The standard terms and conditions must also be interpreted impartially in accordance with the doctrine of good faith, and they must not be interpreted differently for different insurance policyholders. In cases where the standard terms and conditions are not clearly written, they must be interpreted against the insurer, and the exclusion clause of the standard terms and

762) Article 652 of the Korean Commercial Act.
763) Article 657(1) of the Korean Commercial Act.
764) Article 658 of the Korean Commercial Act.
765) Article 659 of the Korean Commercial Act.
766) Article 660 of the Korean Commercial Act.

conditions must be narrowly defined.

4. Statute of Limitations for Insurance Claim

Upon the occurrence of an insured accident, the relevant insured and the beneficiary of the relevant insurance can claim for the applicable insurance money. Exercise of the right to claim payment of the amount of insurance coverage must be barred by expiration of statute of limitations, if it not exercised for three years, and the right to claim return of premiums or reserves must be also barred by expiration of statute of limitations, if it not exercised for three years. In addition, the right to claim payment of premiums must be barred by expiration of statute of limitations, if it not exercised for two years.[767)]

IV. Regulations of Insurance Companies under the IBA

1. License for Insurance Business

The IBL generally regulates insurance companies. A person who intends to run the insurance business must obtain a license from the FSC according to the following types of insurance business:[768)]

(i) Types of life insurance business:
(a) Life insurance,
(b) Pension insurance including retirement insurance, and
(c) Other types of insurance business prescribed by Presidential Decree.

(ii) Types of non-life insurance business:
(a) Fire insurance,
(b) Maritime insurance including aviation and transportation insurance,
(c) Automobile insurance,
(d) Surety insurance,

767) Article 662 of the Korean Commercial Act.
768) Article 4(1) of the Insurance Business Act.

(e) Reinsurance, and
(f) Other types of insurance business prescribed by Presidential Decree.

(iii) Types of Type 3 insurance business:
(a) Injury insurance,
(b) Disease insurance,
(c) Nursing insurance, and
(d) Other types of insurance business prescribed by Presidential Decree.

A person who has obtained a license above is deemed to have obtained the license on the reinsurance of the relevant type of insurance. A person who has obtained an insurance license for all types of insurance constituting life insurance business or non-life insurance business, excluding surety insurance and reinsurance is deemed to have obtained the license for the types of insurance constituting Type 3 insurance business, and also deemed to have obtained the license for the types of insurance newly created for the relevant life insurance business or non-life insurance business unless he has disturbed the soundness of economic order. A person who is entitled to obtain a license for the insurance business is limited to a stock company, a mutual company and a foreign insurer, and the branch office in Korea of any foreign insurer which has obtained a license for insurance business is deemed an insurance company incorporated pursuant to the IBA.

2. Requirements for Insurance License

Any person or entity wishing to perform insurance business must obtain a license from the FSC, and the Article 6 of the IBA details the requirements to obtain the license. In particular,[769]

(i) The minimum capital requirement for an insurance company with a comprehensive insurance business license is KRW thirty billion, Where the insurance company intends to sell part of the types of insurance business licenses, the amount of the capital or fund may be otherwise prescribed by Presidential Decree in the amount of not less than five billion won. For an insurance company that markets or solicits by telephone, mail or computer communication only, the minimum capital requirement is reduced to two-thirds of the above.

769) Article 6(1) of the Insurance Business Act.

(ii) An insurance company must have a professional workforce and a suitable infrastructure (*e.g.*, IT facilities). In cases where an insurance company outsources some of its work (*e.g.*, review of insurance contracts, maintenance of IT facilities or investigation of insurance fraud), the outsourced work must also be done in compliance with the same requirement.

(iii) An insurance company's business plan must be reasonable, and must not be contrary to public policy.

(iv) An insurance company's large shareholders must not be disqualified for any grounds under the Article 5(1) of the Act on Corporate Governance of Financial Companies. They must also have the financial soundness and ample funding capacities without any record of harming the economic order.

A foreign insurance company seeking to obtain an insurance business license in Korea must meet the following requirements:[770)]

(i) It must have operating funds equivalent to or more than the above-mentioned minimum capital requirements for domestic insurance companies,

(ii) It must be in the same insurance business area in a foreign country in accordance with the law of that respective jurisdiction as the insurance business area it seeks to enter in Korea,

(iii) Its assets and financial and business soundness must be adequate to operate business insurance in Korea, and it must be recognized internationally, and

(iv) It should satisfy the requirements of (ii) and (iii) above relating to domestic insurance companies.

In order to obtain an insurance business license, an insurance company may first apply for a provisional license upon which the FSC may place conditions.[771)] The company must indicate the type of insurance that it would offer under its company name. Companies not in the business of offering insurance may not use words in their company names or logos that may show or imply that they are an insurance company.[772)]

Companies cannot operate both life insurance and non-life insurance business at

770) Article 6(2) of the Insurance Business Act.

771) Article 7 of the Insurance Business Act.

772) Article 8 of the Insurance Business Act.

the same time.[773] However, there are exceptions for any of the following types of insurance:

(i) Reinsurance of life insurance business and reinsurance of Type 3 insurance business,

(ii) Types of insurance prescribed by Presidential Decree which is permitted to be concurrently operated in accordance with other statutes and regulations,[774] and

(iii) Any insurance added to the types of Type 3 insurance in accordance with the standards prescribed by Presidential Decree.[775]

3. Non-admitted Insurer and Broker

The IBA regulates the requirements for being in insurance business, and if such requirements are not satisfied, the FSC will not issue a license. An insurer may not conduct insurance business without a valid business license, the failure of which could result in imprisonment for up to five years or fines of up to KRW fifty million.[776]

According to the IBA, insurance brokers must be duly registered with the FSC to perform the intermediate execution of insurance contracts.[777] As insurance brokers are involved in the execution of insurance contracts, in many aspects they are similar to insurance agents. However, insurance brokers differ from insurance agents, who act on behalf of a particular insurance company, in that they liaise with multiple insurance companies. The IBA prohibits insurance brokers from

773) Article 10 of the Insurance Business Act.

774) For example, (i) Insurance contract to set up a pension savings account under Article 20-3(1)(b), with the exception of the items, of the Income Tax Act, and (ii) Insurance contract under the Article 29(2) of the Act on the Guarantee of Employees' Retirement Benefits, and retirement insurance contracts under the Article 2(1) of the Addenda to the Act on the Guarantee of Employees' Retirement Benefits. However, an insurance company that sells only some of the types of insurance constituting the non-life insurance business, excluding reinsurance and surety insurance and an insurance company that operates only Type 3 insurance business are prohibited from concurrent operation (*see* Article 15(1) of Enforcement Decree of the IBA).

775) The insurance added to the types of Type 3 insurance means insurance that covers death caused by a disease in the form of special agreement of a Type 3 insurance and which satisfies all of the following requirements: (i) Insurance maturity must be at 80 or younger years old, (ii) Upper limit of the insurance must be KRW 200 million per person, and (iii) Maturity repayment must not exceed the total sum of paid premiums (*see* Article 15(2) of Enforcement Decree of the IBA).

776) Article 200(1) of the Insurance Business Act.

777) Article 89(1) of the Insurance Business Act.

being affiliated with one particular insurance company.[778] Accordingly, insurance brokers have no authority to execute insurance contracts or collect insurance premiums on behalf of insurance companies.

4. Distribution of Insurance Products

According to the IBA, the term 'insurance product' means a contract stipulating the payment of insurance money and other benefits to an insured in the event that an incident for which the insured is protected against occurs.[779]

Under the Article 2(1) of the IBA, an insurance product can be any of the following:

(i) Life insurance product: a contract that promises to pay stipulated money and other benefits to an individual in relation to the survival or death of an individual,

(ii) Non-life insurance product: a contract that promises to pay stipulated money and other benefits to an insured for a loss including any loss resulting from non-performance of contractual liabilities or statutory duties and obligations, resulting from a contingency excluding a disease, an injury and nursing thereof, and

(iii) Type 3 insurance product: a contract that promises to pay stipulated money and other benefits to an insured for any disease, injury or nursing thereof for the purpose of guaranteeing any risk.

5. Compulsory Insurance

While most insurance contracts can be freely entered into between parties no matter who they are companies or persons, there are some types of insurance that must be purchased mandatorily. In particular, when a party is planning to be involved in an act that may cause damage to others, that party may be required to purchase insurance to ensure that it has the capacity to reimburse the damage.

The IBA does not have a separate section that compels the execution of insurance contracts. A party involved in a specific act or business, should check whether purchasing insurance is mandatory by reviewing the relevant laws. For

778) Article 92 of the Insurance Business Act.

779) Article 2(1) of the Insurance Business Act.

example, under the Guarantee of Automobile Accident Compensation Act, a mandatory purchase of insurance is required: Any motor vehicle owner must purchase a liability insurance policy or enter into a liability mutual aid agreement which covers an amount insured that must be paid to a third party who has died or been injured due to the operation of the motor vehicle.[780)]

V. Other Considerations

The amendment of the Act on the Establishment of Financial Services Commission was put into effect on April 17, 2018. This amendment was enacted to promote mediation for insurance-related disputes and to respond to criticism that the short length of the time-bar for an insurance claim was inadequate to protect the rights of the legitimate insurance consumers. In accordance with the amendment, if a person applies for mediation to the FSS in an insurance dispute, the time-bar on the person's claim will stop running. The time-bar will then start running again when the person accepts the mediated proposal or when the mediation proceedings end without a resolution. Meanwhile, the International Accounting Standards Board has decided to postpone the implementation of IFRS17 by one year to 2022. As interest rates keep declining, however, insurers are still under pressure to inject capital before the implementation of IFRS17, and the need for the Government to take measures and put in policies to ease the financial burden on insurers.[781)]

As a result, a partial amendment to the IBA has been proposed and is pending in the National Assembly. The proposed amendment includes (i) improvements to introduce IFRS17 and K-ICS in 2023, (ii) improvements to streamline the document submission process so that policyholders of medical insurance may claim insurance proceeds with the electronic documents that medical suppliers would directly provide to insurers, (iii) streamlining the policyholders' insurance information request process, including information on surrender value, and obliging insurers to comply with such request, (iv) improvements to allow electronic financial business operators under the Electronic Financial Transactions

780) Article 5 of the Guarantee of Automobile Accident Compensation Act.

781) Peter Rogan, “the Insurance and Reinsurance Law Review (Edition 7),” the Law Reviews: Law Business Research Ltd, April 2019, p.312.

Act to register as an insurance agency, and (v) while prohibiting insurers from conducting its own claim adjustment, in principle, establishing exceptions for inevitable cases to improve efficiency of claim adjustment or to achieve the purpose of claim adjustment for security, urgency and other reasons.[782)]

VI. Case Study on Insurance Law

1. Case Study on Confirmation of Nonexistence of Obligation; Insurance Proceed[783)]

1) Main Issue and Holding

Where a contest for the existence or scope of contractual obligation exists between the parties to an insurance contract, whether the insurance company may get the legal interest of confirmation to file a lawsuit for negative confirmation against the beneficiary of insurance (affirmative).

2) Summary of Supreme Court Decision

[Majority Opinion] There should exist the legal interest of confirmation as the requirements for the protection of a right in a lawsuit for confirmation, and the legal interest of confirmation is merely admitted when there are insecurity and risk existing in the right or legal status of the Plaintiff and judgment of confirmation against the Defendant is the most effective and appropriate means in eliminating such insecurity and risk, and thus if disputes on the right and legal relation of the Plaintiff tend to result in insecurity and risk to the legal status of the Plaintiff, the legal interest of confirmation can be seen to exist. Therefore, where a contest for the existence or scope of contractual obligation exists between the parties to an insurance contract, the insurance company is deemed to get the legal interest of confirmation to file a lawsuit for negative confirmation against the beneficiary of insurance to eliminate legal insecurity caused thereby.

---

782) Jay Ahn, Hyun Wook Shin, Kevin L Todd and Byung Min Choi, "Insurance and Reinsurance in South Korea: Overview," Practical Law, February 1, 2022.

783) Supreme Court en banc Decision 2018Da257958, 257965, decided on June 17, 2021.

[Dissenting Opinion] The public function of the legal interest of confirmation or the effect of a lawsuit for negative confirmation on a creditor should be also considered when determining whether the legal interest of confirmation may be admitted in a lawsuit for negative confirmation, and thus the legal interest of confirmation that enables a creditor to file a lawsuit for negative confirmation cannot be seen to be admitted on the sole basis of the fact that a contest exists between the parties to a contract in all contractual relations.

Examining the publicity of insurance, special regulations on insurance business, the contents of insurance contract and resultant legal status of the party to a contract in light of the foregoing legal doctrine, it cannot be seen that there are insecurity and risk existing in the legal status of the insurance company on the sole basis of the fact that insurance policy holder, the insured, the beneficiary of insurance, etc. (hereinafter 'insurance policy holder, etc.') contend for the occurrence of insurance accident or the scope of insurance money against the insurance company, and a lawsuit for negative confirmation that the insurance company filed against insurance policy holder, etc. on the sole basis of such fact should be seen to lack the legal interest of confirmation in that it corresponds to the utilization of the litigation system contrary to equity in terms of the nation and public interest unless there are special circumstances. Eventually, the legal interest of confirmation cannot be admitted on the sole basis of the circumstance that the insurance policy holder, etc. contend for the existence or scope of the responsibility for the payment of insurance money, and a lawsuit for confirmation can be filed as the legal interest of confirmation is recognized only when there are 'special circumstances' to see that there is the legal interest to immediately confirm the existence or scope of the responsibility for the payment of insurance money additionally other than that.

In such a case, 'special circumstances,' for instance, can be admitted where there is a circumstance that the insecurity or risk that is unexpected in the insurance contract is caused to the insurance company as the insurance policy holder, etc. demand the payment of insurance money in the way that lacks social reasonability beyond the scope prescribed by the insurance contract or related statutes. Furthermore, where there is a circumstance to see that as the conclusion of an insurance contract or a claim for insurance money constitute insurance fraud, the insurance company is or will be likely to be the victim of the crimes or torts corresponds to where the insecurity or risk that is unexpected in an insurance contract is caused to the insurance company and thus can be admitted as a 'special circumstance.'

2. Case Study on Employee Status of Branch Manager of Insurance Company[784)]

1) Main Issue and Fact

There has been an ongoing controversy surrounding the employee status of 'branch managers' who have been delegated that role by insurance companies. On April 14, 2022, the Supreme Court rendered several conflicting decisions on this issue, drawing attention from various insurance companies.

The plaintiffs, who worked as 'branch managers' for Insurance Company A, argued their employee status primarily based on the fact that they were subject to regular performance management by Company A. In response, there could be detailed arguments to highlight (i) the typical work carried out by 'branch managers,' (ii) the reason Company A delegated work to the plaintiffs, and (iii) whether the parties were aware of the purpose and unique nature of the contract in this instance.[785)]

2) Summary of Supreme Court Decision

The Seoul High Court, the appellate court, clarified that "the act of encouraging performance or taking contractual measures against poor performers should not be hastily deemed as proof of employment relationship." The Supreme Court also affirmed such decision of the Seoul High Court, which resulted in a meaningful standard for determining employee status of a 'branch manager.'[786)] Additionally, the Supreme Court provided the following grounds for denying the employee status of a branch manager of Company A:[787)] Although the Company

784) Supreme Court Decision 2021Du33715, decided on April 14, 2022.

785) Kim & Chang, "Supreme Court Decision on Employee Status of Branch Manager of Insurance Company," Insights, 2022.04.21.

786) Seoul High Court Decision 2019Na204860, decided on January 26, 2021 and Supreme Court Decision 2021Da218205, decided on April 14, 2022.

787) Supreme Court Decision 2021Da218205, decided on April 14, 2022. *See* also Supreme

presented and encouraged each branch manager's performance target, there are no grounds to conclude that the Company engaged in substantial supervision and control over the method of achieving such a performance target. It is difficult to conclude that the Company managed the time of arrival/departure from work for branch managers. As commissions were paid based on performance, the amount of commission for each month varied significantly. There was a minimum guaranteed amount of compensation, but the amount of such guarantee was not significant or temporary in nature.

The Supreme Court has recently rendered conflicting decisions on the same issue of 'employee status of branch managers' due to the differences in the circumstances leading up to the introduction of the branch manager system, the parties' awareness of the purpose of the contract, the way in which insurance companies communicated with the branch managers, and the way in which the branch managers were compensated or supported by the insurance companies.

3) Comments on Supreme Court Decision

Therefore, in such disputes about employee status, it is imperative to respond carefully and systematically so that the nature of the underlying contract can be appropriately highlighted from the early stages.[788)]

Related Legal Issues and Questions:

1. What is the main laws for the insurance sector in Korea?
2. How is an insurance contract regulated under the Korean Commercial Act?
3. How is an insurance business regulated under the Insurance Business Act?
4. Why do we need an insurance?
5. Why do we need the insurance regulation and supervision?

Court Decision 2021Da246934, decided on April 14, 2022 and Supreme Court Decision 2020Da287310, decided on April 14, 2022.

788) Kim & Chang, *op. cit.*

CHAPTER 15
EMPLOYMENT AND LABOR LAW

The employment laws, also known as labor laws are those that mediate the relationship between workers, employing entities, trade unions, and the Government. In Korea, the main source of employment laws is the Labor Standards Act, but various other many laws also govern the relevant specific areas. Accordingly, applicable laws related to employment and labor must be considered in order to review the certain employment cases. In this Chapter, it is important to understand what kinds of employment laws there are in Korea and which law should be applied to a certain employment case. Even though the employment and labor law is not a main area of a business law, it is important even in a business law because employers and employees are always main actors in businesses and companies.

I. Introduction to Employment and Labor Law

1. Main Source of Laws for Employment

The employment laws, also known as labor laws are those that mediate the relationship between workers, employing entities, trade unions, and the Government.[789] Collective employment law generally relates to the tripartite relationship among employee, employer, and union.

The Article 32 of the Constitution of Korea establishes some basic principles of employment law, which include declaring that all citizens have the right to work, contemplating legislation providing for minimum wages and working conditions to ensure human dignity, prohibiting gender discrimination in employment and work conditions, allowing for special protection for working minors, and

789) Richard A. Mann and Barry S. Roberts, *op. cit.*, p.867.

allowing for preferential work opportunities for military personnel and policemen or their family members following injury or death in the line of duty.

> Article 32 of the Constitution of Korea
> (1) All citizens shall have the right to work. The State shall endeavor to promote the employment of workers and to guarantee optimum wages through social and economic means and shall enforce a minimum wage system under the conditions as prescribed by Act.
> (2) All citizens shall have the duty to work. The State shall prescribe by Act the extent and conditions of the duty to work in conformity with democratic principles.
> (3) Standards of working conditions shall be determined by Act in such a way as to guarantee human dignity.
> (4) Special protection shall be accorded to working women, and they shall not be subject to unjust discrimination in terms of employment, wages and working conditions.
> (5) Special protection shall be accorded to working children.
> (6) The opportunity to work shall be accorded preferentially, under the conditions as prescribed by Act, to those who have given distinguished service to the State, wounded veterans and police officers, and members of the bereaved families of military service members and police officers killed in action.

In Korea, the main source of employment laws is the Labor Standards Act (LSA, 근로기준법). The purpose of the LSA is to establish the standards for terms and conditions of employment in conformity with the Constitution, thereby securing and improving the fundamental living standards of employees and achieving a well-balanced development of the national economy.[790] Accordingly, the LSA governs the most fundamental and important matters in the employment and labor area, such as the minimum working conditions for the employees including the standard for working hours, recess hours, wages, overtime pay, vacation, as well as the standard for termination or other disciplinary actions.

2. Other Related Laws for Employment and Labor

In addition, various other laws govern the relevant specific areas in Korea. For

790) Article 1 of the Labor Standards Act.

example, (i) for a minimum wages, the Minimum Wage Act (최저임금법), (ii) for a trade unions and labor-management council, the Trade Union and Labor Relations Adjustment Act (Trade Union Act, 노동조합 및 노동관계조정법) and the Act of the Promotion of Employees' Participation and Cooperation (Workers Participation Act), (iii) for severance payment, the Act on the Guarantee of Employees' Retirement Benefits, (iv) for a fixed-term and part-time employees, the Act on the Protection, Etc. of Fixed-Term and Part-Time Employees, (v) for a temporary agency workers, the Act on the Protection, Etc. of Temporary Agency Workers, and (vi) for a protection of job applicant's rights and interests, the Fair Hiring Procedure Act.[791)]

II. Employment and Labor

1. Employee and Equal Treatment

1) Type of Employee

Under the LSA, the term 'employee' means broadly a person, regardless of the kind of occupation, who offers labor to business or a workplace for the purpose of earning wages, and the term 'employer' means a business owner, or a person responsible for the management of business, or a person who acts on behalf of a business owner with respect to matters relating to employees.[792)]

The type of employee or worker that is protected depends on the applicable law which distinguishes: fixed-term versus permanent workers; part-time versus full-time workers; employees versus temporary agency or outsourced workers and recently, even platform workers. Regardless of the type of employee, both employees and employers must comply with collective bargaining agreements (CBA), rules of employment (ROE), rules of employment and terms of labor contracts, and be obliged to fulfill them in good faith.[793)]

791) This Act applies only to the hiring procedures of business or a place of business which employs a regular workforce of at least 30 employees (*see* Article 3 of the Fair Hiring Procedure Act).

792) Article 2(1)(a) and (b) of the Labor Standards Act.

793) Article 5 of the Labor Standards Act.

2) Anti-discrimination Laws

(1) Employees are protected by the general principle of equality under the Constitution of Korea and other employment-related legislation. Basically, the LSA prohibits discrimination based on employee's gender, nationality, religion, or social status. According to the LSA, an employer must neither discriminate against employees on the basis of gender, nor take discriminatory treatment in relation to terms and conditions of employment on the ground of nationality, religion, or social status.[794] This is almost same as in the Title VII of the Civil Rights Act of 1964 and its amendments, which prohibit job discrimination against employees, applicants, and union members on the basis of race, color, national origin, religion, and gender at any stage of employment.[795]

There are also many other laws which prohibit discrimination of employees. The Act on Equal Employment Opportunity and Work-Family Balance Assistance Act (Gender Equality Act, 남녀고용평등과 일·가정 양립 지원에 관한 법률) prohibits discrimination based on an employee's gender, marital status, and pregnancy. Additional statutes prohibit discrimination of employees based on their age, nationality, employment status or disability status. For prohibiting discrimination of employees in aged workers, the Act on the Prohibition, Etc. of Age Discrimination in Employment and Elderly Employment Promotion will apply first, for prohibiting discrimination of employees in foreign workers, the Act on the Employment, Etc. of Foreign Workers (외국인근로자의 고용 등에 관한 법률) will apply first, and for prohibiting discrimination of employees in disabled workers, the Act on the Employment Promotion and Vocational Rehabilitation of Persons with Disabilities will apply first.

For prohibiting discrimination of employees in fixed-term or part-time employees, the Act on the Protection, Etc. of Fixed-Term and Part-Time Employees will apply first, and for prohibiting discrimination of employees in temporary agency workers, the Act on the Protection, Etc. of Temporary Agency Workers will apply first, Further, both Acts specifically address concerns applicable to atypical workers and explicitly prohibit discriminatory treatment of such workers.

---

794) Article 6 of the Labor Standards Act.

795) Frank B. Cross and Roger LeRoy Miller, *id.*, p.493; Richard A. Mann and Barry S. Roberts, *op. cit.*, p.870; Denis Keenan and Sarah Riches, Business Law (8th edition), Pearson Longman, 2007, p.539.

In particular under the Framework Act on Gender Equality (Gender Equality Act, 양성평등기본법), subject to penalties, employers must conduct sexual harassment prevention training annually, process and investigate all complaints regarding sexual harassment, take appropriate protective measures for victims such as changing their work location, providing paid leave, etc., and take appropriate measures against harassers including disciplinary actions, changing their work location, etc.

(2) Direct discrimination where employers treat two distinct groups (*e.g.*, based on gender, type of employment, etc.) differently without reasonable causes, is explicitly prohibited by the applicable legislation. Indirect discrimination where employers set policies that apply to everyone but are disadvantageous only to a certain group of employees in effect is explicitly prohibited by a few of the legislation discussed above (*e.g.*, the Gender Equality Act) or generally prohibited under the Constitution of Korea.

(3) Employers may defend against a discrimination claim by demonstrating a reasonable cause, if any. The employees may enforce their discrimination rights by applying for a correction order to the Labor Relations Commission (LRC, 노동위원회)[796] or the National Human Rights Commission (NHRC, 국가인권위원회), or by seeking damages to the civil court.

If the employee files for a correction order to the LRC, the employee may seek an order for reformation of the relevant policy that the discrimination was based and also claim the difference in wages resulting from the discrimination. By filing a civil lawsuit, an employee may seek monetary compensation for any monetary loss caused by the unlawful discrimination. Employers can settle claims at any time before or after claims are initiated but before the LRC, the NHRC or the court issues an order.

2. Labor Contract

The LSA explicitly stipulates that a labor contract which has established terms

796) There are 3 types of Labor Relations Commission: (i) National Labor Relations Commission, (ii) Local Labor Relations Commissions and (iii) Special Labor Relations Commissions (KOTRA, Labor Laws in Korea 2022, KOTRA Publication No. 22-010, January 2022, p.141).

and conditions of employment not in compliance with the standards of the LSA must be null and void to that extent.[797] Those parts made null and void will be governed by the standards of the LSA. While the LSA does not mandate a labor contract to be executed for most employees, it does require the following key terms of the employment to be provided in writing by the employer:[798]

(i) Wage information including constituent items, calculation method, and payment method,

(ii) Contractual work hours,

(iii) Holidays,

(iv) Annual paid leaves,

(v) Other terms and conditions of employment prescribed by Presidential Decree.

The same must also apply to any alteration of the matters above after entering into a labor contract. The terms and conditions of employment of part-time employees must be determined on the basis of relative ratio computed in comparison to those work hours of full-time employees engaged in the same kind of work at the pertinent workplace.[799] However, the provisions on holidays[800] and annual paid leaves[801] under the LSA will not apply to employees whose contractual work hours per week on an average of four weeks (in cases where their working periods are less than four weeks, such period of working) are less than 15 hours.

When any of the terms and conditions of employment as expressly set forth is not observed, the employee concerned is entitled to claim damages on the ground of the breach of the terms and conditions of employment and may terminate the labor contract forthwith.[802] When an employee intends to claim damages in such cases, he may file a claim with the Labor Relations Commission, and, if the

797) Article 15(1) of the Labor Standards Act. A standard labor contract is usually used not to have any problems, and it can be found from KOTRA, Labor Laws in Korea 2022, *op. cit.*, 16.

798) Article 17 of the Labor Standards Act.

799) Article 18(1) of the Labor Standards Act.

800) Article 55 of the Labor Standards Act. Before a particular holiday arrives, an employee may designate an alternative holiday for replacement and replace the original holiday with a working day according to the Article 55(2) of the LSA. In such case, the original holiday is a contractual workday, and therefore holiday work allowance may not be paid even if labor is provided (*see* KOTRA, Labor Laws in Korea 2022, *op. cit.*, p.52).

801) Article 60 of the Labor Standards Act.

802) Article 19(1) of the Labor Standards Act.

labor contract has been terminated, the employer concerned must provide travel expenses for returning home to the employee who changes his residence for the purpose of taking up a new job.

3. Minimum Employment Terms and Conditions

The LSA is the main employment-related legislation which prescribes the minimum standard of terms and conditions that employers must observe (*e.g.*, weekly maximum work hours, recess hour, and rules for annual paid leave, holidays, overtime restriction and wage payment).[803] The terms and conditions of employment prescribed by the LSA must be the minimum standards for employment, and the parties to labor relations may not lower the terms and conditions of employment under the pretext of compliance with this Act.[804] In addition, supplemental statutes such as the Minimum Wage Act and the Act on the Guarantee of Employees' Retirement Benefits provide additional details on the mandatory minimum requirements.

Where a CBA exists, any other ROE or employment contract containing terms and conditions in contradiction to the CBA will be null and void. Any terms and conditions of employment may be negotiated through collective bargaining, while wages, work hours, and paid leave are generally some of the main focus items thereof. The bargaining usually takes place at the company level, even when the employees are members of a larger umbrella trade union organization.

III. Trade Union and Industrial Relations

1. Rules relating to Trade Union

Under the Trade Union Act, the term 'trade union' means an organization or

803) *See* Articles 1 and 2 of the Labor Standards Act. In a wage payment on extraordinary occasions, for example, where a worker asks for wage payment for the service already provided by him before the monthly payday due to childbirth, disease, disaster or an extraordinary situation (*e.g.*, wedding, death or an inevitable situation requiring him to stay away from his workplace for more than a week) prescribed by Presidential Decree of the LSA, the employer must comply with the request (*see* KOTRA, Labor Laws in Korea 2022, *op. cit.*, p.20).

804) Article 3 of the Labor Standards Act.

associated organizations of workers, which is formed in voluntary and collective manner upon the workers' initiative for the purpose of maintaining and improving their working conditions and enhancing their economic and social status.[805)] Workers may decide, on their own, whether to establish a trade union, its type, and whether to join it. Workers' rights of association are guaranteed. Workers are free to form their trade union and may have plural trade unions in a business entity.[806)] Any person intending to establish such trade union must submit a report to the relevant Government body, which must issue a certificate of report within three days.[807)]

Upon receipt of certificate of report, the trade union is deemed to have been established as of when the Government body received the report for establishment. A trade union must make a report of modifications of contents to the relevant Government body within thirty days from the date when a change occurs in any of the matters reported with respect to establishment.

2. Rights of Trade Union and Industrial Actions

Legally established trade union has the rights to the bargaining and collective agreement, the execution of CBA and the industrial actions against an employer.

1) The representative of a trade union must have the authority to bargain and make a collective agreement with the employer or employers' association for the trade union and its members. A collective agreement may not provide for an effective term exceeding three years, and when the effective term is not specified in a collective agreement or exceeds the period of three years, it will be three years.[808)]

---

805) Article 4(d) of the Trade Union and Labor Relations Adjustment Act. However, the following organizations may not be regarded as a trade union: (i) Where an employer or other persons who always act in the interest of the employer is allowed to join it, (ii) Where most of its expenditure is supported by the employer, (iii) Where its activities are only aimed at mutual benefits, moral culture and other welfare undertakings, (iv) Where those who are not workers are allowed to join it. In this case, a dismissed person may not be regarded as a person who is not a worker, until a review decision is made by the National Labor Relations Commission when he has made an application for remedies for unfair labor practices, and (v) In case where its aims are mainly directed at political movements.

806) KOTRA, Labor Laws in Korea 2022, *op. cit.*, p.103.

807) *See* Articles 10 and 12 of the Trade Union and Labor Relations Adjustment Act.

808) Article 32 of the Trade Union and Labor Relations Adjustment Act.

Any part of rules of employment or a labor contract that violate standards concerning working conditions and other treatment of workers as prescribed in a collective agreement must be null and void.[809] Matters not covered in a labor contract and the part which is null and void must be governed by those standards of a collective agreement.

2) Any industrial action may not be inconsistent with the LSA and subordinate statutes or other social order with respect to its purpose, method and procedure.[810] A member of a trade union may not take part in any industrial action which is not led by the trade union.

A trade union must not conduct industrial actions, unless decided with concurrent votes of a majority of the union members by a direct, secret, and unsigned ballot. Where a representative bargaining trade union has been determined, any industrial action may not be taken unless it is determined with the consent of a majority by a direct, secret and unsigned ballot of the total members, limited to members belonging to the relevant business or place of business, of the trade unions which have participated in such procedures.[811] From among workers engaged in a major business of the national defense industry designated by the Defense Acquisition Program Act, those who are involved in production of electricity, water, or a work of mainly producing national defense goods must not conduct industrial actions. The acts of stopping, discontinuing or impeding the justifiable maintenance and operation of the essential business must be the prohibited industrial actions.[812] The essential business means the business whose suspension or discontinuance may seriously endanger the safety of the lives, health or bodies of the public and the daily life of the public.

Upon the occurrence of a labor dispute, one party to labor relations must notify thereof to the other party in writing.[813] Any industrial action may not be conducted without completing adjustment procedures, excluding the adjustment procedures after a decision is made to end the adjustment, An employer may conduct a lock-out only after the trade union commences an industrial action.[814]

---

809) Article 33 of the Trade Union and Labor Relations Adjustment Act.
810) Article 37(1) of the Trade Union and Labor Relations Adjustment Act.
811) Article 41(1) of the Trade Union and Labor Relations Adjustment Act.
812) Article 42-2(2) of the Trade Union and Labor Relations Adjustment Act.
813) Article 45(1) of the Trade Union and Labor Relations Adjustment Act.
814) Article 46 of the Trade Union and Labor Relations Adjustment Act.

3) Otherwise, the Trade Union Act and relevant court precedents set forth the following legal principles regarding industrial actions:

(i) The leader of such action must be qualified to be the representative of the workers in collective bargaining,

(ii) The purpose of the labor dispute action must be to promote and facilitate self-governing negotiations between the labor and management for the improvement of working conditions,

(iii) The labor dispute action must commence when the employer rejects the collective bargaining in response to the specific request of workers for the improvement of working conditions and upon approval of the action by concurrent votes of a majority of the trade union members by a direct, secret and unsigned ballot, and

(iv) The means and way of the labor dispute action must be harmonious with the employer's property right and must not constitute violence.

(v) The means of industrial actions may include strike, sabotage, production management, boycott, picketing, sit-in, work-to-rule, etc. on the part of the trade union, and lockout[815] on the part of an employer.[816]

3. Labor-Management Council

1) Under the Workers Participation Act, a labor-management council (Council, 노사협의회) means a consultative body formed to help improve the welfare of workers and ensure the sound development of enterprise through the participation and cooperation by workers and employers.[817] In principle, the trade union is composed of workers often with a contentious relationship with the company, whereas the labor-management council, composed of both the labor and management, is intended to be a cooperative forum. When a trade union represents the majority of the employees, its designees serve as the members representing workers and therefore, the council may be utilized as the preliminary step in preparation of collective bargaining. The Workers Participation Act requires employers with 30 or more regular employees to establish the council

815) A 'lockout' is an act against workers' industrial actions. It refers to an employer's temporary rejection of the work provided by workers.

816) KOTRA, Labor Laws in Korea 2022, *op. cit.*, p.129.

817) Article 3(a) of the Act of the Promotion of Employees' Participation and Cooperation.

that consists of three to 10 representatives from the management and employees.[818]

The Workers Participation Act classifies the main rights and responsibilities of the council as the following:

(i) Matters for report including overall management, production, and manpower plans, and financial status of the company,

(ii) Matters for approval including establishment of plan for education or training, establishment of welfare facilities and fund, etc., and

(iii) Matters for consultation including setting up or amendment of work rules, employee stock option plans, installation of surveillance facilities, etc.

Members representing workers must be those elected by workers, and if a trade union composed of a majority of workers is available, the representative of the trade union and persons commissioned by the said trade union. Members representing employers must be the representative of the business or workplace concerned and persons commissioned by such representative.[819]

2) Matters requiring consultation by a council must be as any of the followings:[820]

(i) Improvement of productivity and distribution of results achieved,

(ii) Recruitment, placement, education and training of workers,

(iii) Settlement of workers' grievances,

(iv) Safety, health and improvement of other working environment, and promotion of workers' health,

(v) Improvement of personnel and labor management systems,

(vi) General rules of employment adjustment, such as manpower transposition, retraining and dismissal due to managerial or technological reasons,

(vii) Administration of working hours and recess hours,

(viii) Improvement of systems for payment mode, system, structure, etc. of remuneration,

---

818) Article 4(1) of the Act of the Promotion of Employees' Participation and Cooperation.

819) Article 6 of the Act of the Promotion of Employees' Participation and Cooperation.

820) Article 20(1) of the Act of the Promotion of Employees' Participation and Cooperation.

(ix) Introduction of new machinery and technologies, or improvement of work processes,

(x) Establishment or amendment of work rules,

(xi) Employee stock ownership plan and other assistance to increase workers' property,

(xii) Matters on remuneration to relevant worker for an employee invention, etc.,

(xiii) Improvement of workers' welfare,

(xiv) Installation of surveillance equipment for workers within a workplace,

(xv) Protection of motherhood for women workers and matters to help combine work and home life,

(xvi) Prevention of sexual harassment on the job under subparagraph 2 of Article 2 of the Equal Employment Opportunity and Work-Family Balance Assistance Act and sexual harassment by clients, etc.,

(xvii) Other matters regarding cooperation between labor and management.

A council may pass resolutions as to matters above.

3) With respect to matters falling under any one of the followings, an employer must undergo a resolution by the council:[821)]

(i) Establishment of a basic plan for education and training and ability development of workers,

(ii) Establishment and management of welfare facilities,

(iii) Establishment of an in-house employee welfare fund,

(iv) Matters which are not resolved by the grievance handling committee; and

(v) Establishment of various labor-management joint committees.

4. Employee's Representation at the Board of Directors

Labor related laws do not provide any entitlement of employees to be represented at the board of directors level. However, there has been some movement to promote employee representation in the meetings of board of directors through a 'labor director,' This movement has not progressed to all private companies as of yet and is currently limited to public institutions only.

821) Article 21 of the Act of the Promotion of Employees' Participation and Cooperation.

The Act on the Management of Public Institutions (공공기관의 운영에 관한 법률) was amended on February 3, 2022 (Act No. 18795, effective from August 4, 2022) in order to reflect a labor director representing employees in the board of directors.[822)]

IV. Employee's Leave Rights

1. Annual Paid Leave

Every employer must grant any employee who has worked not less than 80 percent of one year a paid leave of 15 days.[823)] Every employer must grant any employee who has continuously worked for less than one year or who has worked less than 80 percent of one year one paid-leave day for each month during which he has continuously worked. Every employer must grant any employee who has continuously worked for not less than three years the paid-leave days that are calculated by adding one day for every two continuously working years not including the first one year to the 15 paid-leave days. In such cases, the total number of paid-leave days, including the additional paid-leave days, must not exceed 25 days.

In cases of annual paid leaves, any of the three following periods is deemed the period of attendance at work:[824)] (i) Period during which an employee takes time off due to any injury or sickness arising out of duty, (ii) Period during which a woman in pregnancy takes time off due to the maternity leave, and (iii) Period during which an employee takes time off on child-care leave.

The annual paid leave is terminated by time limitation if it is not taken for one year. Of course, this is not apply where the paid leave is not taken for reasons attributable to the employer.

2. Maternity Leave

According to the LSA, the minimum maternity leave is a total of 90 days

822) Article 25(3)(b) of the Act on the Management of Public Institutions.
823) Article 60(1) of the Labor Standards Act.
824) Article 60(6) of the Labor Standards Act.

(120 days for multiple birth) with a minimum of 45 days provided after the childbirth (60 days for multiple birth).[825] Maternity leave is paid leave either through the employer or it is subsidized by the Government. Also, women are protected against termination during pregnancy and up to 30 days following childbirth.

After the end of the maternity leave, the employer must reinstate the employee who returns from maternity leave to the same work or to the work at the same wage level as the employee's position prior to the leave.[826] Up to 10 days of paid paternity leave is also guaranteed to fathers under the Gender Equality Act.[827]

3. Parental Leave

An employee is entitled to 'childcare leave' up to one year where the employee's child is aged eight years or younger and below third grade.[828] An employee eligible for childcare also has the right to request 'working hours reduction' between 15 and 30 hours a week for up to one year.[829] The employer must grant the leave unless it is impossible to employ a substitute employee or the normal operation of its business is significantly impeded. The remaining period of the childcare leave above is added to the working hours reduction period.

An employee is also entitled to 'family care leave' up to 90 days, to take care of his parents, spouse, children, or parents of his spouse on the grounds of their illness, accident, or senility, etc.[830]

---

825) Article 74(1) of the Labor Standards Act.

826) Article 74(6) of the Labor Standards Act.

827) Article 18-2(1) of the Act on Equal Employment Opportunity and Work-Family Balance Assistance Act.

828) Article 19(1) of the Act on Equal Employment Opportunity and Work-Family Balance Assistance Act.

829) 19-2(3) of the Act on Equal Employment Opportunity and Work-Family Balance Assistance Ac.

830) Article 22-2(4) of the Act on Equal Employment Opportunity and Work-Family Balance Assistance Act.

V. Termination of Employment

1. Restrictions on Unfair Dismissal

In the common law doctrine of 'employment at will,' either party may terminate the employment relationship at any time and for any reason, unless doing so would violate the provisions of an employment contract or a statute. This common law doctrine is still in widespread use in the US, and only one state (Montana) does not apply the doctrine.[831)]

However, in Korea, an employer may not, without justifiable cause, dismiss, lay off, suspend, or transfer an employee, reduce his wages, or take other punitive measures against him.[832)] While there is no clear definition of just cause, the courts have described it as a "cause that is attributable to the employee which, under the socially accepted principles, makes the continuation of the employment impossible." Categories, where just cause may be found, would depend on the totality of the circumstances and may include, but are not limited to: serious and repeated violations of internal employment regulations; conviction of a serious crime; falsification of one's resume and detrimental reliance by the company; disclosure of trade secrets; serious sexual harassment; and end of an applicable fixed-term contract. In practice, however, especially in the case of termination for disciplinary reasons, the labor authorities or the courts prefer to see a history of a progressive disciplinary process leading up to termination.

Meanwhile, an employer is permitted to execute fixed-term employment agreements with terms not exceeding two years. In such cases, the employment agreement will terminate automatically upon the expiration of the fixed term. However, if an employer executes a fixed-term employment agreement with an employee that exceeds two years, then such employee will be deemed a permanent employee absent special circumstances. Due to the fact that it is extremely difficult for employers to dismiss permanent employees, employers usually make initial hires based on a fixed-term employment agreement of two years with the option of converting such initial hires into permanent employees after two years if they have demonstrated satisfactory performance.

---

831) Frank B. Cross and Roger LeRoy Miller, *op. cit.*, p.474.

832) Article 23(1) of the Labor Standards Act.

In addition, an employer may not dismiss an employee during a period of suspension of work for medical treatment of an occupational injury or disease and within 30 days immediately thereafter, and any woman before and after childbirth may not be dismissed during a period of suspension of work and for 30 days immediately thereafter. However, this will not apply where the employer has paid a lump sum compensation as provided for under the Article 84 or where the employer may not continue to conduct his business.

2. Notice of Termination of Employment

When an employer intends to dismiss an employee including dismissal (해고) for management reasons, he must give the employee a notice of dismissal at least 30 days in advance of such dismissal, and, if the employer fails to give such advance notice, he must pay such employee a 30 days' ordinary wage[833] (통상임금) at the least.

However, where any of the followings is applicable, this will not apply:[834]

(i) Where the period during which the employee has worked continuously is less than three months,

(ii) Where continuation of the business is impossible due to natural disasters, incidents or other unavoidable circumstances, and

(iii) Where the employee has intentionally caused serious damage to the business or property loss. When an employer intends to dismiss an employee, he must notify the employee in writing of grounds and timing for the dismissal.[835]

The dismissal of an employee will become effective only upon a written notice. Where an employer has given an employee an advance notice of dismissal above in writing, stating grounds and timing for dismissal, the employer is deemed to have given written notification. In addition, if there are any other procedures set forth in the CBA or internal policies, such as holding a disciplinary action committee, the employer must also abide by such procedure.

---

833) 'Ordinary wage' means monetary valuation of work provided by a worker during given work hours per a labor contract and, in the category of ordinary wage, include redundancy pay, overtime allowance, holiday pay and the other types of work stipulated in the LSA as 'to be paid' (*see* Supreme Court Decision 2012Da89399, decided on December 18, 2013).

834) Article 26 of the Labor Standards Act.

835) Article 27(1) of the Labor Standards Act.

Can employers require employees to serve a period of garden leave during their notice period when the employee remains employed but does not have to attend for work? While there is no explicit reference to the concept of garden leave in Korean employment laws, to the extent that such period is with pay, employers would likely be justified in imposing such leave.[836)]

3. Protection of Employees against Dismissal

Under the LSA, an employer may not dismiss an employee without just cause, which is generally a very high standard for employers to satisfy. The burden of proof rests with the employer to show just cause, if contested. However, consent from a third party is not required prior to dismissal.

All employees employed at a business enjoy the protection of just cause for dismissal discussed above. In addition, an employer cannot dismiss an employee during, or within 30 days following, a maternity leave or any period of leave for medical treatment due to an industrial injury or disease.[837)]

As mentioned above, there must be just cause to dismiss an individual employee. Specifically for business-related reasons, just cause is deemed to exist if all the requirements, including urgent managerial necessity,[838)] can be shown.

While there is no compensation owed to an employee specifically for dismissal, any employee is entitled to a retirement benefit regardless of the reason for separation.[839)] The current default retirement benefit is a corporate pension, or statutory severance if no such pension is in place. Depending on the type of retirement benefit applicable, the payment to the employee is approximately 30 days' average wages for each year of continuous employment.

4. Remedies for Employee against Dismissal

When an employee is subjected by the employer to any unfair dismissal, etc., he may request a remedy therefor from the LRC.[840)] Such request for remedy

836) *See* KOTRA, Labor Laws in Korea 2022, *op. cit.*, p.38.
837) Article 23(2) of the Labor Standards Act.
838) Article 24 of the Labor Standards Act.
839) Article 34 of the Labor Standards Act.

must be made within three months from the date of the unfair dismissal, etc. If an employee is successful in his claim before the LRC, the employer must reinstate and back pay the employee within the period ordered, which generally does not exceed 30 days. An employer who does not follow the reinstatement order, pending appeal, may be subject to administrative penalties, or criminal sanctions for failure to comply with the final order for reinstatement.

Any employee who has been dismissed may also claim wrongful termination, where a successful employee is entitled to reinstatement and back pay. Employers can settle dismissal claims with the employees before or after the claims are filed. However any prior agreements to waive employee rights to claim reinstatement or monetary compensation from employers before such claims have vested are unenforceable.

5. Business Sale and Employee Transfer

1) In case of an asset transfer, if an asset is fundamental to the business such that its transfer can be construed as a business transfer, the whole employment relationship will be automatically transferred to the buyer unless employees object. Whether the asset transfer is construed as a business transfer is determined by the Korean courts on a case-by-case basis and is focused on whether the asset is fundamental to the business of the company such that the asset transfer brings about transfer of the business as an ongoing concern.

2) In cases where an employee refuses to transfer with the business or there is a disagreement on the terms of the transfer to the buyer, an employee retains the right to remain employed with the seller unless the seller can legally terminate the employee. As the employment is automatically transferred from the seller to the buyer in a business transfer, the ROE and the CBA that comprehensively prescribes the terms and conditions of employment are also transferred as-is to the buyer.

Pursuant to the Workers Participation Act and relevant statute, the employer must, in good faith, inform the decision involved in the merger or any other decision fundamental to the company's business management to the employees. However, the law sets no penalty for violation of such duty. If the CBA contains

840) Article 28 of the Labor Standards Act.

any provision for prior consultation with respect to the merger or business transfer, the employer must, in good faith, consult with the labor unions regarding the plan for transfer or merger and provide monetary compensation or employment guarantee to the employees. However, breach of such duty has no influence on the validity of the business transfer or merger. Employers can only dismiss employees for just-cause, and redundancy created by a business or asset transfer does not necessarily satisfy it. In order for a redundancy-based termination to be valid, all of the following must be satisfied: (i) urgent business necessity, (ii) best efforts to avoid employee dismissal, (iii) fair and reasonable criteria to select employees for dismissal, and (iv) at least 50 days advanced consultation with the labor union.[841)]

Employees transferring to the buyer as part of a business transfer are entitled to retain the same terms and conditions of employment applicable prior to the transfer unless agreed otherwise.

6. Protecting Business Interests Following Termination

Post-termination restrictions including non-compete, non-solicitation, and confidentiality covenants are, in principle, valid and enforceable provided that the scope of such restrictions may be limited by the reasonableness standard. As noted above, post-termination restrictions are limited by a reasonableness standard, which is determined on a case-by-case basis. To the extent a court finds that the scope of a post-termination restriction is excessive, it has the discretion to reduce such scope without voiding the entire restriction. Financial compensation is not statutorily required for a post-termination restriction. However, the courts generally consider compensation as a factor in determining reasonableness of such covenants.

Restrictive covenants may be enforced with an injunction to enjoin the restricted activity or a claim seeking damages for violation thereof. For violations of post-termination confidentiality covenants that protect trade secrets under the Unfair Competition Prevention and Trade Secret Protection Act (부정경쟁방지 및 영업비밀보호에 관한 법률), an employer may also press criminal charges against the employee.

841) Article 24 of the Labor Standards Act.

VI. Case Study on Employment Law

1. Unfair Dismissal and Unfair Labor Practice[842)]

1) Main Issues and Holdings

In a case where the whole business is transferred after an employee was fired before the date on which a business is transferred without justifiable cause, whether a transferee who acquired the whole business succeeds the labor relation with the employee fired by a transferor without justifiable cause (affirmative in principle).

On this occasion, where there is a special agreement between the parties of the transfer of the business that an employee fired without justifiable cause shall be excluded from the object of succession, whether the special agreement is valid only when there is a justifiable reason stipulated in the Article 23(1) of the LSA (affirmative), and whether the transfer of the business per se can be recognized as a justifiable reason to exclude an employee from succession (negative).

2) Summary of Decision

In a case where an employee was fired before the date on which a business is transferred without justifiable cause, the labor relation between a transferor and the employee is still valid, and if the whole business is transferred after the employee was fired, it is actually impossible for the fired employee to be reinstated in his/her former office in the relationship with the transferor, and thus a transferee, who acquires the whole business, maintaining the identity of the whole business according to a contract for the transfer of the business, in principle, succeeds the labor relation with the employee fired by the transferor without reasonable grounds. In a case where the whole business is transferred, if there is a special agreement between the parties of the transfer of the business that an employee fired without justifiable grounds shall be excluded from the object of succession, the labor relationship may not be succeeded according thereto, but such a special agreement is substantially the same as another

842) Supreme Court Decision 2018Du54705, decided on November 5, 2020.

dismissal, and thus is valid only when there exists a justifiable cause stipulated in the Article 23(1) of the LSA, and the transfer of business per se cannot be recognized as a justifiable reason.

3) Conclusion

Therefore, the final appeal shall be dismissed in entirety, and the cost of final appeals shall be assessed against the losing parties, respectively. It is so decided as per Disposition by the assent of all participating Justices on the bench.

2. Violation of Duty of Reemployment[843)]

1) Main Issues and Holdings

(1) In a case where an employer seeks to hire an employee who will perform the same task as was done by a dismissed employee at the time of dismissal within the period of three years from the day on which the employer fired the dismissed worker pursuant to the Article 24 of the LSA, whether the employer has a duty to offer preferential reemployment to the dismissed employee (affirmative in principle), and in such a case, where the employer hired a third person without confirming the dismissed employee's intention to enter into an employment contract, whether the employer in such a case violated the duty of preferential reemployment prescribed in the Article 25(1) of the LSA (affirmative in principle).

(2) In the case where: (a) Party A worked as a rehabilitation teacher at the welfare facility for people with disabilities, run by Foundation B, and was laid off for managerial reasons; (b) Foundation B hired rehabilitation teachers several times within the period of three years from Party A's dismissal, but it neither notified Party A of the recruitment nor confirmed Party A's intention to re-enter into an employment contract; and (c) the point of time at which Foundation B violated the duty of preferential reemployment stipulated in the Article 25(1) of

843) Supreme Court en banc Decision 2016Da13437, decided on November 26, 2020. *See* also Supreme Court Decision 2013Da14965, decided on November 26, 2015 and Supreme Court Decision 2015Da232859, decided on March 22, 2017.

the LSA was disputed, the case holding that Foundation B's duty to offer preferential reemployment came into effect, at the latest, around the time when it hired the second person for the role of rehabilitation teacher providing life support service, which had been performed by Party A at the time of his dismissal.

(3) In a case where the employer does not perform the duty to offer preferential reemployment prescribed in the Article 25(1) of the LSA, whether the dismissed employee is legally entitled to seek a judgment against the employer in substitution for the declaration of intention to offer employment (affirmative), and whether the employment relationship is established between the employee and the dismissed worker when such a judgment becomes final and conclusive (affirmative). In such an instance, whether the dismissed employee is entitled to file a claim for damages for the employer's noncompliance with the duty of preferential reemployment for lost wages arising from the time at which the employer's duty of preferential reemployment came into effect until the establishment of the employment relationship (affirmative).

(4) In a case where: (a) the dismissed employee files a claim for damages, on account of the employer's noncompliance with the duty of employment, the amount of which commensurate with the amount of wages that the employee could have received had the employer performed its duty of employment; and (b) if a considerable causal relationship between the benefits accrued by the employee by performing work for other workplaces and the employer's noncompliance with the duty of employment is recognized, whether the said benefits ought to be deducted when calculating the amount of damages (affirmative). In such an instance, whether the provision on shutdown allowances stipulated in the Article 46 of the LSA is applicable (negative).

2) Reasoning

(1) Judgment on the Plaintiff's grounds of final appeal

A. The Article 25(1) of the LSA states that "[w]hen an employer who has dismissed an employee under the provisions of Article 24 intends to hire, within three years of the date of the dismissal, any employee who will perform the same duty as the dismissed employee did at the time of such dismissal, he/she shall preferentially rehire the employee dismissed under the Article 24, if the employee so desires." Considering the substance of Article 25(1) of the LSA and the legislative intention to protect dismissed employees, who lost their jobs because of managerial reasons without any reasons attributable to them, by guaranteeing an opportunity to get reinstated, the employer, who seeks to hire an employee for the same role as was performed by a dismissed employee at the time of dismissal, is obligated to offer preferential reemployment to the said dismissed employee, barring special circumstances, such as the dismissed employee's declaration of a contrary intention or the existence of objective reasons making it difficult to conclude an employment contract.

In such an instance, if the employer hired a third party without confirming the dismissed employee's intention to enter into an employment contract, the said employer is considered to have breached the duty of reemployment prescribed in the Article 25(1) of the LSA, unless there were special circumstances, such as the dismissed employee would not have wanted to enter into an employment contract or there were objective reasons making it difficult to expect the employer to enter into an employment contract.

B. The reasoning of the lower judgment and the record reveal the following facts and circumstances.

(1) The Defendant is a foundation that runs a welfare facility ○○○ for people with disabilities. The Plaintiff worked at ○○○ since February 1, 2004, as a rehabilitation teacher under the department of life services and was laid off, along with Nonparty 1, on June 1, 2010, for managerial reasons.

(2) Subsequently, the Defendant hired: ① Nonparty 2 as a rehabilitation teacher tasked with administrative duties on December 1, 2010; ② Nonparty 3 as a rehabilitation teacher tasked with administrative duties on July 1, 2011; ③ Nonparty 4 as a rehabilitation teacher tasked with administrative duties on August 1, 2011; ④ Nonparty 5 as a rehabilitation teacher tasked with administrative duties on September 1, 2011; ⑤ Nonparty 6 as a rehabilitation teacher tasked with administrative duties on October 1, 2011; ⑥ Nonparty 7 as a rehabilitation teacher tasked with administrative duties and Nonparty 8 as the director of the administrative office, respectively, on November 1, 2011; ⑦ Nonparty 9 as a

rehabilitation teacher under the department of life services on February 1, 2012; ⑧ Nonparty 10 as a rehabilitation teacher under the department of life services and Nonparty 11 as a rehabilitation teacher tasked with administrative duties, respectively, on April 1, 2013; and ⑨ Nonparty 12 as a rehabilitation teacher under the department of life services on May 1, 2013.

(3) There is no evidence indicating that the Plaintiff was unreachable by the Defendant because of a change in address or contact details after the dismissal of the Plaintiff. Nonetheless, the Defendant neither notified the Plaintiff of the recruitment nor confirmed the Plaintiff's intention to re-enter into an employment contract when employing employees as above.

(4) There is no evidence of the existence of the objective reasons suggesting that the Plaintiff would not have wanted to enter into an employment contract or making it difficult to expect the Defendant to conclude an employment contract with the Plaintiff.

C. These circumstances are examined in light of the legal doctrine seen earlier. The Defendant fired the Plaintiff and Nonparty 1 for managerial reasons and subsequently hired rehabilitation teachers several times without notifying the Plaintiff of the recruitment and the conditions of employment and confirming the Plaintiff's intention to enter into an employment contract. Therefore, it can be said that the Defendant's duty of preferential reemployment of the Plaintiff came into effect, at the latest, at around November 1, 2011, when, after laying off the Plaintiff and Nonparty 1, the Defendant hired the second person for the role of rehabilitation teacher under the department of life services, the same position with which the Plaintiff was tasked at the time of his dismissal.

D. Nevertheless, based on the grounds stated in its reasoning that there is no basis for requiring the Defendant to notify the Plaintiff of the recruitment procedure in form of individual notifications and confirm the Plaintiff's intention therefor, the lower court determined that the Defendant's duty of preferential reemployment came into effect, and the Defendant's violation of the said duty occurred, on April 1, 2013, which came after the Plaintiff's declaration of intention of getting reinstated and when the Defendant newly hired employees. In so determining, the lower court erred by misapprehending the legal doctrine concerning the Article 25(1) of the LSA and thereby adversely affected the judgment. The grounds of final appeal pointing to this error are with merit.

(2) Judgment on the Defendant's grounds of final appeal

A. The determination on the arguments in the grounds of final appeal relating to the time at which the duty of preferential reemployment came into effect (Ground of final appeal Nos. 1 and 2). This part of the grounds of final appeal challenges the lower court's findings of fact and determination under the premise that the Defendant's duty of preferential reemployment of the Plaintiff did not come into effect until after the Plaintiff expressed the intention of reinstatement to the Defendant and the Defendant hired new employees. However, as seen earlier, the lower court's judgment concerning the time at which the duty of preferential reemployment came into effect is unviable. Hence, without further proceeding to examine, this part of the Defendant's grounds of final appeal is unacceptable.

B. The determination on the argument in the grounds of final appeal relating to general damage (Ground of final appeal No. 3). An employer has a duty of preferential reemployment of dismissed employees under the Article 25(1) of the LSA. Hence, a dismissed employee is legally entitled to seek a judgment against the employer in substitution for the declaration of intention of employment, and the employment relationship between the employer and the dismissed employee is established when such a judgment becomes final and conclusive. Also, the dismissed employee may file a claim for damages for the employer's noncompliance with the duty of preferential reemployment for lost wages arising from the time at which the employer's duty of preferential reemployment came into effect until the establishment of employment relationship.[844)] The lower court determined that the amount of general damage incurred by the Plaintiff because of the Defendant's violation of the Article 25(1) of the LSA was the amount of wages the Plaintiff could have received had the Defendant performed the duty of preferential reemployment. The examination of the reasoning of the lower judgment in light of the legal doctrine seen earlier reveals no error on the part of the above lower judgment based on the misunderstanding of the scope of damages and a considerable causal relationship.

---

844) *See* Supreme Court Decision 2013Da14965, decided on November 26, 2015.

C. The determination on the argument in the grounds of final appeal relating to the offset of the harm done by the benefit (Ground of final appeal No. 4).

(1) In a case where the obligee or victim who incurred damages from default or an act of tort obtained benefits for the same cause, the said benefits must be deducted when calculating the amount of damages, as required by the concept of equity. To offset the harm done by the benefits obtained when calculating the amount of damages, the victim must have obtained new benefits from the act that serves as the cause of the liability for damages, and there has to be a considerable causal relationship between the said benefits and the act that served as the cause of the liability for damages. In a case where: (a) the dismissed employee files a claim for damages, on account of the employer's noncompliance with the duty of employment, the amount of which commensurate with the amount of wages that the employee could have received had the employer performed its duty of employment; and (b) a considerable causal relationship is recognized between the profits accrued by the dismissed employee by performing work for other workplaces instead of the employer and the employer's noncompliance with the duty of employment, such profits must be deducted when calculating the amount of damages arising from the employer's noncompliance with the duty of employment.[845] In the meantime, in a case where the employment relationship is dissolved and remains no longer effective, such as in the case where the dismissed employee seeks damages arising from the employer's noncompliance with the duty of employment, the provision on shutdown allowances under the Article 46 of the LSA is inapplicable.[846]

(2) The lower court considered that, during the period in which the income the Plaintiff earned by getting himself employed by another workplace (midterm income) exceeds 30 percent of the amount of monthly wage the Plaintiff could have earned if reemployed, the amount corresponding to 70 percent of the monthly wage constituted loss after the deduction of the midterm income, and rejected the Defendant's argument that the midterm income must entirely be deducted from the amount of loss incurred by the Plaintiff.

(3) The reasoning of the lower judgment is examined in light of the legal doctrine seen earlier. The Plaintiff obtained benefits, that is, midterm income, by providing labor, which the Plaintiff was supposed to provide to the Defendant, to

845) *See* Supreme Court Decision 2015Da232859, decided on March 22, 2017.
846) *See* Supreme Court Decision 91Da44100, decided on July 24, 1992.

another workplace while the Defendant failed to implement its duty of preferential reemployment. Hence, such benefits are considered to have a considerable causal relationship with the Defendant's noncompliance with the duty of preferential reemployment. Therefore, when calculating the amount of loss incurred by the Plaintiff, the midterm income earned by the Plaintiff during the period temporally corresponding to the period alleged by the Plaintiff as the period during which the loss occurred must entirely be deducted. Nonetheless, the lower court determined that the midterm income can be deducted only within 30% of the amount of the monthly wage. In so determining, the lower court erred by misapprehending the legal doctrine concerning the offset of the harm done by the benefit obtained, and thereby adversely affected the judgment. The ground of final appeal pointing to this error is with merit.

D. The determination on the argument in the grounds of final appeal concerning the extinguishment of the duty of employment (Ground of final appeal No. 5). Based on the grounds stated in its reasoning, the lower court determined that, insofar as the Defendant's duty of preferential reemployment of the Plaintiff came into effect within three years from the day of dismissal due to managerial reasons, the Defendant's duty of preferential reemployment which already came into effect cannot be considered to have been extinguished, notwithstanding that three years have passed since the day of the Plaintiff's dismissal. The examination of the reasoning of the lower judgment in light of the record does not reveal any error on the part of the lower court's judgment by misapprehending the legal doctrine concerning the Article 25(1) of the LSA.

E. The determination on the argument in the grounds of final appeal concerning the good faith principle and abuse of rights (Ground of final appeal No. 6). Based on the grounds stated in its reasoning, the lower court determined that the Plaintiff's filing of the instant lawsuit cannot be considered as a breach of the good faith principle or abuse of rights. The examination of the reasoning of the lower judgment in light of the record does not reveal any error in the above lower judgment arising from misunderstanding of the legal doctrine concerning the good faith principle or abuse of rights.

3) Conclusion

Therefore, the part of the lower judgment concerning a claim for damages is reversed, and this part of the case is remanded to the lower court. The remaining appeals brought by the Defendant are dismissed. It is so decided as per Disposition by the assent of all participating Justices on the bench.

Related Legal Issues and Questions:

1. What is a main source of laws on employment and labor in Korea?
2. How can employees be protected against their unlawful termination of employment?
3. How can employees be protected against any anti-discrimination during the employment?

CHAPTER 16
INTERNATIONAL INVESTMENT LAW

An international investment law mostly governs foreign direct investment and the resolution of disputes between foreign investors and sovereign states. The 'OECD Guidelines for Multinational Enterprises' as one of international sources of law are principles and standards for corporate social responsibility in a harmonious manner with society and the policies of host countries. A foreign direct investment is another area of international investment laws and is made by a firm or individual in one country into business interests located in another country. When a commercial dispute arises in relation to international investment or even to any commercial contract between private parties, it can be resolved through court proceedings or alternative dispute resolutions such as arbitration, mediation, etc. Meanwhile disputes between foreign investors and states are resolved, among others, by the International Center for Settlement of Investment Disputes which is the forum designated most frequently. In this Chapter, it is important to understand how international investments can be carried out and how disputes between parties can be resolved.

I. Introduction to International Investment Law

An international investment law (국제투자법) is one of the fastest growing fields of public international law. It governs foreign direct investment and the resolution of disputes between foreign investors and sovereign States.[847] Over the last two decades, there has been exponential growth both in the formation of investment treaties and in the invocation of their unique systems of dispute settlement against developed and developing states alike.

847) Ralph H. Folsom, Michael Wallace Gordon, Michael P. Van Alstine, Michael D. Ramsey, International Business Transactions: A Problem-Oriented Coursebook (12th edition), West Academic Publishing, 2015, p.911.

Due to economic globalization and the rise of foreign direct investments, the regulation of the field has become a key area of international law. Under international investment agreements, states parties agree to provide a certain degree of protection to investors who are nationals of contracting states, or their investments. Such protection generally includes compensation in case of expropriation, fair and equitable treatment, non-discrimination and full protection and security, among others.[848)]

Further, with the acceleration of economic globalization and the increasing activities of multinational enterprises, multinational enterprises broadly impact areas such as company policies of the host counties, labor, environment and consumer protection.

Under this background of international investment, this chapter addresses, among other issues in an international investment law, the question of whether the rules and regulations on investment can be found in international level and state's level, and of how the disputes on international investment can be settled between investors and states and thus they should migrate to international investment law and arbitration. Mostly, they can be answered from the best resources for locating primary and secondary resources to research international investment law. One of them could be resources for the OECD Guidelines for Multinational Enterprises as an international standard, the foreign investment including foreign direct investment as an state's standard, and the dispute resolution including an investor-state dispute settlement and arbitral institutions.

II. OECD Guidelines for Multinational Enterprises

1. International Investment Laws of the OECD

1) On the international investment aspects, there are many implementations by multinational enterprises. These are corporate organizations that own or control production of goods or services in two or more countries other than their home countries. For example, there are many multinational companies and worldwide or global enterprises including Apple, Samsung Electronics, Disney, franchise companies

848) Valentina Vadi, Proportionality, Reasonableness and Standards of Review in International Investment Law and Arbitration, April 27, 2018., p.1.

such as Baskin Robbins, Dunkin Donuts, McDonald's, etc.

On the perspective of international investment, the OECD announced one of guidelines for multinational enterprises. That is the 'OECD Guidelines for Multinational Enterprises'[849] (MNE Guidelines) which are principles and standards for corporate social responsibility to ensure that the multinational enterprises will operate their business in a harmonious manner with society and the policies of host countries. The MNE Guidelines are an annex to the OECD Declaration on International Investment and Multinational Enterprises. Originally, the OECD Declaration and the MNE Guidelines were adopted in 1976. The OECD Guidelines were subsequently revised in 1979, 1982, 1984, 1991, 2000 and 2011.

The MNE Guidelines are internationally recognized recommendations for social responsibility jointly addressed to multinational enterprises by adhering Governments. The MNE Guidelines are legally nonbinding and thus, in legal sense, correspond not to a hard law, but to a soft law. However, the OECD Investment Committee and its Working Party on Responsible Business Conduct encourage implementation of them among adherents. Accordingly, although the MNE Guidelines are not legally enforceable, the adhering countries including Korea have implemented them in their countries and established the National Contact Points (NCPs) in each country. They also promote the MNE Guidelines and ensure effectiveness of them by dealing with issues raised in relation to the implementation of them.

For multinational enterprises, observing the MNE Guidelines is a good way to establish itself in a host country and to maximize their performance. It is expected for both multinational enterprises which operate in home and also operate abroad to observe the MNE Guidelines voluntarily and actively.[850]

2) In addition, businesses can play a major role in contributing to economic, environmental and social progress, especially when they minimize the adverse impacts of their operations, supply chains and other business relationships. The MNE Guidelines recommend that enterprises conduct due diligence in order to identify, prevent or mitigate and account for how actual and potential adverse impacts are addressed.[851]

---

849) OECD, "OECD Guidelines for Multinational Enterprises (2011 Edition)," May 25, 2011 at <http://mneguidelines.oecd.org/mneguidelines/>.

850) Korea National Contact Point (KNCP), "OECD Guidelines for Multinational Enterprises," at <http://www.ncp.or.kr/servlet/kcab_encp/info/1000>.

The 'OECD Due Diligence Guidance for Responsible Business Conduct,' which was adopted on May 31, 2018 during the annual OECD Ministerial Meeting, provides practical support to enterprises on the implementation of the MNE Guidelines by providing its due diligence recommendations and associated provisions. Implementing these recommendations can help enterprises avoid and address adverse impacts related to workers, human rights, the environment, bribery, consumers and corporate governance that may be associated with their operations, supply chains and other business relationships. It also seeks to promote a common understanding among Governments and stakeholders on due diligence for responsible business conduct. The 'UN Guiding Principles on Business and Human Rights,' as well as the 'ILO Tripartite Declaration of Principles Concerning Multinational Enterprises and Social Policy,' also contain due diligence recommendations, and it can help enterprises implement them.[852)]

3) The 'OECD Investment Committee' (Committee) is the primary body responsible for overseeing the functioning of the MNE Guidelines and implementation of all OECD investment instruments. The Committee consists of member states' senior officials from treasuries, economics, trade and industry, and foreign affairs ministries and central banks. All OECD member states are members of the Committee. Argentina and Brazil are observers and the 13 non-Members that have subscribed to the OECD Declaration participate in the work of the Committee on issues related to the MNE Guidelines. A Working Party on Responsible Business Conduct was established in 2013 as a subsidiary body of the Committee to help implement the MNE Guidelines and strengthen the system of National Contact Points.

2. The MNE Guidelines

1) What are the MNE Guidelines?

The MNE Guidelines are joint recommendations provided to multinational enterprises by the OECD member countries and adhering Governments and they

---

851) OECD, "OECD Due Diligence Guidance for Responsible Business Conduct," 2018, available at <http://mneguidelines.oecd.org/>.

852) *Id.*

provide standards of good practice and can enable the MNE Guidelines to have a positive impact and also simultaneously minimize adverse impact on economy, society and the environment.

The MNE Guidelines widely cover business ethics including Labor Relations, Environment, Information Disclosure, Competition, Taxation, Science and Technology, Anti-Corruption and Consumer Protection. In addition, the OECD has developed specific guidance in a number of sectors such as the OECD Due Diligence Guidance for Responsible Business Conduct, in order to help enterprises implement the MNE Guidelines and proactively identify risks of adverse impacts.

2) Outline of the MNE Guidelines

The MNE Guidelines cover business ethics on a range of issues, including employment and industrial relations, human rights, environment, information disclosure, combating bribery, consumer interests, science and technology, competition, and taxation

The following summary of Chapters I through X is provided for reference purposes only and all sections of the MNE Guidelines should be referred to for the details.

[Summary of the MNE Guidelines][853)]

1. Chapter I Concepts and Principles

- Global applicability of the Guidelines
- Voluntary and non-legal nature of the Guidelines
- Definition of multinational enterprise and applicability of the Guidelines to all parts of the enterprise
- Guidelines apply equally to foreign and domestic enterprises and reflect good practice for all
- Expectations of small and medium-sized enterprises
- Government protectionism and questioning a country's comparative advantage
- Obeying the domestic laws of host countries
- Equal treatment of foreign and domestic enterprises by Governments
- Dispute resolution between enterprises and Governments

- Governments' obligations to create a National Contact Point to promote adherence to the Guidelines

2. Chapter II General Policies

- Obeying policies of the host country and considering views of stakeholders
- Contributing to the achievement of sustainable development
- Respecting human rights consistent with host Governments' obligations and commitments
- Encouraging local capacity building
- Encouraging human capital formation
- Refraining from seeking or accepting exemptions to regulatory requirements
- Upholding good corporate governance principles and applying good corporate governance practices
- Adopting self-regulatory practices and management systems that foster trust
- Promoting employee awareness of, and compliance with, company policies
- Protecting 'whistle-blowers'
- Abstaining from improper involvement in local political activities

3. Chapter III Disclosure

- Disclosing information on activities, structure, financial situation and performance
- Applying high-quality standards for disclosure, accounting and auditing practices
- Applying high-quality standards for non-financial information including environmental and social reporting
- Disclosing basic company information
- Disclosing material information
- Disclosing information on value statements or codes of conduct including information on social, ethical and environmental policies
- Disclosing information on systems for managing risks and complying with laws and on statements or codes of conduct
- Disclosing information on relationships with employees and other stakeholders

4. Chapter IV Employment and Industrial Relations

- Respecting employees' right to organize and engaging in constructive negotiations
- Abolishing child labor
- Eliminating forced or compulsory labor
- Non-discrimination based on race, color, sex, religion, political opinion, national

extraction or social origin
- Providing facilities for effective negotiation of collective bargaining agreements
- Providing information for meaningful negotiation on employment conditions
- Promoting consultation and cooperation among employers and employees
- Providing true and fair information on company performance
- Observing standards on a level equal or better to comparable employees in the country of operation
- Implementing measures to ensure the health and safety of employees
- Employing local personnel and providing training
- Providing reasonable notice of major changes such as facility closure or large-scale dismissals
- Unfairly influencing negotiations on employment conditions or employees' right to organize
- Negotiating on matters of mutual concern and authorizing management to take decisions

5. Chapter V Environment

- Taking account of the need to protect the environment, public health and safety (EH&S) and contributing to the wider goal of sustainable development
- Maintaining an environmental management system including evaluation of EH&S impacts, establishment of objectives or targets to improve performance and verification of progress towards EH&S objectives or targets
- Providing information on EH&S impacts to employees and the public
- Consulting with communities on EH&S policies and their implementation
- Evaluating activities, goods and services for their EH&S impacts over the full life cycle
- Taking precaution to prevent serious harm to the EH&S
- Maintaining plans to prevent or reduce serious environmental and health damage and maintain systems to report to authorities
- Continually seeking to improve environmental performance
- Researching ways to improve environmental performance
- Providing training to employees on EH&S matters including handling hazardous materials and preventing accidents
- Contributing to the development of environmental policies

6. Chapter VI Combating Bribery

- Not offering bribes to obtain or retain business or other undue advantage

- Not offering or giving into demands to pay officials or others a portion of a contract payment
- Maintaining a list of payments to public bodies and state-owned enterprises including making this information available to authorities
- Enhancing transparency of activities
- Promoting awareness of and compliance with company policies against bribery and extortion
- Maintaining management systems that discourage bribery and corrupt practices
- Implementing accounting and audit practices to prevent corrupt practices
- Not making illegal contributions to political candidates or parties including complying with domestic disclosure requirements

7. Chapter VII Consumer Interests

- Acting in accordance with fair business practices and ensuring safety and quality of goods and services
- Ensuring goods and services meet agreed and legally required standards for consumer health and safety
- Providing clear and accurate information to enable consumers to make informed decisions
- Providing transparent and effective procedures to address consumer complaints and resolving disputes
- Not engaging in activities that are misleading, fraudulent or unfair
- Respecting consumer privacy
- Cooperating with officials to prevent or remove threats caused by their products

8. Chapter VIII Science and Technology

- Ensuring activities are compatible with the science and technology (S&T) policies of the host country
- Contributing to the development of local and national S&T capacity
- Carrying out S&T development work in host countries and hiring people from host countries to encourage training• Granting licenses for the use of intellectual property rights or technology transfer that are reasonable
- Cultivating relationships with educational and research institutions through collaborative research

9. Chapter IX Competition

- Obeying competition laws and regulations

- Not entering into anti-competitive agreements with competitors
- Not fixing prices
- Not making rigged bids • Not establishing output restrictions or quotas
- Not sharing or dividing markets
- Taking into account the anti-competition laws of other countries whose economies could be negatively impacted by anti-competitive activity

10. Chapter X Taxation

- Paying taxes in a timely manner
- Obeying tax laws and regulations in every country with operations
- Providing information to authorities for determining tax obligations
- Applying the arm's length principle to the use of transfer pricing

3. National Contact Points

To ensure the effectiveness of the MNE Guidelines, the OECD Council adopted the 'Decision of the Council on the OECD Guidelines for Multinational Enterprises,' therefore adhering countries must establish National Contact Points (NCPs) which will deal with tasks related to the implementation of the MNE Guidelines.[854)]

The Korean Government, hereby, has enacted the 'Regulations for the Implementation of OECD Guidelines for Multinational Enterprises by National Contact Point' in 2001 in accordance with the decision of the OECD Council and has established the Korean NCP.

For the implementation of the MNE Guidelines, the Korean NCP performs the following functions:[855)]

---

853) Colleen Freeman, Cornelia Heydenreich, Serena Lillywhite, "Guide to the OECD Guidelines for Multinational Enterprises' Complaint Procedure Lessons from Past NGO Complaints," the OECD Watch, November 2006, pp.44-46.

854) OECD, "OECD Guidelines for Multinational Enterprises (2011 Edition)," *op. cit.*, p.71.

855) Korea National Contact Point (KNCP), *op. cit.*

(i) Promotional activities: The Korean NCP provides the original text of the guidelines, Korean translations and other references. The Korean NCP makes an effort to raise awareness of the guidelines for potential interested parties such as the business community, worker organizations and environmental organizations.

(ii) Dispute resolution related to the implementation of the guidelines: Though the guidelines are non-binding and voluntary, parties concerned are able to file a complaint related to the implementation of the guidelines. The Korean NCP will review the issues raised and offer assistance to help the parties resolve the issues.

(iii) Co-operation with other NCPs and Reporting to the OECD: The Korean NCP will co-operate with other NCPs to resolve the issues raised. Also, the Korean NCP will report its activities to the OECD annually, and the OECD will review the implementation activities of each NCP.

All Governments adhering to the MNE Guidelines are required to set up an NCP and ensure it has the financial and human resources to function, and does so in a visible, accessible, transparent and accountable way. As of 2020, there are NCPs in 49 countries,[856] which have collectively handled over 500 cases related to responsible business conduct issues in over 100 countries and territories.

III. Foreign Direct Investment

1. Foreign Direct Investment in General

1) What is a Foreign Direct Investment?

A foreign direct investment (FDI, 외국인직접투자) is an investment made by a firm or individual in one country into business interests located in another

856) Argentina, Australia, Austria, Belgium, Brazil, Canada, Chile, Colombia, Costa Rica, Croatia, Czech Republic, Denmark, Egypt, Estonia, Finland, France, Germany, Greece, Hungary, Iceland, Ireland, Israel, Italy, Japan, Jordan, Kazakhstan, Korea, Latvia, Lithuania, Luxembourg, Mexico, Morocco, Netherlands, New Zealand (OECD, "National Contact Points for Responsible Business Conduct Providing Access to Remedy: 20 years and the road ahead," 2020, pp.61-62).

country. Generally, the FDI takes place when an investor establishes foreign business operations or acquires foreign business assets in a foreign company. For example, the Apple's investment in China and the Samsung Electronics' investment into factories in Vietnam and Indonesia are good examples to understand the FDI. The FDI can be to start a new business or invest in an existing foreign owned business. However, since the FDI frequently involves more than just a capital investment, it must be distinguished from portfolio investment in which an investor merely purchases equities of foreign-based companies.[857] It may include provisions of management or technology as well.

The FDIs are commonly and actively utilized in open economies that offer a skilled workforce and above-average growth prospects for the investor, as opposed to tightly regulated economies or closed markets. The key feature of the FDI is that it establishes either effective control of or at least substantial influence over the decision-making of a foreign business.

The FDIs can be made in a variety of ways, including the opening of a subsidiary or associate company in a foreign country, acquiring a controlling interest in an existing foreign company, or by means of a merger or joint venture with a foreign company. The threshold for the FDI that establishes a controlling interest, per the MNE Guidelines, is a minimum 10 percent ownership stake in a foreign-based company.[858] However, that definition is flexible, as there are instances where effective controlling interest in a firm can be established with less than 10 percent of the company's voting shares. In general, anything under 10 percent stake is classed as part of a stock portfolio. For instance, this covers the small amount of stocks that the average citizen may have invested and anything too small to influence any level of control of the firm.

2) Types of Foreign Direct Investment

The FDIs are commonly categorized as being horizontal, vertical or conglomerate. A horizontal FDI is establishing the same type of business in another country, while a vertical FDI is related but different, and a conglomerate FDI is an unrelated business venture.

---

857) James Chen, "Foreign Direct Investment (FDI)," available at <HENhttps://www.investopedia.com/terms/f/fdi.asp>.

858) OECD, "OECD Guidelines for Multinational Enterprises (2011 Edition)," *op. cit.*

1) A horizontal type of the FDI refers to the investor establishing the same type of business operation in a foreign country as it operates in its home country. In other words, a business invests in a foreign firm that produces similar goods. For example, Nike, a US based firm, may purchase Puma, a Germany based firm, or a cell phone provider based in Korea may open stores in the U.S. or China. All they are both in the same industry and therefore would be classified as a form of a horizontal FDI.

Samsung in Korea -> investment -> phone seller in B country

2) A vertical type of the FDI is one in which different but related business activities from the investor's main business are established or acquired in a foreign country, such as when a manufacturing company acquires an interest in a foreign company that supplies parts or raw materials required for the manufacturing company to make its products. In other words, a business invests in a foreign firm that it may supply or sell too. For example, Hershey's, a US chocolate manufacturer, may look to invest in cocoa producers in Brazil. This is known as backwards vertical integration because the firm is purchasing a supplier, or potential supplier, in the supply chain.[859] As an example of forwards vertical integration. a firm invests in a foreign company that is further along in the supply chain and, for example, Hershey's may look to purchase a share in New York where it sells its products.

Hershey's in US -> investment -> chocolate supplier in B country

3) A conglomerate type of the FDI is one where a company or individual makes a foreign investment in a business that is unrelated to its existing business in its home country. In other words, it is not linked in any direct way to the investors business. For example, Walmart, a US retailer, may invest in BMW, a

859) Bypaul Boyce, "Foreign Direct Investment (FDI): Definition, 3 Types, Benefits and Disadvantages," September 23, 2020.

German automobile manufacturer. Since this type of investment involves entering an industry in which the investor has no previous experience, it often takes the form of a joint venture with a foreign company already operating in the industry. This may seem strange, but offer big businesses an opportunity to expand and diversify into new areas. In certain situation, some big businesses may come to a point where the demand for its fundamental business starts to decline. In order to survive, they must invest in new ventures.[860] Even big businesses with strong demand may look to new industries where growth and return on investment are significantly larger.

Walmart in US -> investment -> automobile manufacturer in B country

2. Pros and Cons for Foreign Direct Investment

1) Benefits from Foreign Direct Investment

Some benefits from the FDI may, among others, include boost to international trade, reduced local tensions, sharing of resources, diversification, lower cost and increased efficiency, tax incentives, and employment and economic boost.

(1) Boost to international trade: The FDI promotes international trade as it allows production to flow to parts of the world which are more cost effective. As a result, it could create new jobs in the host region and boosted trade between the nations.

(2) Reduced regional and global tensions: As a result of the interconnected supply chain by the FDI, it is in the interest of all parties to ensure the stability of its trading partners. Accordingly, the FDI can create a level of dependency between countries, which in turn can create a level of peace. In other words, if nations are reliant on each other for their income, then the likelihood of war is also reduced.

860) *Id.*

(3) Sharing of technology, knowledge, and culture: The FDI allows the transfer of technology, knowledge, and culture. By coming in from a different cultural background and perspective, often, efficiencies can be achieved. Furthermore, technology can be transferred over in a number of ways. Employees in host country can benefit from having first-hand access to the new technology. Since the technology could be outright purchased from a foreign nation, it could be reverse-engineered or provide inspiration for domestic development.

(4) Diversification: From the businesses perspective, the FDI reduces risk through diversification. By investing in other nations, it spreads a company's exposure. In other words, it is not so reliant only on home country. By diversifying and investing in foreign markets, it allows businesses to reduce domestic exposure. While there may be a decline in demand for one, there may be growth in another.

(5) Lower costs and increased efficiency: The FDI can benefit from lower labor costs. Businesses will often try off-shore production to nations abroad that offer cheaper labor. Where labor costs are lower, a productivity of labor must be also considered. The foreign investors will take such factors into account and, in most cases, the labor is so much cheaper than most of the productivity differentials are eliminated. In other words, more employees will be needed to make the same number of goods, but the total cost to produce is lower, and as a result, the FDI is generally associated with lower costs and increased cost-effectiveness.

(6) Tax incentives: Reduced levels of corporation tax can save big businesses billions each and every year. Countries with lower tax regimes are usually those that are favored. Furthermore, there are also tax incentives by which the foreign Government offers tax breaks to foreign investors in a bid to encourage the FDI.

(7) Employment and economic boost: When money is invested in another country, it creates jobs, new companies, and new factories or buildings. This brings about new opportunities for local residents and can stimulate further growth. With greater levels of employment being made available, it creates a greater level of purchasing power in the wider economy. In turn, this stimulates

employment in other markets and industries.

2) Disadvantages from Foreign Direct Investment

There must be some other cons when the FDI is considered. Among others, representative disadvantages to the FDI include foreign control, loss of domestic jobs, and risk of political or economic change.

(1) Foreign control: One of the main fears, particularly among developing nations, is that they can essentially be brought and controlled by foreign powers. This is why some countries place strict restrictions on the FDI.

(2) Loss of domestic jobs: When significant sums of money are transferred to another, it is an investment that would have been used in the home country and market. Consequently, the FDI may boost employment in foreign nations, but may temporarily reduce it at home country.

(3) Risk of political or economic change: When investing abroad, particularly in developing nations such as the Middle East and Africa as examples, there is huge risk that is associated. For example, there may be huge political upheaval or a regional war. This may consist of a new Government that is not so favorable to foreign investors. Consequently, there could be an element of significant risk.

IV. Foreign Investment in Korea

1. Introduction

The FDI in Korea is defined as an investment with an investment threshold contributed by foreigners amounting to at least KRW 100 million and being 10% or more of the total amount.[861] Foreigners are able to do business in Korea without restraint, except as otherwise prescribed by regulations. In other words,

861) Article 2(1)(d) of the Foreign Investment Promotion Act.

Foreign investors are guaranteed a legitimate right to manage their business operations in Korea freely. To this goal, the Korean Government has prepared a system to protect foreign investors. Korea's foreign investment policy is in accordance with global standards based on the recommendations and agreements of international organizations such as the OECD, the UNCTAD and the WTO. It provides various incentives to foreign investors that create high-quality jobs or encourage domestic economic growth. As such, it is positively expected that the Korean Government constantly strives to create a business-friendly investment.

According to the Foreign Investment Promotion Act (FIPA, 외국인투자촉진법) as a main source of law for foreign investment in Korea, the FDI in Korea includes the acquisition of stocks of domestic companies, long-term loans (five or more years) from parent companies outside Korea, and investments in non-profit corporations in the fields of science and technology. Cases in which a foreign company uses unappropriated earned surpluses for building new or additional factories are now also considered as the FDI. Objects of investment to acquire stocks or shares include foreign currency, capital goods, proceeds from acquired stocks, etc., and industrial property rights.

While Korea's market is open to foreign investors, there are various businesses prohibited and restricted from foreign investments. Out of a total of 1,196 business categories listed under the Korean Standard Industrial Classification (KSIC), the FDI in Korea is permitted in 1,135 categories.[862] Foreign investment is prohibited in 61 business categories including legislation, public administration, diplomacy, and national defense, etc.[863] Among the permitted business categories, restrictions on shareholding ratio, etc. apply in 29 categories and there are three prohibited business categories - nuclear power generation, radio broadcasting, and terrestrial tv broadcasting. For restricted business categories, each criteria for permission must be satisfied enough for the FDI.[864]

Compared to the increase of the FDI in the past, the FDI in Korea seems to

862) Investment Consulting Center of the KOTRA, Business in Korea 2022, KOTRA publication No. 22-018, January 2022, p.9.

863) Businesses Prohibited from Foreign Investment by the Regulations on Foreign Investment (*see* Public Notice No. 2022-127 of the Ministry of Trade, Industry and Energy) under the Article 4(3) of the Foreign Investment Promotion Act.

864) Businesses Restricted from Foreign Investment and Criteria for Permission by the Regulations on Foreign Investment (*see* Public Notice No. 2022-127 of the Ministry of Trade, Industry and Energy) under the Article 4(3) of the Foreign Investment Promotion Act.

be set to decline from the around 2020 as the corona virus pandemic continues to affect business activities across the world.

2. Types of Foreign Investment

The foreign investment under the FIPA must be any of the followings:[865)]

1) Where a foreigner holds stocks or shares of a Korean corporation or enterprise including a Korean corporation in the process of establishment, as prescribed by Presidential Decree,[866)] by any of the following methods in order to establish a continuous economic relationship with the Korean corporation or enterprise, such as participating in the management of the Korean corporation or enterprise, in accordance with the FIPA:

(i) Acquisition of stocks, etc. newly issued by the Korean corporation or enterprise, and

(ii) Acquisition of previously issued stocks or shares of the Korean corporation or enterprise.

2) A loan with maturity of not less than five years based on the loan maturity prescribed in the first loan contract, which is provided to the relevant foreign invested company by any of the following entities:[867)]

(i) The overseas parent company of the foreign invested company or a company that has a capital investment relationship with such company, and

(iii) A foreign investor or a company that has a capital investment relationship with such investor.

---

865) Article 2(1)(d) of the Foreign Investment Promotion Act.

866) Article 2(2) of the Enforcement Decree of the Foreign Investment Promotion Act. A foreign investment under the Article 2(1)(d)(i) of the FIPA refers to any of the followings and the investment amount is at least KRW 100 million. However, where a business fails to meet the requirements due to partial transfer of stocks or shares or capital reduction, etc. after it has been registered as a foreign invested company, it will be also deemed a foreign investment: (i) Where a foreigner owns at least 10/100 of the total number of voting stocks issued by, or of the total equity investment of, a Korean company, and (ii) Where a foreigner who owns stocks, etc. of a Korean company dispatches or appoints an executive officer to or at such company.

867) Article 2(1)(d)(ii) of the Foreign Investment Promotion Act.

3) Where a foreigner contributes to a non-profit corporation pursuant to the FIPA in order to establish a continuous cooperative relationship with the corporation which satisfies the certain standards and which is a Korean corporation or enterprise in the field of science and technology.[868)]

4) Where a foreign invested company uses its unappropriated earned surplus for the certain purposes, such as the creation or extension of its factory facilities. In this case, the foreign invested company is deemed a foreigner under the FIPA, and the amount of foreign investment must be the amount calculated by multiplying the amount used and the foreign investment ratio.[869)]

5) Other contributions to a non-profit corporation by a foreigner, which the Foreign Investment Committee recognizes as a foreign investment in accordance with the certain standards regarding the business contents, etc. of the non-profit corporation.[870)]

However, where mostly discussing the FDI in practice, there are generally two types of foreign investment. They are opening a domestic branch of a foreign company and establishing a foreign invested company. The biggest difference between them is whether registered capital is invested or not. That also decides the payment of dividends. The earnings and losses of a domestic branch of a foreign company are aggregated to those of its headquarters, after taxes for some countries, the earnings of a foreign invested company, however, could be remitted to its headquarters only when it determines dividends.

In terms of tax liabilities, domestic branches of foreign companies and foreign invested companies both should pay taxes including corporate tax and VAT. The types of investment should be decided based on the scale of investment, equity structure and business outlook of the industry.

3. The Procedure of the FDI Establishment

Based on equity share acquisition of new or existing shares, the most popular

868) Article 2(1)(d)(iii) of the Foreign Investment Promotion Act.
869) Article 2(1)(d)(iv) of the Foreign Investment Promotion Act.
870) Article 2(1)(d)(v) of the Foreign Investment Promotion Act.

type in the FDI, overall procedures are as follows.

[The FDI Procedures in Case of Equity Share Acquisition][871)]

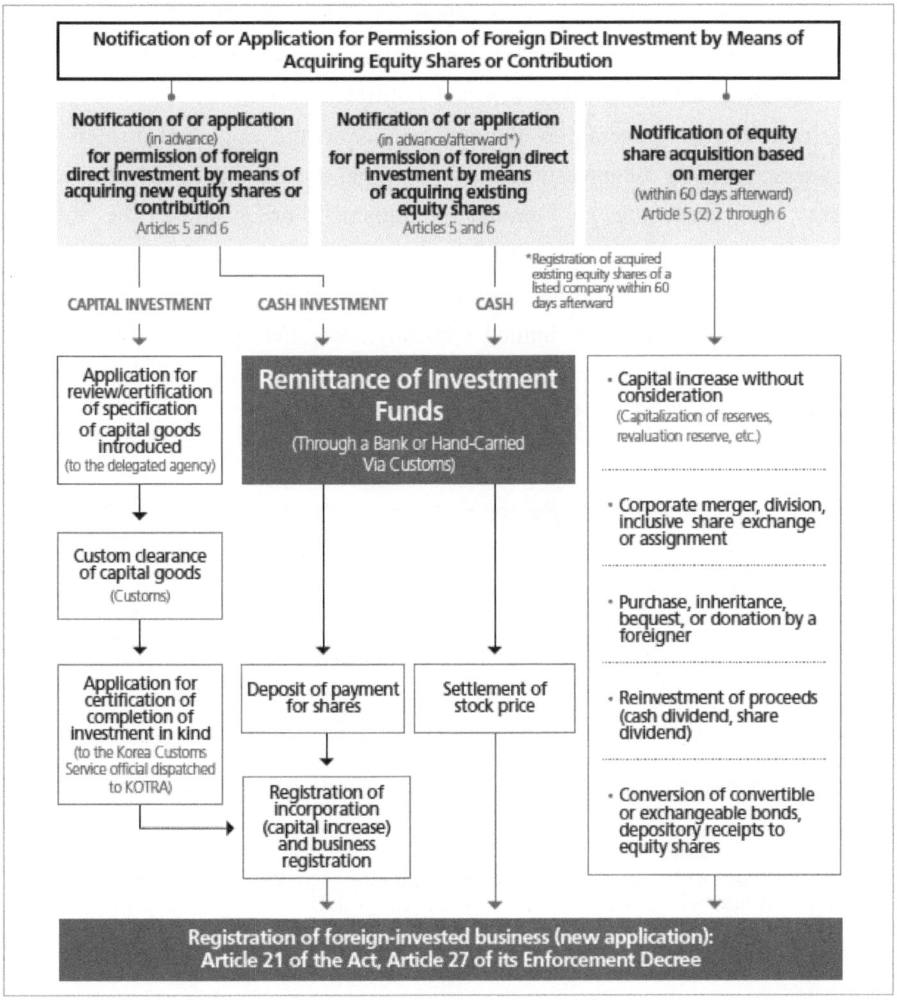

When a foreigner or foreign corporation establishes a corporation in Korea, investing certain amount of money, it can enjoy the benefit of tax benefits. To be recognized as a foreign invested company under the Foreign Investment Promotion Act, a foreigner must invest not less than KRW one hundred million

871) Investment Consulting Center of the KOTRA, *op. cit.,* p.29.

in the local corporation and acquire not less than 10 percent of the company's stocks with voting rights. Where a foreign investment is less than KRW one hundred million it cannot be registered as a foreign invested company and is subject to the Foreign Exchange Transaction Law (외국환거래법) not the FIPA. It is required to submit foreign currency security acquisition reports while a foreign invested company submits foreign invested notification.

It is suggested, in general, to thoroughly review the important matters before the business decision of investment, and to make sure about all the required documents and procedures in foreign investment. For example, the following matters must be considered during the preparation of investment: the products or services and categories of business in Korea, the type of corporation whether it would be a stock company, a limited company. etc., the scale of investment and equity structure whether the investment meets the requirements of the FIPA, and the site of business.

[Incorporation Procedures for the Foreign Invested Company][872]

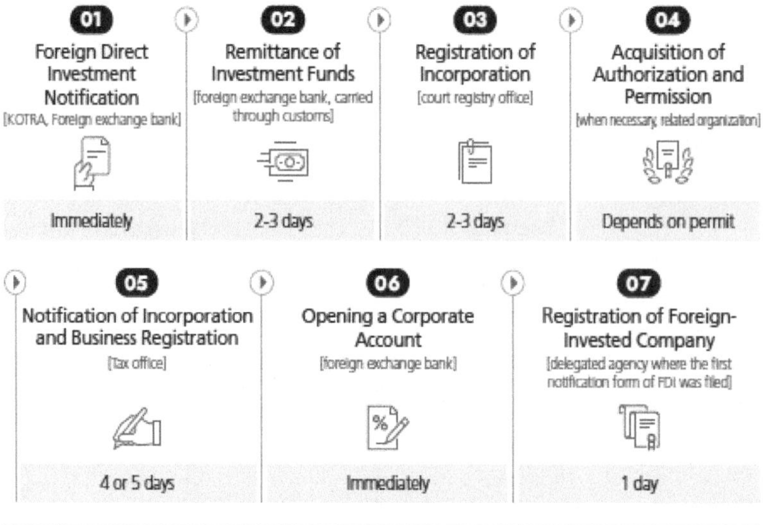

872) Investment Consulting Center of the KOTRA, *op. cit.*, p.30.

1) Foreign Direct Investment Notification

First of all, a foreign investor is required to pre-notify the FDI to the Foreign Investor Support Center in KOTRA or a foreign exchange bank.

According to the Article 30(4) of the FIPA, the Article 39(2) of the Enforcement Decree of the FIPA, and the Article 4 of the Enforcement Decree of the Act on Special Measures for the Promotion of Venture Business (벤처기업육성에 관한 특별조치법), various requirements and forms depending on the objects of investment must be satisfied when a foreign investor makes the FDI notification.

2) Remittance of Investment Funds

A foreign investor may remit investment funds by wire transfer to a temporary account at a domestic bank from overseas or hand-carry the foreign currency through customs directly. In the latter case, the investor must declare the funds at the customs office and receive a 'certificate of declaration of foreign currency.'

In principle, the remitted investment funds must undergo the procedure for deposit of funds for payment for shares and then a certificate of deposit of payment for shares is submitted to the court. However, in case of companies valued less than KRW 1 billion, it is possible to submit a certificate of balance after opening an account in the name of an investor. In this case, the funds can be freely withdrawn for business purposes from the following day.

3) Registration of Incorporation

The registry division in the court accepts the application for the registration of incorporation and it takes two to three days for the registration. The required documents can be checked on the list of application forms and required documents from the Registry of Supreme Court Internet Register Office.

This procedure is the same with what is required for domestic company establishment. However, where the shareholders or executives are foreigners, more documents must be prepared. The required documents differ based on the fact weather the foreign shareholders or executives stay in Korea.

4) Authorization and Permission

Where deemed necessary for business, a foreign investor must acquire the authorization and permission for the business from the competent authorities: *e.g.*, District Office, Health Center, Ministry of Food and Drug Safety, etc. The processing period may vary depending on the sort of authorization and permission for the type of business.

5) Notification of Incorporation and Business Registration

After completing registration of incorporation, notification of incorporation and business registration are required to the tax office having jurisdiction over the place of tax payment.

Once the business registration certificate is issued, opening a corporate bank account is required as a next step. Then, paid-in capital must be transferred to the corporate bank account.

6) Opening a Corporate Bank Account

A foreign investor may open a corporate bank account at a foreign exchange bank immediately. However, the choice of bank requires careful consideration since opening additional accounts at another bank is restricted for twenty business days.

Transferring paid-in capital to corporate bank account is usually carried out right after the foreign investment notification, but it does not matter if it has done before the notification. However, exchanging the capital for Korean Won must be after notification.

7) Registration of Foreign Invested Company

After the registration of incorporation, a foreign invested company registration must be undertaken at the KOTRA or at a foreign exchange bank where the notification was first made as the last step of the FDI incorporation. The registration must be completed within sixty days following the payment of the object of investment. Various requirements and forms must be satisfied when a foreign investor makes the FDI company registration.

Now, a foreign investor can start his business in Korea as a foreign invested company. For a foreign investor, the D-8 corporate investment visa is issued and granted for an investment exceeding KRW one hundred million.

4. Incentives for Foreign Invested Company

1) Tax Benefits for the FDI

Foreign investors can enjoy various tax benefits. A foreign invested company and business eligible for tax reductions or exemptions are defined in detail under the Article 121-2 of the Restriction of Special Taxation Act and the Article 116-2 of its Enforcement Decree.

A foreign invested company that intends to receive a tax reduction or exemption or change the details of a business must file an application to the Minister of Economy and Finance or to the administrative authority of a free trade zone when the company is located in such a zone.[873] Foreign investors who intend to concurrently send notification of a foreign investment and apply for tax reductions or exemptions may file a foreign investment notification form and an application form for tax reductions or exemptions to a foreign exchange bank or the KOTRA.[874]

In the case of a new investment, the deadline for application is the last day of the taxable year in which the business commenced. If the details of the business which has been granted a tax reduction or exemption have changed, an application for change must be filed no later than two years from the day that the reasons for the change arose. Properties acquired and owned by foreign invested companies to operate registered businesses are eligible for acquisition tax and property tax reductions or exemptions.[875]

In the case of capital goods imported through the notification of foreign investment by the acquisition of newly issued stocks, etc. among capital goods that are used in businesses subject to tax reductions or exemptions, customs

873) Article 121-2(6) of the Restriction of Special Taxation Act.

874) Article 51-3 of the Enforcement Rules of the Restriction of Special Taxation Act, Public Notice No. 2017-10 of the Ministry of Economy and Finance (April 4, 2017), and Article 5-2 of the Regulations Defining Tax Exemptions for Foreign Investment.

875) Article 78-3 of the Restriction of Special Local Taxation Act.

duties, individual consumption tax, and value-added tax are exempted under the Restriction of Special Taxation Act.[876)]

There are also other tax support for foreigners as follows.[877)]

(i) Income tax reductions for foreign engineers: The income earned by foreign engineers offering services in Korea is subject to a 50% income tax reduction for a period of five years from the date they started offering services. Foreign engineers engaged in materials, parts, and equipment businesses are subject to a 70 percent income tax reduction for a period of three years from the date they started offering services, and a 50 percent reduction for two years thereafter.

(ii) Special taxation for foreign workers: The income tax on the income of foreign workers including foreign executives or employees but excluding daily employed workers earned from the date they started offering services until the taxable period, which ends within five years, may be calculated by multiplying the relevant earned income by 19 percent, instead of applying the general income tax rate. This sunset provision is applied to foreigners who will have begun to offer services in Korea for the first time by December 31, 2023.

(iii) Workers at regional offices: The income tax on the income of foreign workers at regional offices earned from the date they started offering services until the taxable period, which ends within five years, may be calculated by multiplying the relevant earned income by 19 percent. This special taxation also applies to foreigners who first begin to offer services in Korea after December 31, 2023.[878)]

(iv) Application of special taxation: Any foreign worker who intends to make a year-end settlement of earned income tax or file a final return of global income tax must submit a wage and salary income earner's return on any income and tax deductions as well as an application for a flat tax rate for foreign workers to the withholding agent, the taxpayers' union, or the head of the tax office with

---

876) Article 121-3 of the Restriction of Special Taxation Act.
877) Investment Consulting Center of the KOTRA, *op. cit.,* p.97.
878) Article 18-2 of the Restriction of Special Taxation Act.

jurisdiction over the place of tax payment.[879]

2) Location Support

Location support provided to facilitate and attract foreign investment consists of foreign investment zones under the Foreign Investment Promotion Act, free trade zones under the Act on Designation and Management of Free Trade Zones, and free economic zones under the Special Act on Designation and Management.

Among these, foreign investment zones are further classified into complex-type, individual-type, and service-type zones. Specific details of location support available for foreign investment, such as requirements, eligible businesses, and incentives (*e.g.*, rental fees, taxes, customs or cash) vary depending on the purpose of designation. It is recommended that investors carefully review and analyze investment locations, even for planned sites with seemingly simple procedures for factory establishment, authorization, and permission.[880]

3) Cash Grants

Foreign investments made by the acquisition of new stocks and with ratios of foreign investment 30 percent or greater are eligible for cash grants. Investments with long-term loans are excluded. Cash grants can be provided for the following purposes and businesses.[881]

(i) New growth engines: New growth engines and source technologies, materials and production processes directly related to new growth engine technologies.[882]

(ii) High technologies: Establishment of new or additional factories for high technologies and high-tech products.[883]

---

879) Article 16.2 of the Enforcement Decree of the Restriction of Special Taxation Act and Form No. 8 of the Enforcement Rules of the Restriction of Special Taxation Act.

880) Investment Consulting Center of the KOTRA, *op. cit.*, p.103.

881) *Id.*, p.112.

882) Article 121-2(1)(a) of the Restriction of Special Taxation Act, Table 7 of its Enforcement Decree and Table 14 of its Enforcement Rule.

883) Article 5 of the Industrial Development Act, Public Notice No. 2019-121 of the

(iii) Materials and parts: Textiles, pulp, chemicals, medicine, rubber, plastics, nonmetallic minerals, primary metals, metal processing, electronic parts, computers, imaging · audio · telecommunication equipment, medical · precision · optical instruments, electrical equipment, machinery equipment, automobiles · trailers, other transportation equipment, furniture, etc.[884)]

(iv) Job creation: Manufacturing · construction · transport · information service businesses that employ 300 or more people; wholesale and retail · lodging · financial insurance · specialized science and technology · leisure service businesses that employ 200 or more people; education services, other personal service businesses, etc. that employ 100 or more people; and real estate and lease businesses that employ 50 or more people.[885)]

(v) R&D centers: New or additional research facilities that are engaged in new growth engine technologies, high technologies and high-tech products, and parts and materials businesses that hire five or more full-time research staff members with master's degrees in relevant fields or bachelor's degrees and at least three years of research experience.[886)]

(vi) Regional offices: Regional offices that are established by global companies to support and manage production, sales, logistics, and HR, etc. of two or more overseas corporations (at least KRW three trillion of total sales of an overseas parent company, at least 50 percent of foreign investment ratio, at least ten full-time workers per core function of business, etc.), and that are deliberated upon by the Foreign Investment Committee and designated by the Minister of Trade, Industry and Energy.[887)]

(vii) Others: Businesses that are engaged in industries that are specialized in certain regions that create jobs and strengthen the competitiveness of local industries, and that are acknowledged for their contributions to economic

---

Ministry of Trade, Industry and Energy (July 26, 2019) and Table 1 of the Range of High Technology and High-Tech Products.

884) Article 2 of the Act on Special Measures for the Promotion of Specialized Enterprises, etc. for Materials and Components and Table 1 of its Enforcement Rule.

885) Table 2 of the Enforcement Decree of the Foreign Investment Promotion Act.

886) Article 14-2(1)(e) of the Foreign Investment Promotion Act.

887) Article 9-3 of the Enforcement Decree of the Foreign Investment Promotion Act.

development in the regions.[888)]

Cash grants can be provided for the costs and subsidies available for the following items according to the relevant laws:[889)]

(i) Purchase costs or rental fees for land or buildings to establish factories or research facilities,

(ii) Construction costs to establish factories or research facilities,

(iii) Purchase costs for capital goods and research equipment and materials to be used for projects or research in factories or research facilities,

(iv) Installation costs for infrastructure, such as electricity and telecommunication facilities, necessary to establish factories or research facilities, and

(v) Employment subsidies and education and training subsidies.

V. Dispute Resolution between Private Parties

1. Introduction

When a dispute arises in relation to international investment or even to any commercial contract between private parties, excluding a state, it can be resolved through court proceedings or alternative dispute resolution (ADR) such as arbitration, mediation, etc.[890)] As technology advances, a dispute resolution can also take place online or by using technology in certain cases. An online dispute resolution is a growing field of a dispute resolution and uses new technologies to solve disputes. It also involves the application of traditional dispute resolution methods to disputes which arise online.

The ADR generally depends on the agreement by the parties to use the ADR processes, either before or even after a dispute has arisen. The ADR has experienced steadily increasing acceptance and utilization because of a perception of greater flexibility, costs below those of traditional litigation, and speedy resolution of disputes, among other perceived advantages.[891)] However, some have

---

888) Articles 2(d) and 5 of the Special Act on Balanced National Development.

889) Article 20-2 of the Enforcement Decree of the Foreign Investment Promotion Act.

890) Ralph H. Folsom, Michael Wallace Gordon, Michael P. Van Alstine, Michael D. Ramsey, *op. cit.*, p.1140.

891) Richard Schaffer, Beverley Earle and Filiberto Agusti, International Business Law and

criticized these methods as taking away the right to seek redress of grievances in the courts, suggesting that extrajudicial dispute resolution may not offer the fairest way for parties not in an equal bargaining relationship, for example in a dispute between a consumer and a large corporation. In addition, in some circumstances, an arbitration and other ADR processes may become as expensive as a litigation or more so.[892)]

In case of investment contract between private parties, however, there is no court exclusively designed to resolve investment disputes, and there is no arbitral institution or procedure that exclusively deals with investment disputes in Korea. In turn, any disputes related to international investment or commercial contract whether parties are foreigners or nationals must be resolved in the civil court or through arbitration proceedings in the same way as other general cases.[893)]

In Korea, when a Korean court finds that a dispute has substantial connection with Korea, it has international jurisdiction over the dispute.[894)] More specifically, under the Korean laws, the Korean court has jurisdiction to hear a case when a foreigner's residence or an investment company's principal place of business is located at the place where the Korean court has jurisdiction. This can be changed by the parties' agreement on the jurisdiction and the choice of law. Meanwhile, arbitration cases are generally resolved through arbitration proceedings at the Korean Commercial Arbitration Board (KCAB, 대한상사중재원).

When the parties have expressly or impliedly agreed to a governing law, that law must apply. In other words, the parties' agreement on the governing law will be considered valid. In cases where there is no agreed governing law, the applicable governing law is determined pursuant to the Korean Private International Act (KPIC, 국제사법).

2. Litigation

1) Once the court decides it has a jurisdiction to hear the case, any disputes between parties may be initiated before the court.[895)] Legal proceedings or

---

Its Environment (6th edition), Thomson South-Western, 2005, p.75.

892) Robert Bradgate and Fidelma White, Commercial Law, Oxford Uni. Press, 2008, p.488.

893) ICLG, "Fintech Laws and Regulations Korea 2022," *op. cit.*

894) Article 2(1) of the Act on Private International Law.

litigation (소송) are commenced by a plaintiff's submission of a complaint to a first instance court with competent jurisdiction, and the plaintiff will submit relevant supporting documents along with the complaint. While it is not required to notarize documents to be submitted to the court, powers of attorney and certificates of corporate nationality, which need to be submitted in cases where a foreign corporate entity is a party to the litigation, must be notarized.

A plaintiff will be required to pay stamp tax and service of process fees when commencing a lawsuit, and stamp tax will take up a substantial portion of the court costs. Stamp tax is calculated in accordance with a formula set by the Act on the Stamps attached for Civil Litigation, Etc. based on the claim amount.[896] In cases where the plaintiff is not a Korean resident and does not have an office in Korea, the Korean court can order, ex officio or pursuant to the defendant's application, the plaintiff to provide security for legal costs under the Civil Procedure Act (민사소송법).[897] The amount of security for legal costs will be calculated in accordance with the rules set forth by the Supreme Court based on the total legal costs including attorneys' fees that will be incurred at each level of court. As the defendant is entitled not to respond to the complaint until the plaintiff has paid the security for legal costs, it is general practice that plaintiffs pay security for legal costs in order to continue with the proceedings. The winning party can recover its legal costs albeit not fully from the losing party.

While the time frame is subject to change depending on the complexity of a case, it generally takes eight to ten months from the commencement of the proceedings for the first instance court to render its judgment. In cases of appeal proceedings, it generally takes six to eight months until the Appellate Court's judgment. Finally, it takes approximately one to two years until the Supreme Court renders its judgment.

2) After the case is closed with a final judgment, a civil compulsory execution may be followed pursuant to the Civil Execution Act (민사집행법), A compulsory execution must be based on the final judgment which has become final and conclusive, or on the final judgment with declaration of a provisional execution.[898] A compulsory execution based upon the final and conclusive

895) Richard Schaffer, Beverley Earle and Filiberto Agusti, *op. cit.*, p.79.
896) Articles 2, 3 and 4 of the Act on the Stamps attached for Civil Litigation, Etc.
897) Article 117 of the Civil Procedure Act.

judgment of a foreign court or a trial the effect of which is recognized as the same therewith may be conducted only if a Korean court has permitted such compulsory execution by means of a judgment of execution.[899)]

3) What if it is foreign judgment? If a judgment is rendered in foreign court, it cannot move directly against the other party's assets in a different country. Only a domestic court in the other party's country can do so.[900)] In Korea, a lawsuit seeking a judgment of execution for a foreign judgment must be dismissed without prejudice if it falls under any of the following:[901)]

(i) When it has not been proved that the final and conclusive judgment, etc. of a foreign court has become final and conclusive, or

(ii) When the final and conclusive judgment, etc. of a foreign court fails to fulfill the conditions under the Article 217 of the Civil Procedure Act.

Article 217 (Recognition of Foreign Country Judgments) of the Civil Procedure Act

(1) A final and conclusive judgment rendered by a foreign court or a judgment acknowledged to have the same force shall be recognized, if all of the following requirements are met:

(i) That the international jurisdiction of such foreign court is recognized under the principle of international jurisdiction pursuant to the statutes or treaties of the Republic of Korea;

(ii) That a defeated defendant is served, by a lawful method, a written complaint or document corresponding thereto, and notification of date or written order allowing him or her sufficient time to defend (excluding cases of service by public notice or similar), or that he or she responds to the lawsuit even without having been served such documents;

(iii) That the approval of such final judgment, etc. does not undermine sound morals or other social order of the Republic of Korea in light of the contents of such final judgment, etc. and judicial procedures;

(iv) That mutual guarantee exists, or the requirements for recognition of final judgment, etc. in the Republic of Korea and the foreign country to which the foreign

898) Article 24 of the Civil Execution Act.

899) Article 26(1) of the Civil Execution Act.

900) Ralph H. Folsom, Michael Wallace Gordon, Michael P. Van Alstine, Michael D. Ramsey, *op. cit.*, p.1227.

901) Article 27(2) of the Civil Execution Act.

country court belongs are not far off balance and have no actual difference between each other in important points.

(2) A court shall ex officio investigate whether the requirements under paragraph (1) are satisfied.

3. Arbitration

1) Introduction

An international commercial arbitration (국제상사중재) is the binding resolution of the merits of business disputes between or among transnational parties through the use of one or more arbitrators rather than the courts. There must be some reasons why the use of an arbitration has grown.[902)] One or more parties may distrust a foreign legal system or wish to avoid long delays in the court systems. They may desire resolution of the dispute by someone with expertise in their business. They may wish to exercise more control by specifying the rules that will govern the dispute. They may also wish to avoid the current problem of the lack of internationally recognized standards on the enforceability of foreign judgments.

An issue to the scope of an arbitration clause is the question of arbitrability which involves determining which types of dispute may be resolved by arbitration and which must go to court. This determination will need to be made initially by the arbitral tribunal, but may ultimately be made by courts of particular states applying national laws. Despite the principle of party autonomy there are disputes, which by their very nature, must be determined by the courts. For example, non-commercial or non-money matters, such as insolvency, criminal proceedings, divorce, registration of land or patents, generally have no arbitrability and thus may not go to the arbitration.

An arbitration agreement is the foundation of the arbitration process.[903)] Several important matters can be stated in relation to such agreements. First of all, an

902) Denise Collins, Business Law (3rd edition), Oxford Uni. Press, September 2006, p.355.

903) Richard Schaffer, Beverley Earle and Filiberto Agusti, *op. cit.*, p.76.

agreement to arbitrate or an arbitration clause is considered to be a contract independent of the contract in which it is contained. On this basis, the arbitral tribunal has jurisdiction to rule on its own jurisdiction even if the underlying contract has been terminated or is set aside. The arbitration clause survives termination of the underlying contract. An arbitration agreement will commonly deal with such matters as the types of disputes which fall within its terms, the seat of the arbitration, the law in accordance with which the dispute will be determined, the number of arbitrators, and their appointment, the language of the arbitration, and whether it will be an institutional or ad hoc arbitration.

2) Types of Arbitration

(1) Institutional vs. Ad Hoc

There are essentially two kinds of arbitration which are ad hoc or institutional. An institutional arbitration is entrusted to one of the major arbitration institutions to handle the case, while an ad hoc arbitration is conducted independently and without such an organization or an institution, according to the rules specified by the parties.[904)]

(2) State vs. Private Parties

An arbitration may also be differentiated by those that involve states as a party, and those that do not. Special institutions are available for arbitrations in which states are a party. The Permanent Court of Arbitration in the Hague was formed to handle arbitrations exclusively involving states, but since 1992 has broadened its mandate to include disputes involving states and private parties, as well as disputes involving international organizations. The International Center for the Settlement of Investment Disputes (ICSID) is also concerned with disputes between a state and its foreign investors, and has an international reputation.

(3) Specialized vs. General Purpose Institutions

A number of arbitral mechanisms address arbitrations in a particular industry or

---

904) Robert Bradgate and Fidelma White, *op. cit.*, p.489.

concerning a particular subject matter. An example of industry-specific arbitration is the set of the special rules governing construction industry disputes by the American Arbitration Association. The World Intellectual Property Organization (WIPO) Arbitration and Mediation Center and the Court of Arbitration for Sport are examples of subject matter-specific dispute resolution.

3) Major General Purpose Institutions and Arbitration Rules

Major international commercial arbitration organizations with years of experience include the International Chamber of Commerce (ICC) in Paris, the London Court of International Arbitration (LCIA) and the American Arbitration Association (AAA). The Vienna International Arbitral Center (VIAC) has gained a reputation for arbitrating disputes involving parties from Central Europe. Other organizations include the China International Economic and Trade Arbitration Commission (CIETAC), also known as the Arbitration Court of the China Chamber of International Commerce (CCOIC), Japan International Dispute Resolution Center (JIDRC) and the Korean Commercial Arbitration Board (KCAB).[905]

While most arbitral institutions have their own international arbitration rules, another important development in the spread of international arbitration was the adoption in 1976 of the United Nations Commission on International Trade Law (UNCITRAL) Arbitration Rules, which were intended for parties wishing to arbitrate without the use of an international arbitral institution.[906] The UNCITRAL Model Law on International Commercial Arbitration, adopted on June 21, 1985 and amended in 2006, serves as the basis for many countries' arbitration legislation.[907]

In another recent trend, many countries have adopted new arbitration laws or amended existing laws to remove impediments to the arbitration process in hopes of attracting more global business. Most statutes since 1980 have also included

---

905) *See* Denise Collins, *op. cit.*, p.371.

906) Robert Bradgate and Fidelma White, *op. cit.*, p.506.

907) Along with the New York Convention, the other most influential international legal instrument in the context of international commercial arbitration is the UNCITRAL Model Law. The Model Law is not legally effective or enforceable on its own but is simply a template for legislation for an arbitration law (a lex arbitri) which may be enacted by individual states. It draws heavily from the New York Convention and the UNCITRAL Arbitration Rules.

'trade usage' as a permissible source of arbitration law, again in an effort to attract more global business.

4) International Recognition and Enforcement of Foreign Arbitral Award

(1) New York Convention

Countries may agree to enforce foreign arbitration awards in many ways. Some examples are bilateral agreements, multilateral agreements and bilateral investment treaties. However, the widespread adoption of the 'New York Convention on the Recognition and Enforcement of Foreign Arbitral Awards' (New York Convention) has greatly facilitated the growth of arbitration.[908] It is said that the single most important reason for the success of international commercial arbitration as the preferred method for resolving international commercial disputes is the New York Convention.[909] It limits the grounds upon which arbitral awards may be attacked, and is primarily concerned with two matters: (i) the recognition of and giving effect to arbitration agreements, and (ii) the recognition and enforcement of international (non-domestic) arbitral awards.

The New York Convention gives both recognition and effect to arbitration agreements by:

(i) requiring a court of a contracting state to refer a dispute which has come before it, and which falls within the scope of an arbitration agreement to arbitration. Parties are not free to litigate disputes that they have agreed to arbitrate, and

(ii) enabling the successful party to enforce the award, which is the culmination of the arbitration process, if the losing party will not voluntarily comply with it. The successful party is able to easily and simply obtain recognition and enforcement of an award in any country which is a party to the New York Convention in accordance with that country's arbitration laws ideally where the losing party may have assets, and there are only a limited number of grounds by which enforcement of an award may be refused.

---

908) Ralph H. Folsom, Michael Wallace Gordon, Michael P. Van Alstine, Michael D. Ramsey, *op. cit.,* p.1291.

909) Min Kyu Lee, "Enforcement of Annulled Arbitral Awards in Korea: Where are We and Where Should We Go?" Journal of Korean Law, Vol. 18, December 2018, p.207.

(2) Korea's Position on New York Convention

Korea is also a party to the New York Convention. Accordingly, an arbitral award (중재판정) duly delivered by the KCAB can be recognized and enforced in other countries that are also parties to the New York Convention, and foreign arbitral awards rendered by other countries that are parties to the New York Convention will be also recognized and enforceable in Korea. Further, Korean courts will even recognize arbitral awards rendered in foreign countries that are not parties to the New York Convention by applying standards similar to those used to determine the enforceability of foreign judgments in Korea. Foreign arbitral awards must satisfy the requirements under the Article 217 (Recognition of Foreign Country Judgments) of the Civil Procedure Act in order to be recognized and enforced in Korea, as already reviewed in the litigation above.

5) Arbitration in Korea

(1) KCAB Arbitration

In Korea, an institutional arbitration is carried out by the KCAB. In arbitration proceedings through the KCAB, parties will appoint one or multiple arbitrators from among the arbitrators recommended by the KCAB. While arbitration proceedings through the KCAB do not differ much from court procedures in international arbitration proceedings where a foreign company or foreign personnel are involved, the parties can choose the language to be used in the proceedings. An arbitral award will have the same effect as a judgment, and arbitration proceedings will not be generally as costly as court proceedings. Moreover, an arbitral award is rendered more promptly than a court judgment.

The KCAB amended, in 2016 and came into effect on June 1, 2016, its International Arbitration Rules to secure autonomy and fairness of arbitration tribunals and to promote effectiveness of international arbitration. Such rules are not markedly different from the previous version, with the exception of the procedure for an emergency arbitrator. By appointing an emergency arbitrator, parties can now ask for immediate preservation and temporary injunction even before the constitution of an arbitration tribunal.

On the other hand, an expedited arbitration is one of arbitration forms that is carried out in a shortened time frame and at reduced cost by accelerating and simplifying key aspects of the proceedings so as to reach a final decision on the merits in a cost and time effective manner. Fast arbitration services are offered by many arbitral institutions including the KCAB, and can also be found in certain areas tailored for specific needs, such as sport arbitration, commodity arbitration, domain name disputes or construction cases.[910] From the Korean perspective, the KCAB's International Arbitration Rules need further to respond to the recent developments of the UNCITRAL and to be updated specially in the scope of expedited procedure, time limits and the scope of written examination. This will be able to confirm the developments of other international arbitral institutions' arbitration rules including expedited arbitration and to improve the rules and usage of expedited procedure in Korea.[911]

(2) Model Arbitration Agreement

(i) Model Clause for Future Disputes[912]

Any disputes arising out of or in connection with this contract shall be finally settled by arbitration in accordance with the International Arbitration Rules of the Korean Commercial Arbitration Board. (i) The number of arbitrators shall be [one / three] (ii) The seat, or legal place, of arbitral proceedings shall be [Seoul / South Korea] (iii) The language to be used in the arbitral proceedings shall be [language]

910) ICC, "ICC Arbitration Rules in force as from 1 March 2017 and Mediation Rules in force as from 1 January 2014," CAS, "Code of Sports-related Arbitration (in force as from 1 January 2019)," WIPO, "Uniform Domain Name Dispute Resolution Policy(UDRP)." and UNCITRAL, "Report of Working Group II(Dispute Settlement) on the work of its seventy-first session (New York, 3-7 February 2020)," A/CN.9/1010, February 12, 2020.

911) Byung-Tae Kim, "International Approach to Expedited Arbitration and Its Implications to Korea - Focusing on the UNCITRAL Perspective (in Korean)," HUFS Law Review, Vol. 44 No. 3, August 2020, p.296.

912) KCAB International, "Model Clause of KCAB," Retrieved on December 20, 2022 from <http://www.kcabinternational.or.kr/>.

(ii) Model Agreement for Existing Disputes[913)]

> We, the undersigned parties, hereby agree that the following dispute shall be referred to and finally determined by arbitration in accordance with the KCAB International Arbitration Rules:
> [brief description of the dispute]
> (i) The number of arbitrators shall be [one / three]
> (ii) The seat, or legal place, of arbitral proceedings shall be [city / country]
> (iii) The language to be used in the arbitral proceedings shall be [language]

(3) Arbitration Procedure under the Revised International Arbitration Rules of the KCAB[914)]

(i) Arbitration Agreement

Any parties may file a Request for Arbitration where the contract in dispute contains an effective arbitration agreement or when the parties agree in writing to resolve their disputes by arbitration. Where a case is 'international,' the KCAB International Arbitration Rules will apply by default, unless the parties agree otherwise.

(ii) Request for Arbitration

Claimant must pay a fixed filing fee when submitting its Request for Arbitration. Upon receiving the Request, the Secretariat of the KCAB notifies the respondent, who has 30 days to submit an Answer. The Secretariat will provide a pre-estimate of the arbitration expenses including administrative and arbitrator fees which the parties must pay in equal shares prior to the commencement of proceedings. This advance will be re-calculated once proceedings are brought to a close.

---

913) *Id.*

914) KCAB International, "Arbitration Procedure," Retrieved on December 20, 2022 from <http://www.kcabinternational.or.kr/>.

(iii) Submission of Answer or Filing Counterclaims

When submitting the Answer, the respondent may also file a counterclaim, which may be consolidated with the existing claim and the amount in dispute will be the sum of both claims. The respondent will be charged a separate filing fee for its counterclaim. If the respondent disputes the jurisdiction of the arbitral tribunal or otherwise believes there is no basis upon which the arbitration may be conducted, they may make this submission in the Answer.

(iv) Constitution of Arbitral Tribunal

In principle, disputes under the KCAB International Arbitration Rules must be decided by a sole arbitrator chosen by the parties, unless the parties agree otherwise. When asked by the parties, the Secretariat must provide a list of arbitrators with the necessary expertise and impartiality. If the parties are unable or unwilling to appoint an arbitrator, the Secretariat will make the appointment on their behalf. To this end, the KCAB may consult the International Arbitration Committee (IAC), which will assist in the appointment of a tribunal. In the event of a challenge by one party to the appointment of an arbitrator, the Secretariat will decide on the challenge, having first consulted the IAC.

(v) Hearing

The Tribunal is fully in charge of hearings. Unless and until the Tribunal directs otherwise, all communications, written or verbal, must take place directly between parties or between each party and the Tribunal.

(vi) Delivery of Arbitral Award

Once the hearings have concluded, an arbitral award is rendered by the tribunal. When all outstanding arbitration expenses have been paid, the Secretariat must deliver the arbitral award to the parties.

(vii) Enforcement of an Award

An Award rendered by the Tribunal is binding upon the parties. The

Secretariat will deliver to the competent court the arbitral award and a copy of the document proving that the arbitral award has been delivered to the parties. Parties may obtain a writ of execution based on the arbitral award either in a Korean Court or abroad.

(4) Sample of Arbitration Form

(i) Form for Request of Arbitration[915]

Claimant:
Address:
Representative Director:
E-mail:
Tel: / Fax:

Respondent:
Address:
Representative Director:
E-mail:
Tel: / Fax:

Basis of the Request (Claim)
1. The Respondent shall pay to the Claimant the sum of ____.
2. The Arbitration Cost shall be borne by the Respondent.

Grounds of the Request (Claim)

The Claimant is a Korean Corporation engaged in sea and air freight forwarding business. The Claimant and the Respondent executed "Sea and Air Cargo Transportation Agency Contract ('Agency Agreement') on November 01, 20XX (see the attached Exhibit A-1),

Based on this 'Agency Agreement,' the Claimant and the Respondent had transported sea and air cargo reciprocally and had settled the freight charge accounts within 1 month. The Respondent failed to make payment on the accounts outlined below and had no special reasons.

915) KCAB International, "Model Clause of KCAB," Retrieved on December 20, 2022 from <http://www.kcabinternational.or.kr/>.

The exact calculation is as follows:
- Accounts amount: ________
- Period: from June 20XX to December 20XX

The Claimant met the Respondent in ____ on June 14, 20XX and verified the amount owed and the detail statement for cargo business. The Respondent and the Claimant agreed that the Respondent would pay to the Claimant _____ before September 30, 20XX and that all disputes arising from the Respondent's inability to fulfill the above obligations would be resolved by arbitration. (see the attached Exhibit A-2)

The Respondent did not pay the freight charge. Accordingly, the Claimant requested arbitration to be conducted by the Korean Commercial Arbitration Board as set forth in the Purport.

It is recommended that the address of the Parties correspond to the address on the certified registration book. It is also recommended to write all valid contacts of the Respondent. i.e. telephone number of the office, fax number, e-mail address, cell phone number of the person in charge. The Statement of Claim must be signed by the representative of the Party or the person in charge who submitted the Power of Attorney. It is recommended to write an enumerated list of exhibits so that the arbitrator can mention any individual piece of evidence in the award.

(ii) Form for Method of Proofs[916)]

Exhibit A-1: Agency Agreement
Exhibit A-3: Letter
Exhibit A-4: Fax dated February 7, 20XX
Exhibit A-5: Dunning letter dated May 11, 20XX
Exhibit A-6: Fax dated May 27, 20XX

(Company's Name)
----

916) *Id.*

(Signature)
(Name)
Representative Director

It is recommended to check and mark the arbitration clause included in the contract and signed by all of the parties. The Power of Attorney (위임장) or equivalent document must be signed by the representative of the party. This must be accompanied by proof of employment when an employee of the party attends the hearing instead of the representative.

4. Mediation

(1) As an another one of the ADRs, a typical mediation procedure may be generally conducted by a court. A mediation can be held upon the parties' application or at the court's discretion during legal proceedings, and a case may be referred to the Mediation Committee whereby parties will come to a reasonable level of agreement. A mediation decision, once finalized, has the same legal effect as other court judgments. In cases where parties are unable to come to an agreement through mediation, they can continue with court proceedings and resolve the matter through a court judgment.

(2) In Korea, a mediation may be also conducted by non-judiciary organizations or institutions. For example, if there are financial disputes between parties, a financial dispute mediation is available to resolve disputes arising between customers and financial institutions that are subject to the FSS supervision. The 'Committee for the Mediation of Financial Disputes' (Mediation Committee, 금융분쟁조정위원회) under the Financial Supervisory Service (FSS) deliberates and resolves on matters concerning the mediation of finance-related disputes arising among the institutions, financial consumers and other interested persons pursuant to the Act on the Protection of Financial Consumers (금융소비자 보호에 관한 법률).[917)]

When a dispute arises in connection with finance, an institution subject to

917) Article 33(1) of the Act on the Protection of Financial Consumers.

mediation, a financial consumer, or other interested person may apply for the mediation of the dispute to the governor of the FSS.[918] Upon the receipt of an application for the mediation of a dispute, the governor of the FSS may notify relevant parties of the issues of the application and may recommend settlement by agreement to them. However, if the issues of the application fall under any of the followings, it does not need to recommend settlement by agreement or refer the dispute to the Mediation Committee:[919]

(i) If the governor of the FSS finds that the issues of the application is not appropriate to settle by mediation,

(ii) If the issues of the application have no practical merit in proceeding with recommendation of settlement by agreement or mediation, in light of objective evidence, etc., and

(iii) Other cases as similar to those referred to in (i) or (ii) above.

When a dispute is not settled by agreement within 30 days from the filing date of an application for the mediation of a dispute, the governor of the FSS must refer the dispute to the Mediation Committee, without delay. When a dispute is referred to the Mediation Committee for mediation, the Mediation Committee must deliberate on the dispute and prepare a draft mediation agreement within 60 days. When the Mediation Committee completes a draft mediation agreement, the governor of the FSS may propose the draft mediation agreement to the applicant and involved parties to recommend them to accept it. If the applicant and involved parties do not accept a draft mediation agreement within 20 days from the date the draft mediation agreement is proposed to them, the draft mediation agreement will be deemed not accepted. When both parties accept a draft mediation agreement, the draft mediation agreement will be as effective as judicial compromise.[920]

918) Article 36(1) of the Act on the Protection of Financial Consumers.
919) Article 36(2) of the Act on the Protection of Financial Consumers.
920) Article 39 of the Act on the Protection of Financial Consumers.

VI. Dispute Resolution between Foreign Investor and State

1. Introduction

An investor-state dispute settlement is a system through which individual companies can sue host states for alleged discriminatory practices. If an investor from one country (home state) invests in another country (host state), both of which have agreed to an investor-state dispute settlement, and the host state violates the rights granted to the investor, then the investor may bring the matter before an arbitral tribunal or other dispute resolution institutions. Only foreign investors can sue states under the investment treaties, because states are the parties to the treaty, and only states can be held liable to pay damages for breach of the treaty. States have no corresponding right to bring a claim against a foreign investor under such treaties, because investors are not parties to the treaty and therefore cannot be in breach of it. An investor-state dispute settlement cannot overturn domestic laws which violate foreign investment treaties but it can grant monetary damages to investors adversely affected by such laws.

A investor-state dispute settlement is an instrument of public international law. Provisions for international dispute settlement between foreign investors and host states are generally contained in national legislation, bilateral investment treaties, international investment agreements, and in some international trade treaties.

2. Arbitration for Investor-State Dispute Settlement

1) International investment agreements, investment treaties and national laws governing foreign investments often designate a forum or arbitration rules for arbitrating disputes between foreign investors and host states. In general, international arbitration between a foreign investor and a host state results from their agreement to solve their disputes in this manner. This agreement may provide claimants with a choice of one or more institutions and the corresponding governing rules. This agreement may take the form of a contractual provision including those in a legal stability contract or a subsequent arbitral agreement, but increasingly it is the result of a foreign investor accepting a state's standing offer to arbitrate disputes in international investment agreements (IIAs), primarily bilateral investment treaties (BITs) and free trade agreements (FTAs) with an

investment chapter.[921)]

As of January 1, 2022, Korea has signed 99 BITs of which 84 are currently in effect. Korea is also a party to 18 effectuated FTAs.

2) Among others, the International Center for Settlement of Investment Disputes (ICSID), is the forum designated most frequently.[922)] The ICSID is an arbitral forum in which independent arbitral tribunals, conciliation commissions and fact-finding committees resolve investment disputes between a foreign investor and a host state. The ICSID arbitration most often takes place under the 'Convention on the Settlement of Investment Disputes between States and National of other States' (ICSID Convention) and the 'ICSID Rules of Procedure for Arbitration Proceedings' (ICSID Arbitration Rules). The ICSID Convention is an international treaty ratified and in force for 161 States.

A claimant may only submit an arbitral claim under the ICSID Convention and the ICSID Arbitration Rules when both the country of nationality of the investor and the host state are parties to the ICSID Convention. The ICSID Convention arbitral award may not be appealed or subjected to other recourse except to an annulment request for limited grounds under the ICSID Convention. In addition, a final arbitral award by the ICSID will be recognized and its pecuniary obligations will be enforced by every ICSID Convention party as a final judgment of one of its courts. The ICSID arbitration may also take place pursuant to the ICSID Additional Facility Rules when either the country of nationality of the investor or the host state is not a party to the ICSID Convention.

3) However, an investor-state dispute settlement can also take place under the auspices of international rules and arbitral tribunals that regularly administer

---

921) According to the United Nations Conference on Trade and Development (UNCTAD), there are over 3,300 IIAs in force. States often make information about IIAs and FTAs and they are party to available online to promote investment and increase the transparency of their investment climate. Foreign affairs and trade ministries, relevant sectoral authorities, and trade and investment promotion authorities are natural sources for this information. The most up-to-date database of BITs and FTAs is the International Investment Treaties Navigator of the UNCTAD. The WTO's Regional Trade Agreements Information System is also a reliable source on existing FTAs.

922) Hernando Otero, "UPDATE: International Arbitration Between Foreign Investors and Host States (Investor-State Arbitration)," March/April 2022, Retrieved on January 10, 2023 from <https://www.nyulawglobal.org/globalex/International_Arbitration_Foreign_Investors_Host_States1.html>.

investor-state arbitrations. There are distinguished arbitral institutions and rules which have international reputation in the field of arbitration such as:

(i) London Court of International Arbitration,

(ii) Hong Kong International Arbitration Center,

(iii) Arbitration Institute of the Stockholm Chamber of Commerce,

(iv) Australian Centre for International Commercial Arbitration,

(v) International Chamber of Commerce (the 'ICC') International Court of Arbitration,

(vi) Permanent Court of Arbitration,

(vii) Singapore International Arbitration Center,

(viii) United Nations Commission on International Trade Law Arbitration Rules (UNCITRAL Arbitration Rules)[923]

(ix) Korean Commercial Arbitration Board (the 'KCAB') and its International Arbitration Rules.

More comprehensive listing of arbitral institutions worldwide can be found from various international directory of dispute resolution centers,[924] which can be browsed alphabetically or geographically.

If the relevant investment treaty or law does not designate a forum, the parties may select an arbitral institution of their choice to administer the arbitration, or they may proceed without the assistance of an arbitral institution.

Confidentiality provisions in investment treaties, such as the Article 48(5) of the ICSID Convention, preclude public disclosure of arbitral decisions and awards, unless all parties to the arbitration consent. Therefore by no means all awards and decisions are available. Arbitral decisions and awards that have been publicly disclosed may be accessed in many databases.[925]

In all cases, each IIA or FTA must be reviewed to confirm whether it affords

---

923) A common choice provided in international investment agreements is to submit an arbitral claim under the UNCITRAL Arbitration Rules. They provide for a non-institutional procedural framework for proceedings. The parties to the dispute, however, often resort to arbitral institutions such as the ICSID or the Permanent Court of Arbitration to assist the administration of proceedings.

924) International Council for Commercial Arbitration, "Arbitral Institutes Directory,“ Retrieved on January 12, 2023 from <https://www.arbitration-icca.org/institutes>; UN Commission on International Trade Law, "Arbitration Centers," Retrieved on January 12, 2023 from <https://uncitral.un.org/en/texts/arbitration/contractualtexts/arbitration/centres>.

925) For example, ICC Dispute Resolution Library, Kluwer Arbitration, Westlaw, New York Convention Case Law Database, CISG Online, and CLOUT database.

foreign investors the choice of submitting their claims against host states to international arbitration.

VII. Case Study on International Investment Law

1. KNCP Case on Samsung Heavy Industries' Crane Accident[926)]

1) Case Summary

(1) In connection with the crane accident of the Martin Linge Project, the Samsung Heavy Industries Martin Linge Project Crane Accident Workers Support Team and the Korean Transnational Corporations Watch (hereinafter, 'KTNC Watch') made a submission to the KNCP, Norwegian NCP and French NCP on March 29, 2019 against Samsung Heavy Industries (SHI), Total, Technip FMC and Equinor claiming that the Respondent SHI had no safety measures in place for crane crash accidents, such as passages for overlapping areas and crane crash prevention measures (Ⅱ. General Policies A. 10 and Ⅳ. Human Rights 1, 4), managers under the responsibility of SHI were negligent in directing work tasks, and a sufficient number of signal personnel were not assigned for the Goliath crane and the signal personnel were also negligent in their surveillance.

(2) In this case, the KNCP notified the concerned NCPs that it would proceed with this specific instance, focusing on matters relating to the company headquartered in Korea. The French and Norwegian NCPs also proposed that they would conduct a relevant procedure against the companies based in their countries and share the progress or results of their handling of the specific instance. Accordingly, the NCPs agreed that the KNCP would handle the instance against the Respondent SHI based in Korea while the Norwegian NCP would deal with the instance against the Respondents Total, Technip FMC and Equinor headquartered in Europe.

(3) The KNCP determined that further investigation and good offices were

926) Korean National Contact Point (KNCP), Martin Linge Project Crane Accident Workers Support Team *v.* Samsung Heavy Industries etc. October 26, 2022.

necessary, comprehensively considering (i) the facts that this instance is based on an accident within the place of business of SHI and there is a link between the enterprise's activities and the issue raised in the specific instance, (ii) the materials submitted by the parties and (iii) the parties' response to the situation. Accordingly, the KNCP offered good offices for mediation among the parties during the period from November 19, 2019 to June 9, 2022, but they failed to reach a settlement.

(4) The KNCP recommends the Respondent SHI to take remedial measures for any additional victims not included during the course of the investigation; devise a plan to actively seek out victims and remedial measures to be taken upon the occurrence of any future industrial accidents; conduct due diligence on countermeasures for such accidents; reflect the Guidelines in the course of such due diligence, and submit the implementation results of such recommendations within six months.

2) Comment

As the procedures initiated by the NCPs are not legally binding in accordance with the OECD Guidelines and the NCPs are not judicial bodies, the NCPs cannot directly order compensation nor compel parties to participate in a conciliation or mediation process. The same applies to the KNCP's final statement.

2. CLOUT[927] Cases relating to Korea

1) CLOUT Case No. 1293: New York Convention IV(1), IV(2)[928]

In the case at hand the plaintiff was seeking enforcement of an arbitration decision by the Tokyo Maritime Arbitration Commission in Busan, Korea. As per

927) In order to support consistency in decisions and awards on its texts, the UNCITRAL established a system in 1988 to collect and disseminate information on court decisions and arbitral awards relating to UNCITRAL texts: the Case Law on UNCITRAL texts, known as the CLOUT. Each case in the CLOUT includes a short summary of the case, termed 'CLOUT Abstracts.' The CLOUT Abstracts are published in collections known as 'CLOUT issues,' available in the United Nations Official Documents system. Basic case information and individual CLOUT abstracts are also published in the searchable CLOUT Database, freely accessible worldwide.

928) Busan District Court Decision 2011Gahap8532, decided on October 26, 2011.

the Article IV(1) of the New York Convention, the plaintiff was to submit the following: (a) the duly authenticated original award or a duly certified copy thereof, and (b) the original agreement referred to in Article II NYC or a duly certified copy thereof. Further, as required under the Article IV(2) of the New York Convention, the plaintiff should have submitted a translation of the award, because in this case the award was not made in the official language of the country in which the award was being relied upon.

Though the plaintiff failed to submit a translation of the award, the court ruled that the award could be enforced, unless other exceptional circumstances existed, because the defendant did not file any objection concerning the existence or content of the award, and the mere failure to submit a translated copy is not a sufficient ground to reject a demand of execution.

2) CLOUT Case No. 1294: New York Convention V(1)(d)[929]

The plaintiff, a company from the Philippines, initiated action for enforcement of the arbitral award decided against the defendant, a Korean company, by the Construction Industry Arbitration Commission (CIAC) in the Philippines.

The Korean court found that the plaintiff and the defendant had originally contracted to submit any dispute to arbitration subject to the arbitration provisions of the International Chamber of Commerce (ICC) and that an award rendered under the CIAC arbitration rules fell outside this agreement.

The court held that the case was within the scope of the Article V(1)(d) of the New York Convention, according to which if the composition of the arbitral authority or the arbitral procedure is not in accordance with the agreement of the parties or, failing such agreement, with the law of the country where the arbitration took place, enforcement of the award can be refused. On this basis the court rejected the plaintiff's claim for enforcement of the award.

---

929) Supreme Court Decision 2011Da41352, decided on August 19, 2011 (First instance: Seoul Central District Court 2010Gahap17142, and Second instance: Seoul High Court 2010Na72375).

3) CLOUT Case No. 1296: New York Convention V(2)(b)[930]

The plaintiff, a company of the Marshall Islands, sought execution of the arbitral award rendered by the London Court of International Arbitration against the defendant, a Korean company. The defendant argued that the amount of the award was excessive and contravened the public policy of Korea, and should not be enforced, pursuant to the Article V(2)(b) of the New York Convention.

The court held that the party seeking denial or enforcement bears the burden of proof in relation to raising a public policy defense. In the present case, the amount of the award amounted to two-thirds of the original contract fee. The court held that this fact alone was not sufficient to establish that it was contrary to the moral or other social orders of Korea. The defendant's claims were thus rejected.

Related Legal Issues and Questions:

1. What is a main source of laws on international investment in Korea?
2. How is the FDI processed in Korea?
3. What are requirements for the FDI under the Foreign Investment Promotion Act?
4. How can we resolve the disputes between private parties?
5. How can we resolve the disputes between foreign investor and state?
6. How can a foreign arbitral award be recognized and enforced in another countries? What about in Korea?

930) Changwon District Court 2009Gahap194, decided on November 18, 2010.

[Appendix: Model Articles of Incorporation]

Model Articles of Incorporation[931)]

Chapter I General Provision

Article 1 (Corporate Name)

The name of the Company shall be ____ in Korean and ____ in English (hereinafter referred to as 'the Company').

Article 2 (Purposes)

The purposes of the Company are to conduct the following businesses:

1. _____
2. _____
3. _____
4. Business ancillary to the foregoing 1 through 4.

Article 3 (Head Office and Branches)

① The Head office of the Company shall be located in Seoul.

② The Company may have branches, business offices, local corporations either in or out of the country as required in accordance with the Board of Directors' meeting.

Article 4 (Method of Public Notices)

Public notices of the Company shall be given in the ____ Newspaper published in ____.

Chapter II Shares and Stock Certificates

Article 5 (Total Number of Shares to be Issued)

The total number of shares of stock to be issued by the Company shall be 80,000 (eighty thousand).

Article 6 (Value per Share)

Each share to be issued by the Company shall have a value of (5,000) won per share.

Article 7 (Total Number of Shares to be Issued upon Incorporation)

The number of shares to be issued at the time of the Company's incorporation shall be 20,000 (Twenty Thousand).

Article 8 (Types of Shares and Stock Certificates)

① All shares to be issued by the Company shall be registered common shares.

② The stock certificates of the Company shall be in the following 8 (eight) denominations: One-stock certificate, five-stock certificate, ten-stock certificate, fifty-stock certificate, one-hundred stock certificate, five- hundred-stock certificate, and one-thousand

931) The Articles of Incorporation (정관) are essential in a company and always required for the review of corporate structure and liability in the business law. This appendix for the model Articles of Incorporation is derived and updated from the 'KOTRA, Guide to Establishing a Business in Korea. KOTRA Publication No. 16-079, 2016.' There are also many other samples or models for the Articles of Incorporation available in professional materials or on the internet, which are no big differences among them in contents.

and ten-thousand-stock certificates, respectively.

③ Notwithstanding the foregoing Paragraphs ① and ②, the Company may issue shares with a different denomination by a resolution of the General Meeting of Shareholders.

Article 9 (Subscription Rights)

① A shareholder shall have subscription rights concerning new shares issued by the Company in proportion to his/her/its percentage of shares held.

② Notwithstanding the foregoing, the Company may allot new shares to those other than the existing shareholders as per the resolution of the General Meeting of Shareholders for the purpose of achieving management-related purposes such as the introduction of new technology and improvement of financial structure, in accordance with Article 418 (Terms of Preemptive Rights, Designation and Public Notice of Record Date for Allotment), Paragraph 2 of the Commercial Act.

③ The Board of Directors shall decide how to dispose of odd lots that may arise in the process of new stock allotment or shares of stock that may arise as a result of a shareholder's forfeiture or loss of subscription rights with its resolution.

Article 10 (Capitalization of Surplus Reserves)

The Company may issue new shares following capitalization of all or part of its surplus reserves by a resolution of the Board of Directors. However, resolution of the General Meeting of Shareholders is necessary where there are special reasons such as management-related reasons of the Company.

Article 11 (Issue Price of New Shares)

Concerning the Company's issuance of new shares, their price may be set either partially or wholly at a level equal to, or higher than, the face value of the stock as decided by the Board of Directors.

Article 12 (Record Date of Dividend Payout of New Shares)

Concerning the Company's issuance of new shares on the occasion of a capital increase with/without consideration or stock dividend payment, they shall be deemed to have been issued at the end of the business year preceding the year in which the new shares were issued.

Article 13 (Stock Transfer)

① In the event of an application for stock transfer, registration or cancellation of pledge of right, or indication or cancellation of trust assets, the applicant should sign a form provided by the Company and submit it along with the stock certificate. In the event that stocks are acquired for reasons other than transfer, a document stating the reason should
also be submitted.

② The Company may have a stock transfer agent by a resolution of the Board of Directors, for the purpose of stock transfer, registration or cancellation of pledge of right, indication or cancellation of trust assets, etc.

Article 14 (Transfer of Shares and Requirement for Setting up Against)

① The transfer of a share shall be accompanied by the relevant stock certificate unless the Company has not issued a stock certificate.

② The transfer of a share shall not be set up against the Company unless the name and the address of the acquirer are not entered on the shareholders' ledger.

Article 15 (Report of Shareholder's Address, Name and Seal/Signature)

① A shareholder and registered pledgee (including his/her legal proxy, and the company representative in the case of a company) shall report his/her name, address and seal or signature to the Company.

② In the event that the party stated in the foregoing Paragraph ① resides in a foreign country, he/she shall designate a temporary address or a proxy in Korea through which he/she can receive the Company's notices, and report it to the Company.

③ A change in the matters stated in the foregoing Paragraphs ① and ② shall also be reported to the Company.

Article 16 (Reissuance of Stock Certificate)

① To apply for reissuance of a stock certificate due to split or consolidation of shares, or loss, damage or mutilation of the certificate, the applicant shall sign an application for stock certificate reissuance and submit it together with the relevant stock certificate.

② A party who requests the reissuance of a stock certificate due to loss (including cases where the damage or mutilation of a stock certificate is so extreme that the stock certificate cannot be authenticated) shall attach the original copy or certified copy of court judgment of nullification of the stock certificate to the application for stock certificate reissuance and submit the documents.

Article 17 (Closure of Shareholders Ledger and Record Date)

① No change shall be made in the contents of the shareholders' ledger in the period ranging from the day following the end date of each business year through to the end of the day on which the periodical General Meeting of Shareholders concerning the said business is held.

② Those listed on the shareholders' ledger as of the end date of a business year shall be the shareholders eligible to exercise their rights at the periodical General Meeting of Shareholders concerning the business year.

③ The Company may suspend alterations of the contents of the shareholders' ledger, if required for the convocation of an extraordinary General Meeting of Shareholders or for the determination of those who can exercise their rights as dividend recipients, shareholders or registered pledgees by designating a period not exceeding three (3) months as per the resolution of the Board of Directors. The Company may designate shareholders or pledgees listed on the shareholders' ledger on a specified day as those eligible to exercise their rights.

④ Where the Company has designated a specific period or day as prescribed by the foregoing Paragraph ③, the Company shall put up the relevant public notice at least two (2) weeks prior to the beginning of such period or date.

Article 18 (Rules for Managing Stock-Related Matters)

The details and procedures concerning the management of stocks, stock certificates, and stock certificate reissuance fee, etc. shall be determined by the rules for managing stock-related matters adopted by the resolution of the Board of Directors.

Chapter III Corporate Bonds

Article 19 (Issuance of Bonds)

① The Company may issue corporate bonds as per the resolution of the Board of Directors.

② The types of corporate bonds issued by the Company shall be the following three: ordinary bonds, convertible bonds (CBs), and bonds with warrants (BWs).

Article 20 (Entrustment of Matters concerning Corporate Bond Offering)

The Company may select a business to entrust matters concerning corporate bond offering as per the resolution of the Board of Directors.

Article 21 (Issuance of CBs)

① As prescribed by Article 513 (Issuance of Convertible Bonds) of the Commercial Act, the Company may issue CBs to persons other than existing shareholders of the Company in any of the following cases following a resolution of the Board of Directors:

1. Issuance by general public offering;
2. Issuance in order to attract foreign direct investment due to a management-related need under the Foreign Investment Promotion Act;
3. Issuance to an affiliated business for technological transfer;
4. Issuance to domestic financial institutions, corporations or individuals for urgent fund supply.

② The Board of Directors may determine that the CBs referred to in Paragraph ① may be issued on condition that conversion rights will be attached to only a portion of the CBs.

③ The shares to be issued upon conversion shall be registered as common shares. The conversion price, which shall be equal to or more than the face value of the shares, shall be determined by the Board of Directors at the time of issuance of the CBs.

④ The conversion period shall be from the day following the issuance date of the CBs to the day immediately preceding the redemption date thereof. However, the conversion period
may be adjusted within the above period as per the resolution of the Board of Directors.

⑤ For the purpose of any distribution of dividends or interest on shares issued upon conversion, Article 12 (Record Date of Dividend Payout of New Shares) hereof shall apply mutatis mutandis.

⑥ Any matters concerning the issuance of CBs not covered by the foregoing Paragraphs ① through ⑤ shall be fixed as per the resolution of the Board of Directors.

Article 22 (BWs)

① The Company may issue BWs to persons other than the existing shareholders of the Company to the extent that the total face value of the bonds shall not exceed an amount equal to 4 (four) times the net asset value stated in the most recent balance sheet in any of the following cases:

1. Issuance by general public offering;
2. Issuance in order to attract foreign direct investment due to a management-related need under the Foreign Investment Promotion Act;
3. Issuance to an affiliated business for technological transfer;
4. Issuance to domestic financial institutions, corporations or individuals for urgent fund supply.

② The Board of Directors may determine that the BWs referred to in Paragraph ① may be issued on condition that conversion rights will be attached to only a portion of the CBs.

③ The shares to be issued upon the exercise of subscription rights shall be registered common shares. The issue price, which shall be equal to or more than the face value of the shares, shall be determined by the Board of Directors at the time of issuance of the BWs.

④ The period for the exercise of subscription rights shall be from the day following the issuance date of the BWs to the day immediately preceding the redemption date thereof.
However, the period for the exercise of subscription rights may be adjusted within the above period as per the resolution of the Board of Directors.

⑤ For the purpose of any distribution of dividends or interest on shares issued upon the exercise of subscription rights, Article 12 (Record Date of Dividend Payout of New Shares) hereof shall apply mutatis mutandis.

⑥ Any matters concerning the issuance of BWs not covered by the foregoing Paragraphs ① through ⑤ shall be fixed as per the resolution of the Board of Directors.

Article 23 (Provisions Applied Mutatis Mutandis to the Issuance of Bonds)
Article 13 (Stock Transfer) and 15 (Report of Shareholders' Address, Name and Seal/Signature) shall apply mutatis mutandis in the case of issuance of bonds.

Chapter IV The General Meeting of Shareholders

Article 24 (Convocation of the General Meeting)
① The General meetings of the shareholders of the Company shall be of two types: Ordinary and Extraordinary.
② The ordinary General Meeting of Shareholders shall be held within three (3) months of the end of each business year, while the extraordinary General Meeting of Shareholders may be convened at any time when required.
Article 25 (Decision to Convene a General Meeting)
The General Meeting of Shareholders shall be convened by the Representative Director pursuant to a resolution of the Board of Directors unless otherwise stipulated in other regulations.
Article 26 (Notice of Convocation of a General Meeting)
The written notice of the Convocation of a General Meeting of Shareholders stating the date, time, place and agenda thereof shall be sent to all shareholders 10 (ten) days prior to the date set for the General Meeting of Shareholders. The written notice may be replaced by an electronic document with all individual shareholders' consent.
Article 27 (Place of Convocation)
The General Meeting of Shareholders shall be held in the city where the headquarters is located or at another place close to it if required.
Article 28 (Chair of the General Meeting of Shareholders)
The Representative Director shall serve as the Chair of the General Meeting of Shareholders.
Article 29 (Chairman's Authority to Maintain Order)
① The Chairman of the general meeting of shareholders may order persons who intentionally speak or behave in an obstructive manner or who disrupt the proceedings of the meeting to stop or retract a speech or to leave the meeting.
② The Chairman of the general meeting of shareholders may also restrict the length and frequency of speeches made by the shareholders if it is deemed necessary for the smooth progress of the General Meeting of Shareholders.
Article 30 (Exercise of Voting Rights)
① Each shareholder shall have one (1) voting right for each share he/she owns.
② A shareholder may exercise his/her vote through a proxy.
③ The proxy holder shall present to the Company documentary evidence (the power of attorney) of his/her authority to act as a proxy prior to the commencement of each General Meeting of Shareholders at which he/she acts as a proxy.
④ A shareholder may exercise his/her voting right in writing without being present at a General Meeting. In this case, the Company shall have a written form and the reference data required to help shareholders to exercise their voting rights included in the notice of a forthcoming meeting sent to individual shareholders.
⑤ A shareholder intending to exercise his/her voting right in writing as stated in the foregoing Paragraph ④ shall fill in the necessary form and submit it to the Company by the day preceding the day of a General Meeting.
⑥ Persons who have a special interest concerning the resolution of a General Meeting cannot exercise their voting rights.
Article 31 (Method of Resolution)

Unless otherwise stipulated in the laws and these Articles of Incorporation, the passage of a resolution shall have the consent of a majority of shareholders present in terms of the voting rights and at least a quarter of the total number of shares of stock issued.

Article 32 (Minutes of a General Meeting of Shareholders)

① The Chairman of the General Meeting of Shareholders shall record meeting minutes.

② The substance of the proceedings of the General Meeting of Shareholders and the results thereof shall be recorded in the minutes, and shall be preserved at the headquarters of the Company and made available to others, after being affixed with the name and seal impression or signature of the Chairman as well as the Directors present.

Chapter V Directors and the Board of Directors

Article 33 (Number of Directors)

The Company shall have at least 3 (three) Directors.

Article 34 (Election of Directors)

① The Director(s) of the Company shall be elected at the General Meeting of Shareholders.

② The election of the director(s) shall require the consent of a majority of shareholders present in terms of the voting rights and at least a quarter of the total number of shares of stock issued.

③ In the event that two (2) or more Directors are to be elected, the cumulative voting system provided for in the Commercial Act shall not be applicable.

Article 35 (Terms of Directors)

The term of office of a Director shall be three (3) years; provided that, the term of office of a Director shall be extended up to the close of the ordinary General Meeting of Shareholders, if the term expires prior to the General Meeting convened in respect of the last account settlement period.

Article 36 (Election of the Representative Director)

The Company may appoint one or more Representative Directors as per the resolution of the Board of Directors.

Article 37 (Duties of the Representative Director)

The Representative Director shall represent the Company in its business in general and take charge of the general affairs of the Company. When there is more than one Representative Director, it shall be decided as per the resolution of the Board of Directors whether they will represent the Company individually or jointly.

Article 38 (Duties of Directors)

① A Director shall assist the Representative Director and carry out the duties assigned to him/her by the Board of Directors.

② In the event of the absence or disability of the Representative Director or when the office is vacant, the Directors shall act in his/her place by order of seniority.

Article 39 (Obligation of Directors)

① Directors shall carry out their duties in good faith under the relevant laws and the Articles of Incorporation.

② Directors shall not disclose to a third party any information pertaining to the Company during and after their service in the Company.

Article 40 (Director's Obligation to Report)

Upon identifying any matter that will clearly inflict a loss or damage to the Company, a director shall immediately report the matter to the Auditor or the General Meeting of Shareholders if there is no Auditor.

Article 41 (Board of Directors)

① The Company shall have a Board of Directors to make decisions on matters of importance to the Company.

② The Representative Director shall be the chairman of the Board of Directors.

③ When convoking a meeting of the Board of Directors, the Representative Director or a director assigned by the Board of Directors shall put up a notice at least 3 (three) days in advance. The procedure may be omitted when unanimously agreed upon by all the directors and the auditor.

Article 42 (Resolution of the Board of Directors)

① The passage of a resolution of the Board of Directors shall require the presence of a majority of the Directors and the consent of a majority of those present.

② A Director who has a special interest concerning a matter being contemplated by the Board of Directors shall not be allowed to exercise his/her voting right on the matter.

Article 43 (Meeting Minutes of the Board of Directors)

① The Company shall keep minutes concerning the meetings of the Board of Directors.

② The meeting minutes shall record the agenda and proceedings of a meeting of the Board of Directors, and those against the submitted agenda and the reasons for the objection. The minutes shall be signed by the auditor and directors present at the meeting.

Article 44 (Directors' Remuneration and Severance Allowance)

Remuneration of the Directors shall be fixed by the resolution of the General Meeting of Shareholders.

Chapter VI Auditors

Article 45 (Auditors)

① The Company may have one or more Auditors.

② The election of an Auditor shall require affirmative votes by a majority of the voting rights of the shareholders present at the meeting and more than a quarter of the total number of stocks issued. However, when a shareholder's total number of shares held exceeds 3 (three) percent of the total number of shares issued with voting rights, such a shareholder shall not exercise the voting rights concerning the portion of shares exceeding 3 (three) percent in the election of an Auditor.

Article 46 (The Term of Auditors)

The term of the auditor(s) shall be effective up to the end of the ordinary General Meeting of Shareholders concerning the last accounting settlement period within the 3 (three) years following his/her inauguration.

Article 47 (Auditors' Duties)

① The Auditors shall carry out an inspection of the Company's accounting and other affairs in general.

② The Auditors may express their opinion at a meeting of the Board of Directors.

③ The Auditors may ask for the convocation of an extraordinary General Meeting of Shareholders, by submitting a document stating the reason for and purpose of the meeting to the Board of Directors.

④ The Auditors may ask an affiliate company to submit a business report if required to carry out their duties. In such a case, the affiliate shall comply with the request. The Auditors may check the status of the affiliate's business operation or assets, if the affiliate company fails to comply with such a request in a timely fashion or if the Auditors find it necessary to check the contents of the report thus submitted.

Article 48 (Audit Minutes)

① The Auditors shall draw up audit minutes.

② The Auditors shall record the details and results of their inspection activities on the

minutes, which shall be signed by the Auditors who performed the inspection.
Article 49 (Remuneration and Severance Allowance of Auditors)
The remuneration and severance allowance of the Auditors shall be determined by a resolution of the General Meeting of Shareholders.

Chapter VII Accounting

Article 50 (Business Year)
The Company's business year shall be from January 1 through December 31 of each year.
Article 51 (Financial Statements and Annual Report)

① The Representative Director shall draw up the following documents, supplementary statements and the annual report and obtain the approval of the Board of Directors:

1. Balance sheet
2. Income statement
3. Surplus appropriation statement or deficit disposition statement

② The Representative Director shall submit the documents stated in the foregoing Paragraph ① to the Auditors 4 (four) weeks prior to the commencement of the ordinary General Meeting of Shareholders.

③ The Auditors shall submit their audit report to the Representative Director within 3 (three) weeks of their receipt of the documents stated in the foregoing Paragraph ①. ④ The Representative Director shall keep the documents stated in the foregoing Paragraph ① and the audit report in a proper place at the Headquarters for 5 (five) years and shall also keep photocopies thereof in a proper place at the branch offices for 3 (three) years from one week before the commencement of the ordinary General Meeting of Shareholders.

⑤ The Representative Director shall submit the documents stated in the foregoing Paragraph ① to the ordinary General Meeting of Shareholders for approval and also submit the annual report to the ordinary General Meeting of Shareholders.

⑥ After obtaining the General Meeting of Shareholders' approval as stated in the foregoing Paragraph ⑤, the Representative Director shall put the balance sheet, along with an independent Auditor's opinion, on public notice without delay.

Article 52 (Disposal of Retained Earnings)
The Company shall dispose of its retained earnings before appropriations as of the end of each business year for the following:

1. Legal reserve
2. Other statutory reserve
3. Dividends
4. Voluntary reserves
5. Other surplus appropriations

Article 53 (Dividend Payout)

① The Company may make its dividend payout in either cash or stock.

② The dividend payout stated in the foregoing Paragraph ① shall be made to those shareholders listed on the shareholder ledger or to pledgees registered as of the end of each account settlement period.

③ In the case of stock dividends, if the Company has issued several classes of shares, a different class of shares from the class the shareholders currently hold may be allotted by a resolution of the General Meeting of Shareholders.

④ The Company may carry out the interim dividend payout in accordance with Article 463-3 (Interim Dividend) of the Commercial Act.

⑤ No interest shall accrue concerning the dividend payout.

Article 54 (Elimination of Dividend Rights)
① Dividend rights shall be eliminated, if the rights are not exercised for 5 (five) consecutive years.
② Upon the expiry of the prescription of dividends stated in the foregoing Paragraph ①, such dividends shall be returned to the Company.

Chapter VIII Others

Article 55 (Corporate Counselor and Advisor)
The Company may have a Corporate Counselor or Advisor as per the resolution of the General Meeting of Shareholders.
Article 56 (Regulations and Rules)
The Company may enact regulations and rules concerning the general operation of the Company's business as per the resolution of the Board of Directors.
Article 57 (Matters not Covered by the Articles of Incorporation)
Any matters not covered by this Articles of Incorporation shall follow the resolution of the General Meeting of Shareholders and the relevant laws, including the Commercial Act.

Additional Rules

Article 1 (Date of Enforcement)
This Articles of Incorporation shall take effect on the day of notarization (or on the __ day of ____, 2022).
Article 2 (Initial Business Year)
The Company's initial business year shall be from the date of incorporation through December 31 of the same year.
Article 3 (Name, Resident Registration Number and Address of the Promoters)
The full name, resident registration number and address of the promoters for the establishment of the company are set forth at the end hereof:

For the establishment of ____ Company Ltd., the Articles of Incorporations shall be prepared, and all the promoters shall affix their names and seals herein below:

Date: On the ____ day of, 20 Promoter ○○○ (Signature)
Resident registration number: (-)
Address:
Promoter ○○○ (Signature)
Resident registration number: (-)
Address:
Foreign Promoter ○○○ (Signature)
Resident registration number: (-)
Address:
Foreign Promoter ○○○ from (country) (Signature)
Date of birth:
Address:

References

[Books and Articles]

Bang-Shik Lee, Central Banking System (in Korean), July 1994

Bank Department of the Bank of Korea, "Study on the Introduction of the Financial Holding Company," April 2000

Bank for International Settlements (BIS), "Basel III: International framework for liquidity risk measurement, standards and monitoring," Press Release, December 2010

Bank of Korea, Financial Institutions in Korea as of December 2015, December 2015

Bank of Korea, Financial System in Korea, December 2018

Basel Committee on Banking Supervision, "A New Capital Adequacy Framework," Basel Committee Publications No. 50, June 1999

Basel Committee on Banking Supervision, "Overview of The New Basel Capital Accord," Consultative document issued for comment by 31 May 2001, January 2001

Basel Committee, "Minimum Capital Requirements for Market Risk," January 14, 2019

Bloomberg, "2021 Bloomberg Innovation Index," 2022

Byoung Kook Min, Chang Hee Lee and James M. West, "Special Report," International Financial Law Review: Special Supplement, September 1992

Bypaul Boyce, "Foreign Direct Investment (FDI): Definition, 3 Types, Benefits and Disadvantages," September 23, 2020

Byung-Tae Kim, "Cyber Shareholder's Meeting (in Korean)," in the Series of Stock Company (II), Bubmoonsa, March 2022

Byung-Tae Kim, "International Approach to Expedited Arbitration and Its Implications to Korea - Focusing on the UNCITRAL Perspective (in Korean)," HUFS Law Review, Vol. 44 No. 3, August 2020

Byung-Tae Kim, Korea's Banking Law Reform: Post Asian Crisis, Kluwer Law International, 2003

Byung-Tae Kim, "Act on Special Cases concerning Internet-only Bank and Its Legal Issues (in Korean)," Advanced Commercial Law Review, Vol. 86, April, 2019

Byung-Tae Kim, "Compulsory Electronic Voting System and Its Problems (in Korean)," Business Law Review, Vol. 27 No. 3, September 2013

Byung-Tae Kim, "Fit and Proper Test for Large Shareholders under the 'Act on Special Cases concerning Internet-only Bank' (in Korean)," Korean Journal of Banking and Financial Law, Vol. 13 No. 2, November 2020

Byung-Tae Kim, "Korea's New Challenge to the Internet-only Banking System, Korean Journal of Banking and Financial Law, Vol. 8 No. 2, November 2015

Byung-Tae Kim, "The Current Banking Regulations in Korea on the Legal Perspective, Sungkyunkwan Journal of Science & Technology Law, VOL. 6 No. 2, Fall 2012

CAS, “Code of Sports-related Arbitration (in force as from 1 January 2019)”

Cheol Park, Soo Cheol Park, “The Behavior of Stock Prices on Ex-Dividend Day in Korea,” Korean Journal of Financial Management, Vol. 26 No. 1, March 2009

Chloe Jung-Myung LEE and Ross Harman, “Introduction to FinTech Laws and Regulations in South Korea,” Lee & Ko, October 18, 2022

Choi Junesun, Company Law (16th edition) (in Korean), February 2021

Christian N. Watson, “The Growth of Internet-Only Banks: Brick and Mortar Branches Are Feeling the 'Byte',” North Carolina Banking Institute, April 2000

Chung Chan-Hyung, Commercial Law (I) (24th edition) (in Korean), Parkyoungsa, February 2021

Chung Joon-Woo, “A Review of Current Issues Concerning the Appointment and Dismissal of Directors under the Commercial Act (in Korean),” Inha Law Review, Vol. 20 No. 2, June 2017

Chung Byung-Duck, “Review of The Supreme Court of Korea Case concerning relating to Provision and Commercial Transaction under the Korean Commercial Act in 2014 (in Korean),” The Commercial Cases Review, Vol. 28 No. 3, September 2015

Chung Joon-Woo, “The Critical Review of Offering and Administration of Corporate Bonds under the Commercial Law (in Korean),” Korea Economic Law Review, Vol. 13 No. 1, 2014

Colleen Freeman, Cornelia Heydenreich, Serena Lillywhite, “Guide to the OECD Guidelines for Multinational Enterprises' Complaint Procedure Lessons from Past NGO Complaints,” the OECD Watch, November 2006

Committee on Banking Regulations and Supervisory Practices, Revised Basle Concordat on Principles for the Supervision of Bank's Foreign Establishments, May 1983

Constitutional Court of Korea, “Search Guide,” Retrieved on January 12, 2023 from <https://english.ccourt.go.kr/>

David Ellis, “Online Banking is Becoming the Most Popular Way to Bank,” The Business of Surveillance: Balancing Concerns over Ubiquitous Technology, February 12, 2007, at <http://iblsjournal.typepad.com/illinois_business_law_soc/2007/02/virtual_bank_re.html>

Denis Keenan and Sarah Riches, Business Law (8th edition), Pearson Longman, 2007

Denise Collins, Business Law (3rd edition), Oxford Univ. Press, September 2006

Department of Economic and Social Affairs of the UN, E-Government Survey 2022: The Future of Digital Government, 2022

Depository Trust & Clearing Corporation (DTCC), “DTCC 2021 Annual Report,” Retrieved on January 15, 2023 from <https://www.dtcc.com/about/annual-report>

Dong-Won Ko, “Legal Review on Regulations on the Scope of Banking Business in Korea (Korean paper),” The Korean Commercial Law Review, Vol 26 No.3, 2007

Dong-Wook Won, “The Situation and Future Tasks of the Korean Banking Law (Korean paper),” The Korean Journal of Financial Law, Vol. 8 No. 1, 2011

Edward L. Symons and James J. White, Banking Law (Third Edition), West Publishing Co., 1995

Ewan Maclntyre, Business Law (3rd edition), Pearson Longman, 2007

Federation of Korean Industries, “Analysis on the Protection Measures for a Corporate Management,” Press Release (in Korean), October 10, 2022

Finance & Economy Times, "People & Opinion: The Success of an Internet-only Bank depends on Prospective Regulations (in Korean)," July 13, 2015

Financial Services Commission, "Financial Measures to Curb Speculation in Cryptocurrency Trading," Press Release, January 23, 2018

Financial Services Commission, "Financial Regulatory Sandbox Launched," Press Release, April 1, 2019

Financial Services Commission, "FSC Approves Internet-only Bank License for Toss Bank," December 16, 2019

Financial Services Commission, "FSC approves Korea's 1st Internet-only bank," Press Release. December 14, 2016

Financial Services Commission, "Guidelines on Financial Companies' Investment in Fintech Business," September 4, 2019

Financial Services Commission, "New Open Banking System in Korean Banking Sector," Press Release, October 30, 2019

Financial Services Commission, "Notice of Revision to 「Regulation on Financial Institutions' Outsourcing of Data Processing Business & IT Facilities」," Press Release, June 10, 2015

Financial Services Commission, "Open Banking Service Launched for Banks and Fintech Businesses," Press Release, December 18, 2019

Financial Services Commission, "Open Banking Services Available from Savings Banks," Press Release, April 28, 2021

Financial Services Commission, "Plan to Introduce Internet-only Banks in Korea," Press Release, June 19, 2015

Financial Services Commission, "Preliminary Approval Granted to Kakao and KT Consortiums for Internet-only Bank," November 29, 2015

Financial Services Commission, "The Results of Preliminary Applications for Internet-only Banks (in Korean)," Press Release, October 1, 2015

Financial Services Committee, "Fintech and Digital Finance Policy for 2020," Press Releases, February 26, 2020

Financial Statistics Information System (FISIS), "Number of Companies by Financial Sector," at <https://efisis.fss.or.kr>

Financial Supervisory Service, "Capital Ratios of Banks and Bank Holding Companies, Third Quarter 2022," Press Release, December 6, 2022

Fintech Center Korea, "Sandbox Case," at <ttps://sandbox.fintech.or.kr/>.

Fn Hub Korea (International Financial Market Dept.), "Continuous Financial Innovation," at <https://www.fss.or.kr/fhkeng/main/main.do>.

Fn Hub Korea, "Regulatory Update / Latest Buzz," Monthly Newsletter of Fn Hub Korea by the FSS, Vol 131, April 2022

Frank B. Cross and Roger LeRoy Miller, The Legal Environment of Business: Text and Cases (8th edition), South-Western Cengage Learning, 2012

FSC Announcement, No. 2010-40, November 16, 2010

FTA Korea, "Korea's FTAs," Retrieved on January 15, 2023 from <www.fta.go.kr>

G.H. Treitel, The Law of Contract (10th Edition), Sweet & Maxwell, 1999

Global Water Intelligence, "The Global Water Tariff Survey 2021," 2021

Government of Korea, "Letter of Intent of the Government of Korea," December 3, 1997, available at <http://www.imf.org/external/np/loi/120397.htm>

Hal S. Scott & Philip A. Wellons, International Finance Transactions, Policy and Regulation(7th edition), 2000

Hankyoreh, "[Editorial] Behind Lone Star Case is Failure of Korea's Financial Supervisory System," September 1, 2022

Heritage Foundation, "Highlights of the 2022 Index of Economic Freedom," 2022

Hernando Otero, "UPDATE: International Arbitration Between Foreign Investors and Host States (Investor-State Arbitration)," March/April 2022, Retrieved on January 10, 2023 from <https://www.nyulawglobal.org/globalex/International_Arbitration_Foreign_Investors_Host_States1.html>

ICC, "ICC Arbitration Rules in force as from 1 March 2017 and Mediation Rules in force as from 1 January 2014,"

ICLG, "Fintech Laws and Regulations Korea 2022," Retrieved on January 5, 2023 form <<https://iclg.com/practice-areas/fintech-laws-and-regulations/korea>

IEA, "Domestic Electricity Prices in the IEA," 2020

Iinvestkorea, "Invest Guide," at <https://www.investkorea.org/>

IMF, "IMF Data Mapper," Retrieved on January 12, 2023 from <https://www.imf.org/external/datamapper>

International Bank for Reconstruction and Development of the World Bank, "Doing Business 2020: Comparing Business Regulation in 190 Economies," 2020

International Council for Commercial Arbitration, "Arbitral Institutes Directory," Retrieved on January 12, 2023 from <https://www.arbitration-icca.org/institutes>

Investment Consulting Center of the KOTRA, Business in Korea 2022, KOTRA publication No. 22-018, January 2022

Investopedia. "CREST," August 24, 2021

James Chen, "Foreign Direct Investment (FDI)," at <HENhttps://www.investopedia.com/terms/f/fdi.asp>

James, "The Future of Fintech in South Korea," the QARA, May 25, 2018.

Jay Ahn, Hyun Wook Shin, Kevin L Todd and Byung Min Choi, "Insurance and Reinsurance in South Korea: Overview," Practical Law, February 1, 2022

Jennifer Maree, "Banking in the 21st Century: Cyberspace and Internet Banks - Redefining Compliance with the Community Reinvestment Act," Banking Law Journal, October 2002

Jessica Susan Bogtrotter, "Understanding South Korean Business Culture and Etiquette," Korea Times, April 27, 2021

Ji-Hong Joo, "Analysis of the Supreme Court Cases in 2021: The Law of Obligations (in Korean)," Human Rights and Justice, Vol. 505, May 2022

Joon Young Kim, Samuel Yim, Gye-Jeong Kim and Ina Chung, "FinTech in South Korea: Overview," Kim & Chang, 2022

Joseph J, Norton, Devising International Banking Supervisory Standards, Graham & Trotman / Martinus Nijhoff Publishers, 1996

Joseph J. Norton, "Gramm-Leach-Bliley Act of November 1999: Overview of Selective Legislative and Regulatory Issues," Essay in International Financial and Economic Law, CCLS-London, 2000

Jung-Hai Moon, "A Study on the Cases of the Supreme Court on the Commercial Act in 2020," Ewha Law Journal, Vol. 25 No. 2, December 2020

Junho Kim, "The Challenges and Outlook of Trial by Jury in Korea," Journal of Korean Law, Vol. 8, June 2009

KCAB International, "Model Clause of KCAB," Retrieved on December 20, 2022 from <http://www.kcabinternational.or.kr/>

Ki Jong Lee, General Principles of Korean Commercial Law, Sam Young Sa, October 2020

Kim & Chang, "Supreme Court Decision on Employee Status of Branch Manager of Insurance Company," Insights, April 21, 2022

KITA, "Medicines Exports by Month," 2021

Korea Development Bank, "KDB Data Plaza: Foreign Banks in Korea," available at <http://www.kol.co.kr/~kdbmst/ focus/for_bank.html>

Korea Exchange, "Listing Requirements for the KOSDAQ Market"

Korea Federation of Banks, "Standards of Internal Regulations on Corporate Governance," January 26, 2015

Korea Herald, "Applications for Internet-only Banks Begin," September 30, 2015

Korea Insurance Research Institute, "Korean Insurance Industry Trend 2Q 2022," June 2022

Korea JoongAng Daily, "Split off proposal could help protect shareholder rights," September 5, 2022

Korea Legislation Research Institute, "Legislative System," Retrieved on January 3, 2023 from <https://elaw.klri.re.kr/>

Korea National Contact Point (KNCP), "OECD Guidelines for Multinational Enterprises," at <http://www.ncp.or.kr/servlet/kcab_encp/info/1000>

Korea Securities Depository, "E-voting & E-proxy," 2011

Korea Times, "Korea ordered to pay Lone Star $216.5 mil. in investor-state suit," August 31, 2022

Korea Times, "KT, Kakao, Interpark Consortiums Apply for Internet-only Bank License," October 1, 2015

Korea Times, "Regulator Starts Receiving Applications for Internet-only Banks," September 30, 2015

Korea Times, "Lone Star Ruling regarded as '50% Defeat' for Korean Gov't," September 1, 2022

Korean Culture and Information Service, Facts About Korea, Ministry of Culture, Sports and Tourism, 2020

KOTRA, Guide to Establishing a Business in Korea. KOTRA Publication No. 16-079, 2016

KOTRA, Labor Laws in Korea 2022, KOTRA Publication No. 22-010, January 2022

KOTRA, "Guide to Establishing a Business in Korea," 2016

KOTRA, "Invest Korea," Retrieved on January 12, 2023 from <https://www.investkorea.org/ik-en/pgm/i-295/statistics/front/list.do>

Kwan Hoon Kwak, "The Study on Possibilities, Limitations and Improvement of the Use of Dividend in Kind (in Korean)," Commercial Law Review, Vol. 33 No.1, 2014

Kwon, O., J. Park, and B. Kim. "Fintech, Cryptoassets, and Central Bank Digital Currency in the Republic of Korea," ADBI Working Paper No. 1018, October 2019

Kyung-Hoon Chun "Understanding Korean Corporate Law and Governance," Journal of Korean Law, Vol. 21, August 2022

Lee Ik Joo, "Foreign Banks in Korea (Korean paper)," Monthly Review of the Korea Exchange Bank, Vol XXV No.7, July 1991

Lee, Janet & Shailer, Greg. "The Effect of Board-Related Reforms on Investors' Confidence," Australian Accounting Review, Vol. 18 No. 2, June 2008

Legal Information Institute, "Commercial Law: An Overview," Retrieved January 18, 2023 from <https://www.law.cornell.edu/wex/commercial_law>

Lim, Soomin, "The Cumulative Voting Rule in Taiwan," The Korean Association of Comparative Private Law, Vol. 27 No. 3, August 2020

LS Sealy and BJA Hooley, Commercial Law: Text, Cases, and Materials (4th edition), Oxford Univ. Press, 2009

Michelle Jamrisko, Wei Lu, and Alexandre Tanzi, "South Korea Leads World in Innovation as U.S. Exits Top Ten," Bloomberg, February 3, 2021.

Min Kyu Lee, "Enforcement of Annulled Arbitral Awards in Korea: Where are We and Where Should We Go?" Journal of Korean Law, Vol. 18, December 2018

Ministry of Economy and Finance, Public Notice No. 2017-10, April 4, 2017

Ministry of Finance and Economy(MOFE), "Effect of OECD Membership and Future Tasks," October 1996

Ministry of Trade, Industry and Energy, "Businesses Restricted from Foreign Investment and Criteria for Permission by the Regulations on Foreign Investment," Public Notice No. 2022-127

National Assembly Research Service, "Sale of Stocks by the Lone Star Fund and Non-financial Business Operators or Not? (Korean paper)," Issue & Point, No. 325, November 17, 2011

National Law Review, "South Korea," available at <https://www.natlawreview.com/jurisdiction/all-international/south-korea>

Neal R. Bevans, Business Law: A Hands-On Approach, Thomson Delmar Learning, 2006

OECD, "Education at a Glance 2021," September 16, 2021

OECD, "G20/OECD Principles of Corporate Governance," 2015

OECD, "National Contact Points for Responsible Business Conduct Providing Access to Remedy: 20 years and the road ahead," 2020

OECD, "OECD Corporate Governance Factbook 2021," available at <https://www.oecd.org/corporate/OECD-Corporate-Governance-Factbook.pdf>

OECD, "OECD Due Diligence Guidance for Responsible Business Conduct," 2018 at <http://mneguidelines.oecd.org/>.

OECD, "OECD Guidelines for Multinational Enterprises (2011 Edition)," May 25, 2011 at <http://mneguidelines.oecd.org/mneguidelines/>

O'Sullivan, Arthur & Sheffrin, Steven M. "Economics: Principles in Action," Upper Saddle River, N.J.: Pearson Prentice Hall, 2003

Park Eungyoung, "Case Study on the Duty to Notify of the Alteration or Increase of Risks under the Korean Commercial Act (in Korean)," Law Review, Vol. 58, 2015

Park, Sei-hwa, "A Shareholder's Right in Share Transfer Prior to Issuing Share Certificates and Preferred Position Relation between First and Second Transferees - A Review of a Korean Supreme Court Case (in Korean)," Analysis of Recent Cases, Vol. 721, February 2017

Peter Rogan, "The Insurance and Reinsurance Law Review (7th edition)," the Law Reviews:

Law Business Research Ltd, April 2019
R. David, JEC. Brierley, Major Legal Systems in the World Today: An Introduction to the Comparative Study of Law, Simon & Schuster Inc., 1978
Ralph H. Folsom, Michael Wallace Gordon, Michael P. Van Alstine, Michael D. Ramsey, International Business Transactions: A Problem-Oriented Coursebook (12th edition), West Academic Publishing, 2015
Research Department of the Bank of Korea, "The Main Points of Reshaping the Central Banking and Financial Supervision System in Korea," January 1998
Reuer, Jeffrey J., Arino, Africa, "Strategic alliance contracts: dimensions and determinants of contractual complexity," Strategic Management Journal, Vol. 28 No. 3, March 2007
Richard A. Mann and Barry S. Roberts, Smith & Roberson's Business Law (13th edition), Thomson West, 2006
Richard Schaffer, Beverley Earle and Filiberto Agusti, International Business Law and Its Environment (6th edition), Thomson South-Western, 2005
Rory Van Loo, "Making Innovation More Competitive: The Case of Fintech," UCLA Law Review, Vol. 65 No. 1, February 1, 2018
Sang Hoon Han, "Double Sales of Real Estate and the Breach of Trust in Korean Criminal Act sec. 355(2) Focusing on the Categorization of 'Another's Business' and the Efficient Breach of Contract Theory (in Korean)," Justice, Vol. 192, 2022
Sang Hwan Lee & Chan Moon Park, "Korea," Banking Regulatory Review, 2010
Sangche Lee, "Internet-only Banks: Uncertain Innovation," Economic Papers, Vol. 7 No. 1, 2015
Seog Roon Lee and Jung Soo Lee, Korean Banking Institutions (Korean book), 1997
Seung-Ki Shin, Beom-Jun Kim, "'Obtaining a Pecuniary Advantage' Requirement for Establishing the Crime of Breach of Trust (in Korean)," Korea Law Review, No. 95, 2019
Soo Hyun Ahn, "A Review of the Korean Supreme Court Case on the General Provision and Commercial Activities under the Commercial Act announced in 2008 (in Korean)," Commercial Cases Review, Vol. 21 No. 4, December 31, 2008
Stella Lim, Pedro Choi, "South Korea Dividends More to be Discovered," APAC Thematic Report, S&P Global Market Intelligence, June 17 2022
Sumatriani SUMATRIANI, Gagaring PAGULUNG, Darwis SAID, Grace T. PONTOH, Jamaluddin JAMALUDDIN, "The Effects of Shareholders' Rights, Disclosures, and Transparency on Firm Value," The Journal of Asian Finance, Economics and Business, Vol. 8 No. 3, 2021
Supreme Court of Korea, "The Judiciary," Retrieved on January 12, 2023 from <https://eng.scourt.go.kr/>
Sweet & Maxwell, "English Common Law is the Most Widespread Legal System in the World," November 2008
Tae Hee Lee, "Special Report," Special Supplement of the International Financial Law Review, September 1991
Thakur, Madhuri, Vaidya, Dheeraj (ed.), "Legal Capital," CFA Institute, August 29, 2020
UN Commission on International Trade Law, "Arbitration Centers," Retrieved on January 12, 2023 from <https://uncitral.un.org/en/texts/arbitration/contractualtexts/arbitration/centres>
UNCITRAL, "Report of Working Group II(Dispute Settlement) on the work of its

seventy-first session (New York, 37 February 2020)," A/CN.9/1010, February 12, 2020
UNCTAD, "COVID-19 boost to e-commerce sustained into 2021, new UNCTAD figures show," April 25, 2022
Valentin Todorov, "Competitive Industrial Performance Index 2020: Country Profiles," July 3, 2020
Valentina Vadi, Proportionality, Reasonableness and Standards of Review in International Investment Law and Arbitration, April 27, 2018
WIPO, "Uniform Domain Name Dispute Resolution Policy (UDRP)"
World Bank, "Ease of Doing Business Score," Retrieved on January 18, 2023 from <https://www.doingbusiness.org/data/doing-business-score>
World Intellectual Property Organization, "June 2022-2021 Intellectual Property Statistics," WIPO IP Facts and Figures 2021, 2022
World Intellectual Property Organization, "Yearly Intellectual Property Statistics," WIPO IP Facts and Figures 2021, 2022
Yonhap News Agency, "S. Korea Ordered to Pay Lone Star US$216.5 mln in Investor-state Suit," August 31, 2022
Young Shim, Korean Bank Regulation and Supervision: Crisis and Reform, Kluwer Law International, 2000
Young-Cheol Lee, "Elliott v. Samsung C&T: Evaluating Challenges to the Legality and Fairness of the Samsung C&TCheil Industries Merger," Business Law Review, Vol. 31 No. 4, December 2017
Yunjong Moon, "Introduction and Progress of Korean Open Banking," International Cooperation Center of the KFTC, December 17, 2020

[Cases]

Busan District Court Decision 2011Gahap8532, decided on October 26, 2011
Constitutional Court Decision 2017Hun-Ba369, decided on November 29, 2018
Changwon District Court 2009Gahap194, decided on November 18, 2010
Gimbel v. Signal Cos., 316 A.2d 599, 608 (Del. Ch. 1974)
In Sokoloff v. National City Bank of New York, 130 Misc, 66, 224 N.Y.S. 102 (1927), affirmed 223 A.D. 754, 227 N.Y.S. 907 (1928), affirmed 250 N.Y. 69, 164 N.E. 745
Korean National Contact Point (KNCP), Martin Linge Project Crane Accident Workers Support Team v. Samsung Heavy Industries etc. October 26, 2022
LSF-KEB Holdings SCA and others (Lone Star) *v.* Republic of Korea, ICSID Case No. ARB/12/37
Pan-American Bank & Trust Co. v. National City Bank, 6 F.2d 762 (1925) 269 U.S. 554, 46 S.Ct. 18, 70 L.Ed. 408
Seoul Appellate Court Decision 94Na12526, decided on February 15, 1995
Seoul Central Court Decision 2010Gahap17142, decided on July 9, 2010
Seoul Central Court Decision 2014GaHap38116, decided on October, 16, 2015
Seoul High Court Decision 2010Na72375, decided on April 14, 2011
Seoul High Court Decision 2016Na2089876, decided on July 7, 2017
Seoul High Court Decision 2019Na204860, decided on January 26, 2021
Supreme Court Decision 2000Da37326, decided on June 25, 2004
Supreme Court Decision 2000Da42786, decided on February 26, 2003

Supreme Court Decision 2000Da60890, decided on August 23, 2002
Supreme Court Decision 2000Du9731, decided on November 27, 2001
Supreme Court Decision 2001Da52407, decided on June 14, 2002
Supreme Court Decision 2001Da53059, decided on April 11, 2003
Supreme Court Decision 2003Da65438, 65445, decided on October 28, 2004
Supreme Court Decision 2003Da69638, decided on October 28, 2005
Supreme Court Decision 2004Da25123, decided on December 10, 2004
Supreme Court Decision 2004Da49570, decided on November 23, 2006
Supreme Court Decision 2005Da5812, decided on June 1, 2007
Supreme Court Decision 2005Da602, decided on July 22, 2005
Supreme Court Decision 2005Da602, decided on July 22, 2005
Supreme Court Decision 2006Da19603, decided on November 30, 2007
Supreme Court Decision 2006Da33333, decided on October 11, 2007
Supreme Court Decision 2007Da60080, decided on December 13, 2007
Supreme Court Decision 2007Da89722, delivered on April 11, 2008
Supreme Court Decision 2007Da90982, decided on September 11, 2008
Supreme Court Decision 2007Do8373, decided on April 11, 2008
Supreme Court Decision 2008Da14633, decided on April 14, 2011
Supreme Court Decision 2008Da96963, 96970, decided on February 25, 2010
Supreme Court Decision 2008Da96963, decided on February 25, 2010
Supreme Court Decision 2008Do9410, decided on January 15, 2009 (overruled)
Supreme Court Decision 2008Do9436, decided on May 29, 2009
Supreme Court Decision 2008GaHap6916, decided on January 23, 2009
Supreme Court Decision 2009Ma1600, decided on March 25, 2010
Supreme Court Decision 2010Da13541, decided on June 24, 2010
Supreme Court Decision 2010Da20532, decided on October 28, 2010
Supreme Court Decision 2010Da49380, decided on November 15, 2012
Supreme Court Decision 2011Da28342, decided on February 14, 2013
Supreme Court Decision 2011Da41352, decided on August 19, 2011
Supreme Court Decision 2012Da89399, decided on December 18, 2013
Supreme Court Decision 2013Da14965, decided on November 26, 2015
Supreme Court Decision 2013Da14965, decided on November 26, 2015
Supreme Court Decision 2013Da217108, decided on July 24, 2014.
Supreme Court Decision 2014Da53745, decided on August 29, 2016
Supreme Court Decision 2014Do1104, decided on July 20, 2017
Supreme Court Decision 2014Du335, decided on November 26, 2015
Supreme Court Decision 2015Da232859, decided on March 22, 2017
Supreme Court Decision 2015Da232859, decided on March 22, 2017
Supreme Court Decision 2015Da71795, decided on March 24, 2016
Supreme Court Decision 2017Da207499, decided on July 18, 2017
Supreme Court Decision 2017Da251564, decided on April 9, 2020
Supreme Court Decision 2017Da258237, decided on September 10, 2019
Supreme Court Decision 2018Du54705, decided November 5, 2020.
Supreme Court Decision 2019Da276338, decided on June 30, 2021
Supreme Court Decision 2019Da293449 Decided on April 15, 2021

Supreme Court Decision 2020Da287310, decided on April 14, 2022
Supreme Court Decision 2021Da218205, decided on April 14, 2022
Supreme Court Decision 2021Da246934, decided on April 14, 2022
Supreme Court Decision 2021Du33715, decided on April 14, 2022
Supreme Court Decision 89Nu916, decided on September 12, 1989
Supreme Court Decision 91Da44100, decided on July 24, 1992
Supreme Court Decision 92Da29696, decided on October 13, 1992.
Supreme Court Decision 92Nu16942, decided on July 27, 1993
Supreme Court Decision 94Da14629, decided on August 9, 1994
Supreme Court Decision 97Da21604, decided on January 19, 2001
Supreme Court Decision 99Da35737, decided on January 28, 2000
Supreme Court Decision 99Do1141, decided on June 25, 1999
Supreme Court en banc Decision 2016Da13437, decided on November 26, 2020
Supreme Court en banc Decision 2016Da251215, decided on March 23, 2017
Supreme Court en banc Decision 2018Da257958, 257965, decided on June 17, 2021
Supreme Court Order 2003Ma1575, decided on December 24, 2004
Supreme Court Order 2005Ma541, decided on November 8, 2005 (overruled)
Supreme Court Order 2013Ma657, decided on July 21, 2014
United States v. First National City Bank, 379 U.S. 378, 85 S.Ct. 528, 13 L.Ed.2d 365 (1965)

Index

C

G

H

I

J

K

U

V

W

Byung-Tae Kim (김병태)

Professor of Law (Youngsan University, Korea)
Attorney at Law (Member of NY Bar, USA)
Arbitrator (Korean Commercial Arbitration Board, KCAB)
Committee Member (Busan, Yangsan and Ulsan, Korea)
Examination Board (Bar Exam and other national exams)
Ex-President of Korean Banking & Financial Law Association
Ex-Dean of College of Law, Youngsan University

BA in Law & Business Administration, Kyung Hee Univ. (Korea)
Master of Law, Kyung Hee Univ. Graduate School (Korea)
LL.M., Southern Methodist Univ. School of Law (USA)
S.J.D., Southern Methodist Univ. School of Law (USA)

KOREAN BUSINESS LAW

Published by SAM YOUNG SA. 335, Achasan-ro, Gwangjin-gu,
Seoul, Republic of Korea.
March 2, 2023

ISBN 978-89-445-0567-6-93360
Price ₩40,000
Printed in Korea